Study Guide

to accompany

ESSENTIALS OF BUSINESS LAW

Third Edition

Len Young Smith
Richard A. Mann
Barry S. Roberts

Prepared by

Georgia L. Holmes
Associate Professor and Chair of Business Law
Mankato State University
Member, Minnesota Bar

Barry S. Roberts
Professor of Business Law
University of North Carolina at Chapel Hill
Member, North Carolina and Pennsylvania Bars

Richard A. Mann
Professor of Business Law
University of North Carolina at Chapel Hill
Member, North Carolina Bar

West Publishing

St. Paul   New York   Los Angeles   San Francisco

∞

Purpose and Use of the Study Guide

This Study Guide can be a valuable supplement to your textbook and classroom attendance. It was written to help you understand and recall the information presented in Smith, Mann, and Roberts' *Essentials of Business Law*, Third Edition. You should carefully read the appropriate chapter in your textbook before attempting to answer the questions in this guide.

The Study Guide supplements the cases and problems in the text. The problems in the Study Guide cover a greater range of difficulty than those in the text, although the overall level of difficulty is similar. Some of the problems in the workbook are similar to those in the text, but none of them are identical. The Study Guide contains the following components for each chapter:

1. A brief statement about the purpose of the chapter.

2. Chapter checkpoints to insure that you have learned the major points of the chapter.

3. A list of key terms from the chapter to which you are to supply definitions.

4. True/False review questions on major chapter concepts.

5. Multiple choice questions on major chapter concepts.

6. Short essay questions.

The Study Guide includes sample test banks containing cumulative questions and integrated questions at the end of each part.

The authors sincerely hope that you will find the study of business law to be interesting and rewarding as well as challenging.

STUDY TIPS FOR THE STUDENT

How to Study Law

Those who have never studied law before may find that the study of law is different from the study of other social sciences. Not only must you know a rule of law and the source of that law, but you must also know how to apply it. Students sometimes find themselves frustrated by terms in the text such as "in most cases," "ordinarily" or "usually." Sometimes students need to know more than one rule, because there may be a majority rule of law and a slightly different minority rule of law. This is because much of business law is based on State law. Sometimes that law is State common law; sometimes that law is State statutory law. In either case, because there are many States, the student may be confronted with a situation where the law differs from State to State. There are also general rules of law that are mentioned in the text. However, law is complex and for every general rule, there are frequently exceptions. Students must learn to be precise in applying the rule or the exception to the rule. Sometimes too, the general rule has been modified by statute. Students must recognize these situations and mention in any exam answer that the general rule may have been superceded by a statute or a common law exception.

In studying each chapter, you should consider the following procedures:

1. Skim the chapter noting the main headings. Note the terms that are defined in the margins.

2. Read the chapter carefully before class.

3. After attending class and taking notes on the lecture, re-read the chapter.

4. Underline, take notes, and outline the most important points in the chapter.

5. Write definitions to the terms listed in the study guide.

6. Answer the true/false, multiple choice, and essay questions.

7. Check your answers with those in the back of the study guide.

8. Review the questions, paying particular attention to the ones that were missed.

Law Exams

To do well on law exams, you must know both the rule (or rules) of law and the application of those rules. When taking a law exam, you must also carefully budget your time. You should take an orderly, systematic approach to both your studying for and taking of the exam.

In taking law exams, issue spotting is essential. The best way to recognize issues is by reading the text, including the cases, and then by working through the case problems at the end of each chapter. In working out problems on an exam, don't always accept an obvious issue as being the only issue in the problem. There may be more than one issue that should be considered and analyzed, and there may be more than one rule of law that needs to be cited and applied. Frequently instructors will grade essay exams based upon the number of issues spotted by a student and by the student's ability to recognize that more than one rule applies to a particular fact situation. Preciseness, specificity, and organization are the keys to doing well on a law exam. Finally, you should recognize that in law there is not always a "correct" answer. In these instances, the instructor may be looking for your analysis of the issues raised by the facts rather than a specific legal conclusion.

Table of Contents

INTRODUCTION TO LAW

PURPOSE

This chapter introduces the nature, classification and sources of law in the American legal system. The chapter discusses the concept of law in a general sense, and then examines the classifications and sources of American business law. Most of the chapter deals with the science of law, known as jurisprudence, and introduces the student to important basic terminology, concepts and principles that are essential to an understanding of later chapters.

CHAPTER CHECKPOINTS

After reading and studying this chapter, you should be able to:

1. Give a definition of law and distinguish between "law" and justice" and "law" and "morality."

2. Define substantive law and procedural law and give examples of rules of substantive law and rules of procedural law.

3. Distinguish between civil law and criminal law and between law and equity.

4. Define the term "stare decisis" and discuss its importance to common law systems of law such as the one we have in the United States.

5. List the sources of American law and discuss how the Uniform Commercial Code and the Restatements fit into the American legal system.

CHAPTER OUTLINE

A. Nature of Law - Law is an instrument of social control whose function is to regulate within certain limitations, human conduct and human relations.
  1. Definition of Law - Predictions of the way a court will decide legal questions or "a rule of civil conduct by the supreme power in a State, commanding what is right, and prohibiting what is wrong."
  2. Legal Sanctions - These are the means of enforcing legal judgments.

1

3. Laws and Morals - Law and morality are two intersecting circles that are not the same.
4. Functions of Law - The functions of law are maintaining stability in the social, political and economic system through dispute resolution; protection of property; and the preservation of the State.
5. Law and Justice - These are separate and distinct concepts, although without law, there can be no justice in the sense of fair, equitable and impartial treatment of competing interests and desires with due regard for the common good.

B. Classification of Law
1. Substantive and Procedural - Substantive law is the basic law creating rights and duties; procedural law consists of rules for enforcing substantive law.
2. Public and Private - Public law is the law dealing with the relationship between government and individuals; private law is the law involving relationships among individuals and legal entities.
   a. Right - The legal capacity to require another person to perform or refrain from performing an act.
   b. Duty - A legal obligation requiring a person to perform or refrain from performing an act.
3. Civil and Criminal - Civil law is the law dealing with the rights and duties of individuals among themselves; criminal law is the law that involves offenses against the entire community.

C. Sources of Law
1. Constitutional Law - A constitution is the fundamental law of a government establishing its powers and limitations. The U.S. Constitution is the supreme law of the land.
2. Judicial Law - Common law systems such as the U.S. and England rely heavily on the judiciary as a source of law and on the adversary method for settling disputes in contrast to civil law systems which are based on Roman law and comprehensive legislative enactments called Codes.
   a. Common law - The body of law developed by the courts that serves as precedent for determination of later controversies.
   b. Equity - The body of law based upon principles distinct from common law and providing remedies not available at law.
   c. Restatements of law - Authoritative statements of the common law of the United States which are drafted by the American Law Institute.
3. Legislative Law - Laws adopted by legislative bodies; the primary source of new law since the end of the nineteenth centry.
4. Treaties - Agreements between or among independent nations.
5. Executive Orders - Laws issued by the President or the governor of a State.
6. Administrative Law - Law dealing with the establishment, duties and powers of agencies in the executive branch of government.

D. Legal Analysis - This refers to the method of analyzing and briefing Federal and State judicial decisions.

DEFINITIONS

1. Sanctions

2. Substantive law

3. Procedural law

4. Public law

5. Private law

6. Civil law

7. Criminal law

8. Adversary system

9. Common law system

10. Civil law system

11. Stare decisis

12. Maxim

13. Restatements

14. Administrative law

15. Legislative law

16. Equity

17. Constitution

18. Right

19. Duty

20. Inquisitional system

TRUE/FALSE

_T_ 1. A person may break the law even though his conduct is not immoral. _T_

_F_ 2. In a criminal trial, the government must show that the defendant is guilty by a preponderance of the evidence. _F_

_F_ 3. A State statute may be valid even though it violates the Federal constitution. _F_

_T_ 4. The courts of equity arose to provide relief to those who had no adequate remedy at common law. _T_

_T_ 5. Over the past century, the emphasis in law-making has shifted from judge-made (common) law to legislatively-enacted (statutory) law. _T_

_T_ 6. The courts may review the decisions of administrative agencies even though such agencies have their own adjudication procedures. _T_

_F_ 7. Because of the many statutes enacted by the legislatures of the States and by the Federal government, the American legal system is considered to be a civil law system.

_F_ 8. Under the principle of separation of powers, only the courts have the power to promulgate Federal laws.

_T_ 9. The most serious crime a person can commit is treason.

_T_ 10. The law is constantly changing in an effort to meet the evolving needs of society.

_T_ 11. In a civil action, the plaintiff must show that the defendant is liable by a preponderance of the evidence.

_F_ 12. The constitutionality of any law is ultimately decided by the President of the United States.

_F_ 13. Business law is primarily public law.

_F_ 14. The Uniform Commercial Code is a Federal Statute that was adopted by Congress to make uniform the law among the States.

_F_ 15. Law is a guarantee of justice.

MULTIPLE CHOICE

_b_ 1. A primary function of the legal system is to:
   a.   provide work for judges and lawyers.
   b.   insure that legal rules are enforced.
   c.   insure that no dispute is settled without an unreasonable delay.
   d.   none of the above.

_d_ 2. A court may enforce the law through the use of such sanctions as:
   a.   fines.
   b.   seizure and sale of property.
   c.   imprisonment.
   d.   all of the above.

_d_ 3. A person who is injured by the wrongful act of another may bring a civil suit to:
   a.   recover money damages.
   b.   have the wrongdoer thrown in jail.
   c.   order the wrongdoer to engage in or desist from certain conduct.
   d.   (a) and (c), but not (b).

_d_ 4. While the principle of stare decisis provides that courts will follow their precedents in making subsequent decisions, nevertheless a court may decline to follow its precedents:
   a.   to correct an erroneous decision.
   b.   to choose among conflicting precedents.
   c.   in recognition of the fact that the needs of society change over time.
   d.   all of the above.

_C_ 5. Which of the following is NOT a characteristic of a court equity?
    a. It may provide injunctive relief.
    b. It may reform or rescind a contract.
    c. It presides over jury trials.
    d. It applies the clean hands doctrine.

_a_ 6. Which of the following is NOT an administrative agency?
    a. Congress of Industrial Organizations.
    b. National Labor Relations Board.
    c. Social Security Administration.
    d. Securities and Exchange Commission.

_b_ 7. The appeals court decision in the case of State v. Dawson, 282 S.E. 2d 284, may be found at:
    a. page 282 of volume 284 of the Southeastern Reporter, second series.
    b. page 284 of volume 282 of the Southeastern Reporter, second series.
    c. pages 282-284 of volume 2 of the Southeastern Reporter.
    d. None of the above.

_a_ 8. In a criminal trial, which of the following is NOT required?
    a. The defendant must testify in his own behalf.
    b. Criminal guilt must be proven beyond a reasonable doubt.
    c. Mens rea.
    d. A wrongful act.

_d_ 9. Sources of State law include:
    a. administration rules and regulations.
    b. State constitutions and statutes.
    c. judicial decisions.
    d. all of the above.

_b_ 10. In the criminal trial of State of West Virginia v. Dawson, the party bringing the action was:
    a. Dawson.
    b. the State of West Virginia.
    c. the victim of the crime.
    d. the Federal government.

_c_ 11. The highest source of law in the United States is:
    a. an executive order of the President.
    b. an interstate compact.
    c. the Federal constitution.
    d. the State constitutions.

_a_ 12. The most successful attempt by the National Conference of Commissioners on Uniform State Laws and the American Law Institute has been the:
    a. Uniform Commercial Code.
    b. Uniform Limited Partnership Act.
    c. Model Business Corporation Act.
    d. Uniform Probate Code.

(C) 13. The person who brings a civil lawsuit must prove the case:
- a. beyond a reasonable doubt.
- b. beyond all uncertainty.
- c. by a preponderance of the evidence.   *C*
- d. beyond a shadow of a doubt.

(d) 14. Which of the following is not an equitable remedy?
- a. Injunction.
- b. Reformation.
- c. Rescission.   *d*
- d. Money damages.

(c) 15. Bill Businessman files a lawsuit against Carl Contractor for breach of contract. This case is a/an:
- a. equitable action.
- b. criminal proceeding.
- c. civil lawsuit.   *✓*
- d. public law case.

SHORT ESSAY:

1. What are the major differences between common law systems and civil law systems?

Com Law orig in England and is derived from Judicial decisions. Civil law derived from Roman law and is based on comprehensive legislative enactments

2. Explain the principle of stare decisis. *It applies the principal that Courts should apply rules decided in prior cases in deciding substantially similar cases*

3. Explain the purposes of administrative agencies. *Their functions are concerned with genl matters of public health, safety + welfare inc. police, military, taxation, coinage of money, trade + commerce. They create more legal rules + decide more controversies than all legislatures + courts*

4. Why are constitutions such important sources of law? *They are the fundamental law of government + establish its powers + its limitations of power + allocates*

5. How are the Restatements of Law and the Uniform Commercial Code similar? How are they different?

_____
_____
_____
_____

THE JUDICIAL SYSTEM

PURPOSE

The purpose of this chapter is to introduce the student to procedural law and to the process of dispute resolution. The first part of the chapter discusses the structure and function of the Federal and State court sytems. The second part deals with jurisdiction, or the power of a court to hear and decide a case. The last part of the chapter describes the process by which a civil lawsuit is begun and then proceeds through the court system. This last part also discusses mediation and arbitration as alternatives to the civil lawsuit.

CHAPTER CHECKPOINTS

After reading and studying the chapter, you should be able to:

1. Outline the courts in a State court system and in the Federal court system.

2. Identify and define the various types of jurisdiction and compare the subject matter jurisdiction of the State courts to that of the Federal courts.

3. Distinguish between "jurisdiction" and "venue" and explain why the two are frequently confused by beginning students of law.

4. Outline using correct terminology the process by which a civil lawsuit is begun and proceeds through the court system.

5. Discuss and compare the relative advantages and disadvantages of court adjudication, arbitration and mediation/conciliation.

CHAPTER OUTLINE

A. The Court System - The U.S. has a dual court system.
   1. The Federal Courts - Article III of the U.S. Constitution vests the judicial power of the United States in one Supreme Court and such lower courts as Congress may establish.
      a. District Courts - These are trial courts of general jurisdiction in the Federal system that can hear and decide most legal controversies.

    b. Courts of Appeal - There are eleven numbered circuits plus the D.C. circuit; each has a court which primarily hears appeals from the district courts and reviews orders of certain administrative agencies; three judge panels can reverse, modify or affirm the decision of the lower court.

    c. The Supreme Court - Consists of a Chief Justice and eight Associate Justices who sit in Washington, D.C.; it has original jurisdiction in some cases, but it is primarily an appellate court that hears a few cases by way of appeal by right and most of its cases by discretionary writ of certiorari.

    d. Special Courts - Courts having jurisdiction over cases in a particular area of Federal law include the U.S. Claims Court, the Tax Court, the U.S. Bankruptcy Court and the U.S. Court of Appeals for the Federal Circuit.

2. State Courts - Each of the fifty States and the District of Columbia has its own independent court system; State courts can hear and decide cases under the common law, State statutes and many cases of Federal law.

    a. Inferior Trial Courts - Usually hear minor criminal cases such as traffic offenses, civil cases involving small amounts of money and preliminary hearings in more serious criminal cases.

    b. Small Claims Court - Inferior trial courts which hear only civil cases involving a limited amount of money; usually an appeal de novo can be taken to the trial court of general jurisdiction.

    c. Trial Courts - Each State has trial courts of general jurisdiction, which may be called county, district, superior, circuit, or common pleas court. In New York, this court is known as the Supreme Court.

    d. Appellate Courts - Except for those cases reviewed by the U.S. Supreme Court, the decision of this Court is final.

B. Jurisdiction - The authority of a court to hear and decide a case.

1. Subject Matter Jurisdiction - The authority of a court to decide a particular kind of case.

    a. Exclusive Federal Jurisdiction - Jurisdiction that permits only one court (State or Federal) to hear a case is exclusive. Federal courts have exclusive jurisdiction over Federal crimes, bankruptcy, antitrust, patent, trademark and copyright cases.

    b. Concurrent Jurisdiction - Authority of more than one court to hear a case. State and Federal courts have concurrent jurisdiction over Federal question cases and Diversity of citizenship cases.

    c. Exclusive State Jurisdiction - State courts have exclusive jurisdiction over all other matters to which the Federal judicial power does not reach.

    d. Stare Decisis in the Dual Court System - This presents certain problems when there are parallel court systems.

2. Jurisdiction Over the Parties - The power of a court to bind the parties to a suit.

    a. In Personam Jurisdiction - Jurisdiction based upon claims against a person in contrast to jurisdiction over his property; obtained by serving process within the State of pursuant to a "long-arm" statute.

    b. In Rem Jurisdiction - Jurisdiction based on claims against property; must give reasonable notice and an opportunity to contest the claim.

    c. Attachment Jurisdiction - Also known as quasi in rem jurisdiction; allows seizure of a person's property within the State to obtain payment of a claim against a defendant.

    d. Venue - The location where a lawsuit should be brought.

C. Civil Procedure - Rules to resolve a dispute in a just, prompt, and inexpensive way.

1. The Pleadings - A series of responsive, formal, written statements by each side to a lawsuit; consist of the summons, complaint, answer and reply.

2. Pretrial Procedure - Discovery is the pre-trial exchange of information between opposing parties to a lawsuit; depositions, written interrogatories, production of documents, examination by a physician, requests for admission of facts are part of discovery. The case may be disposed of by summary

judgment if the evidence is so clear that no trial is needed. If a trial is necessary, a pre-trial conference between the judge and the attorneys representing the parties will be held.

3. Trial - There may be a jury trial or court trial; a jury trial begins with jury selection and voir dire, then proceeds to opening statements, direct examination, cross examination, possibly a motion for directed verdict. If there is no appeal, the holder of the judgment can demand enforcement by means of a writ of execution or by garnishment.

4. Appeal - Notice of appeal must be filed; briefs and arguments are submitted to the reviewing court; oral arguments may be made; the reviewing court may reverse, modify or remand the case.

D. Alternative Dispute Resolution - Nonjudicial methods of dealing with disputes have arisen to overcome the disadvantages of litigation. These methods are especially suitable where privacy, speed, preservation of continuing relations and control of the process are important to the parties.

1. Arbitration - Consensual arbitration is voluntarily entered into by the parties. Compulsory arbitration is required by statute in specific types of disputes. Arbitration is a nonjudicial proceeding where a neutral third party selected by the disputants renders a binding decision.

2. Conciliation and Mediation - Conciliation is a nonbinding process in which a third party acts as an intermediary between the disputing parties; mediation is a nonbinding process in which a third party acts as an intermediary between the disputing parties and proposes solutions for them to consider.

DEFINITIONS

1. Appeal by right

2. Writ of certiorari

3. Subject matter jurisdiction

4. Exclusive jurisdiction

5. Concurrent jurisdiction

6. Diversity of citizenship

7. Removal jurisdiction

8. Pleadings

9. Complaint

10. Summons

11. Statute of limitations

12. Demurrer

13. Answer

14. Denial

15. Counterclaim

16. Reply

17. Arbitration

18. Conciliation

19. Mediation

20. Default judgment

21. Discovery

22. Summary judgment

23. Directed verdict

24. Voir dire

25. Judgment n.o.v.

26. Judgment on the pleadings

27. Appellant

28. Appellee

29. In personam

30. Long Arm Statute

31. In rem

32. Attachment jurisdiction

33. Venue

TRUE/FALSE

 1. Each State has at least one Federal district court.

 2. The U.S. Supreme Court consists of a panel of three judges.

 3. The United States can be sued in the Claims Court.

4. State court judges in most States receive lifetime appointments from the Governor.

5. Federal court judges receive lifetime appointments from the President.

_T_   6. A corporation maay be a citizen of more than one State for diversity of citizenship purposes.   _T_

_T_   7. A State court may have exclusive jurisdiction to hear a case involving diversity of citizenship.   _T_

_F_   8. There is no right to trial by jury in civil cases.   _F_

_F_   9. The decision of an arbitrator is final and not subject to review by the courts.   _F_

_F_ 10. The function of a grand jury is to determine the guilt or innocence of the accused.   _F_

_T_ 11. A criminal defendant may not be tried twice for the same crime.   _T_

_T_ 12. A motion for a new trial may be granted if the trial court judge committed prejudicial error during the trial.   _T_

_F_ 13. The parties to a lawsuit may not waive the right to a jury trial.   _F_

_T_ 14. The Federal courts have exclusive jurisdiction of cases involving Federal questions.   _T_

_F_ 15. If a court has subject matter jurisdiction over a case, it will always have jurisdiction to decide the case.   _F_

MULTIPLE CHOICE

_C_   1. To render a binding decision, a court need not have:
   a. subject matter jurisdiction.
   b. jurisdiction over the parties to the dispute.
   c. exclusive jurisdiction.
   d. venue.

_b_   2. The main function of the appellate courts is to:
   a. keep criminals out of jail.
   b. review the decisions of the trial courts for prejudicial error.
   c. hear the testimony of witnesses.
   d. determine questions of fact.

_C_   3. The citizenship of an individual is:
   a. the State of his birth.
   b. the State where he is employed.
   c. the State where he is domiciled.
   d. any State where he has been domiciled.

_d_   4. Diversity of citizenship exists when:
   a. the plaintiff and defendant are citizens of different states.
   b. a foreign country brings an action against U.S. citizens.
   c. U.S. citizens bring an action against citizens of a foreign country.
   d. all of the above.

5. In a case where the appropriate State and Federal courts have concurrent jurisdiction to hear the matter, the plaintiff may bring the action:
   a. in the State court only.
   b. in the Federal court only.
   c. in the State court or the Federal court.
   d. none of the above.

6. A party to a civil action who feels that there are no issues of fact to be determined by trial would most likely move for:
   a. a new trial.
   b. a summary judgment.
   c. a directed verdict.
   d. a judgment notwithstanding the verdict.

7. After a criminal trial in which the defendant has been acquitted, the State may:
   a. try the defendant for a separate offense.
   b. try the defendant a second time for the same offense.
   c. appeal for the acquittal.
   d. none of the above.

8. The defendant in a criminal trial may:
   a. be tried without a jury.
   b. be convicted by a jury of less than 12 jurors.
   c. appeal his conviction.
   d. all of the above.

9. In a civil action, the plaintiff is the party more likely to file:
   a. an answer.
   b. a reply.
   c. a counterclaim.
   d. a demurrer.

10. In a civil action, proper service of the summons establishes:
    a. the court's venue.
    b. the court's subject matter jurisdiction over the controversy.
    c. the court's jurisdiction over the person of the defendant.
    d. all of the above.

11. Jurisdiction of a court over a party to a lawsuit is:
    a. in personam.
    b. in rem.
    c. attachment.
    d. venue.

12. When a Federal district court hears a case solely under diversity of citizenship jurisdiction, the Federal courts apply _____ law.
    a. Federal statutory
    b. U.S. Constitutional
    c. State
    d. common

C   13. Which of the following is included in the "discovery" stage of a lawsuit?
    a.   Voir dire.
    b.   The pleadings.
    c.   Depositions.
    d.   Venue.

b   14. A motion to dismiss for failure to state a claim is also known as a/an:
    a.   answer.
    b.   demurrer.
    c.   peremptory challenge.
    d.   motion for a directed verdict.

b   15. Paul Plaintiff has a judgment that he would like to collect from David Defendant. He may do so by means of:
    a.   a contempt of court order.
    b.   writ of execution.
    c.   writ of certiorari.
    d.   appeal by right.

SHORT ESSAY

1. What is the difference between an appeal by right and an appeal by writ of certiorari? _____

2. In a civil trial, what procedure does the judge use in deciding whether to grant or deny a motion for a directed verdict? _____

3. Compare the relative advantages and disadvantages of court adjudication, arbitration and mediation/conciliation. _____

4. Outline the major courts in the Federal court system and in the State court system of the State where you live. _____

5. Outline using correct terminology the process by which a civil lawsuit is begun and proceeds through the court system. _____

CHAPTER 3

CONSTITUTIONAL AND ADMINISTRATIVE LAW

PURPOSE

This chapter introduces the student to some basic terminology and concepts found in the U.S. Constitution. The process of judicial review by which the U.S. Supreme Court reviews legislation, acts of the executive branch, and the decisions of inferior courts is also discussed in the chapter. The sources of Federal power and the limitations on governmental power are summarized with particular emphasis on the Federal Commerce Power, which forms the basis for most Federal regulation of business, and the Bill of Rights, which places limits on governmental power. The Fourteenth Amendment Due Process and Equal Protection Clauses and the judicial tests used in applying these clauses to challenges of governmental power are also summarized. These two clauses and the tests used in applying them have particular relevance to the area of administrative law, because administrative agencies are governmental agencies that have the authority to affect the rights of private parties through their operations.

CHAPTER CHECKPOINTS

After reading and studying this chapter, you should be able to:

1. Discuss the principles of judicial review and preemption and their interrelationship.

2. List the powers possessed by the Federal government and identify the Constitutional source of each power.

3. List the limitations on government action and identify the Constitutional source of each limitation.

4. Identify the three tests used by courts in applying the Equal Protection Clause when deciding whether to uphold or to set aside a statute or administrative rule.

5. List the three basic functions of administrative agencies, discuss the Administrative Procedures Act, and identify the limits placed upon administrative agencies.

CHAPTER OUTLINE

I. Constitutional Law - The fundamental law of a particular level of government; it establishes the structure of government and defines political relationships within it.

A. Basic Principles
1. Federal Supremacy and Preemption - The Federal Constitution as the "supreme law of the land" takes precedence over all other law. Under Federal preemption the Federal government has the first right to regulate matters within its powers to the possible exclusion of State regulation.
2. Judicial Review - This is the power of the courts to determine the constitutionality of any legislative or executive act.
3. Separation of Powers - This is the allocation of powers among the legislative, executive and judicial branches of government.
4. State Action - Most protections in the U.S. Constitution and its amendments apply only to governmental action as opposed to actions taken by private individuals.

B. Powers of Government - Legislation enacted by Congress must be based on a specific power granted to the Federal government by the Constitution.
1. Federal Commerce Power - The exclusive power granted to the Federal government by the U.S. Constitution in Article I, Section 8 to regulate commerce with foreign countries and among the States.
2. State Regulation of Commerce
    a. Regulations - The commerce clause restricts the States' power to regulate activities if the result obstructs or unduly burdens interstate commerce; the balancing factors are: (1) the necessity and importance of the regulation; (2) the burden imposed on interstate commerce; and (3) the extent of discrimination against interstate commerce in favor of local concerns.
    b. Taxation - The commerce clause in connection with the import-export clause limits the power of the States to tax; once goods enter the stream of interstate or foreign commerce, the power of the State to tax ceases and does not resume until the goods are delivered or their movement terminates.
3. Federal Fiscal Powers
    a. Taxation and Spending - The Federal government has broad power to tax limited by the following: (1) direct taxes other than income taxes must be apportioned among the States; (2) custom duties and excise taxes must be uniform throughout the United States; and (3) no duties may be levied on exports from any State. The spending of Congress is broad and will be upheld so long as it does not violate a specific constitutional limitation on Federal power.
    b. Borrowing and Coining Money - Article I, Section 8 gives Congress the power to borrow and coin money.
    c. Eminent Domain - This is the power of the government to take private property for public use upon payment of fair compensation. It supplements the government's power to tax.

C. Limitations on Government - Restrictions on governmental powers are not absolute limitations but instead will be scrutinized under one of three tests which are the rational relationship test, the strict scrutiny test and the intermediate test.
1. Contract Clause - Article I, Section 10 contains a prohibition against the State's retroactively modifying public and private contracts.
2. First Amendment - The First Amendment's guarantee of free speech is not absolute.
    a. Commercial Speech - Expression related to the economic interest of the speaker and its audience receives a lesser degree of constitutional protection.
    b. Defamation - Public figures who pursue a cause of action for the tort of defamation or injury to their reputation by publication of false statements must prove actual malice or proof that the defendant had knowledge of the falsity of the communication or acted in reckless disregard of its truth or falsity.
3. Due Process - The Fifth and Fourteenth Amendments prohibit the Federal and State governments respectively from depriving any person of life, liberty, or property without due process of law.

a. Substantive Due Process - This refers to the requirement that governmental action be compatible with individual liberties; where fundamental rights are involved strict scrutiny till be used.

b. Procedural Due Process - This requires that governmental action depriving a person of life, liberty or property be done through a fair procedure.

4. Equal Protection - Requires that similarly situated persons be treated similarly by governmental actions.

a. Rational Relationship Test - Applies to economic legislation and requires only that it is conceivable that the legislation bears some rational relationship to a legitimate governmental interest furthered by the legislation; applied to economic regulation.

b. Strict Scrutiny Test - Far more exacting than the rational relationship test and requires that the legislature's classification is necessary to promote a compelling or overriding governmental interest; applied where fundamental rights and suspect classifications are involved.

c. Intermediate Test - Imposes a level of scrutiny more rigorous than the rational relationship test but less demanding than the strict scrutiny test; applies to legislation based on gender, legitimacy and usually citizenship.

II. Administrative Law - That branch of public law that governs the powers and procedures of administrative agencies, as well as the review of agency actions.

A. Federal Administrative Agencies - Governmental entities other than courts and legislatures having authority to affect the rights of private parties through their operations. These agencies are frequently criticized but the scope of administrative law has expanded enormously and much of Federal, State and local law in this country is established by these agencies which have sometimes been labelled the "fourth branch of government."

B. Operation of Administrative Agencies - The term "administrative process" refers to the entire set of activities in which administrative agencies engage while carrying out their rulemaking, enforcement, and adjudicative functions. The power of all three separate branches of government are exercises by these agencies.

1. Rulemaking - The process by which an administrative agency promulgates rules of law is governed by the Administrative Procedures Act.

a. Legislative Rules - Often called regulations and are in effect "administrative statutes." They must not violate any provision of the U.S. Constitution such as the requirement of due process; must be promulgated in accordance with the procedures set forth in the APA.

b. Interpretive Rules - Statements issued by the agency which explain how the agency construes its governing statute. Interpretive rules are exempt from the APA but are not law in that they are not automatically binding on private parties.

c. Procedural Rules - These are also exempt from the APA and establish rules of conduct for practice before the agency, identify an agency's organization and describe its method of operation.

2. Enforcement - Agencies have the power to investigate conduct to determine if there has been a violation of the statute or of the agency's legislative rules. Agencies have great discretion to compel disclosure of information.

3. Adjudication - The formal procedure by which an agency resolves a matter. It involves applying legal rules to facts; an administrative hearing is tried to an administrative law judge who decides both the facts and law to be applied.

C. Limits on Administrative Agencies

1. Judicial Review - The court may either compel agency action unlawfully withheld or set aside impermissible agency action. The scope of judicial review is limited to reviewing questions of

law; the court is restricted in its scrutiny of questions of fact or policy.

2. Legislative Control - The legislature may exercise control through its budgetary power; by amending the agency's enabling statute; by establishing general guidelines such as the APA; by reversing or changing an agency rule through legislation; through review of agencies by Congressional oversight committees; and through the Congressional power to confirm high-level administrative appointments.

3. Control by Executive Branch - The president has the power to appoint and remove the chief administrator of agencies, but he has less control of independent agencies. The president also submits a budget to Congress and can impound monies or restructure agencies unless disapproved by Congress.

DEFINITIONS

1. Federal preemption

2. Judicial review

3. Separation of powers

4. Commerce power

5. Fiscal power

6. Contract clause

7. Administrative process

8. Equal protection

9. Administrative law

10. Adjudication

11. Interpretative rules

12. Procedural rules

13. State action

14. Eminent domain

15. Defamation

16. Procedural due process

17. Substantive due process

18. Rational relationship test

19. Strict scrutiny test

20. Intermediate test

21. Administrative agency

22. Order

23. Legislative rules

TRUE/FALSE

F   1. Interpretative rules establish an administrative agency's organization and method of operation.

T   2. The doctrine of Federal preemption requires that a conflicting State regulation give way to the Federal rule.

F   3. States are not permitted to regulate commerce in any way.

F   4. Federal fiscal poers are derived from the Commerce Clause.

F   5. The right of eminent domain permits the taking of private property by government without fair compensation.

T   6. Defamation is a civil wrong.

T   7. Procedural due process refers to the decision-making process that enforces substantive laws.

T   8. Under the Fourteenth Amendment's rational relationship test, there is a strong presumption that the legislation is constitutional.

F   9. Administrative law is a branch of private law.

T   10. The tenth amendment reserves powers to the States that are not specifically delegated to the Federal government.

F   11. While goods are in the stream of interstate commerce, they may be taxed by individual States.

F   12. The United States Court has held that commercial speech falls outside the protection of the First Amendment.

F   13. The rational relationship test is the most exacting test used by the U.S. Supreme Court.

T   14. The Fifth and Fourteenth Amendments both contain due process clauses.

F   15. Commercial speech is given no protection under the U.S. Constitution.

MULTIPLE CHOICE

c 1. Which of the following is not a Federal fiscal power?
   a. Power to tax and spend.
   b. Power to borrow and coin money.
   c. Power of eminent domain.
   d. All of the above are Federal fiscal powers.

d 2. For a public official to recover in a defamation action, she must show that the defamatory remarks were made with:
   a. no malice.
   b. an evil motive.
   c. a criminal intent.
   d. actual malice.

b 3. The equal protection clause is contained in the:
   a. Fifth amendment.
   b. Fourteenth amendment.
   c. First amendment.
   d. Fourth amendment.

c 4. Substantive due process rights would include all of the following except:
   a. right of privacy.
   b. right to interstate travel.
   c. right to have certain evidence excluded from a trial.
   d. right to vote.

d 5. For the purposes of procedural due process, the term "property" includes:
   a. real property and personal property only.
   b. real property and entitlements only.
   c. personal property and entitlements only.
   d. real property, personal property, and entitlements.

c 6. In equal protection cases involving fundamental rights or suspect classifications, which test would be used for review by the Supreme Court?
   a. rational relationship test
   b. procedural due process test
   c. strict scrutiny test
   d. substantive relationship test

a 7. The power of eminent domain is contained in the:
   a. Fifth amendment.
   b. Fourth amendment.
   c. Fourteenth amendment.
   d. First amendment.

b   8. The procedure by which an agency sets forth rules is specified in the:
          a. Federal Procedures Act.
          b. Administrative Procedures Act.
          c. Federal Rule-making Act.
          d. Federal Trade Commission Act.

d   9. A decision by an administrative agency may be overturned if the agency:
          a. exceeded its authority.
          b. acted arbitrarily or capriciously.
          c. reached conclusions not supported by substantial evidence.
          d. all of the above.

c 10. Which of the following is the only amemndment to apply to private individuals?
          a. First amendment
          b. Fourth amendment
          c. Thirteenth amendment
          d. Fourteenth amendment

a 11. The protection of the _____ Amendment applies to cases involving the tort of defamation.
          a. First
          b. Fourth
          c. Fifth
          d. Ninth

c 12. Which of the following would be considered property for purposes of procedural due process?
          a. Social security payments
          b. Food stamps
          c. Both social security and food stamps
          d. Neither social security nor food stamps

d 13. Limits placed on administrative agencies include:
          a. judicial review of agency actions.
          b. appointment of administrators by the President.
          c. control of the budget by Congress.
          d. all of the above.

b 14. Which of the following is a true statement with regard to the Commerce Clause of the U.S. Constitution?
          a. It expressly excludes State regulation of interstate commerce.
          b. It expressly permits Federal regulation of interstate commerce.
          c. It expressly excludes State regulation and expressly permits Federal regulation.
          d. The U.S. Constitution makes no statement regarding regulation of commerce.

d 15. Which of the following Amendments to the U.S. Constitution places limits upon government?
          a. The First amendment.
          b. The Fourteenth amendment.
          c. The Contract Clause.
          d. All of the above place limits upon government.

SHORT ESSAY

1. How does the burden of proof in a defamation case involving a public figure differ from cases where a private person is involved? _____
   _____
   _____
   _____

2. What is the difference between substantive due process and procedural due process? _____
   _____
   _____
   _____

3. In equal protection cases, how does the rational relationship test compare with the strict scrutiny test?
   _____
   _____
   _____

4. Explain the constitutional basis supporting Federal preemption of State law. _____
   _____
   _____
   _____

5. How does the Commerce Clause restrict the ability of States to regulate interstate commerce? _____
   _____
   _____
   _____

CHAPTER 4

CRIMINAL LAW

PURPOSE

Whereas civil law defines duties, the violation of which constitutes a wrong against the injured party, the criminal law establishes duties, the violation of which is a wrong against the whole community. Civil law is a part of private law; criminal law is a part of public law. In a civil case, the injured party sues to recover compensation for the injury sustained. In a criminal case, a public prosecutor brings a case against a person for a wrong against society. If the person accused is convicted, the wrongdoer will be punished by a fine or imprisonment or both. Some conduct may be both a crime and a civil wrong, or tort. The purpose of this chapter is to introduce the general principles of criminal law and to define and classify some of the most common crimes involving property. The purpose is also to summarize some of the common defenses to criminal charges and to outline the usual procedure followed in a criminal case from the time the case is begun to the time the case comes to trial. Because many of the defenses raised in criminal cases and much of the procedure that is followed stems from provisions in the Bill of Rights, the chapter discusses a number of provisions found in the U.S. Constitution.

CHAPTER CHECKPOINTS

After reading and studying the chapter, you should be able to:

1. Distinguish between a tort and a crime and identify the essential elements of a crime.

2. Compare the procedure used in initiating and pursuing a civil case to the procedure used in initiating and pursuing a criminal case.

3. Identify and define the common property crimes and the common defenses to crimes.

4. Identify the protections for criminal defendants found in the U.S. Constitution and the source of each of these constitutional rights.

5. Outline the steps in a criminal prosecution using appropriate legal terminology.

CHAPTER CHECKPOINTS

After reading and studying the chapter, you should be able to:

1. Distinguish between a tort and a crime and identify the essential elements of a crime.

2. Compare the procedure used in initiating and pursuing a civil case to the procedure used in initiating and pursuing a criminal case.

3. Identify and define the common property crimes and the common defenses to crimes.

4. Identify the protections for criminal defendants found in the U.S. Constitution and the source of each of these constitutional rights.

5. Outline the steps in a criminal prosecution using appropriate legal terminology.

CHAPTER OUTLINE

A. Nature of Crimes - A crime is any act or omission forbidden by public law in the interest of protecting society and made punishable by fines, imprisonment or death in a judicial proceeding brought by the government.
    1. Essential Elements - A crime consists of two elements: (a) the wrongful or overt act (actus reus); and (b) the criminal intent (mens rea). Some statutory crimes require only objective fault; many regulatory statutes have dispensed with the mental element and impose criminal liability without fault.
    2. Classification - Historically, crimes were classified as wrongs in themselves or morally wrong (mala in se) or not morally wrong but declared wrongful by law (mala prohibita); from the standpoint of seriousness, crimes are classified as felonies (serious crimes), misdemeanors and petty crimes.
        a. White-Collar Crime - Defined by the Justice Department as nonviolent crime involving deceit, corruption, or breach of trust.
        b. Liability of the Employer - Vicarious liability is liability imposed on one person for the acts of another person. An employer is vicariously liable for acts of his employees if the employer directed, participated in, or approved of the acts.
        c. Liability of the Corporation - Historically, corporations were not held criminally liable, because they did not possess the requisite criminal intent. Today, corporations can be convicted of crimes and punished by means of fine; individuals in the corporation can be found guilty of crimes.
        d. Computer Crime - A special type of white collar crime; unauthorized access to a computer is a Federal crime.
        e. Racketeer Influenced and Corrupt Organizations Act - Enacted in 1970 to terminate the infiltration by organized crime into legitimate businesses; it imposes severe civil and criminal penalties when a business commits two or more predicted acts within a 10 year period.

B. Offenses Against Property
    1. Larceny - The trespassory taking and carrying away of personal property of another with the intent to deprive the victim permanently of the goods.
    2. Embezzlement - The improper taking of another's property by one who was in lawful possession of it.
    3. False Pretenses - The crime of obtaining title to property of another by means of materially false representations of fact, with knowledge of their falsity and made with intent to defraud.
    4. Robbery - Larceny with the additional elements that (a) the property is taken from the victim or in the immediate presence of the victim, and (b) it is accomplished through either force or threat of force. If

a deadly weapon is used, the crime may constitute aggravated robbery.

5.   Extortion and Bribery - Extortion is sometimes called blackmail and is generally held to be the making of threats for the purpose of obtaining money or property. Bribery is the offer of money or property to a public official to influence the official's decision.

6.   Burglary - The breaking and entering of a dwelling house at night with the intent to commit a felony was the common law definition. Most modern statutes require an entry into a building with the intent to commit a felony in the building.

7.   Forgery - The intentional falsification or false making of a document with the intent to defraud.

8.   Bad Checks - A statutory crime that varies greatly from jurisdiction to jurisdiction.

C. Criminal Defenses

1. Defense of Person or Property

a.   Self-Defense - An individual may use reasonable force to protect himself against an attack if he reasonably believes that he is in immediate danger of unlawful bodily harm and that the use of force is necessary to protect himself from such harm.

b.   Defense of Another - An individual has a complete defense against criminal prosecution if he uses reasonable force in defense of another provided he reasonably believes the other to be in immediate danger of unlawful bodily harm and that use of such force is necessary to prevent this harm.

c.   Defense of Property - An individual has the right to use reasonable force to protect her property but cannot use a deadly mechanical device such as a spring gun.

2. Incapacity - Sometimes a defense based upon lack of criminal intent.

a.   Insanity - A troubling defense in the legal system. The traditional test is the M'Naghten test. Under this test, a person is not criminally liable if at the time of committing the act, he did not understand the nature and quality of the act or could not distinguish between right or wrong. Under the irresistable impulse test, a person is not liable if he had a mental disease that prevented him from controlling his conduct, even though he understood the nature of his act. The ALI's Model Penal Code Test differs from the other two in that it requires only a substantial lack of capacity, whereas the others require a complete impairment of capacity or self-control.

b.   Infancy - A child under the age of seven is conclusively presumed to be incapable of committing a crime. Between seven and fourteen, there is a rebuttable presumption that the child is incapable of committing a crime. Above the age of fourteen, there is a rebuttable presumption that a child is capable of committing a crime.

c.   Intoxication - Most States follow the voluntary/involuntary test which makes involuntary intoxication a defense but not voluntary intoxication.

3. Other Defenses

a.   Duress - A person who is threatened with immediate, serious bodily harm to himself or another unless he engages in criminal conduct other than murder may raise the defense of duress.

b.   Mistake of Fact - A person who reasonably believes the facts to be such that his conduct would not constitute a crime may use this defense to justify her conduct.

c.   Entrapment - This defense arises when a law enforcement official induces a person to commit a crime when that person would not have done so otherwise.

D. Criminal Procedure

1.   Steps in Criminal Prosecution - Varies somewhat from State to State, but generally includes arrest, booking and formal notice of charges; preliminary hearing to determine probable cause; indictment or information in less serious cases; arraignment and trial by jury to establish whether there is guilt beyond a reasonable doubt.

2.   Fourth Amendment - Protects individuals against unreasonable searches and seizures.

3.   Fifth Amendment - Protects persons against self-incrimination, double jeopardy, and being charged

with a capital or infamous crime except by grand jury indictment.

4. Sixth Amendment - Provides that the Federal government shall provide the accused with a speedy and public trial by an impartial jury, shall inform the accused of the nature and cause of the accusations, shall be afforded the opportunity to confront witnesses against her, shall be afforded with compulsory process for obtaining witnesses in her favor, and shall have the assistance of counsel for her defense.

DEFINITIONS

1. Intent

2. Preliminary hearing

3. Arraignment

4. Information

5. RICO

6. White-collar crime

7. Probable cause

8. Larceny

9. Embezzlement

10. Robbery

11. Extortion

12. Burglary

13. Incapacity

14. False pretenses

15. Duress

16. Mistake of fact

17. Entrapment

18. Exclusionary rule

19. Self-defense

20. Mens rea

21. Actus reus

TRUE/FALSE

F   1. Criminal law is a part of private law. F

F   2. To prove that a crime has been committed, it is necessary only to demonstrate that the defendant had the required criminal intent. F

T   3. A felony is any crime punishable by death or imprisonment in the penitentiary. T

T   4. Voluntary manslaughter is the intentional, unjustified killing of another committed under extenuating circumstances. T

F   5. Assault is the unlawful touching of another person. F

F   6. To establish the crime of larceny, it is not necessary to prove that there was an intent to deprive the victim permanently of her goods. F

F   7. False pretenses is a common law crime. F

T   8. The exclusionary rule prohibits illegally seized evidence from being introduced into court. T

T   9. The right to a jury trial is provided by the Sixth Amendment. T

F   10. In a criminal trial, the prosecution must establish guilt by a preponderance of the evidence. F

F   11. The right to a jury trial is found in the Fifth Amendment. F

F   12. Duress can never be raised as a defense to the commission of a crime. F

T   13. A woman may use deadly force to protect herself against an attack that threatens death or serious bodily harm. T

F   14. A person who breaks into a vacant house and steals valuable household items has committed robbery. F

T   15. Reasonable, but not deadly, force can be used to defend one's property. T

MULTIPLE CHOICE

C   1. The defense available to a criminal defendant who has been threatened with immediate, serious bodily harm is:
a. mistake of fact.
b. entrapment.
c. duress.
d. infancy.

_C_   2.   Generally, a crime consists of which of the following?
      a.   A wrongful or overt act.
      b.   The requisite criminal intent.
      c.   Both a and b.
      d.   None of the above.

_a_   3.   A crime punishable by a fine or imprisonment in local jail is called a:
      a.   misdemeanor.
      b.   felony.
      c.   white collar crime.
      d.   mala in se.

_d_   4.   Which of the following crimes involves an intentional misrepresentation of fact in order to cheat
           another?
      a.   Extortion.
      b.   Robbery.
      c.   Burglary.
      d.   False pretenses.

_b_   5.   A law requiring motorists to yield the right of way would be classified as:
      a.   mala in se.
      b.   mala prohibits.
      c.   a felony.
      d.   none of the above.

_C_   6.   Which of the following is not an essential element of larceny?
      a.   Trespassing taking.
      b.   Carrying away of another's personal property.
      c.   Under the threat of serious physical harm.
      d.   With the intent to deprive the victim permanently of the goods.

_d_   7.   Which of the following is NOT a defense to a criminal act?
      a.   Infancy.
      b.   Intoxication.
      c.   Self-defense.
      d.   Mistake of law.

_a_   8.   Individuals are protected against unreasonable searches and seizures by the:
      a.   Fourth Amendment.
      b.   Fifth Amendment.
      c.   Sixth Amendment.
      d.   Fourteenth Amendment.

_d_   9.   The right to a twelve member jury is provided by:
      a.   the Sixth Amendment.
      b.   the Fourth Amendment.
      c.   the Fourteenth Amendment.
      d.   custom.

b 10. Which of the following crimes includes all the elements of the crime of larceny?
a. Burglary.
b. Robbery.
c. Extortion.
d. False pretenses.

d 11. A warrant is not required for a search by the police when:
a. they have just witnessed a crime.
b. they have a report from an informant that someone has stolen goods at her house.
c. they would like to wiretap the phone of a suspected drug dealer.
d. Two of the above (a and b).

b 12. Violations of RICO would be considered:
a. petty crime.
b. white collar crime.
c. computer crime.
d. civil violations.

d 13. The rule which prohibits the introduction of illegally seized evidence is the:
a. mala in se rule.
b. predicate act rule.
c. due process rule.
d. exclusionary rule.

d 14. How are crimes distinguished from other forms of unlawful conduct?
a. They are prosecuted by the victims.
b. They are offenses against society as a whole.
c. They are punishable by a fine and/or imprisonment.
d. They are offenses against all of society and are punishable by a fine and/or imprisonment.

C 15. Which of the following is considered to be the most serious?
a. A petty misdemeanor.
b. A gross misdemeanor.
c. A felony.
d. A tort.

SHORT ESSAY

1. Outline the steps in a criminal prosecution using appropriate terminology. _____
   _____
   _____
   _____
   _____

2. Under what circumstances may an individual use deadly force? _____
   _____
   _____
   _____
   _____

3. Explain the voluntary/involuntary test followed by most states in allowing intoxication as a defense to criminal conduct. _____

   _____

   _____

   _____

   _____

4. Under the Fourth Amendment, a search warrant is not required in what situations? _____

   _____

   _____

   _____

   _____

5. Distinguish between a tort and a crime. _____

   _____

   _____

   _____

   _____

CHAPTER 5

INTENTIONAL TORTS

PURPOSE

The purpose of this chapter is to introduce the student to the law of intentional torts. The law of torts reallocates losses caused by human misconduct. In general, a tort is committed when a person owes a duty to another, breaches that duty and when that breach proximately causes injury to the other person's body or property. Torts may be inflicted intentionally, negligently, or without fault (strict liability). This chapter summarizes the general common law of intentional torts. All of the torts studied in this chapter require the element of intent. As defined in tort law, "intent" is not necessarily the desire to harm, but the desire to cause the consequences of an act or to know that the consequences of an act are substantially certain to result from it.

CHAPTER CHECKPOINTS

After reading and studying this chapter, you should be able to:

1. Define "intent" as used in the law of intentional torts and recognize fact situations where intent to commit a tort exists.

2. List and define six intentional torts that cause injury or damage to the person.

3. Identify and define three business torts that interfere with economic interests.

4. Identify the two broad categories of defenses to intentional torts.

5. Discuss the standards applied in determining the amount of force that a person may use in defending oneself, another person, or one's property.

CHAPTER OUTLINE

I. Intent - For intentional tort purposes, intent means that a person does an act knowing its consequences or that he believes such consequences are substantially certain to result from the act.
   A. Injury or Damage to the Person
      1. Battery - The intentional infliction of harmful or offensive bodily contact constitutes a battery.
      2. Assault - The intentional infliction of fear of immediate bodily harm or offensive contact is an

assault.

3. False Imprisonment - Intentional interference with a person's freedom of movement by unlawful confinement is false imprisonment.
4. Infliction of Emotional Distress - Extreme and outrageous conduct intentionally or recklessly causing severe emotional distress is known as either outrageous conduct or the intentional infliction of emotional distress.
5. Defamation - This tort consists of injury to a person's name or reputation by means of the publication of a false statement. Slander is oral defamation. Libel is defamation that is communicated by writing, television, radio or the like.
6. Invasion of Privacy - Four distinct torts are included within invasion of privacy.
    a. Appropriation - The unauthorized use of another person's name or likeness for one's own benefit constitutes the tort of appropriation.
    b. Intrusion - Unreasonably and highly offensive interference with the seclusion of another is the tort of intrusion.
    c. Public Disclosure of Private Facts - Offensive publicity given to private information about another person is the public disclosure of private facts.
    d. False Light - Offensive publicity placing another in a false light constitutes this tort.
    e. Defenses - Absolute, conditional and constitutional privilege are the allowable defenses.

B. Interference with Property Rights
    1. Real Property - Land and anything attached to it, such as buildings, trees, and minerals is real property.
        a. Trespass - Wrongful entry onto another's land.
        b. Nuisance -Nontrespassory invasion of another's interest in the private use and enjoyment of his land.
    2. Personal Property - Any type of property other than an interest in land is considered personal property.
        a. Trespass - An intentional dispossession or unauthorized use of the personal property of another is considered a trespass to personal property.
        b. Conversion - The intentional exercise of dominion or control over another's personal property is considered to be conversion.

C. Interference with Economic Interests
    1. Interference with Contractual Relations - Intentionally causing one of the parties to a contract not to perform the contract.
    2. Disparagement - Publication of false statements resulting in harm to another's monetary interests.
    3. Fraudulent Misrepresentation - A false statement made with knowledge of its falsity and intent to deceive constitutes the tort of fraudulent misrepresentation, which is also known as fraud in the inducement when associated with a contract.

II. Defenses to Intentional Torts
    A. Consent - Unless the conduct exceeds the consent given, consent to participate in or view a game or consent to a criminal act will result in no tort being committed.

    B. Privilege
        1. Self-Defense - Privilege exists whether or not the danger actually exists, provided that the defendant's action is based on what a person of average courage would have thought under the circumstances. One may stand her ground and use deadly force if the attack occurs in her own residence; otherwise, she is only privileged to use reasonable force, not intended or likely to cause death or serious bodily harm to defend herself against a threatened harmful or offensive contact or

confinement.

2. Defense of Others – One is privileged to defend third persons from harmful or offensive contact to the same extent that one is privileged to protect oneself.

3. Defense of Property – The possessor of property is privileged to use reasonable force, not intended or likely to cause death or serious bodily harm, to protect real or personal property; may not use indirect means, such as mechanical devices, that employ deadly force unless such force could have been used in the possessor's presence.

DEFINITIONS

1. Tort

2. Intent

3. Battery

4. Assault

5. False imprisonment

6. Outrageous conduct

7. Defamation

8. Libel

9. Slander

10. Absolute privilege

11. Conditional privilege

12. Constitutional privilege

13. Appropriation

14. Intrusion

15. False light

16. Trespass to personal property

17. Nuisance

18. Conversion

19. Trespass to real property

20. Interference with contractual relations

21. Disparagement

22. Consent

23. Exemplary or punitive damages

TRUE/FALSE

_F_ 1. The purpose of tort law is to punish the wrongdoer.

_F_ 2. A person may be assaulted even though he is not afraid for his safety.

_T_ 3. A person may be falsely imprisoned even though he is not aware of the confinement.

_F_ 4. Appropriation of a person's name or likeness must be unreasonable to constitute an invasion of privacy.

_F_ 5. Truth is a complete defense to the tort of unreasonable publication of private facts.

_T_ 6. A person may be liable for trespass to real property even though he causes no actual damage to the property itself.

_T_ 7. A person may be liable for trespass to personal property even though he causes no actual damage to the property itself.

_T_ 8. Truth is a complete defense to the tort of disparagement.

_F_ 9. Infants are not held liable for their intentional torts because they are unable to form the requisite intent.

_F_ 10. A person may use deadly force to protect his property.

_F_ 11. A spring-gun rigged to shoot an intruder is a permissible method for defending an unoccupied house.

_T_ 12. Arthur has a grudge against Bill. When Bill asks him to write a letter of reference to a prospective employer, Arthur readily agrees. He makes untrue statements in the letter, which prevent Bill from getting the job. Arthur is guilty of defamation.

_T_ 13. Harold Homeowner signs a consent form to allow Dr. Bright to perform surgery on his left knee. Through a mixup, Dr. Bright operates on Harold's right elbow. Dr. Bright is guilty of battery.

_F_ 14. Bill Businessman rigs a burglar alarm that drenches an intruder with red dye. The dye is harmless except that it ruins the clothes of the person drenched. If an intruder gets drenched, Harold has committed the tort of battery.

_T_ 15. Sarah Student is detained by a sales clerk and store manager at Marlin's Department Store and accused of shoplifting. The sales clerk is mistaken, having confused Sarah with someone else. Sarah is locked in a room and prevented from leaving. Marlin's is guilty of false imprisonment.

MULTIPLE CHOICE

___C___ 1. A has committed a battery if he:
   a. gently taps B on the shoulder to get his attention.
   b. accidentally steps on B's foot.
   c. pinches B on the bottom to get her attention.
   d. (a) and (c) but not (b).

___a___ 2. A has committed an assault if he:
   a. aims an unloaded gun at B and tells her that he is going to shoot her.
   b. tells B that he is going to shoot her the next time he sees her with C.
   c. kisses B while she is sleeping.
   d. all of the above.

___C___ 3. A is liable for defamation if she:
   a. tells B that C is an adulteress when C is an adulteress.
   b. tells D, her husband, that C is an adulteress when C actually is not an adulteress.
   c. tells E that C is an adulteress when C actually is not an adulteress.
   d. none of the above.

___b___ 4. Publication or publicity is NOT an element of:
   a. defamation.
   b. intrusion.
   c. public disclosure of private facts.
   d. false light.

___d___ 5. A is liable for trespass to real property if he:
   a. unknowingly crosses B's land while jogging.
   b. plays his stereo so loudly that C, his neighbor, can't sleep at night.
   c. tosses a gum wrapper and a cigarette butt onto D's front yard.
   d. (a) and (c) but not (b).

___d___ 6. A is liable for interference with contractual relations if she:
   a. intends to interfere with the performance of another's contract.
   b. knows that her actions are substantially certain to interfere with the performance of another's contract.
   c. intends to interfere with another's prospective contractual relation.
   d. all of the above.

___a___ 7. A is liable for fraudulent misrepresentation if she:
   a. induces B to rely justifiably on her false statements of fact.
   b. induces B to rely justifiably on her false statements of opinion.
   c. induces B to rely unjustifiably on her false statements of fact.
   d. induces B to rely unjustifiably on her true statements of fact.

___C___ 8. A person may defend himself by the use of deadly force:
   a. anytime he is in his own home.
   b. if he reasonably believes his property is in danger.
   c. if he reasonably believes his life is in danger and he has no means of escape.
   d. (a) and (c) but not (b).

_b_   9. If A attacks B, B is privileged to:
        a. retaliate.
        b. defend himself by the use of reasonable force.
        c. defend himself by the use of whatever force he chooses.
        d. counterattack.

_d_   10. The tort of conversion:
        a. includes the intentional destruction of personal property.
        b. includes the use of personal property in an unauthorized manner.
        c. entitles the possessor to recover the full value of the converted property.
        d. all of the above.

_c_   11. As used in tort law, _____ denotes that the actor desires to cause the consequences of his act.
        a. assault
        b. retaliation
        c. intent
        d. privilege

_b_   12. Arthur throws his garbage over the fence into Brian's yard. Arthur has committed the tort of:
        a. nuisance.
        b. trespass to real property.
        c. outrageous conduct.
        d. conversion.

_b_   13. In a defamation case, the defendant raises an issue involving the First Amendment to the U.S. Constitution. This is the defense of:
        a. consent.
        b. privilege.
        c. self-defense.
        d. defense of public property.

_d_   14. Intentional torts that involve interference with property rights include:
        a. battery and assault.
        b. false imprisonment and trespass.
        c. defamation and invasion of privacy.
        d. nuisance and trespass to real property.

_b_   15. Oral defamation is also known as:
        a. libel.
        b. slander.
        c. nuisance.
        d. outrageous conduct.

SHORT ESSAYS

1. What is the difference between trespass and nuisance? _trespass interferes with exclusive possession of the property nuisance interferes with the owner's full use + enjoyment ie. dirt smoke foul smells noise_

2. Explain the meaning of "intent" as used in the law of torts. _____

_____

_____

_____

3. What is the underlying rationale for having such privileges as self-defense and absolute immunity from liability for defamation? _____

_____

_____

_____

4. Arnold needs money to buy drugs, so he beats up Benjamin and steals his wallet. (a) What, if any, torts has Arnold committed? Explain. (b) What, if any, crimes has Arnold committed? Explain. (c) How much force can Benjamin use to defend himself? Explain. (d) If Carl sees Arnold attack Benjamin, how much force can he use to defend Benjamin? _____

_____ torts trespass _____

_____

assault + battery

reasonable force, not deadly
bean no weapon

NEGLIGENCE AND STRICT LIABILITY

PURPOSE

This chapter introduces the student to the law of negligence and strict liability. Liability based upon negligence results from the failure to exercise reasonable care under the circumstances which proximately causes injury to another person or his property. Negligence liability is based upon fault, but it is not based upon the intent to do or fail to do the act which causes the injury. Liability based upon strict liability is liability without fault and without intent to commit an act which causes harm. Instead it is based upon the nature of the activity in which a person is engaging.

CHAPTER CHECKPOINTS

After reading and studying this chapter, you should be able to:

1. List and discuss the basic elements of negligence.

2. Define the reasonable man standard and explain how it applies to children, the physically disabled, those with mental deficiencies, those with superior skill or knowledge, emergency situations, and statutory violations.

3. Explain and compare the duty of care which a property owner has to trespassers, licensees, and invitees.

4. Define the term "res ipsa loquitur" and explain its application to a case involving negligence.

5. Define the term "proximate cause" and explain its application in the Palsgraf case.

6. Explain causation in fact; how the "but for" test is applied to determine causation in fact; and how unforeseeable circumstances and superceding causes limit causation in fact.

7. Define and compare contributory negligence to comparative negligence.

8. Define assumption of the risk and explain how it applies to a case which might otherwise involve negligence. Distinguish assumption of the risk from contributory negligence.

9. List the activities which give rise to strict liability.

10. Identify the defenses that are available to a defendant in a cause of action based upon strict liability.

CHAPTER OUTLINE

I. Negligence - A person is negligent if he fails to exercise reasonable care under the circumstances. According to the Restatement, negligence is "conduct which falls below the standard established by law for the protection of others against unreasonable risk of harm."
   A. Duty of Care
      1. Reasonable Man Standard - This is an objective and external standard which is the duty of care required to avoid being negligent. It is the standard of a fictitious individual who is always careful and prudent and never negligent.
         a. Children - To avoid negligence, children must conform to the standard of a reasonable child of like age, intelligence and experience under like circumstances.
         b. Physical disability - A person who is ill or physically disabled must conform to the standard of a reasonable man under like disability.
         c. Mental deficincy - No allowance is made for insanity or other mental deficiency.
         d. Superior skill or knowledge - A person who is qualified to practice a profession or trade that requires special skill and expertise is required to use the same care and skill normally possessed by members of that profession or trade.
         e. Emergencies - In sudden, unexpected events that call for immediate action, the standard is that of a reasonable man under the circumstances -- the emergency is considered part of the circumstances.
         f. Violation of statute - If the statute is found to apply, the violation of it is negligence per se.
      2. Duty to Act - Except in special circumstances, no one is required to aid another in peril.
      3. Special Duties of Possessors of Land
         a. Duty to trespassers - A trespasser is a person who enters or remains on the land of another without permission or privilege to do so. The owner is not free to inflict intentional injury on a trespasser, but except for children there is no duty to maintain the land in a reasonably safe condition.
         b. Duty to licensees - A licensee is a person privileged to enter or remain on land by virtue of the consent of the lawful possessor; includes social guests. The possessor must warn the licensee of dangerous activities and conditions of which the possessor has knowledge and which the licensee does not and is not likely to discover.
         c. Duty to invitees - An invitee is a person invited upon land for a business purpose. The duty of the possessor is to exercise reasonable care to protect them against dangerous conditions they are unlikely to discover.
      4. Res Ipsa Loquitur - Means "the thing speaks for itself." Permits the jury to infer both negligent conduct and causation.

   B. Proximate Cause - Judicially imposed limitations on a person's liability for the consequences of his negligence.
      1. Causation in Fact - The defendant's negligence must be the actual cause of the plaintiff's injury. Under the "but for rule," the conduct is a cause of an event if the event would not have occurred in the absence of the person's negligent conduct. The "substantial factor test" states that the conduct is a cause of the event if the conduct is a substantial factor in bringing about the harm.
      2. Limitations on Causation in Fact - Unforeseeable consequences and superceding causes are taken into account.

   C. Injury - The plaintiff must prove that the defendant's negligence caused harm to a legally protected

interest.
1. Defenses
   a. Contributory Negligence - The failure of a plaintiff to exercise reasonable care that legally causes him harm. An exception to this general rule is the "last clear chance rule."
   b. Comparative Negligence - Rules adopted by most States that divide damages between the plaintiff and the defendant where the negligence of each has caused the harm.
   c. Assumption of the Risk - The plaintiff's express or implied consent to encounter a known danger.

II. Strict Liability - Liability for injuries caused even though the defendant has not acted intentionally or negligently.
   A. Activities Giving Rise to Strict Liability
      1. Abnormally Dangerous Activities
      2. Keeping of Animals
         a. Trespassing animals
         b. Non-trespassing animals
      3. Products Liability - A recent trend in the law.

   B. Defenses
      1. Contributory Negligence - Ordinary contributory negligence is not a defense.
      2. Comparative Negligence - Allowed by some States in cases of product liability.
      3. Assumption of Risk - If voluntary, assumption of the risk is a defense.

DEFINITIONS

1. Negligence

2. Reasonable man

3. Duty of care

4. Proximate cause

5. Negligence *per se*

6. Trespasser

7. Licensee

8. Invitee

9. *Res Ipsa Loquitur*

10. Causation in fact

11. Contributory negligence

12. Last clear chance

13. Comparative negligence

14. Assumption of risk

15. Strict liability

16. Abnormally dangerous activities

17. But for rule

18. Superseding cause

19. Last clear chance

TRUE/FALSE

____ 1.   A may be liable for B's injuries even though A exercises reasonable care to prevent B's injuries.

____ 2.   A person is under an affirmative duty to aid another in peril whenever he can do so at no risk to his own safety.

____ 3.   A possessor of land may inflict intentional injury upon a trespasser to eject him upon discovery of his presence on the land.

____ 4.   Negligent conduct is a legal cause of harm if the harm would not have occured but for the negligent conduct.

____ 5.   A peson will be liable for the foreseeable consequences of his negligence even though the actual harm results in an unforeseeable manner.

____ 6.   A person may be liable for negligently inflicting emotional distress even though no bodily harm results from the distress.

____ 7.   A plaintiff who has proved all the required elements of a negligence action may nevertheless be deined recovery.

____ 8.   Whether an activity is considered abnormally dangerous or not usually depends on the circumstances under which the activity is conducted.

____ 9.   The contributory negligence of the plaintiff is a defense to most actions based on strict liability.

____ 10. A person who knowingly and voluntarily parks his car in a blasting zone has assumed the risk of and may not recover for damage to his car caused by the blasting.

____ 11. The "but for" rule is a test for determining causation in fact.

____ 12. A person with a mental deficiency will be held to the same reasonable man standard as a person of normal intelligence.

_T_ 13. The possessor of land owes a higher duty of care to a licensee than to a trespasser. _T_

_____ 14. The Palsgraf case involved issues of contributory negligence.

_T_ 15. For purposes of strict liability, an elephant would be a wild animal. _T_

MULTIPLE CHOICE

_d_ 1. The reasonable man standard of care takes into account the defendant's:
  a. physical disabilities.
  b. mental deficiency.
  c. superior knowledge.
  d. (a) and (c) but not (b).

_c_ 2. The standard of care applicable to a child is that of:
  a. the reasonable man.
  b. a reasonable man who is incapable of exercising the judgment of an adult.
  c. a reasonable person of like age, intelligence, and experience. _c_
  d. a reasonable person who is mentally deficient.

_b_ 3. Assume F violates a statute which is intended to protect restaurant patrons from food poisoning by requiring restaurant owners to install special refrigeration equipment. F may be sued under a standard of care based upon this statute if:
  a. A, a patron, falls down a poorly lit staircase on his way to the salad bar.
  b. B, a patron, becomes violently ill after eating tainted fruit salad.
  c. C, a patron, chokes on a chicken bone which was in his fruit salad.   _b_
  d. D, a waitress, dies after eating tainted fruit salad.

_b_ 4. A is under an affirmative duty to come to the aid of B who is in danger if:
  a. A is B's best friend.
  b. A is responsible for B's predicament. _b_
  c. A is a doctor.
  d. none of the above.

_a_ 5. A possessor of land is liable for the injuries to his licensee if he fails to:
  a. warn her of a known defect which she is unlikely to discover.
  b. repair a known defect.
  c. warn her of a known defect which she is likely to discover.   _a_
  d. discover a defect.

_c_ 6. A plaintiff who sues under *res ipsa loquitur* must show that:
  a. the event which occured would not normally occur in the absence of negligence.
  b. other possible causes have been eliminated by the evidence.
  c. both of the above.
  d. none of the above.   _c_

___d___ 7. A may be relieved of liability for negligent harm to B if an intervening act:
  a. occurs after A's negligent conduct.
  b. is a cause in fact of B's injury.
  c. is a normal consequence of the situation created by A's negligent conduct
  d. (a) and (b) but not (c)

___C___ 8. In a State which does NOT recognize the doctrine of comparative negligence, A may recover from B for injuries proximately caused by B's negligence and A's contributory negligence if:
  a. B's fault was greater than A's fault.
  b. B's fault was less than A's fault.
  c. B had the last clear chance to avoid the injury.
  d. none of the above.

___C___ 9. A, the owner of a dog, is strictly liable to B for harm caused by the dog if it:
  a. digs up B's flower bed.
  b. bites B when it has never attacked or bitten anyone before.
  c. bites B when it has bitten someone before.
  d. bites B when A knows that it frequently chases bicycle riders.

___a___ 10. If A's abnormally dangerous activity injures B, B may not recover for her injuries if she:
  a. assumed the risk of harm.
  b. was more at fault than A.
  c. had the last clear chance to avoid the danger.
  d. was contributorily negligent.

___C___ 11. If proven, _____ prohibits an injured plaintiff from recovering damages.
  a. comparative negligence
  b. res ipsa loquitur
  c. contributory negligence
  d. but for rule.

___C___ 12. The worker's compensation laws place liability upon the employer that is:
  a. comparative.
  b. contributory
  c. strict
  d. absolute

___b___ 13. When a 16-year-old minor commits a tort:
  a. his parents are responsible.
  b. the minor is responsible if he is involved in an adult activity.
  c. will be held to the same reasonable man standard as a five-year-old.
  d. two of the above, (a) and (b).

___C___ 14. Carl Customer goes to Marlin's Department Store to shop. Carl is a _____ while he is shopping.
  a. trespasser
  b. licensee
  c. business visitor
  d. public invitee

b   15. Sarah Student goes to Tom Terrific's house for a party. Sarah is a:
- a. trespasser.
- b. licensee.
- c. public invitee.
- d. business invitee.

SHORT ESSAY

1.   When may the courts apply a statutory standard of care in determining negligence? _____
_____
_____
_____
_____

2.   What are the elements which a plaintiff must prove in an action for negligence? *a duty,*
a breach of said duty, proximate cause &
injury or harm + protect of negligent interfer
_____

3.   What is the difference between causation in fact and proximate cause? _____
_____
_____
_____
_____

4.   List the activities that give rise to strict liability. *explosives (dang. actuals)*
_____ *wild animals*
_____ *product defects*
_____

5.   Compare the application of the reasonable man standard to children and persons of mental deficiency.
How does it differ? _____
_____
_____
_____

PART I

SAMPLE EXAMINATION

_C_ 1. Harold Homeowner has a pet lion cub in a cage in his backyard. One of the neighbor children comes over to play. As the child is petting the animal, it nips him. The child is taken to the hospital emergency room where he receives two stitches. Harold is liable for this injury based on:
a. negligence.
b. intentional tort.
c. strict liability.
d. contributory negligence.

_a_ 2. Harold Homeowner has a pet lion cub in a cage in his backyard. One of the neighbor children comes over to play. As the child is petting the animal, it nips him. Under this fact situation, the child is a:
a. trespasser.
b. business invitee.
c. social invitee.
d. licensee.

_a_ 3. The Federal courts have exclusive jurisdiction over _____ cases.
a. bankruptcy
b. Federal question
c. diversity of citizenship
d. bankruptcy, Federal question and diversity of citizenship.

_C_ 4. The phrase used in negligence law which means "the thing speaks for itself" is:
a. stare decisis.
b. negligence per se.
c. res ipsa loquitur.
d. quasi in rem.

_C_ 5. A decree of an equity court ordering a party to perform a contractual act is known as:
a. an injunction.
b. reformation.
c. specific performance.
d. rescission.

_d_ 6. The U.S. Supreme Court interprets the _____ as granting virtually complete power to Congress to regulate the economy and business.
a. contract clause
b. equal protection clause
c. Federal power to tax and spend
d. commerce clause

_b_ 7. State courts have exclusive jurisdiction over _____ cases.
a. copyright
b. divorce
c. contract
d. diversity

a 8. The nonbinding process in which a third party acts as an intermediary between the disputing parties and proposes solutions for them to consider is known as:
   a. mediation.
   b. arbitration.
   c. conciliation.
   d. consensual arbitration.

d 9. The location where a lawsuit should be brought is known as:
   a. forum non-conveniens.
   b. in personam jurisdiction.
   c. in rem jurisdiction.
   d. venue.

b 10. The _____ protects all individuals against unreasonable searches and seizures and is intended to protect the privacy and security of individuals against arbitrary invasions by government officials.
   a. First Amendment
   b. Fourth Amendment
   c. Fifth Amendment
   d. Sixth Amendment

d 11. Sarah Student attends a professional basketball game with her boyfriend. When the forward passes the ball, the guard misses and the ball strikes Sarah, injuring her and permanently scarring her face. Sarah sues the team. A defense that the team is likely to raise is:
   a. contributory negligence.
   b. comparative negligence.
   c. proximate cause.
   d. assumption of the risk.

c 12. Albert, a citizen of California, is injured in an auto accident, which occurs in Colorado and involves another car which is driven by Barbara, a citizen of Nebraska. Albert's medical expenses and property damage amount to $75,000. Albert sues in Federal court based upon diversity jurisdiction.
   a. No diversity of citizenship exists, because both Albert and Barbara are U.S. citizens.
   b. Diversity exists because Albert is a citizen of California and the accident occured in Colorado.
   c. Diversity exists because Albert is a citizen of California and Barbara is a citizen of Nebraska.
   d. The Federal court will dismiss the suit, because the amount in controversy is less than the minimal jurisdiction amount.

d 13. For purposes of procedural due process, "property" includes:
   a. social security payments.
   b. food stamps.
   c. land.
   d. All of the above are considered property.

c 14. The intentional exercise of dominion or control over another's personal property that so seriously interferes with the other's right of control and which justly requires the payment of full value for the property is known as:
   a. theft.
   b. trespass to personal property.
   c. conversion.
   d. two of the above, (a) and (b).

b 15. Patricia Plaintiff has a case which can be brought in either the State or the Federal court. Jurisdiction in the case is:
   a. in rem.
   b. concurrent.
   c. exclusive
   d. quasi in rem.

d 16. The constitutional protection which guarantees the right to a speedy, public trial by jury is found in the:
   a. First Amendment.
   b. Fourth Amendment.
   c. Fifth Amendment.
   d. Sixth Amendment.

a 17. At the _____, the accused is informed of the charge against him and enters his plea.
   a. arraignment
   b. preliminary hearing
   c. information
   d. trial

c 18. At common law, _____ was defined as a breaking and entering of a dwelling house with the intent to commit a felony.
   a. theft
   b. robbery
   c. burglary
   d. stealing

b 19. The first right of the Federal government to regulate matters within its powers to the possible exclusion of State regulation is known as:
   a. Federal supremacy.
   b. Federal preemption.
   c. judicial review.
   d. State action.

b 20. The Elmville City Council has passed an ordinance stating that no person of Iranian extraction shall be allowed to purchase property within the city limits. Mohammed Abou came to the U.S. as a student ten years ago from Iran. He has now graduated, works as an engineer in Elmville and would like to buy a house there. His attorney tells him the ordinance is unconstitutional and should be challenged. If Mohammed sues to challenge the ordinance, the court will apply the _____ standard.
   a. rational relationship
   b. strict scrutiny
   c. intermediate
   d. beyond a reasonable doubt

CHAPTER 7

INTRODUCTION TO CONTRACTS

PURPOSE

Knowledge of contract law is important to anyone involved in business, but is especially important for anyone in management. Virtually every business transaction and many of the everyday personal transactions into which we enter involve one or more contracts. Ordering something from a catalog, buying an item at a store, agreeing to work as an employee or hiring someone to work as an employee, opening a bank account, and signing a purchase agreement to buy real estate all involve contracts. This chapter summarizes the basic requisites of a binding contract and introduces the student to the sources of contract law and the basic terminology involved in contract law.

CHAPTER CHECKPOINTS

After reading and studying this chapter, you should be able to:

1. Define the term "contract."

2. List the sources of contract law and discuss their interrelationship.

3. List the essential elements of a contract.

4. Identify and define the various classifications of contracts.

5. Define the term "quasi contract," explain why it is not a contract, and why the law allows for its enforcement as if it were a contract.

6. Discuss some of the major changes that have occured in contract law during the twentieth century and why in the opinion of some there has been the death of the contract.

CHAPTER OUTLINE

A. Development of the Law of Contracts
   1. Common Law – Contracts are primarily governed by State common law. An orderly presentation of this law is found in the Restatements of the Law of Contracts.

2.   Uniform Commercial Code - Article 2 of the UCC governs sales of goods. A sale is the transfer of ownership from seller to buyer. Goods are tangible personal property.

3.   Types of Contracts Outside the Code - The Code does not apply to employment contracts, service contracts, insurance contracts, contracts involving real estate, and contracts involving patents and copyrights, all of which are governed by general common law.

B.   Definition of Contract - A binding agreement that the courts will enforce. The Restatement defines a contract as "a promise or a set of promises for the breach of which the law gives a remedy, or the performance of which the law in some way recognizes as a duty." A breach is the failure to properly perform a contractual obligation.

C.   Essentials of a Contract
1.   Manifestation of Mutual Assent
2.   Consideration
3.   Legality of Object
4.   Capacity of the Parties

D.   Classification of Contracts
1.   Formal and Informal Contracts - A formal contract is an agreement which is legally binding because of its particular form or mode of expression; informal contracts are all oral or written contracts other than a formal contract.
2.   Express and Implied Contracts - An express contract is an agreement of parties that is stated in words either in writing or orally; an implied in fact contract is one where agreement of the parties is inferred from their conduct.
3.   Bilateral and Unilateral Contracts - A bilateral contract is one in which both parties exchange promises; a unilateral contract is one in which only one party makes a promise.
4.   Void, Voidable and Unenforceable Contracts - A void contract is no contract at all and is without legal effect. A voidable contract is not wholly lacking in legal effect; it can be avoided by one or both parties based upon fraud or other grounds. An unenforceable contract is one for which the law does not provide a remedy such as one where the Statute of Frauds requirements have not been met or where the Statute of Limitations has run.
5.   Executed and Executory - An executed contract is one that has been fully performed by all of the parties. An executory one has not been fully performed.

E.   Quasi Contract - An obligation based upon contract that is imposed by law to avoid injustice; also called an implied in law contract.

DEFINITIONS

1.   Sale

2.   Goods

3.   Contract

4.   Formal contract

5.   Informal contract

6. Express contract

7. Implied contract

8. Bilateral contract

9. Unilateral contract

10. Void contract

11. Voidable contract

12. Unenforceable contract

13. Executed contract

14. Executory contract

15. Quasi contract

16. Breach

TRUE/FALSE

F 1. Contracts are governed primarily by Federal law.

T 2. As defined by the Uniform Commercial Code, a sale is a contract involving the transfer of title to goods from seller to buyer for a price.

F 3. A contract to provide legal services for a fee is governed by Article 2 of the Uniform Commercial Code.

F 4. As defined by the Uniform Commercial Code, goods are movable, tangible and intangible personal property.

T 5. Where general contract law has not been specifically modified by the Code, the common law of contracts continues to apply.

T 6. An informal contract is any contract, whether oral or written, that does not depend upon mere formality for its legal validity.

F 7. A contract may be formed orally or by a writing, but it may not be inferred merely from the conduct of the parties.

F 8. The courts will presume that the parties intended to form a unilateral contract when it is unclear whether a unilateral or a bilateral contract has been formed.

F 9. A voidable contract has no legal effect and is unenforceable by any party to the contract.

_T_   10. An executory contract is one in which there are one or more unperformed promises by any party to the contract.

_T_   11. A quasi contract is not a contract, but rather is an obligation imposed regardless of the intention of the parties in order to assure a just and equitable result.

_F_   12. All express contracts are also formal contracts.

_F_   13. Today a formal contract needs to be under seal in order to be legally effective.

_T_   14. Thomas says to Steve, "If you will paint my garage, I will pay you $75." Steve replies, "It's a deal." Under these facts, Thomas and Steve are both promisors and promisees.

_T_   15. A promissory note signed in connection with a bank loan is a formal contract.

MULTIPLE CHOICE

_a_   1. All of the following are relevant to defining the principles of contract law EXCEPT:
   a. Federal common law.
   b. State common law.
   c. Restatement, Second, Contracts.
   d. Uniform Commercial Code.

_b_   2. The Uniform Commercial code defines goods as:
   a. movable, tangible and intangible personal property.
   b. movable, tangible personal property.
   c. immovable or movable tangible personal property.
   d. immovable tangible personal property.

_d_   3. The Uniform Commercial Code does NOT apply to:
   a. a contract to purchase a television set.
   b. a contract to sell a textbook.
   c. a contract to purchase a car.
   d. an employment contract.

_b_   4. A written contract induced by fraud is:
   a. void at the election of the defrauded party.
   b. voidable at the election of the defrauded party.
   c. void at the election of the fraudulent party.
   d. voidable at the election of the fraudulent party.

_a_   5. An executed contract is one in which:
   a. all duties under it have been performed by all parties to the contract.
   b. at least one party has performed all of its duties under the contract.
   c. there are one or more unperformed promises by any party to the contract.
   d. the contract is wholly unperformed by one or more of the parties.

d 6. Each of the following is an essential element of a binding promise EXCEPT:
a. manifestation of mutual assent.
b. consideration.
c. capacity of the parties.
d. a writing signed by the parties.

c 7. A promise or a set of promises for the breach of which the law gives a remedy, or the performance of which the law in some way recognizes as a duty, is best described as:
a. a promise.
b. an agreement.
c. a contract.
d. none of the above.

a 8. A manifestation of the intention to act or refrain from acting in a specified way is best described as:
a. a promise.
b. an agreement.
c. a contract.
d. none of the above.

c 9. A contract that is neither express nor implied in fact, but rather is implied in law is called:
a. a formal contract.
b. a unilateral contract.
c. a quasi contract.
d. an executed contract.

d 10. The general law of contracts applies to contracts involving:
a. the services of an accountant.
b. an employment relationship.
c. the sale of a television set.
d. the services of an accountant and an employment relationship.

d 11. A contract in which both parties exchange promises is a/an:
a. formal contract.
b. quasi contract.
c. implied in fact contract.
d. bilateral contract.

a 12. An illegal agreement to pay a bribe to a legislator in return for his vote on an upcoming bill would best be termed a/an:
a. void agreement.
b. valid contract.
c. voidable contract.
d. unenforceable contract.

c 13. A contract agreed to by a person under legal guardianship would best be described as:
a. binding.
b. voidable.
c. void.
d. unenforceable.

14. Bill Businessman places an ad in the local newspaper saying, "Reward: $50 for return of my golden retriever named Fido." The ad lists his address and telephone number. If Tim Teenager finds Fido and returns him to Bill, there will be:
    a. a formal contract requiring that Bill pay Tim $50.
    b. a bilateral contract, because two people are involved.
    c. an implied in fact contract requiring that Bill pay Tim $50.
    d. a unilateral contract, because Bill has promised to pay $50 but Tim hasn't promised anything.

15. The test to determine whether the parties intended to enter into a contract is:
    a. an objective test.
    b. a subjective test.
    c. an implied in law test.
    d. the reasonable man test.

SHORT ESSAY

1. Discuss how State common law, the Restatement Second, of contracts and Article 2 of the Uniform Commercial code combine to form the law of contracts. _____

    _____

    _____

    _____

2. Arthur Accountant orally agrees to serve as an accountant for Clem Client in exchange for Clem's promise to pay Arthur an annual salary of $15,000. Describe this contract in terms of the following classifications: formal/informal;   express/implied;   unilateral/bilateral;   void/voidable/unenforceable; executory/executed. _____

    _____

    _____

    _____

3. In general, what changes in contract law have occured during the twentieth century? Briefly explain why in your opinion these changes have taken place. _____

    _____

    _____

    _____

4. Define the term "contract." How does a contract differ from a quasi contract? _____

    _____

    _____

    _____

5. Indicate whether each of the following contracts would be governed by the common law of contracts or the UCC. Explain your answer.
    a. a purchase agreement to buy a house
    b. an installment sales agreement to buy a VCR

c.   a written agreement to work as an engineer for a corporation for a period of one year
d.   a life insurance policy

_____

_____

_____

_____

CHAPTER 8

Mutual Assent

PURPOSE

For a contract to exist, the parties must have an agreement. This agreement can be either oral or written. In a bilateral contract, the agreement involves a promise for a promise; in a unilateral contract, the agreement involves a promise for either an act or a forebearance to act. In determining whether there is an agreement, it is necessary to analyze whether there has been an offer and whether there has been an acceptance of that offer by someone to whom it was made. The test for making this determination is the objective standard based upon intent as determined from the words and actions of the parties. Contract law is not concerned with what a party actually thought or by the intention a party meant to convey. Instead it is concerned with what an objective third party would have understood from the words and actions of the party.

This chapter examines the essentials of an offer; the distinction between an offer and an invitation seeking offers; determination of the moment of acceptance; determination of whether acceptance has been by an authorized means of communication; the effect of acceptance following a prior rejection; defective acceptances; silence as acceptance; contracts formed by conduct; and acceptance in an auction sale. This chapter is the first one in which students must learn both the common law contract rules and the rules that are found in Article 2 of the UCC. Students must learn both rules, because both rules are essential to a complete understanding of contract law. Code sections that differ from the common law and that students should study include: the sections involving open terms under the Code; output, requirements and exclusive dealing contracts; firm offers in writing by a merchant; the battle of the forms that occurs when offers made and accepted are not mirror images of each other; and auction sales.

CHAPTER CHECKPOINTS

After reading and studying the chapter, you should be able to:

1. List the essentials of an offer, identify the offeror and the offeree, and recognize when an offer comes to an end.

2. Compare the traditional common law's approach to the requirement of definiteness to that found in Article 2 of the UCC and the Restatement.

3. Define the common law "mirror image rule" and explain how this rule has been modified by the Code's Battle of the Forms provision.

4.   Recognize the effective moment of acceptance of an offer and discuss the effect of the means of acceptance on the moment of acceptance.

5.   Identify a firm offer and explain how the Code's firm offer provision differs from the rule at common law.

CHAPTER OUTLINE

I.   Offer - An offer is defined as an indication of willingness to enter into a contract.
    A.   Essentials of an Offer - An offer must be communicated to the offeree. It must manifest an intent to enter into a contract, and it must be sufficiently definite and certain.
        1.   Communication - The communication must be made or authorized by the offeror to the offeree. Communication can be by conduct as well as words.
        2.   Intent - An offer must show an intent to enter into a contract.
            a.   Invitations seeking offers - Advertisements are generally considered to be invitations seeking offers, because they are not sufficiently definite and certain. Note, however, the Lefkowitz case.
            b.   Objective standard for intent - The standard used to determine whether there is intent to enter into a contract is whether a reasonable man under the circumstances would believe there was intent.
        3.   Definiteness - The terms must be clear enough to provide a court with a basis for determining the existence of a breach and for giving an appropriate remedy.
            a.   Open terms under the Code - With good faith and commercial reasonableness omitted terms may be determined, provided the parties intended to enter into a binding contract.
            b.   Output, requirements and exclusive dealings - Outputs and requirements contracts are valid under the Code so long as there is an objective standard for their application and the parties act in good faith. Exclusive dealing contracts are valid under the Code so long as the seller uses her best efforts to supply the goods and the buyer uses his best efforts to promote the sale of the goods.

    B.   Duration of Offers - An offeree's power to accept an offer continues until the offer terminates.
        1.   Lapse of Time - An offer remains open for the specified time period. If no time is stated, the offer will terminate after a reasonable period of time.
        2.   Revocation - Cancellation of an offer by an offeror brings an offer to an end. An offer made to the general public is revoked only by giving equivalent publicity to the revocation as was given to the offer.
            a.   Option contracts - Contracts which provide that an offer will stay open for a specified period of time are enforceable if they comply with all of the requirements of a contract, including the payment of consideration by the offeree to the offeror.
            b.   Firm offers under the Code - A merchant is bound to hold open an offer to buy or sell goods for a stated period not over three months, if the merchant gives assurance in a signed writing that it will be held open.
            c.   Statutory irrevocability - Some offers such as bids for the construction of a building or public work made to a governmental body are irrevocable.
            d.   Irrevocable offers of unilateral contracts - The offeror is obligated not to revoke the offer for a reasonable time where the requested act necessarily requires time and effort on the part of the offeree.
        3.   Rejection - The refusal to accept an offer is effective when received by the offeror and terminates the power of acceptance.
        4.   Counter-offer - A counter-proposal to an offer terminates the original offer upon its receipt by

the offeror. A conditional acceptance is a counter-offer, but the Code treats acceptances containing terms that vary the offer differently than does common law.

5. Death or Incompetency - Death or incompetency of either the offeror or the offeree terminates the offer.

6. Destruction of Subject Matter - If the subject matter of the offer is destroyed, the offer is terminated.

7. Subsequent Illegality - If the subject matter of the offer becomes illegal, the offer is terminated.

II. Acceptance of Offer - Acceptance is a manifestation of a willingness to enter into a contract on the terms of the offer.

   A. Definiteness - Acceptance must be positive and unequivocal. An acceptance must be the mirror image of the offer. Except as modified by the Code, a deviation from the terms of the offer is a counteroffer rather than an acceptance.

   B. Effective Moment of Acceptance - An offer, revocation, rejection and counter-offer are effective when received. An acceptance is generally effective upon dispatch unless the offer specifically provides otherwise or the offeree uses an unauthorized means of communication.

     1. Authorized Means - Historically, this was the means expressly authorized by the offeror. The Restatement and the Code both now provide that unless the offeror has unambiguously indicated otherwise, acceptance can be in any reasonable manner.

     2. Unauthorized Means - Effective when dispatched provided that it is received within the time the authorized means would have arrived.

     3. Specific Provisions in the Offer - The acceptance must conform to the specification. If the offer states that acceptance will be effective only when received, then that is the moment of acceptance.

     4. Acceptance Following a Prior Rejection - The first communication received by the offeror is the effective one.

     5. Defective Acceptances - Late or defective acceptance does not create a contract.

   C. Mode of Acceptance

     1. Silence as Acceptance - Silence is usually not an acceptance unless it becomes one by custom, usage, or course of dealing. There is no legal duty to reply to an offer.

     2. Contract Formed by Conduct - A contract exists if both parties have acted in a manner that manifests a recognition by them of a contract.

     3. Auction Sales - The auctioneer invites offers to buy. A bid is an offer to buy. The offer is accepted and a contract comes into existence upon the fall of the hammer in the hands of the auctioneer or when the auctioneer says "sold." A bidder can withdraw his bid anytime prior to acceptance; the auctioneer can withdraw the goods unless the auction is without reserve.

DEFINITIONS

1. Offer

2. Offeror

3. Offeree

4. Acceptance

5. Objective standard

6.   Open terms

7.   Output contract

8.   Requirements contract

9.   Exclusive dealing

10. Revocation

11. Option contract

12. Firm offer

13. Rejection

14. Counter-offer

15. Conditional acceptance

16. Mirror image rule

17. Auction sale

TRUE/FALSE

_F_   1.   The person to whom an offer is made is called the offeror.

_T_   2.   In order to have the mutual assent requisite to the formation of a contract, the offeror must have communicated the offer and the offeree must have knowledge of the offer.

_F_   3.   An offer must be stated or communicated by words and cannot be inferred from conduct.

_F_   4.   An offeror's manifestation of intent to enter into a contract is judged by a subjective standard.

_T_   5.   The Uniform Commercial Code imposes an obligation of good faith in the performance or enforcement of every contract within its scope.

_T_   6.   A contract for the sale of goods may contain an open price term.

_T_   7.   If an offer does not state the time within which the offeree may accept, the offer will terminate upon the expiration of a reasonable time.

_F_   8.   In order for an offeror's revocation of his offer to be effective, notice of the revocation must be directly communicated to the offeree before acceptance.

_F_   9.   A rejection is effective at the moment of its dispatch by the offeree.

_T_ 10.   Under the common "mirror image" rule, an offeree's acceptance will not be effective if it deviates from the exact terms of the offer.

11. Under the Uniform Commercial Code, if both parties are merchants, additional terms contained in the offeree's unconditional acceptance will become part of the contract provided they do not materially alter the agreement and are not objected to by either party within a reasonable period of time.

12. Under the Restatement of Contracts and the Code, unless language in the offer, or the circumstances under which it is made indicate otherwise, an offer shall be construed as inviting acceptance in any reasonable manner.

13. When an acceptance is sent following a prior rejection, the first communication sent by the offeree is the effective one.

14. Although an offeree is generally under no duty to reply to an offer, by custom, usage, or course of dealing, silence or inaction by the offeree may operate as an acceptance.

15. At an auction announced to be "without reserve," the auctioneer is free to withdraw the goods from sale at any time prior to a bid's acceptance.

MULTIPLE CHOICE

1. In order for an offer to have legal effect, it must:
   a. be communicated to the offeree.
   b. manifest an intent to enter into a contract.
   c. be sufficiently definite and certain in its terms.
   d. all of the above.

2. An offer can be effectively communicated to an offeree by:
   a. a writing only.
   b. spoken words only.
   c. a writing or by spoken words only.
   d. a writing, by spoken words, or by conduct from which a reasonable person could infer a promise.

3. When an offeree's proposal does not constitute an offer because it fails to manifest an intent to enter into a contract, the offeree's purported acceptance constitutes a/an:
   a. offer.
   b. counter-offer.
   c. contract
   d. rejection.

4. Advertisements, circulars, quotation sheets and other similar business communications usually do not constitute offers because:
   a. they do not contain a promise.
   b. they leave unexpressed many terms which would be necessary to the making of a contract.
   c. both (a) and (b).
   d. none of the above.

C   5. Whether or not a person's words or conduct constitutes an offer is determined according to:
   a. the subjective intent of the offeror.
   b. the subjective intent of the offeree.
   c. the objective, reasonable person standard.
   d. none of the above.

C   6. With respect to agreements for the sale of goods, the Code provides standards by which omitted terms may be ascertained, provided:
   a. the parties actually agreed upon the open term but negligently failed to include it in the written contract.
   b. the parties actually discussed the open term but intentionally failed to include it in the written contract.
   c. the parties intended to enter into a binding contract regardless of whether they actually discussed the open term or not.
   d. the parties did not intend to enter into a binding contract regardless of whether they actually discussed the open term or not.

d   7. If an offer does not specify the time within which it is to be accepted, the offer will terminate:
   a. immediately.
   b. after 24 hours.
   c. after thirty days.
   d. after a reasonable period of time.

d   8. An offeree generally may cancel or revoke his offer at any time prior to its acceptance unless the offer:
   a. is an option contract.
   b. is a merchant's firm offer under the Code.
   c. contemplates a unilateral contract and the offeree has begun the invited performance.
   d. all of the above.

C   9. A rejection of an offer by the offeree is effective:
   a. at the moment that the offeree signs the notice of rejection.
   b. at the moment that the offeree dispatches the notice of rejection.
   c. at the moment that the offer receives the notice of rejection.
   d. none of the above.

b   10. Under the Code, if two parties, at least one of whom is not a merchant, intend to enter into a binding contract but the offeree in his acceptance includes additional terms for the contract, those terms are construed as:
   a. mere surplus and are ignored.
   b. proposals for addition to the contract.
   c. terms of the contract provided they do not materially alter the agreement.
   d. terms of the contract provided they are not material and are not objected to by the offeror within a reasonable time.

11. Under the Code, if the auctioneer knowingly receives a bid by or on behalf of the seller, and if notice has not been given that the seller reserves the right to bid at the auction sale, then any such bid by or on behalf of the seller gives the bidder to whom the goods are sold a right:
    a. to avoid the sale.
    b. to take the goods at the price of the last good faith bid before the sale.
    c. both (a) and (b).
    d. none of the above.

12. Which of the following would be subject to Article 2 of the UCC?
    a. An agreement to clean someone's yard for $25.
    b. An option to buy a vacant lot.
    c. An agreement to buy a used computer from a private party.
    d. None of the above is subject to the UCC.

13. A leading manufacturer of electronic equipment writes a letter to its wholesale distributors offering to sell its most popular VCR for $100 and stating that it will accept orders at that price for 30 days. This is a/an:
    a. option to sell.
    b. auction without reserve.
    c. firm offer.
    d. requirements contract.

14. Anita says to her neighbor Bob, "I'll pay you $10 if you wash my car this weekend." Bob washes the car on Saturday.
    a. This is an implied in fact contract.
    b. This is not a contract, because it is too indefinite.
    c. This is a unilateral contract in which Bob accepted Anita's offer by doing the act requested.
    d. Bob has accepted Anita's offer by his silence.

15. Carol Customer sees an ad in a newspaper for a clock radio at $8. She goes to the store and wants to buy the item advertised in the newspaper at the price quoted. Carol is:
    a. making a counter-offer.
    b. making an offer to buy.
    c. making an acceptance of the store's offer to sell.
    d. making an acceptance of the store's firm offer.

SHORT ESSAY

1. An offer is a definite proposal or undertaking made by one person to another that manifests a willingness to enter into a bargain. Although an offer need not take any particular form to have legal effect, three essentials must be present for it to confer upon the offeree the power to form a contract by accepting the offer. Identify those three essentials and discuss briefly the requirements associated with each. _____

_____
_____
_____
_____

2. An offer confers upon the offeree a power of acceptance that continues until the offer terminates. Identify and discuss briefly seven ways to which an offer may be terminated other than by acceptance.

    _____

    _____

    _____

    _____

3. Compare briefly the traditional and modern theories of definiteness of acceptance of an offer as shown by the common law "mirror image" rule and by the rule of the Uniform Commercial Code. _____

    _____

    _____

    _____

    _____

4. Distinguish between revocation of an offer and rejection of an offer. _____

    _____

    _____

    _____

    _____

5. List two situations where the Code rule differs from the common law. Give both the Code rule and the common law rule. _____

    _____

    _____

    _____

    _____

CONDUCT INVALIDATING ASSENT

PURPOSE

This chapter deals with situations when an apparent acceptance of an offer and consent to a contract will be legally ineffective. The situations studied in this chapter are defenses to a breach of contract action that have developed over the years for various reasons of public policy. In general, the law says in these situations that a person has not really entered into the agreement voluntarily. In some situations what seems to be a contract will be considered to be a void agreement, or one that is totally lacking in legal effect and cannot be enforced by either party. In other situations, a contract will be merely voidable. If a contract is voidable, it can either be enforced or avoided by one party, or in some cases, either party. A person who wants to avoid a voidable contract must act affirmatively to do so, whereas the protected party in a void agreement generally does not need to affirmatively act in order to have the agreement set aside. The chapter also considers some contracts, which are neither void nor voidable, but nevertheless are unenforceable either because they are supposed to be in writing but are not, or because the statute of limitations has lapsed and no court action can be maintained. These contracts are considered to be valid but unenforceable.

CHAPTER CHECKPOINTS

After reading and studying this chapter, you should be able to:

1. Distinguish between void, voidable and unenforceable contracts.

2. Identify fact situations involving duress, undue influence, fraud, misrepresentation, and mistake.

3. List the elements of fraud in the inducement and distinguish between fraud in the inducement and fraud in the execution.

4. Distinguish between duress by threats of physical force and duress by improper threats and discuss the differing legal effect of each type of duress.

5. Distinguish between unilateral mistake of fact and mutual mistake of fact and discuss the legal effect of each type of mistake.

CHAPTER OUTLINE

A. Duress - There are two basic types of duress. Physical duress or coercion involving physical force or the threat of physical force renders the agreement void. Duress by means of improper threats or acts, including economic and social coercion, makes the contract voidable at the option of the coerced party.

B. Undue Influence - Taking unfair advantage of a person by reason of a dominant position based on a relationship of trust or confidence renders a contract voidable.

C. Fraud
   1. Fraud in the Execution - This type of fraud is extremely rare and renders a contract void. It consists of a misrepresentation that deceives the other party as to the nature of the document evidencing the contract.
   2. Fraud in the Inducement - When this type of fraud exists there is a contract, but it is voidable at the option of the party deceived.
      a. False Representation - A false statement or conduct that misleads. Silence ordinarily will not constitute a false representation except in the case of a fiduciary who owes a duty of trust, loyalty and confidence to another.
      b. Fact - There must be a misrepresentation of a material fact; only on rare occasions will the misrepresentation of an opinion form a basis for fraud; an expression of opinion by someone holding himself out as an expert will be considered a statement of fact. Statements of value by a salesperson are generally considered to be puffing or sales talk; a statement of fact should be distinguished from a prediction of the future. Misrepresentations of law are generally not considered to be misrepresentations of fact.
      c. Materiality - A misrepresentation must relate to something of sufficient importance to induce reliance.
      d. Knowledge of Falsity and Intention to Deceive - The misrepresentation must have been made with scienter, which can consist of actual knowledge, lack of belief in the statement's truthfulness, or reckless indifference to its truthfulness.
      e. Justifiable Reliance - There is no fraud if the complaining party's decision was in no way influenced by the misrepresentation.

D. Nonfraudulent Misrepresentation - A majority of courts today permit rescission for negligent or innocent misrepresentation; some courts permit recovery of damages for nonfraudulent misrepresentation. Negligent misrepresentation is made without due care in ascertaining its falsity; innocent misrepresentation is made without knowledge of its falsity but with due care.

E. Mistake - A mistake is an understanding that is not in accord with existing fact. A mutual mistake is one where both parties have a common but erroneous belief forming the basis of a contract; a unilateral mistake is an erroneous belief of only one of the parties to a contract. The law grants relief only where there has been a mutual mistake of material fact by both parties to the contract.
   1. Existence or Identity of Subject Matter - The contract is avoided where the goods suffer casualty without fault of either party. The most famous decision involving mutual mistake is Raffles v. Wichelhaus, known as the "Peerless Case."
   2. Nature of Subject Matter - A contract is voidable where both parties are mistaken as to the subject matter of the contract. A unilateral mistake, which is an erroneous belief on the party of only one of the parties to a contract, is generally not grounds for avoiding the contract. However, a palpable unilateral mistake, which is an erroneous belief by one party which is recognized by the other is grounds for avoiding a contract.
   3. Failure to Read Document - Generally, one who assents to a writing is presumed to know its contents

and cannot escape being bound by contending that she did not read them.

4. Mistake of Law - Generally, in the absence of fraud, one cannot obtain a release from contractual liability on the grounds of not understanding the legal effect of the contract. However, some States treat a mutual mistake of law on the same basis as a mutual mistake of material fact.

DEFINITIONS

1. Duress

2. Undue influence

3. Fraud in the execution

4. Fraud in the inducement

5. Innocent misrepresentation

6. Mutual mistake

7. Palpable unilateral mistake

8. Puffing

9. Scienter

TRUE/FALSE

_T_   1. Duress in the form of physical force renders the resulting agreement void.

_F_   2. Duress in the form of improper threats must be explicit in order to render the resulting contract voidable.

_F_   3. In deciding whether a threat is sufficient to constitute duress, the fact that the act or threat would not affect a person of average strength and intelligence is determinative.

_T_   4. It has generally been held that contracts induced by threats of criminal prosecution are voidable, regardless of whether the coerced party had committed an unlawful act.

_F_   5. A contract resulting at least in part from one party's unfair influencing of another is avoid. _voidable_

_F_   6. Fraud in the inducement consists of a misrepresentation that deceives the defrauded person as to the very nature of the contract being entered into.

_T_   7. Fraud in the inducement will result in the contract being voidable at the election of the defrauded party.

_F_   8. Actionable fraud can usually be based on a statement of opinion as well as a statement of fact.

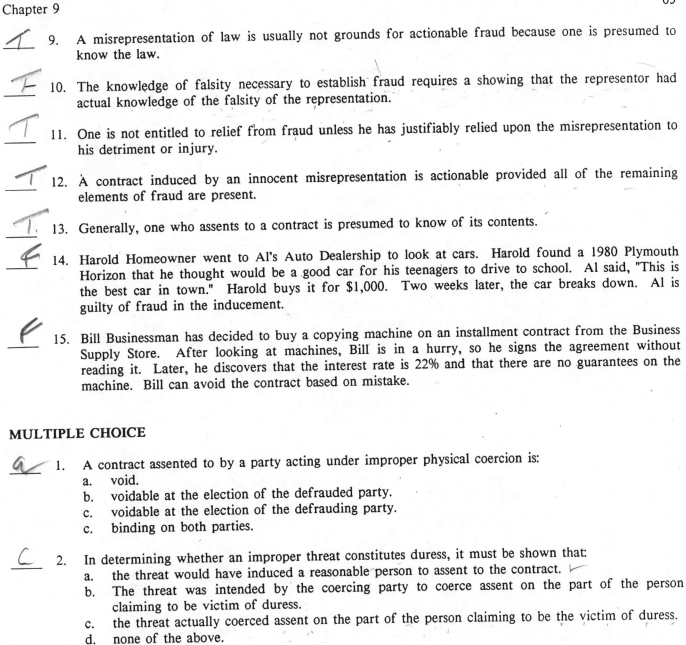

T 9. A misrepresentation of law is usually not grounds for actionable fraud because one is presumed to know the law.

F 10. The knowledge of falsity necessary to establish fraud requires a showing that the representor had actual knowledge of the falsity of the representation.

T 11. One is not entitled to relief from fraud unless he has justifiably relied upon the misrepresentation to his detriment or injury.

T 12. A contract induced by an innocent misrepresentation is actionable provided all of the remaining elements of fraud are present.

T 13. Generally, one who assents to a contract is presumed to know of its contents.

F 14. Harold Homeowner went to Al's Auto Dealership to look at cars. Harold found a 1980 Plymouth Horizon that he thought would be a good car for his teenagers to drive to school. Al said, "This is the best car in town." Harold buys it for $1,000. Two weeks later, the car breaks down. Al is guilty of fraud in the inducement.

F 15. Bill Businessman has decided to buy a copying machine on an installment contract from the Business Supply Store. After looking at machines, Bill is in a hurry, so he signs the agreement without reading it. Later, he discovers that the interest rate is 22% and that there are no guarantees on the machine. Bill can avoid the contract based on mistake.

MULTIPLE CHOICE

a 1. A contract assented to by a party acting under improper physical coercion is:
   a. void.
   b. voidable at the election of the defrauded party.
   c. voidable at the election of the defrauding party.
   c. binding on both parties.

C 2. In determining whether an improper threat constitutes duress, it must be shown that:
   a. the threat would have induced a reasonable person to assent to the contract.
   b. The threat was intended by the coercing party to coerce assent on the part of the person claiming to be victim of duress.
   c. the threat actually coerced assent on the part of the person claiming to be the victim of duress.
   d. none of the above.

C 3. Contracts assented to under each of the following conditions are voidable at the election of the innocent party except:
   a. duress resulting from improper threats.
   b. undue influence.
   c. fraud in the execution.
   d. fraud in the inducement.

_d_   4.   The requisite elements of fraud in the inducement include:
          a.   a false representation of material fact.
          b.   a representation made with knowledge of its falsity and the intention to deceive.
          c.   a false representation justifiably relied upon.
          d.   all of the elements above are required to be shown.

_c_   5.   Silence may constitute a false representation actionable as fraud in all of the following instances except:
          a.   where one party's prior representation was innocently made but later discovered to be false before the making of the contract.
          b.   where a fiduciary relationship exists between the parties.
          c.   where two parties are engaged in an arm's length business transaction characterized by good faith and commercial reasonableness.
          d.   where one party is actively concealing a fact material to the transaction.

_d_   6.   Knowledge of falsity and intention to deceive under fraud in the inducement may be shown by:
          a.   actual knowledge of its falsity.
          b.   lack of belief of the statement's truthfulness.
          c.   reckless indifference as to its truthfulness.
          d.   all of the above.

_d_   7.   In general, the question of "mistake" in the formation of a contract is judged according to:
          a.   the subjective understanding of the mistaken party only.
          b.   the subjective understanding of the innocent party only.
          c.   the subjective understanding of both parties.
          d.   on objective, reasonable person standard.

_b_   8.   The law grants relief in a situation involving mistake only where there has been:
          a.   a unilateral mistake by one party as to the nature of the subject matter of the contract.
          b.   a mutual mistake of material fact.
          c.   a unilateral mistake by one party to the contract occasioned by his failure to read the document before assenting to it.
          d.   a unilateral mistake by one party to the contract as to its legal effect.

_a_   9.   In order for an act or threat to constitute duress, it needs to be at least:
          a.   contrary to public policy.
          b.   tortious but not necessarily criminal.
          c.   a criminal act or threat.
          d.   none of the above.

_b_   10. Contracts entered into by persons in the following relationships would be scrutinized carefully for undue influence except that between:
          a.   husband and wife.
          b.   factory owner and supplier.
          c.   trustee and beneficiary.
          d.   principal and agent.

C   11. Carl Contractor submits a bid that contains an error in addition.
      a.   This is a unilateral mistake. Carl is bound by the error.
      b.   Carl is guilty of fraud in the inducement.
      c.   If the error is an obvious one that the other party knew of when it accepted the contract, Carl can avoid the contract.
      d.   Carl can avoid the contract based upon duress.

C   12. Which of the following would be a statement of fact?
      a.   This is the best typewriter for the price available.
      b.   This is the one that I would recommend.
      c.   This furniture was refinished last year.
      d.   With a few more lessons, you should be able to compete in the regional dance competition.

C   13. The Raffles v. Wichelhaus case, which is popularly known as the "Peerless Case," involved an issue of:
      a.   fraud in the inducement.
      b.   duress by improper threats.
      c.   mutual mistake.
      d.   palpable unilateral mistake.

d   14. When both parties are mistaken as to a material fact regarding the subject matter of the contract, the contract:
      a.   must still be enforced.
      b.   is voidable based on palpable unilateral mistake.
      c.   can only be avoided if both parties agree.
      d.   can be avoided by either party.

b   15. Which of the following would be unable to raise the defense of duress?
      a.   A cowardly person who is easily threatened.
      b.   A person threatened with a civil lawsuit unless he pays an agreed sum of money.
      c.   A person threatened with a criminal prosecution unless he signs an agreement to pay some missing money.
      d.   A person threatened with economic coercion.

SHORT ESSAY

1.   Identify the types of duress and discuss the legal effect of each. _____

      _____

      _____

      _____

      _____

2.   a.   List the elements necessary to establish fraud in the inducement.
      b.   Can the statement of an opinion constitute fraud in the inducement? Explain.
      c.   What is the difference between a false statement of fact and "puffing?" Explain.

      _____

      _____

      _____

      _____

3. X (The Main Street Gazette) and Y (Ned of Ned's Newstand) enter into a contract under which X agreed to ship its newspaper, the <u>Morning Disturber</u>, to Y, a distributor of newspapers in Smalltown, U.S.A. In order to sell a morning newspaper, Y must receive the papers and have them on the newstand by 12 noon. Accordingly, the parties agreed to ship the papers from X's plant in Bigtown, U.S.A., to Smalltown on the "Silver Streak," a train that arrives in Smalltown at 10:00 a.m. Unbeknownst to either party, however, the "Silver Streak's" schedule was to be changed effective the first date of their contract so that it will not arrive in Smalltown until 2 p.m. No other trains pass through Smalltown and shipment of the newspapers by truck or by airplane is impractical. Y sues X for breach of contract when the first shipment of papers arrives too late for him to sell. What result? _____

_____

_____

_____

_____

4. Why does the law apply a subjective standard in determining whether there is duress while requiring that a person alleging fraud in the inducement must have justifiably relied upon the misrepresentations that were made? _____

_____

_____

_____

_____

5. Why does the law treat duress by threats of physical force differently from duress by improper threats?

_____

_____

_____

_____

CHAPTER 10

CONSIDERATION

PURPOSE

For an agreement to be a binding contract, there must be legally sufficient consideration. Consideration is the inducement given to enter into a contract; it is the bargained for element of exchange that is necessary to make a contract binding on the parties. Generally, a promise made without consideration, which is known as a gratuitous promise, is not enforceable. To be legally sufficient, the consideration for a promise must be either a benefit to the promisor or a detriment to the promisee. A promise which is a gift does not meet this test, because it is a detriment to the promisor and a benefit to the promisee. The promisee gives up nothing to make the promisor's promise binding. Generally, if one party is not bound, then neither party is bound. Such is the case wiht a gratuitous promise.

The law of contracts is concerned with whether there is legally sufficient consideration to enforce a contract, but it has little or no interest in whether the consideration is adequate or fair. In general, a contract will be enforced against a person even if that person is getting a bad deal, at least so long as their is no fraud, duress, undue influence, or unconscionability.

This chapter discusses considertion in bilateral and unilateral contracts. It examines what constitutes an illusory promise and analyzed why an output contract, a requirements contract and an exclusive dealing contract are enforceable and are not considered to be illusory.

CHAPTER CHECKPOINTS

After reading and studying this chapter, you should be able to:

1. Distinguish between legal sufficiency of consideration and adequacy of consideration and recognize when there is legally sufficient consideration to enter into a bilateral and a unilateral contract.

2. Distinguish between an illusory promise and a promise that constitutes legally sufficient consideration in fact situations involving outputs and requirements contracts and in those involving exclusive dealing contracts.

3. Explain the concept of bargained-for exchange and discuss whether it is present in fact situations involving past consideration, moral obligation, and third party beneficiaries.

4. Discuss why a contractual agreement to perform a pre-existing public obligation lacks consideration; and why the settlement of a disputed debt for a lesser amount discharges the debt, but the settlement of an

69

undisputed debt for a lesser amount lacks consideration.

5. Identify and discuss contracts that are enforceable even though they are not supported by consideration.

CHAPTER OUTLINE

A. Legal Sufficiency - As a general rule, a contract cannot be performed without legally sufficient consideration. To be legally sufficient, onsideration must be something of value in the eye of the law.
   1. Definition - Consideration is the inducement given to enter into a contract. Legally sufficient consideration must be "either a benefit to the promisor or a detriment to the promisee."
   2. Unilateral Contracts - Since only one promise exists, the promisor gives consideration in the form of the promise while the promisee gives consideration in the form of either an act or a forebearance to act.
   3. Bilateral Contracts - In a bilateral contract each party is both a promisor and a promisee. The promises are consideration provided there is either a legal benefit to the promisor or a legal detriment to the promisee. Usually, where there is a legal detriment to the promisee, there is also a legal benefit to the promisor.
   4. Adequacy - The requirement of legal sufficiency is not at all concerned with whether the bargain was good or bad. Adequacy is not required where the parties have freely agreed to the exchange.
   5. Mutuality of Obligation - A contract is legally binding only if both parties to a contract give consideration.
      a. Illusory Promises - A promise that imposes no obligation on the promisor is illusory.
      b. Output and Requirements Contracts - An output contract is an agreement to sell all of one's production. A requirements contract is an agreement to buy all of one's needs. The Code and the Restatement impose an obligation of good faith and say that no quantity unreasonably different from any stated estimate or if none, any normal prior output or requirements may be demanded.
      c. Exclusive Dealing Contracts - An exclusive dealing contract is one where a manufacturer grants the sole right to sell goos in a defined market to a franchisee or licensee. There is an implied obligation imposed on the manufacturer to use his best efforts to supply the goods and on the distributor to use her best efforts to promote their sale. With these implied obligations there is legaly sufficient consideration.
      d. Conditional Contracts - A conditional contract is one where the obligations are contingent upon the occurence of a stated event. Mutuality exists because neither party need perform if the event does not occur.
   6. Pre-existing Public Obligation - Public duties such as those imposed by tort or criminal law are neither a legal detriment nor a legal benefit. Public officials are under a pre-existing obligation to perform their duties by virtue of their public office. No additional private gain is allowed for performing a public duty.
   7. Pre-existing Contractual Obligation - Performance of a pre-existing contractual duty which is neither doubtful nor the subject of an honest dispute is legally insufficient consideration.
      a. Modification of a Pre-existing Contract - Under the common law, a modification of a pre-existing contract must be supported by mutual consideration to be enforceable. The Code has modified the common law rule by providing that a contract for the sale of goods can be modified without now consideration, if the parties act in good faith.
      b. Settlement of an Undisputed Debt - An undisputed debt is one whose existence and amount are not contested. Under the common law, payment of a lesser sum of money to discharge such a liquidated debt will not support the promise to discharge the debt. An early payment or a payment in a different manner than originally agreed can constitute legally sufficient consideration.
      c. Settlement of a Disputed Debt - A disputed debt is one whose existence or amount is contested.

An unliquidated debt is uncertain or contested in amount. When by mutual agreement a lesser amount is paid, there is mutuality of consideration which is legally sufficient to discharge the original obligation.

    d.   Substituted Contracts Distinguished - In a substituted contract the parties agree to rescind their original contract and to enter into a new one. Substituted contracts are perfectly valid and effective to discharge the original contract and to impose the obligations of the new one.

B. Bargained-For Exchange - A bargain is mutually agreed upon exchange.
    1.   Past Consideration - The element of exchange is absent where a promise is given for an act already done.
    2.   Moral Obligation - A promise made to satisfy a pre-existing moral obligation is unenforceable for lack of consideration. The Restatement, however, takes the position that a promise made following the rendering of emergency services is binding even if it is not supported by consideration.
    3.   Third Parties - Consideration to support a promise may be given to a person other than the promisor if the promisor bargains for that exchange.

C. Contracts Without Consideration - Certain transactions are enforceable without consideration.
    1.   Promise to Pay Debt Barred by the Statute of Limitations - All States have statutes which provide a time period in which a lawsuit must be initiated. A new promise by the debtor to pay the debt renews the running of the statute for a second statutory period.
    2.   Promise to Pay Debt Discharged in Bankruptcy - Such a promise is enforceable without consideration. However, the Bankruptcy Act imposes a number of requirements before the promise may be enforced.
    3.   Promissory Estoppel - This is a doctrine that prohibits a party from denying his promise when the promisee takes action or forbearance based upon the promise. A common application of the doctrine is to charitable subscriptions. The Restatement has relaxed the reliance requirement for charitable subscriptions so that actual reliance need not be shown; probable reliance is sufficient.
    4.   Contracts Under Seal - Under the common law, no consideration for a promise under seal was necessary. Some states still follow this rule.
    5.   Other Promises Which Require No Consideration
        a.   Renunciation - Under the Code and the Restatement, any claim or right arising out of an alleged breach can be discharged by a written waiver or renunciation signed and delivered by the aggrieved party.
        b.   Firm Offer - Under the Code, a written offer signed by a merchant offeror to buy or sell goods is not revocable for lack of consideration for the time stated but not exceeding three months.

DEFINITIONS

1. Consideration

2. Legal detriment

3. Legal benefit

4. Illusory promise

5. Undisputed debt

6. Disputed debt

7. Substituted contract

8. Past consideration

9. Promissory estoppel

10. Firm offer

11. Gratuitous promise

12. Adequacy of consideration

13. Output contract

14. Requirement contract

15. Exclusive dealing contract

16. Conditional contract

17. Unliquidated debt

18. Statute of limitations

19. Promisee

TRUE/FALSE

_____ 1. The doctrine of consideration requires only that the promise or performance of one party be legally sufficient.

_____ 2. To be legally sufficient, the consideration for the promise must be either a legal detriment to the promisor or a legal benefit to the promisee.

_____ 3. The adequacy of consideration is crucial to the issue of legal sufficiency.

_____ 4. A contract under which the parties' obligation to perform arises only on the happening of a stated event lacks the requisite mutuality of obligation if the specified event may never occur.

_____ 5. The performance of a pre-existing contractual obligation that is neither doubtful nor the subject of honest dispute is not legally sufficient consideration.

_____ 6. At common law, a modification of an existing contract does not need to be supported by some new consideration.

_____ 7. The payment of a sum of money in consideration of a promise to discharge a matured undisputed debt for services rendered in an amount larger than the sum paid is legally sufficient consideration to support the promise of discharge.

_____ 8. The bargained-for exchange element of consideration is not satisfied when a promise is given to satisfy a pre-existing moral obligation.

_____ 9. Consideration to support a promise may be given to a third person other than the promisor provided the promisor bargains for that exchange.

_____ 10. In the absence of legal consideration, a promise may nevertheless be enforceable under the doctrine of promissory estoppel even if the promisee has not relied on the promise to his detriment.

_____ 11. Under the Code, a merchant's firm offer to buy or sell goods is not revocable for lack of consideration, during the time stated that it is open or if no time is stated, for a reasonable time, but in either event for a period not to exceed three months.

_____ 12. Under Article 2 of the Uniform Commercial Code, the modification of a contract for the sale of goods requires the furnishing of additional consideration just as required under the common law.

_____ 13. Bill Businessman agrees to buy 2,000 widgets from the Widget Corporation of America next year for $60 a widget if it becomes necessary in his business. This is an illusory contract.

_____ 14. Bill Buyer purchased 500 pairs of shoes from Sam Seller at a contract price of $1,000. Fifty of the shoes were defective and a dispute arose as to the amount due and owing under the contract. Finally, Bill sent a check for $800, marked it paid in full, and sent a letter to Sam explaining his reasons for thinking $800 was fair. Sam didn't respond, but he did cash the check. The debt is discharged.

_____ 15. Bill Businessman has a bad day one Monday morning and signs a contract to buy a piece of real property for $250,000. Later he realizes he has been had, because the property is only worth $100,000. Bill can avoid the contract based on inadequacy of consideration.

MULTIPLE CHOICE

_____ 1. The requirement of consideration is satisfied by _____.
   a. a promise exchanged for a promise
   b. a promise exchanged for an act
   c. a promise exchanged for a forbearance to act
   d. all of the above

_____ 2. To be legally sufficient, the consideration for a promise must be _____.
   a. a legal detriment to the promisee
   b. a legal benefit to the promisor
   c. either a legal detriment to the promisee or a legal benefit to the promisor
   d. both a legal detriment to the promisee and a legal benefit to the promisor.

_____ 3. A contract in which a promise is exchanged for an act or a forbearance to act is called
   _____.
   a. a unilateral contract
   b. a bilateral contract
   c. a gratuitous contract
   d. none of the above

b 4. A promise to purchase such goods as the promisor may "desire" or "wish" to buy is called
_____.
   a. an exclusive dealing contract
   b. an illusory promise
   c. an output contract
   d. a requirements contract

d 5. Which of the following is legally sufficient consideration?
   a. The performance of a pre-existing public obligation.
   b. The performance of a pre-existing contractual obligation.
   c. The settlement of an undisputed matured debt of $10,000 arising out of the purchase of land for $8,500.
   d. The settlement of a debt subject to honest dispute as to its amount.

b 6. A promise made on account of something that the promisee has already done is called_____.
   a. a moral obligation
   b. past consideration
   c. an illusory promise
   d. substituted contract

d 7. Which of the following operates as a sufficient promise by a debtor to pay a debt barred by the statute of limitations?
   a. A voluntary, unqualified admission that the debt was owing.
   b. A partial payment of the debt.
   c. A statement that the statute of limitations will not be pleaded as a defense.
   d. All of the above

b 8. Which of the following is not a requirement under the Bankruptcy Reform Act of 1978 for a promise to pay a debt discharged in bankruptcy to be enforced?
   a. The debtor's promise must be made before the discharge of the debt is granted.
   b. The debtor's promise must be in writing.
   c. The debtor does not revoke the promise within thirty days after the promise becomes enforceable.
   d. The debtor, if an individual, must be informed of his legal right and the effects of his new promise by the bankruptcy court.

b 9. A promise made under circumstances that should lead the promisor reasonably to expect that the promisee will be induced by the promise to act or forebear from acting in reliance on the promise may be enforceable under the doctrine of _____.
   a. gratuitous promises
   b. promissory estoppel
   c. waiver
   d. res ipsa loquitur

d 10. Under the Code, which of the following promises requires consideration to be binding?
   a. A promise under seal.
   b. A written and signed renunciation of a right arising out of a contractual breach.
   c. A good faith modification of an existing contract.
   d. A merchant's firm offer.

b   11. Widget Manufacturing Corporation of America contracts with the Poly Plastic Company of Wisconsin to buy from Poly all of the plastic it will need next year in its manufacturing process. This is an example of a/an _____.
   a.   illusory contract
   b.   requirements contract
   c.   outputs contract
   d.   exclusive dealing contract

c   12. Crime Stoppers offers a reward of $500 for information leading to the arrest and conviction of a criminal who has committed several recent burglaries. Paul Police Officer has been working on the case and applies for the reward based upon information he has gathered while on duty. Paul cannot collect the reward under the _____.
   a.   legal detriment rule
   b.   inadequacy of consideration rule
   c.   pre-existing duty rule
   d.   promissory estoppel rule

d   13. A debt in which the amount owing is not disputed and can be expressed as a sum certain of money is known as a/an_____.
   a.   unliquidated debt
   b.   pre-existing duty
   c.   executed debt
   d.   liquidated debt

c   14. Carl Contractor pledges to contribute $500 to the local United Fund for charity.

   a.   This promise lacks consideration and will not be enforced.
   b.   This promise is a firm offer under the Code and will be enforced.
   c.   There is the probability on reliance by the United Fund and the promise will be enforced under the doctrine of promissory estoppel.
   d.   This promise is a pre-existing public obligation and will be enforced.

b   15. Colleen agrees to pay $10 for David's computer which is worth $300. Colleen's consideration:
   a.   is not legally sufficient.
   b.   appears to be inadequate but is probably legally sufficient.
   c.   is a forebearance.
   d.   is inadequate but the contract will be enforced based on moral obligation.

SHORT ESSAY

1. Discuss briefly what is meant by "mutuality of consideration". Define the terms "legal detriment" and "legal benefit." _____

_____

_____

_____

2. What are the essential elements of consideration? Is the adequacy of consideration a concern in determining legal sufficiency? Explain. _____

_____

_____

3. Are illusory promises enforceable? Why? How do output and requirements contracts differ from illusory promises? _____

_____

_____

_____

4. Sam Student has just graduated from Ivory Towers University and has been offered a graduate assistantship if he wants to pursue a MBA. Big Bucks, Inc., offers him a $35,000 management position if he will move to California and begin work in three weeks. Based on this promise of a job, Sam turns down the graduate assistantship and moves to California. When he contacts Big Bucks, they say they have changed their mind and no longer need him. What recourse does Sam have? Explain. _____

_____

_____

_____

5. In what ways has Article 2 of the UCC altered the common law rules for consideration? Explain. _____

_____

_____

_____

CHAPTER 11

ILLEGAL BARGAINS

PURPOSE

This chapter discusses the requirement that a binding promise or agreement be for a lawful objective. Such a promise or agreement is illegal and unenforceable if the formation or performance of it is criminal, tortious, or otherwise contrary to public policy. Such agreements are properly termed "illegal bargains" or "illegal agreements," because by definition the term "contract" denotes an agreement which is legally enforceable. The chapter divides the topic into agreements that (1) are violations of a statute; and (2) those that are contrary to public policy. It then discusses the effect of illegality including some exceptions to the general rule that illegal agreements are not enforceable.

CHAPTER CHECKPOINTS

After reading and studying the chapter, you should be able to:

1. Identify four types of statutes that frequently raise issues regarding enforceability of an agreement.

2. Distinguish between a regulatory license and a revenue raising license and explain the effect of an unlicensed person's agreement to perform services in situations involving both types of licenses.

3. Identify the two types of situations where restraints of trade typically arise and give an example of enforceable and unenforceable restraints in each type of situation.

4. Define the term "exculpatory clause" and give an example of an enforceable and an unenforceable exculpatory clause.

5. Explain why illegal bargains are generally unenforceable; then list three situations where such an agreement will be enforced despite its illegality.

CHAPTER OUTLINE

A. Violations of Statutes - Generally, agreements declared illegal by statute will not be enforced.
    1. Licensing statutes - A license is a formal authorization to engage in certain practices.

a. Regulatory Statutes - A statute that requires a license to engage in certain practices and that is intended to protect the public against unqualified persons. Two common examples are licensing requirements for doctors and lawyers. An unlicensed person cannot recover for professional services without the required license.

b. Revenue Raising Statutes - A statute that does not seek to protect against unqualified persons but simply seeks to raise money. Agreements for such services are enforceable even when the person who performs the services is unlicensed.

2. Gambling Statutes - A wager is an agreement that one party will win or lose depending upon the outcome of an event in which the only interest is the gain or loss. Courts generally refuse to recognize the enforceability of a gambling agreement, although some States permit certain regulated gambling such as state-run lotteries.

3. Sunday Statutes - Common law allowed contracts entered into on any day to be enforced. Some States have enacted Blue laws that prohibit certain types of commercial activity on Sunday. Weekday ratifications make such contracts enforceable.

4. Usury Statutes - Such laws establish a maximum rate of interest; rates and application vary greatly from State to State. The time-price doctrine allows a seller to have different prices for cash sales and credit sales.

B. Violations of Public Policy
1. Tortious Conduct - A promise to commit a tort is unenforceable on public policy grounds.
2. Common Law Restraint of Trade - At early common law all such agreements are illegal. Today reasonable restraints on trade are enforceable.
    a. Sale of a Business - The seller of a business frequently agrees not to compete in a particular business in a defined area for a stated period of time. Courts will enforce these if they are reasonable as to time period and geographic area.
    b. Employment Contracts - Employees are frequently required to sign employment contracts prohibiting them from competing with their employers during the time of employment and for a stated period following termination. Such agreements are readily enforced during employment; after termination, the employer must demonstrate the restriction is necessary to protect legitimate interests such as trade secrets.
3. Obstructing the Administration of Justice - Such agreements are not enforceable.
4. Corrupting Public Officials - Such agreements are not enforceable.
5. Exculpatory Clauses - An exculpatory clause excuses one party from liability for his own tortious conduct. These clauses are generally looked upon with disfavor, but are frequently enforced, because of the policy of freedom of contract.
6. Unconscionable Contracts - An unconscionable contract is unfair or unduly harsh. The Code and Restatement both limit the enforcement of unconscionable contracts.

C. Effect of Illegality - In most cases, neither party can recover under an agreement, because both parties are *in pari delicto* (in equal fault). Exceptions are as follows:
1. Party Withdrawing Before Performance
2. Party Protected by Statute - For example, an investor protected by a "Blue Sky" law prohibiting the sale of unregistered securities may have the right to recover the money paid.
3. Party Not Equally at Fault - A party who entered into an illegal agreement based upon fraud, duress or undue influence is not equally at fault.

DEFINITIONS

1. Licensing statute

2. "Blue Laws"

3. Usury statute

4. Exculpatory clause

5. Unconscionable contracts

TRUE-FALSE: Circle true or false.

_____ 1. Legality of objective is one of the essential requirements of a binding promise or agreement.

_____ 2. In the absence of a specific statutory provision, an unlicensed person engaged in a business or profession for which a license is required cannot recover for services rendered if the licensing statute was enacted in order to raise revenue.

_____ 3. A regulatory licensing statute is one designed to protect the public against unqualified persons.

_____ 4. Some States have enacted "Blue Laws" that adopt the common law rule that a valid contract may not be entered into on Sunday.

_____ 5. Usury statutes establish the minimum rate of permissible interest that may be contracted for between a lender and a borrower of money.

_____ 6. An exculpatory clause is a contractual clause that exempts a party from liability for his own poor business judgment in entering into a contract.

_____ 7. If a court finds that a part of a contract is unconscionable, it must deny enforcement of the entire contract.

_____ 8. Ordinarily the entire agreement is unenforceable if any part of it is illegal.

_____ 9. Subject to a few exceptions, neither party to an illegal contract can sue the other for breach nor recover for any performance rendered.

_____ 10. First Bank issues a consumer loan to Happy Homemaker at an annual rate of interest of 16%. This is an illegal contract, because First Bank is in violation of State usury law.

_____ 11. Big Bucks, Inc. pays Andrew Attorney to lobby for a law that would increase its annual income. This is an illegal contract.

_____ 12. Donna is in her last semester of dental school. On weekends she cleans the teeth of her friends and relatives and then sends them a bill for $25. This is an illegal contract, because Donna is not a licensed dentist.

_____ 13. Any agreement in restraint of trade is illegal and enforceable.

_____ 14. The President of Big Bucks, Inc. pays a State official $500 to give the corporation's application for a government contract special consideration. This is an illegal contract.

_____ 15. Carol Customer signs a consumer purchase agreement for a VCR in which she agrees to make monthly payments. The contract also provides that if she misses a payment, she will confess judgment and pay all costs necessary in enforcing the contract without raising any defenses against the lender. This is an unconscionable contract.

MULTIPLE CHOICE

_____ 1. An agreement is illegal and unenforceable if its formation or performance is:
   a. criminal.
   b. tortious.
   c. contrary to public policy.
   d. all of the above

_____ 2. A regulatory licensing statute is one intended to:
   a. raise revenue.
   b. protect the public against unqualified persons.
   c. prevent gambling.
   d. prevent certain types of commercial activity on Sunday.

_____ 3. A statute that establishes a maximum rate of permissible interest that might be contracted for between a lender and a borrower of money is called:
   a. a usury statute.
   b. a "Blue Law."
   c. a "Blue Sky" law.
   d. a "savings and loan" law.

_____ 4. At the current time, an agreement not to compete with one's employer during one's employment is enforceable if:
   a. the purpose of the restraint is to protect the employer's business.
   b. the restraint is no more extensive than is reasonably necessary to protect the employer's business.
   c. both (a) and (b).
   d. neither (a) nor (b).

_____ 5. An agreement in a contract that attempts to excuse one party from liability for her own negligence is called:
   a. a clause obstructing the administration of justice.
   b. an exclupatory clause.
   c. a restraint of trade.
   d. an illusory promise.

_____ 6. A State statute that prohibits the sale of unregistered securities is called:
   a. a "Blue Law."
   b. a "Blue Sky Law."
   c. a restraint of trade.
   d. a usury statute.

_____ 7. In considering whether a covenant not to compete included in the sale of a business is reasonable, courts will consider all of the following factors except:
   a. the geographic area covered.
   b. the time period for which the restraint is to be in effect.
   c. the activities that the restraint prohibits the promisor from engaging in.
   d. the price that the promisee paid for the business.

_____ 8. In general, if a promise is illegal:
   a. only the promisor can sue the promisee for breach and recover any performance rendered.
   b. only the promisee can sue the promisor for breach and recover any performance rendered.
   c. neither the promisor nor the promisee can sue the other for breach and recover any performance rendered.
   d. both the promisor and the promisee can sue the other for breach and recover any performance rendered.

_____ 9. All of the following situations represent exceptions to the strict rule of unenforceability of illegal agreements except:
   a. where a party to the illegal agreement withdraws from the transaction prior to the performance.
   b. where one of the parties to the agreement is a party protected by the statute violated.
   c. where the parties are not equally at fault.
   d. where the parties are ni pari dilecto.

_____ 10. The State of Minnesota prohibits car dealers from selling cars on Sunday. This type of law is known as a/an:
   a. Blue law.
   b. restrictive covenant.
   c. exculpatory law.
   d. regulatory licensing law.

_____ 11. Which of the following would most likely be considered a revenue raising licensing law?
   a. A State statute requiring a license to practice medicine.
   b. A city ordinance requiring that all businesses register and pay a yearly licensing fee.
   c. A State statute requiring that beauticians pass an examination and pay a yearly licensing fee.
   d. A State statute requiring that public school teachers complete a required course of study and pay a yearly licensing fee.

_____ 12. Lucky Larson runs an illegal gambling business. Every month he pays a local judge $500 for protection. If Lucky is arrested and convicted in a trial before the same judge, and then sues the judge for breach of contract, what will be the likely result?
   a. The contract will be unenforceable because it is a violation of public policy.
   b. The contract will be enforced, because both parties are in pari delicto.
   c. Lucky will be able to have the contract rescinded and get back the payments he made to the judge.
   d. The judge will be ordered to pay the money to the government as a fine.

_____ 13. A man and a woman make mutual promises to marry. Unknown to the woman, the man is already married.
    a. This is an agreement to commit a crime which renders the agreement void.
    b. Both parties are in pari delicto.
    c. If the woman is unaware of the man's other marriage, she could pursue an action for money damages against him.
    d. Two of the above, (a) and (c).

_____ 14. Ron Realtor owns an apartment complex, which he rents to low income tenants. A clause in the lease agreement states that the tenants will hold Ron harmless from any claim against him by anyone injured in the entryway or common areas of the building.
    a. This is a valid exculpatory clause.
    b. This is an invalid restrictive covenant in restraint of trade.
    c. This is an invalid exculpatory clause.
    d. This is a valid restrictive covenant in restraint of trade.

_____ 15. Bill Businessman buys $50,000 in Saudi Arabian oil futures.
    a. This is an illegal wagering contract.
    b. This is a valid contract.
    c. This contract is a violation of public policy.
    d. This is an unconscionable contract.

SHORT ESSAY

1. Why are illegal agreements not called contracts? Why are they rendered unenforceable? _____

_____

_____

_____

_____

2. What are the two types of licensing statutes? How do they differ in their legal effect if violated? _____

_____

_____

_____

3. What is a restrictive covenant? When are such agreements effective? _____

_____

_____

_____

4. Are unconscionable contracts enforceable? What do the Code and the Restatement say with regard to unconscionable contracts? _____

_____

_____

_____

CONTRACTUAL CAPACITY

PURPOSE

Everyone is regarded as having the capacity to enter into a binding promise or agreement unless the law for public policy reasons holds that an individual lacks such capacity. In this chapter, you learn the classes of persons who lack contractual capacity and the effect on the agreement when one of the parties to it is a member of a protected class. Persons who are adjudged insane and very young children are incompetent to contract. Minors, mentally handicapped persons who have not been adjudged insane, and intoxicated persons possess limited contractual capacity. The contracts of these latter groups are voidable while those of the former groups are totally lacking in validity. Because the contracts of minors, mentally handicapped persons who have not been adjudged insane, and intoxicated persons have some validity, the fact situations that arise are more complex and require that the protected party take some affirmative action to avoid contracts. Therefore, most of this chapter focuses on how a protected party can successfully avoid a contract and the situations when a protected party will be held responsible for a contractual obligation despite having membership in a protected class.

CHAPTER CHECKPOINTS

After reading and studying this chapter, you should be able to:

1. List the classes of persons who have partial contractual capacity and discuss the effect of lack of capacity on the contracts of each class.

2. Recognize necessary items for a minor and discuss a minor's liability for necessary items.

3. Recognize when a minor has disaffirmed a contract in contrast to when a minor has ratified a contract and discuss the effect of a minor's misrepresentation of age on the power to disaffirm.

4. Discuss the liability of minors for torts connected with a contract.

5. Compare the liability of minors to that of incompetent persons and to that of intoxicated persons.

CHAPTER OUTLINE

A. Minors - A minor is a person who is under the age of majority, which is 18 in most jurisdictions today.

1. Liability for Necessaries - A necessary item is one that is needed to maintain a person's station in life. Minors are liable for the reasonable value of necessary items, which may be different from the contract or selling price.
2. Liability of Contracts - A minor's contracts are voidable at the minor's option.
   a. Ratification - The affirmation of the contract may be done upon reaching majority; it makes the contract binding from the beginning. Ratification must validate the whole contract, both as to burdens and benefits. Ratification need not be express; it may be implied from a person's conduct. A minor has no power to ratify a contract while still under age.
   b. Disaffirmance - The exercise of a minor's power to avoid a contract is known as disaffirmance. A minor's contract is voidable at his option. Disaffirmance may be either express or implied; no particular form is necessary so long as the intention not to be bound is conveyed. Some contracts, such as those for student loans, medical care and bank accounts may not be avoided. A minor may have duties upon disaffirmance. Under the UCC, a person with voidable title has the power to transfer valid title to a good faith purchaser for value.
3. Liability for Misrepresentation of Age - The States do not agree whether a minor who fraudulently misrepresents her age when entering into a contract has the power to disaffirm. The prevailing view is that a minor may nevertheless disaffirm. Other States either require the minor to restore the other party to the position she had before the contract or allow the defrauded party to recover damages against the minor in tort.
4. Liability for Tort Connected with Contract - Generally minors are liable for their torts. However, if a tort and a contract are so connected that to enforce the tort action the court must enforce the contract, the minor is not liable in tort.

B. Incompetent Persons
1. Person Under Guardianship - A guardianship is the relationship under which a person (the guardian) is appointed to preserve and control the property of another (the ward). Contracts made by a person under guardianship by court order are void. However, the person dealing with the ward may be able to recover the fair value of any necessaries provided to the incompetent. The guardian may ratify the contracts; the ward may ratify the contacts upon termination of the guardiaship.
2. Mental Illness or Defect - A mentally incompetent person is one who is unable to understand the nature and effect of his acts. A person must be able to comprehend the subject of the contract, its nature, and its probable consequences. Such a person is liable for the reasonable value of necessaries on the principle of quasi contract. The person may ratify or disaffirm contracts during a lucid period.

C. Intoxicated Persons - The effects of intoxication are generally the same as that given to contracts that are voidable because of incompetency. For a contract to be voidable, the other party must know that the intoxicated person is unable to understand the nature and consequences of his actions. The options of ratification or disaffirmance remain, although the courts are more strict with the requirement of restitution on disaffirmance than they are with the agreements of an incompetent person. Intoxicated persons are liable in quasi contract for necessaries furnished.

DEFINITIONS

1. Contractual capacity

2. Minor

3. Necessaries

4. Ratification

5. Disaffirmance

6. Guardianship

7. Mentally incompetent

TRUE/FALSE

_____ 1. As a general rule, a contract entered into by a minor is void and without legal effect.

_____ 2. Recovery for necessaries furnished to a minor is based upon the reasonable value of the item furnished and not the contract price.

_____ 3. A minor cannot ratify a contract until he has attained his majority.

_____ 4. Except in the case of a contract to transfer land, a minor can disaffirm a contract before attaining his majority or within a reasonable time thereafter.

_____ 5. A disaffirmance must be express and cannot be implied from the conduct.

_____ 6. Under the Code, a person buying goods from a minor has the power to transfer valid title to the goods to a good faith purchaser for value.

_____ 7. In most States, a minor who fraudulently misrepresented his age at the time the contract was entered into may nevertheless disaffirm the contract.

_____ 8. If a tort and a contract are so connected that to enforce the tort action the court must enforce the minor's contract, the court will enforce the contract and the minor will be liable in tort.

_____ 9. In order to prove that a person with a mental defect lacks the necessary capacity to enter into a contract, it must be shown that the person is permanently insane.

_____ 10. If property of an individual is under guardianship by court order, contracts entered into by that individual are voidable at his election.

_____ 11. As is the case with minors and incompetents, intoxicated persons are liable in quasi-contract for necessaries furnished during their incapacity.

_____ 12. What is necessary for a minor depends upon that minor's station in life.

_____ 13. Seventeen year old Tim Teenager has just completed a course in business law. He now wants to disaffirm his student loan agreements. Most States allow a minor to avoid contracts for student loans.

_____ 14. Parents are liable for the contracts of their minor children.

MULTIPLE CHOICE

_____ 1. A person lacks contractual capacity if she is:
   a. a minor.
   b. incompetent.
   c. intoxicated.
   d. all of the above.

_____ 2. In nearly all jurisdictions today, the age of majority has been set by statute at:
   a. sixteen years of age.
   b. eighteen years of age.
   c. twenty-one years of age.
   d. twenty-five years of age.

_____ 3. Except for a contract for necessaries, a contract entered into by a minor is:
   a. voidable at the election of the minor.
   b. voidable at the election of the other party.
   c. void and without legal effect.
   d. illegal and unenforceable.

_____ 4. In a contract for necessaries, a minor is liable for:
   a. the list price of the items furnished.
   b. the agreed price of the items furnished.
   c. the reasonable value of the items furnished.
   d. the wholesale cost of the items furnished.

_____ 5. If a minor purchases a car and then continues to use it for one year after obtaining his majority, his action constitutes:
   a. a disaffirmance of the contract.
   b. a ratification of the contract.
   c. a breach of the contract.
   d. none of the above.

_____ 6. A minor may disaffirm a contract for personal property:
   a. before attaining majority.
   b. on the day he attains majority.
   c. within a reasonable time after reaching majority.
   d. all of the above.

_____ 7. A person who lacks sufficient mental capacity to enter into a contract is one who is:
   a. adjudicated incompetent by a court decree.
   b. incompetent, although not adjudicated as such by a court decree.
   c. unable to understand the nature and effect of his act.
   d. all of the above.

_____ 8. One does not possess sufficient contractual capacity to enter into a contract if it is shown that he is:
   a. slightly intoxicated.
   b. unable to understand the nature and consequences of his acts.
   c. intoxication never deprives one of contractual capacity.
   d. none of the above.

___ 9. Which of the following is (are) liable in quasi-contract for necessaries furnished to them during their incapacity?
   a. Emancipated minors.
   b. Persons incompetent but not so adjudicated.
   c. Intoxicated persons.
   d. All of the above.

_____ 10. Which of the following is correct with regard to ratification?
   a. It can occur only by express conduct.
   b. It must be in writing.
   c. It can occur by implied conduct only.
   d. It can only be of the whole contract.

_____ 11. Which of the following is NOT true with regard to necessary items?
   a. A car can be a necessary item.
   b. A loan contract to pay for necessary items will be set aside.
   c. What is necessary will vary from person to person.
   d. The liability for necessary items will be at the reasonable value of the items, which may differ from the contract amount.

_____ 12. When can a minor disaffirm a contract?
   a. Only before reaching the age of majority.
   b. At any time after reaching the age of majority.
   c. At any time either prior to or immediately after reaching the age of majority.
   d. None of the above.

_____ 13. Martha, who is a minor, contracts with Alice, who is an adult.
   a. Alice may disaffirm the contract at any time.
   b. Alice may disaffirm the contract when Martha becomes and adult.
   c. Alice may ratify the contract when Martha reaches the age of 18.
   d. Alice may not disaffirm the contract.

_____ 14. Hester is 95 years old and under the legal guadianship of her daughter. One day she recevies a telephone call from a magazine salesman and orders 10 magazines, so she will have something to read during the day while her daughter works.
   a. This contract is valid.
   b. This contract is voidable.
   c. This contract is void.
   d. This contract is unenforceable.

_____ 15. Tim Teenager agrees to fix Harold Homeowner's computer for $50. Unfortunately, Tim hasn't had a lot of experience and damages the computer beyond repair. Harold wants to sue.
   a. Harold cannot sue, because the tort is not clearly separate from the contract.
   b. Harold can sue under Article 2.
   c. Harold can sue, because the tort was intentional.
   d. Harold cannot sue, because he was contributorily negligent in selecting Tim to do the work.

SHORT ESSAY

1. Define what is meant by the word "necessaries" and state what types of items are "necessaries." _____

     _____

     _____

     _____

2. How does a person's duty on disaffirmance differ if her lack of contractual capacity is a result of her (a) minority; (b) incompetency; or (c) intoxication? _____

     _____

     _____

     _____

3. Under what circumstances will a minor not be responsible for his torts? _____

     _____

     _____

     _____

4. Tim Teenager, who is 17 years old, shows a false ID to the loan officer at First Bank. Based upon the mistaken belief that Tim is of legal age, the bank officer gives Tim a $10,000 loan to buy a used sports car. Tim defaults on the loan two months later after the car has been destroyed in a collision. Tim, who is still 17, informs the bank that he has decided to avoid the contract. What are Tim's rights? What are the bank's rights? _____

     _____

     _____

     _____

CHAPTER 13

CONTRACTS IN WRITING

PURPOSE

In general, oral contracts are just as enforceable as are written contracts. However, there are some exceptions to this general rule. In this chapter, you study (1) the types of contracts that must be in writing to be enforceable; (2) the parol evidence rule; and (3) the rules of contractual interpretation. State statutes of fraud are modeled after a statute passed by the English Parliament in 1677 which required that certain contracts must be evidenced by a writing, signed by the party to be charged. Contracts within the statute and which are not covered by a writing could not be enforced. The statutes of fraud which have been enacted by the States are very similar to this old English statute.

In this chapter, you also study the parol evidence rule. This rule applies when the parties have reduced their agreement to writing. When the parties have reduced their agreement to a complete and final written expression, the parol evidence rule honors this written document by not allowing the parties to introduce any evidence in a lawsuit that would vary or contradict the terms of the written document. There are some situations when this rule does not apply that you must learn, because you cannot understand the rule without fully understanding the exceptions to it. Evidence can be used under both the common law rule and the Code rule or you will have difficulty with the exercises that follow.

The chapter ends with the rules for interpretation of contracts that are found in the Restatement. These rules are a useful aid in determining the meaning of a contract. These rules permit the parties to introduce evidence to resolve ambiguity and to show the meaning of the language employed by the parties in order to determine the intent of the parties.

CHAPTER CHECKPOINTS

After reading and studying the chapter, you should be able to:

1. List and discuss the situations that fall within the general Statute of Frauds.

2. Summarize and discuss the provisions of the UCC Article 2 Statute of Frauds.

3. Define the Parol Evidence Rule, and identify five general types of situations when the rule does not apply and parol evidence can be used even though there is a written contract.

4. Define the terms "course of performance," "course of dealing" and "usage of trade, and discuss their relevance to contractual interpretation and the UCC parol evidence rule.

5. Summarize the rules for interpretation of contracts that are found in the Restatement.

CHAPTER OUTLINE

I. Statute of Frauds - Requires that in order to be enforceable, certain contracts must either be in writing or must be evidenced by a written memorandum signed by the party to be charged (the one you want to sue).
    A. Contracts within the Statute of Frauds - If a contract is "within" the Statute, it must comply with the requirements of the Statute,i.e., a writing is necessary.
        1. Suretyship Provision - A suretyship is a guarantee to pay the debts of another.
            a. Promise must be Collateral - A collateral promise is an undertaking to be secondarily liable, that is, liable if the principle debtor does not perform. "If X doesn't pay, I will," is collateral, because the promisor is not the one who is primarily liable. An original promise (one to become primarily liable) is not collateral.
            b. Main Purpose Doctrine - This is an exception that the courts have developed to the suretyship provision. It is also known as the leading object rule. If the main purpose or object of the promisor/surety is to provide an economic benefit to herself, then the promise is not within the Statute, i.e., no writing is necessary to enforce the promise against the promisor.
            c. Promise made to Debtor - Courts have interpretted the Statute NOT to include promises made to the debtor.
        2. Executor - Administration Provision - An executor is a person appointed to settle a decedent's estate. If an executor or administrator promises to answer personally for a duty of the decedent, the promise is unenforceable unless in writing.
        3. Marriage Provision - The marriage provision does NOT apply to mutual promises to marry. It covers marriage settlement agreements, such as where a man or his parents promise a woman to convey title to property if she marries him.
        4. Land Contract Provision - An interest in land is any right, privilege, power or immunity in real property. It includes ownership interests in land, leases, mortgages, options and easement. Under this provision, a promise to transfer an interest in land must be in writing.
        5. One Year Provision - Contracts that cannot by their terms be performed within one year from the date of making must be in writing.
            a. The Possibility Test - The test for whether an agreement is within the Statute is whether it is possible for the agreement to be performed within one year; the test is not whether it is likely to be performed within one year from its formation.
            b. Computation of Time - The year runs from the time the agreement is made, not from when the performance is to begin.
            c. Full Performance by One Party - When one party has fully performed, most courts hold that the promise of the other party is enforceable even if performance was not possible within one year.
        6. Sale of Goods - The English Statute of Frauds is the prototype for the UCC Article 2 Statute. Under Article 2 of the UCC, a contract for the sale of goods for the price of $500 or more is not enforceable without a writing.
        7. Modification or Rescision of Contracts Within the Statute of Frauds - Oral contracts modifying existing contracts are unenforceable if the resulting contract is within the Statute of Frauds.

    B. Methods of Compliance - The most common method is for the parties to have a written agreement.
        1. A Writing or Memorandum - It need not be a written contract; it must merely comply with the

statutory requirements.
   a. General Contract Provisions - The general statutes require that the writing (1) be signed by the party to be charged or her agent; (2) specify the parties to the contract; (3) specify the subject matter and essential terms of the unperformed promises. The note or memorandum may be formal or informal. The signature may be initialled, printed, or typewritten, and need not be at the bottom of the page. A personal letter or handwritten note would suffice. It may consist of several papers, none of which would be sufficient by itself.
   b. UCC Provisions - The Article 2 Statute of Frauds provision is more liberal. It requires merely a writing (1) sufficient to indicate that a contract has been made between the parties; (2) signed by the party against whom enforcement is sought or by her authorized agent or broker; and (3) specifying the quantity of goods to be sold. An incorrectly stated term will not disqualify the writing.
2. Other Methods of Compliance Under the UCC
   a. Written Confirmation - Between merchants, a written confirmation that is sufficient against the sender is also sufficient against the recipient of the confirmation unless the recipient gives written notice of his objection within ten days of receipt of the confirmation.
   b. Admission - an Admission in pleadings, testimony or otherwise will make the contract enforceable to the quantity of goods admitted.
   c. Specialty Manufactured Goods - An oral contract for specially manufactured goods is enforceable if the seller has made a substantial beginning of their manufacture before any notice of repudiation. To enforce this exception to the writing requirement, the seller must show that the goods are not suitable for resale in the ordinary course of business.
   d. Delivery or Payment and Acceptance - Partial performance validates the contract only for the goods that have been accepted or for which payment has been accepted. A division of authority exists where the contract is indivisible. The better rule is that it makes the entire contract enforceable.

C. Effects of Noncompliance - The oral contract is unenforceable.

II. Parol Evidence Rule
   A. The Rule - When a contract is expressed in a writing that is intended to be the complete and final expression of the rights and duties of the parties, parol evidence of (1) prior oral or written negotiations or agreements of the parties; or (2) their contemporaneous oral agreements that vary or change the written contract are not admissible.

   B. Situations to which the Rule Does Not Apply - The rule is considered to be a substantive rule of law that defines the limits of a contract. It does not apply to the following situations:
      1. A contract that is not an integrated document.
      2. Parol evidence can be used to correct a typographical error.
      3. Parol evidence can be used to show that a contract was void or voidable, i.e., it can be used to establish a defense of lack of capacity, fraud, misrepresentation, duress, undue influence, mistake or illegality.
      4. Parol evidence can be used to show whether a condition precedent that was orally agreed upon at the time of the contract's execution has in fact occurred.
      5. Parol evidence can be used to show a subsequent mutual rescission or modification of the contract. This evidence is subsequent and not prior or contemporaneous.

   C. Supplemental Evidence - Under the Restatement and the Code, a written contract may be explained or supplemented by course of dealing, usage of trade, course of performance or evidence of consistent additional terms.

1. A course of dealing is previous conduct between the parties that establishes a common basis for understanding; i.e., previous contracts between the same parties.

2. A usage of trade is a practice or method of dealing regularly observed and followed in a place, vocation or trade.

3. Course of Performance is the manner and extent to which the respective parties have accepted successive tenders of performance by the other party without objection, i.e., what has been done in prior installments of an installment contract.

III. Interpretation of Contracts - The Restatement defines interpretation as the ascertainment of the meaning of a promise or agreement or a term of the promise or agreement. Rules for interpretation include:

A. All the circumstances are considered and the principal purpose of the parties is given great weight.

B. A writing is interpreted as a whole.

C. Commonly accepted meanings are used unless a different intention is intended.

D. Wherever possible, the intentions of the parties are interpreted as consistent with each other and with course of performance, course of dealing or usage of trade.

E. Technical terms are given their technical meaning.

F. Specific terms are given greater weight than general language.

G. Separately negotiated terms are given greater weight than standardized terms or those not separtely negotiated.

H. The order for interpretation is express terms, course of performance, course of dealing and usage of trade.

I. Where a term has several possible meanings, the term will be interpreted against the party who supplied the contract or term.

DEFINITIONS

1. Surety

2. Collateral promise

3. Main purpose doctrine

4. Parol evidence

5. Course of dealing

6. Usage of trade

7. Course of performance

TRUE/FALSE

_____ 1. A contract "within" the Statute of Frauds need NOT comply with the requirements of the Statute to be enforceable.

_____ 2. If an executor or administrator promises to answer personally for the duty of the decedent, the promise is unenforceable unless in writing.

_____ 3. A promise to a creditor to perform the duties and obligations of a third party is "collateral" and therefore subject to the Statute of Frauds when the promise is to pay only upon the default of the one primarily obligated.

_____ 4. An oral promise made to a debtor to pay his debt to a third party is not enforceable.

_____ 5. All contracts not to be performed within one year of when performance is to begin must be in writing.

_____ 6. The Uniform Commercial Code provides that a contract for the sale of goods for the price of $5,000 or more is enforceable unless it satisfies the requirements of the Statute of Frauds.

_____ 7. In order to comply with the requirements of most Statute of Frauds, the writing or memorandum must be signed by the party to be charged or his agent.

_____ 8. The Parol Evidence Rule applies to all integrated written contracts and deals with what terms are part of the contract.

_____ 9. The Parol Evidence Rule is a rule of evidence that prohibits the parties from subsequently orally modifying their written contract.

_____ 10. Rules of contractual interpretation are incorporated within the Statute of Frauds.

_____ 11. A writing must be signed by both parties in order to meet the memorandum requirements of the Statute of Frauds.

_____ 12. A course of dealing is a practice or method of dealing regularly observed and followed in a place, vocation or trade.

_____ 13. Under the parol evidence rule, words can be introduced in court which vary or contradict the terms of an integrated contract.

_____ 14. Under the "main purpose rule," an oral contract which would ordinarily require a writing can be enforced.

_____ 15. The parol evidence rule does not apply to parol evidence which is used to show a subsequent mutual rescission of a contract.

MULTIPLE CHOICE

_____ 1. The following promises or contracts are within the Statute of Frauds EXCEPT:
   a. the promise of an executor or administrator that he personally will pay all of the decedent's creditors in full.
   b. a promise to marry made in consideration for some promise other than a reciprocal promise to marry.
   c. a promise made by a father to his son by which the father will pay the son's debt in the event of his son's default.
   d. a promise made by a father to his son's creditor to pay the son's debt in the event of his son's default.

_____   2.   All of the following contracts are within the Statute of Frauds and therefore must meet its requirements in order to be enforceable EXCEPT:
   a.   a contract to sell one half acre lots of land in a 60 acre lot subdivision.
   b.   a six month lease of an apartment.
   c.   a deed granting an easement.
   d.   a 30 year mortgage.

_____   3.   A contract for the sale of securities (stocks and bonds) must be in writing to comply with the applicable Uniform Commercial Code Statute of Frauds provision if the value of the securities involved exceeds:
   a. $50.
   b. $500.
   c. $5000.
   d.   none of the above.

_____   4.   All of the following are required of a writing to satisfy the requirements of the general contract Statute of Frauds EXCEPT:
   a.   it must be signed by the party to be charged or his agent.
   b.   it must be signed by the party seeking to enforce the contract or his agent.
   c.   it must specify the parties to the contract.
   d.   it must specify with reasonable certainty the subject matter of the unperformed promises as well as their essential terms.

_____   5.   Under the Statute of Frauds provision of the UCC, if a writing that is otherwise sufficient incorrectly states the quantity term agreed upon by the parties, the contract is:
   a.   unenforceable.
   b.   enforceable, but only to the extent of the quantity of goods stated in the writing.
   c.   enforceable to the extent of the quantity term orally agreed upon by the parties.
   d.   enforceable to the extent determined by the court to be fair and reasonable at the time of enforcement of the contract.

_____   6.   An oral contract for the sale of land:
   a.   is enforceable.
   b.   is enforceable if the party seeking to enforce it has performed all of his promises under the oral contract.
   c.   is enforceable if the party against whom enforcement is sought has performed all of his promises under the oral contract.
   d.   is enforceable if all of the promises of the oral contract have been performed by all of the parties.

_____   7.   If a contract is expressed in a writing that is intended by the parties to be the complete and final expression of their rights and duties under the contract, the parol evidence rule precludes the admission into evidence of all of the following EXCEPT:
   a.   prior oral negotiations or agreements of the parties.
   b.   prior written negotiations of the parties.
   c.   a subsequent oral agreement between the parties to modify the terms of the contract.
   d.   a contemporaneous oral agreement between the parties that varies or changes the written contract.

_____ 8. The parol evidence will bar the introduction of:
   a. evidence that one of the parties to the contract was a minor.
   b. evidence of fraud in the formation of the contract.
   c. evidence of usage and custom that is not inconsistent with the terms of the written agreement.
   d. evidence of a letter written prior to the execution of the final contract setting that the price to be charged for the goods was $2.00 each rather than $2.10 as provided in the final contract.

_____ 9. A party seeking to introduce evidence of a subsequent oral agreement modifying a written employment contract from 2 to 3 years would be:
   a. admissible under both the Statute of Frauds and the parol evidence rule.
   b. inadmissible because of the Statute of Frauds.
   c. inadmissible because of the parol evidence rule.
   d. inadmissible because of both the parol evidence rule and the Statute of Frauds.

_____ 10. Which of the following is not a rule of interpretation?
   a. Words and other conduct are interpreted in light of all the circumstances, and if the principal purpose is acertainable, it is given greater weight.
   b. Unless a different intention is manifested, technical terms and words of art are given their technical meaning.
   c. Express terms, usage of trade, course of dealing and course of performance are weighed in that order.
   d. Separately negotiated or added terms are given greater weight than standardized terms or other terms not separately negotiated.

_____ 11. Arthur writes a letter to Bob in which he promises to pay Clark's debts if Clark doesn't pay.
   a. Arthur's promise is a primary promise.
   b. Arthur's promise is an original promise.
   c. Arthur's promise is a collateral promise.
   d. Arthur's promise falls within the main purpose doctrine.

_____ 12. Which of the following contracts need not be in writing to be enforced?
   a. Arthur agrees to buy Bob's house for $60,000.
   b. Clara's Aunt Amanda promises Clara $1,000 if she will marry Brad.
   c. Bill Buyer agrees to buy $450 in goods from Sam Seller.
   d. Oscar agrees to work for Big Bucks, Inc., for 2 years beginning June 1.

_____ 13. One of the exceptions to the Statute of Frauds occurs when:
   a. there is oral evidence of fraud.
   b. the contract is partially performed.
   c. the Parol Evidence Rule applies.
   d. the contract is partly oral and partly written.

_____ 14. Which of the following would not meet the signature requirement of the Statute of Frauds?
   a. Big Bucks, Inc., signs a contract with a signature stamp.
   b. Bill Buyer has a printed acceptance of order form which contains the name of Sam Seller showing receipt of an order for 200 widgets at a price of $600.
   c. Arthur types his initials at the bottom of a written memorandum.
   d. All of the above meet the signature requirements.

_____ 15. Which of the following is a correct rule regarding contract interpretation?
   a. Printed terms prevail over written terms.
   b. General terms are given greater weight than specific terms.
   c. Course of performance takes priority over course of dealing which takes priority over usage of trade.
   d. The intention of the parties has no relevance to the interpretation of a written contract.

SHORT ESSAY

1. What is the difference between an original promise and a collateral promise? _____
   _____
   _____
   _____

2. Identify two instances in which a contract to transfer an interest in land need not be in writing and give an example of each? _____
   _____
   _____
   _____

3. Compare the requirements for a writing to comply with the general contract Statute of Frauds and the UCC version. Which is easier to satisfy? Why? List four alternative methods of compliance with the UCC version. _____
   _____
   _____
   _____

4. Identify six situations to which the Parol Evidence Rule does not apply. _____
   _____
   _____
   _____

THIRD PARTIES TO CONTRACTS

PURPOSE

In prior chapters, you studied contracts that involved only two parties. In this chapter, you study the rights of third parties who are not parties to the contract, but who have rights or duties under the contract. These rights or duties arise by (1) an assignment of the rights of a party to the contract; (2) a delegation of the duties of a party to the contract; or (3) the express terms of the contract, because that contract was entered into for the benefit of a third person.

The early common law placed a great deal of emphasis on privity of contract. Because of this principle, under ordinary circumstances, only the original parties to a contract may bring an action to enforce it in the event of a breach. However, today third party beneficiaries and assignees are frequently allowed to enforce a contract against the original parties. With some exceptions, a party to a contract today can assign her rights or delegate her duties to a third party. In the case of duties, the obligations created by a contract can be delegated to a third party unless such duties call for the special or personal skills of the original party attempting the delegation.

CHAPTER CHECKPOINTS

After reading and studying the chapter, you should be able to:

1. Distinguish between an assignment of rights and a delegation of duties and identify situations when assignments and delegations are not permitted by the law.

2. Recognize the assignor, the assignee, the delegator, the delegatee, the obligor and the obligee in various fact situations.

3. Discuss the majority rule, the minority rule and the Restatement rule for situations involving successive assignments of the same right and the priorities of assignee claimants.

4. Distinguish third party beneficiary contracts and novations from assignments and delegations.

5. Identify intended beneficiaries, incidental beneficiaries, donee beneficiaries and creditor beneficiaries and discuss the relative rights of each in enforcing a contract.

CHAPTER OUTLINE

I.   Assignment of Rights and Delegation of Duties
    A. Assignment of Rights - an assignment is the voluntary transfer to a third party of the rights arising from the contract. The assignor is the party making an assignment. The assignee is the party to whom the contract rights are assigned. An obligor is a party who owes a duty to the assignor under the original contract. The delegation of a duty is the transfer to a third party of a contractual delegation. The delegator is the party who delegates his duty to a third party. The delegatee is a third party to whom the delegator's duty is delegated. The obligee is the party to whom a duty of performance is owed by the delegator and delegatee.
       1. Requirements of an Assignment - The Restatement defines an assignment as a manifestation of the assignor's intention to transfer a contract right such that the assignor's right to performance is extinguished. No special form or words are needed to create an assignment. No consideration is necessary to make an assignment effective.
          a. Revocability of Assignments - If the assignee gives consideration in exchange for the assignment, then there is a contract. Revocation of the assignment would be a breach of the contract. An assignee may disclaim an assignment when the assignment is gratuitous.
          b. Partial Assignments - A partial assignment is the transfer of a portion of contractual rights to one or more assignees.
       2. Rights that are Assignable - Most contract rights are assignable. The right to the payment of money is frequently assigned.
       3. Rights that are Not Assignable
          a. Assignments that Materially Increase the Risk or Burden - Rights in an automobile liability policy are not assignable.
          b. Assignments of Personal Rights - A contract for personal services that are of a highly personal nature cannot be assigned.
          c. Express Prohibition Against Assignment - At common law, these were enforced; however, today they are strictly construed. The Restatement and Article 2 of the Code say that unless circumstances indicate the contrary, a prohibition of assignment will be construed as barring only the delegation of the assignee's duty of performance and not the assignment of rights.
          d. Assignments Prohibited by Law - Federal and State statutes prohibit or regulate certain assignments such as those of the right to future wages.
       4. Rights of the Assignee
          a. The assignee stands in the shoes of the assignor, but acquires no new rights. The obligor may assert rights of set-off or counter-claim. Waivers of rights against assignees are valid under the Code, but the FTC has invalidated them in consumer credit transactions.
          b. Notice - A valid assignment does not require that notice be given to the obligor, however, such notice is wise.
       5. Implied Warranties of Assignor - Four implied warranties are imposed by law upon the assignor. Any express warranties given by the transferor will also be binding.
       6. Successive Assignments of the Same Right - The majority rule in the U.S. is that the first assignee in point of time prevails over later assignees. In England and a minority of States, the first assignee to notify the obligor prevails.
    B. Delegation of Duties - Duties are not assignable, but their performance may be delegated unless the nature of the duties are personal; the performance is expressly made nondelegable; or the delegation is prohibited by statute or public policy. When a delegation is not permitted, the parties may wish to agree to a novation, which is a new contract substituting a new promisor for an existing promisor and to which the promisee is a party.

II. Third Party Beneficiary Contracts - Contracts in which one party promises to render performance to a third person.

A. Intended Beneficiaries - Third parties intended by the two contracting parties to receive a benefit from their contract.

   1. Gift Promise - A third party is an intended donee beneficiary if the promisee's purpose in bargaining for and obtaining the agreement was to make a gift to the beneficiary. An example is the beneficiary of an insurance policy.

   2. Creditor Beneficiary - A third person is an intended beneficiary if the promisee intends the performance of the promise to satisfy a legal duty owed to the beneficiary, who is a creditor of the promisee.

   3. Rights of Intended Beneficiaries - Some intended beneficiaries are neither donee beneficiaries nor creditor beneficiaries, but they nevertheless can enforce the contract. An intended donee beneficiary may enforce the contract against the promisor only. An intended creditor beneficiary may sue either or both parties.

B. Incidental Beneficiaries - An incidental beneficiary is one whom the parties to a contract did not intend to benefit, but who nevertheless would derive some benefit from its performance. Incidental beneficiaries have no rights under a contract.

DEFINITIONS

1. Rights

2. Duties

3. Assignment of rights

4. Assignor

5. Assignee

6. Obligor

7. Delegation of duties

8. Delegator

9. Delegatee

10. Obligee

11. Partial assignment

12. Successive assignments

13. Third-party beneficiary contract

14. Intended beneficiary

15. Incidental beneficiary

16. Gift promise

17. Creditor beneficiary

TRUE/FALSE

_____ 1. An assignment of rights is a voluntary transfer to a third party of the rights arising from the contract.

_____ 2. After an effective assignment of rights, both the assignor and the assignee have a right to the obligor's performance.

_____ 3. After an effective delegation of duties, both the delegator and the delegatee are liable to the obligee for performance of the contractual duty.

_____ 4. Although no special words or particular form are necessary to create an assignment, an assignment must be supported by consideration to be effective.

_____ 5. For an assignment to be effective, notice of the assignment must be given to the obligor.

_____ 6. A delegation of duties will not be permitted if the duties are of a personal nature.

_____ 7. Under the Restatement and the Code, unless the language or circumstances indicate otherwise, an assignment of "all my rights under the contract" is both an assignment of rights and a delegation of the assignor's duties under the contract.

_____ 8. A third party beneficiary contract usually is not enforceable by an incidental beneficiary.

_____ 9. A third party is an intended beneficiary if the promisee's purpose in bargaining for and obtaining the promisor's promise was to make a gift to the beneficiary.

_____ 10. The rights of an intended beneficiary vest at the time of the making of the contract or at the time he learns of its making, whichever is later.

_____ 11. In an action by the intended beneficiary of a third party beneficiary contract, the promisor may assert any defense that would have been available to him if the action had been brought by the promisee.

_____ 12. A gift assignment is not effective.

_____ 13. Harold Homeowner sells his used car to Tim Teenager and assigns his rights in his auto liability insurance policy to Tim. This is a valid assignment.

_____ 14. Sarah orders a microwave oven from Marlin's Department Store and requests that it be delivered to her sister Theresa. Theresa is a third party intended beneficiary.

_____ 15. The assignor makes no warranties to the assignee.

MULTIPLE CHOICE

_____   1.   A gift assignment is:
   a.   valid even though not supported by consideration.
   b.   not revocable by the assignor.
   c.   not terminated by the assignor's death.
   d.   all of the above.

_____   2.   A transfer of a portion of a person's rights under a contract to one or more assignees is called:
   a.   a gift assignment.
   b.   a revocable assignment.
   c.   a partial assignment.
   d.   none of the above.

_____   3.   Which of the following assignments of contract rights are NOT valid?
   a.   Assignments that would materially increase the risk or burden on the obligor.
   b.   Assignments which would transfer a personal contract right.
   c.   Assignments wich are prohibited by law.
   d.   All of the above.

_____   4.   An assignee of a contract:
   a.   acquires all of the rights of the assignor.
   b.   acquires new, additional rights by virtue of the assignment.
   c.   takes the assigned rights free of all of the defenses to which the rights would be subject in an action by the assignor against the obligor.
   d.   all of the above.

_____   5.   For an assignment to be valid, notice of the assignment must be given to:
   a.   the assignee.
   b.   the assignor.
   c.   the obligor.
   d.   none of the above.

_____   6.   In the absence of an expressed intention to the contrary, an assignor who receives value makes all of the following implied warranties to the assignee with respect to the assigned right EXCEPT:
   a.   that he will do nothing to defeat or impair the assignment.
   b.   that the obligor will pay the assigned debt.
   c.   that the assigned right actually exists.
   d.   that he has no knowledge of any fact that would impair the value of the assignment.

_____   7.   A delegation of contractual duties will not be permitted if:
   a.   the duties are of a personal nature.
   b.   the performance is expressly made non-delegable.
   c.   the delegation is prohibited by statute or by public policy.
   d.   all of the above.

_____ 8. The delegator remains bound to perform his contractual duties even after a delegation unless the delegation is:
   a. a gratuitous delegation.
   b. a delegation for value.
   c. a novation.
   d. none of the above.

_____ 9. A contract in which the promisor agrees to render a certain performance to a third person is called:
   a. a third party beneficiary contract.
   b. an assignment of rights.
   c. a delegation of duties.
   d. a novation.

_____ 10. An intended creditor beneficiary of a third party beneficiary contract has rights against:
   a. the promisee/debtor only.
   b. the promisor only.
   c. both the promisee and the promisor.
   d. neither the promisee nor the promisor.

_____ 11. A life insurance policy naming a spouse as a beneficiary is a common example of a/an:
   a. assignment.
   b. delegation of duties.
   c. third party donee beneficiary contract.
   d. third party incidental beneficiary contract.

_____ 12. Clara sells her house to Donald. The house has a mortgage which is held by First Bank. As part of the transaction, First Bank agrees to discharge Clara from the mortgage and to allow Donald to assume the obligation. This is a/an:
   a. assignment of rights.
   b. delegation of duties.
   c. novation.
   d. third party creditor beneficiary contract.

_____ 13. Arthur and Bob enter into a contract. Bob later delegates his duty of performance to Clark. Which of the following is true?
   a. If Clark fails to perform, Bob has a duty to perform.
   b. Arthur will always have to accept Clark's performance.
   c. The delegation is valid only if all three parties agree.
   d. Bob must compensate Clark for accepting the delegation.

_____ 14. The law does not recognize the rights of a/an:
   a. assignee.
   b. incidental beneficiary.
   c. intended beneficiary.
   d. donee beneficiary.

_____ 15. An assignment of the right to collect payment of money owed under a contract:
   a. will always be invalid.
   b. will only be valid if the obligor consents to the assignment.
   c. requires the approval of the assignee and the obligor.
   d. will usually be valid and enforceable.

SHORT ESSAY

1. Distinguish between an assignment of rights and a delegation of duties. How does an assignor's rights after an assignment differ from a delegator's duties after a delegation? _____

   _____

   _____

   _____

2. Although notice is not required for an assignment to be effective, why should notice of the assignment be given to the obligor? _____

   _____

   _____

   _____

3. What is the majority American rule regarding successive assignments of the same right? Identify the exceptions to that rule. _____

   _____

   _____

   _____

4. Distinguish between an intended creditor beneficiary and an intended gratuitous beneficiary. Against whom can each enforce his rights? _____

   _____

   _____

   _____

PERFORMANCE, BREACH, AND DISCHARGE

PURPOSE

In this chapter, you study the termination of contractual duties and the methods by which a party who has been bound by contractual duties is discharged from those duties. All contracts are subject to certain conditions. These may be precedent, subsequent or concurrent. When they are breached or met, they affect the legal rights of the parties. Many contractual promises are not absolute, but depend upon either the occurence or non-occurence of a condition. In these cases, the obligation to perform depends upon the happening or non-happening of a specific event.

Most contracts are discharged by performance when each party does what she has promised to do. However, performance may be defective in which case there is a breach. In such a case, the defaulting party is not discharged. The consequences to the breaching party depend upon the seriousness of the breach. The contract may also be discharged by the agreement of the parties to a rescission, novation, or an accord and satisfaction. In some situations, the contract may be discharged by operation of law. Such is the case when a party is discharged in bankruptcy, when a statute of limitations has run, or when one party makes a fraudulent, material alteration of a written contract.

CHAPTER CHECKPOINTS

After reading and studying the chapter, you should be able to:

1. Recognize express conditions, implied-in-fact conditions, implied-in-law conditions, concurrent conditions, conditions precedent and conditions concurrent and discuss the effect upon a contract of either the occurence or the failure of occurence of each type of condition.

2. Identify fact situations in which discharge by agreement of the parties occurs and distinguish among a mutual rescission, a substituted contract, an accord and satisfaction and a novation.

3. Identify and discuss the ways in which discharge may be brought about by operaton of law.

4. Compare the common law concept of material breach to the perfect tender rule of the UCC.

5. Distinguish between full performance and tender of performance.

Chapter 15

CHAPTER OUTLINE

A. Conditions - A condition is an event whose happening or non-happening affects a duty of performance.
   1. Express Conditions - An express condition is explicitly set forth in language. It is usually preceded by words such as "provided that," "on condition that," "while," "after," "upon," or "as soon as." An express condition of satisfaction makes performance contingent upon one of the party's approval of the other's performance. If this standard is subjective, then a party can unreasonably withhold approval, provided the opinion is honestly held. An objective standard is based upon whether a reasonable person would be satisfied.
   2. Implied-in-Fact Conditions - These are conditions that are contingencies understood but not expressed by the parties.
   3. Implied-in-Law Conditions - These are not contained in the language of the contract but are imposed by law in order to accomplish a just and fair result.
   4. Concurrent Conditions - These are performances by mutual promisors that are to take place at the same time.
   5. Condition Precedent - An event which must occur or not occur before performance is due.
   6. Condition Subsequent - An event which terminates a duty of performance.

B. Discharge by Performance - A discharge is a termination of a contractual duty. Substantial performance does not discharge a promisor, but at common law it deprives the other party of an excuse for nonperformance. A tender is an offer of performance. In a bilateral contract, the refusal of a tender is a repudiation that discharges the tendering party from further duty to perform the contract.

C. Discharge by Breach - A breach is a wrongful failure to perform the terms of a contract. A breach is always a basis for an action for damages by the injured party.
   1. Breach by One Party as a Discharge of the Other
      a. Material Breach - Nonperformance which significantly impairs the aggrieved party's rights under the contract. An uncured material breach by one party discharges the aggrieved party from any further duty under the contract. An intentional breach is generally held to be material. The Code alters the common law doctrine of material breach by adopting what is known as the perfect tender rule. This rule says that performance must strictly comply with contractual duties.
      b. Substantial Performance - Performance that is incomplete but that does not defeat the purpose of the contract. Substantial performance plus damages will discharge a contractual duty. This doctrine is important in the construction industry.
   2. Prevention of Performance - One party's substantial interference with or prevention of performance by the other constitutes a material breach and discharges the other party to the contract.
   3. Anticipatory Repudiation - A breach of contract before performance is due by announcing that one will not perform or by committing an act which makes it impossible to perform. It is treated as a breach and allows the nonrepudiating party to bring suit immediately as if it were a breach.
   4. Material Alteration of a Written Contract - A material fraudulent alteration of a written contract discharges the entire contract.

D. Discharge by Agreement of the Parties - Before breach, the parties may discharge each other from performance by rescission or substituted contract; after breach, liability may be discharged by an accord and satisfaction.
   1. Mutual Rescission - A rescission is an agreement between the parties to terminate their respective duties under the contract.
   2. Substituted Contracts - A substituted contract is an agreement between the parties to rescind their old contract and replace it with a new contract.
   3. Accord and Satisfaction - Substituted performance under a contract (the accord) and the discharge of

the prior contractual obligation by performance of the new duty (the satisfaction).
4. Novation - A substituted contract involving a new third party promisor or promisee.

E. Discharge by Operation of Law
   1. Subsequent Illegality - If performance becomes illegal or impractical as a result of a change in the law, the duty of performance is discharged.
   2. Impossibility - Means that the performance cannot be done. There are two types of impossibility -- subjective and objective. Subjective impossibility refers to the situation where it is impossible for the promisor to perform due to financial inability or because he personally lacks the capability to do so. Subjective does not excuse the promisor from liability for breach of contract. Objective impossibility means that no one is able to perform. It will generally be held to excuse the promisor or to discharge his duty of performance. Where the purpose of a contract has been frustrated by unexpected circumstances that deprive the performance of the value attached to it by the parties, the courts generally regard the frustration as a discharge. Commercial impracticability means that performance can only be accomplished at unforeseen and unjust hardship. The Restatement and the Code take the view that commercial impracticability will excuse performance, even though the performance is not literally impossible.
   3. Bankruptcy - This is a method of discharge which is available to a debtor who obtains an order of discharge by the bankruptcy court.
   4. Statute of Limitations - All States have statutes providing time limitation within which to bring an action. When the statute of limitations has run, the debt is not discharged, but the creditor cannot maintain an action against the debtor.

DEFINITIONS

1. Discharge

2. Condition

3. Express condition

4. Implied-in-fact condition

5. Implied-in-law condition

6. Concurrent conditions

7. Condition precedent

8. Condition subsequent

9. Material breach

10. "Perfect Tender Rule"

11. Substantial performance

12. Anticipatory repudiation

13. Accord and satisfaction

14. Novation

TRUE/FALSE

_T_ 1. A condition is any operative event the happening or non-happening of which affects one's duty of performance under a contract.

_F_ 2. Even if a contract is expressly made subject to a subjective condition of satisfaction, courts generally will apply an objective, reasonable person standard to evaluate its peformance.

_T_ 3. In the absence of an agreement to the contrary, the law assumes that the respective performances under a conract are concurrent conditions.

_F_ 4. A condition precedent is an operative event the happening of which terminates an existing duty of performance under a contract.

_T_ 5. An uncured material breach by one party excuses the other's non-performance and discharges the aggrieved party from any further duty under the contract.

_F_ 6. The Code has followed the common law doctrine of material breach in adopting the "Perfect Tender Rule."

_T_ 7. A rescission must satisfy all of the essentials of an ordinary contract to be effective.

_F_ 8. A promisor's good faith personal belief that she lacks the necessary capability or competence to perform her contractual duties will excuse her from liability for non-performance.

_T_ 9. Under the Restatement and Code view of impossibility, commercial impracticability will excuse liability of non-performance.

_F_ 10. In most States, the running of the period of the Statute of Limitations discharges the promisor's contractual liability.

_T_ 11. Harold Homeowner has a household insurance policy which requires that he notify the company within two weeks of any loss before he is eligible to receive payment for his loss. The notification requirement is a condition precedent.

_F_ 12. Carl Contractor builds a house for Harold and Happy Homemaker. The contract calls for extra-grade stain resistant carpet. The pattern selected by the Homemakers is not available when the carpeting is supposed to be installed, so Carl substitutes a comparable grade similar carpet. Carl has substantially performed the contract. Substantial performance plus a small amount of damages will discharge Carl's contractual obligations, even if the Homemakers think the substituted carpet ruins the house.

_T_ 13. Sam Seller has a contract with Bill Buyer, which Bill breaches before the time for performance is due. Sam is discharged from his contractual obligation by Bill's breach.

F   14. Carl Contractor has a contract with Big Bucks, Inc., to build a new office complex. The contract
          provides that Carl must furnish a certificate of occupancy and conformity with the fire code before
          Big Bucks has an obligation to pay. The furnishing of the certificate is an implied in fact condition
          subsequent to the construction of the building.

T   15. Brian owes Albert $500. Brian, Albert and Clarence agree that Brian will be discharged from the
          obligation and that Clarence will pay the debt. This is a novation.

MULTIPLE CHOICE

b   1. A condition that is understood by the parties to be part of their agreement, but is not included in
         their express contract, is called:
         a.   an implied-in-law condition.
         b.   an implied-in-fact condition.
         c.   a concurrent condition.
         d.   a condition precedent.

c   2. An operative event that must take place before a duty of performance under the contract is created
         is called:
         a.   an implied-in-law condition.
         b.   a concurrent condition.
         c.   a condition precedent.
         d.   a condition subsequent.

d   3. An uncured material breach of contract:
         a.   gives rise to a cause of action for damages by the aggrieved party.
         b.   operates as an excuse for non-performance by the aggrieved party.
         c.   discharges the aggrieved party from any further duty under the contract.
         d.   all of the above.

c   4. The unjustified failure of one party to perform substantially the obligations of the contract
         constitutes:
         a.   a perfect tender.
         b.   a novation.
         c.   a material breach.
         d.   an accord.

a   5. Which one of the following statements it NOT a correct principle to be applied in determining what
         constitutes a material breach:
         a.   A failure to timely perform a promise is a material breach even if time is not of the essence.
         b.   Partial performance is a material breach if an essential part of the contract is not performed.
         c.   If quantitatively significant, a breach will be considered material.
         d.   An intentional breach of a contract is generally held to be material.

b   6. If, prior to the date that performance is due, a party announces that he will not perform or commits
         an act that renders him unable to perform, he has committed:
         a.   an anticipatory novation.
         b.   an anticipatory repudiation.
         c.   a prevention of performance.
         d.   a material alteration of a written contract.

7. An agreement between three parties to substitute a new promisee or promisor in place of an existing promisee or promisor is called:
   a. a condition subsequent.
   b. a mutual rescission.
   c. an accord and satisfaction.
   d. a novation.

 8. An agreement between the parties to a contract to terminate their respective duties under the contract is called:
   a. a novation.
   b. a mutual rescission.
   c. an accord and satisfaction.
   d. an anticipatory repudiation.

 9. A promisor will be excused from liability for failure to perform under a contract on grounds of impossibility when:
   a. she is financially unable to perform.
   b. she personally lacks the capability or competency to perform.
   c. no one, including the promisor, is able to perform.
   d. all of the above.

 10. The effect of a party's failure to bring an action before expiration of the period of the Statute of Limitations is:
   a. to discharge the promisor from liability.
   b. to act as a mutual rescission.
   c. to bar the remedy.
   d. to act as an accord and satisfaction.

 11. A contract in which the promisee agrees to accept and the promisor agrees to render a substituted performance in satisfaction of an existing contractual duty is called:
   a. a material alteration of a written contract.
   b. an accord.
   c. a substantial performance.
   d. a novation.

 12. Edward has agreed to buy Donna's C.D. player. Edward agrees to pay Donna when the C.D. player is delivered. This transaction involves:
   a. implied in fact conditions subsequent.
   b. implied in law conditions subsequent.
   c. express concurrent conditions.
   d. express conditions precedent.

 13. David and Edward entered into a written contract involving the performance of some marketing services. A week later, they both changed their mind and agreed in writing to cancel the contract. This is an example of:
   a. accord and satisfaction.
   b. novation.
   c. substituted contract.
   d. mutual rescission.

c 14. Clarence owes David $50 for a used television which he bought last year at David's garage sale. The two agree that the debt can be paid by Clarence mowing David's lawn for six weeks. The new contract is a/an:
   a. satisfaction.
   b. novation.
   c. accord.
   d. rescission.

b 15. An offer to perform one's obligation under a contract is a/an:
   a. novation.
   b. tender.
   c. condition precedent.
   d. condition subsequent.

SHORT ESSAY

1. What is a condition? What is the difference between the breach of a promise and the failure of a condition? _____
   _____
   _____
   _____

2. At common law, when is a party excused from liability for non-performance of a contractual duty on grounds of impossibility? How have the Restatement and the Code altered this rule? _____
   _____
   _____
   _____

3. Explain the "perfect tender" rule and how it differs from the common law approach. _____
   _____
   _____
   _____

4. Distinguish between subjective impossibility and objective impossibility. Does either one operate to discharge contractual obligations? _____
   _____
   _____
   _____

REMEDIES

PURPOSE

This chapter discusses the remedies that are available to the injured party when the other party breaches the contract by failing to perform his contractual duties. No remedy will be equal to the promised performance, but the primary objective of contract remedies is to compensate the injured party for the loss resulting from the breach. In this chapter, you study the most common remedies available for breach of contract. These include the legal remedy of money damages and the equitable remedies of specific performance, injunction, and reformation. You also study the remedy of restitution, which is available as an alternative remedy for a party injured by breach and to a party who has avoided a contract for reasons such as lack of capacity, duress, undue influence or fraud. Sometimes an injured party will have more than one remedy available to him. In many such cases, the injured party must elect a remedy and then cannot pursue another inconsistent remedy. Remedies under Article 2 of the Code differ from those available at common law and are not included in this chapter. Instead they are included in Chapter 21.

CHAPTER CHECKPOINTS

After reading and studying the chapter, you should be able to:

1. List and discuss the various types of money damages.

2. Identify and discuss the two ways to measure damages for misrepresentation.

3. Identify the equitable remedies that are available for breach of contract and discuss the circumstances under which these remedies are available.

4. Define restitution and list the situations when restitution is available to the injured party.

5. List and discuss situations where the remedies of the injured party will be limited.

OUTLINE

A. Monetary Damages - This is the most common remedy for breach of contract.
    1. Compensatory Damages - These are contract damages placing the injured party in as good a position as

if the other party had performed. The amount of damages is generally the loss of value to the injured party caused by the other party's failure to perform or by his deficient performance. In general, this is the difference between the value of the promised performance of the breaching party and the value of the actual performance rendered by the breaching party. The value of the promised performance minus the value of the actual performance equals the loss of value.

    a.   Incidental damages are damages arising directly out of a breach of contract, such as costs incurred to acquire substitute goods from another source. Incidental damages are added to the loss of value.

    b.   Consequential damages are damages not arising out of a breach but that are a foreseeable result of the breach such as lost profits and injury to persons or property resulting from defective performance.

    c.   Nominal damages are a small sum of money awarded where a contract has been breached but the loss is either negligible or unproved.

2.   Reliance Damages - Instead of seeking compensatory damages, the injured party may seek reimbursement for loss caused by his reliance on the contract. This results in placing the injured party in as good a position as he would have been in had the contract not been made. These might be preferred where an injured party is unable to establish his lost profits with reasonable certainty or when the contract itself is unprofitable.

3.   Foreseeability of Damages - Compensatory or reliance damages are recoverable only for loss that the party in breach had reason to foresee as a probable result of the breach when the contract was made. The test for foreseeability is an objective test based on what the breaching party had reason to foresee. A leading case on foreseeability of damages is *Hadley v. Baxendale*.

4.   Damages for Misrepresentation

    a.   Fraud - A minority of States allow the party to recover out-of-pocket damages, which is the difference between the value received and the value given. The majority of States permit the defrauded party to receive damages based upon the benefit-of-the-bargain rule, which is the difference between the value received and the value of the fraudulent party's performance as represented.

    b.   Non-fraudulent Misrepresentation - The Restatement of Torts permits out-of-pocket damages but not benefit-of-the-bargain damages where the misrepresentation is not fraudulent.

5.   Liquidated Damages - These are reasonable damages to which the parties agree in advance and insert into the contract. If the liquidated damages clause is a reasonable forecast of the loss that may result from the breach, the provision will be enforced. If the sum bears no reasonable relationship to the amount of probable loss, it is unenforceable as an invalid penalty. If the clause is invalid, a party is entitled to ordinary breach of contract remedies.

6.   Mitigation of Damages - When a breach of contract occurs, the injured party is required to take reasonable steps to lessen or avoid damages.

B.   Remedies in Equity - These remedies are not a matter of right but rest largely in the discretion of the court. They will not be granted where there is an adequate remedy at law.

1.   Specific Performance - This is a court decree ordering the breaching party to render the promised performance. It is not ordinarily available for breach of contract, because the usual remedy for breach is an action at law for money damages. It is available in contracts involving the sale of personal property where the goods are rare or unique, such as for a famous painting or statue, an original manuscript, a patent or copyright, shares of stock in a closely held corporation, or a rare relic or heirloom. Courts will always grant specific performance in case of breach of contract for the sale of real property. Specific performance is not available in contracts for personal services.

2.   Injunctions - An injunction is a court order prohibiting a party from doing a specific act. A person who violates the order may be held in contempt of court and fined or imprisoned. Where damages for breach would be inadequate, a court may grant an injunction against breach of a contractual duty. Where an employee breaches a personal service contract in which the services are unusual in character,

the court may issue an injunction prohibiting the employee from working for another employer as long as the employee would be able to make a living.

C. Restitution - This is the restoration of the injured party to the position he was in before the contract was made. It is available (1) as an alternative remedy for a party injured by breach; (2) for a party in default; (3) for a party who may not enforce the contract because of the Statute of Frauds; and (4) on rescission of a voidable contract.

1. Party Injured by Breach - It is available if the other party totally breaches the contract by nonperformance or repudiation.

2. Party in Default - The party who has partly performed but is in default such that the other party's duty to perform is discharged is entitled to restitution for any benefit she has conferred in excess of the loss she has caused by her breach.

3. Statute of Frauds - Where a contract is unenforceable because of the Statute of Frauds, but the party has nevertheless acted in reliance on the contract, the party may recover in restitution the benefits conferred on the other in reliance on the contract.

4. Voidable Contracts - A party who has avoided a contract for lack of capacity, duress, undue influence, fraud, misrepresentation, or mistake is entitled to restitution for any benefit he has conferred on the party.

D. Limitation on Remedies

1. Election of Remedies - If remedies are inconsistent, a party injured by a breach of contract must elect which remedy he will pursue. If the breaching party changes his position in reliance on the non-breaching party's choice, then the non-breaching party may not change his election.

2. Loss of Power of Avoidance

   a. Affirmance - A party who has the power to avoid a contract for lack of capacity, duress, undue influence, fraud, misrepresentation, or mistake will lose that power by affirming the contract.

   b. Delay - If a party has the power to rescind a contract but does not do so within a reasonable time, then the power of avoidance may be lost.

   c. Rights of Third Parties - The power of avoidance is limited by the intervening rights of third parties. For example, the right to rescind may be lost where a third party good faith purchaser acquires an interest in the subject matter of the contract before the right to rescind has been exercised.

DEFINITIONS

1. Compensatory damages

2. Reliance damages

3. Foreseeability of damages

4. "Out-of-pocket" damages

5. "Benefit-of-the-bargain" damages

6. Nominal damages

7. Punitive damages

8. Liquidated damages

9. Mitigation of damages

10. Specific performance

11. Injunction

12. Restitution

13. Incidental damages

14. Consequential damages

TRUE/FALSE

1. The primary objective of contract remedies is to compensate the injured party for the loss resulting from the contract breach by attempting to provide an equivalent of the promised performance.

2. An injured party may seek reliance damages as well as compensatory damages for a promisor's breach of contract.

3. Damages are recoverable for losses beyond those that the party in breach had reason to foresee as being a probable result of its breach when it entered into the contract.

4. The foreseeability of damages is a subjective test based on the breaching party's actual expectations.

5. Even if an unforeseeable, extraordinary loss results from a breach of contract, the injured party may still recover for any ordinary loss resulting from the breach.

6. Most States permit a party who has been induced to enter into a contract by fraud to recover only "out-of-pocket" damages.

7. Punitive damages are not recoverable for a breach of contract unless the breach also gives rise to a tort for which punitive damages are recoverable.

8. A contract provision by which the parties agree in advance to the damages to be paid in event of breach is enforceable even if it is NOT a reasonable forecast of the loss that would result from the breach.

9. When a breach of contract occurs, the injured party has a duty to take steps to minimize the damages that he may sustain.

10. Specific performance may be ordered even if monetary damages will provide an adequate remedy.

11. Restitution is the return to the injured party of the consideration that the injured party gave to the other party.

12. Under the doctrine of election of remedies, the injured party's choice of one available remedy will

bar his choice of an additional, consistent remedy.

 13. The power of avoidance may be lost if the party having the power does not rescind within a reasonable time.

 14. Compensatory damages are only recoverable for damages that were foreseeable when the contract was made.

15. The majority of States follow the benefit-of-the-bargain rule in awarding damages for fraud.

MULTIPLE CHOICE

1. The remedy which provides for damages to be awarded in an amount equal to the loss of value to the injured party caused by the other party's failure to perform or its deficient performance is called:
   a. compensatory damages.
   b. reliance damages.
   c. nominal damages.
   d. punitive damages.

2. In computing reliance damages, which of the following expenses of the injured party are properly includible:
   a. Expenses incurred in preparing to perform.
   b. Expenses incurred in actually performing.
   c. The value of foregone opportunities to enter into another contract.
   d. All of the above.

3. Money damages are only recoverable for losses that the party in breach had reason to foresee as a probable result of such breach at time that:
   a. the parties began negotiations.
   b. the parties entered into the contract.
   c. the breach occurred.
   d. none of the above.

4. Acting in reliance on X's intentional misrepresentation as to a drill press's capabilities, Y purchases the press from X for $17,000. Although the value of the press, if it had performed as promised, would be $10,000, its actual delivered value is $4,000. Under the benefit-of-the-bargain rule, Y could recover:
   a. nothing.
   b. $3,000.
   c. $6,000.
   d. $7,000.

5. Even if an injured party has not sustained or cannot prove an injury or loss resulting from a breach of contract, the injured party can still recover:
   a. compensatory damages.
   b. reliance damages.
   c. nominal damages.
   d. all of the above.

6. A formal order issued by a court of equity commanding a party to render the performance promised under the contract is called:
a. a decree of specific performance.
b. an injunction.
c. restitution.
d. none of the above.

 7. In which of the following instances is restitution available as a remedy for breach of contract?
a. When one party totally fails to perform its obligations.
b. When a party may not enforce the contract because of the Statute of Frauds.
c. Upon the avoidance of a voidable contract.
d. All of the above.

 8. A party with a power of avoidance may lose that power if he:
a. affirms the contract.
b. delays unreasonably in exercising the power of disaffirmance.
c. the rights of third parties intervene.
d. all of the above.

 9. When a misrepresentation is innocent, the aggrieved party may recover damages under the:
a. "out-of-pocket" damages rule.
b. "benefit-of-the-bargain" damages rule.
c. either (a) or (b).
d. neither (a) nor (b).

 10. A liquidated damages provision will be enforced only if it is:
a. a reasonable estimate of the loss that may result from the breach of contract.
b. a reasonable estimate of the loss that may result from the breach of contract.
c. a substitute for a penalty.
d. none of the above.

_C_ 11. Sam Seller contracts to sell 200 tables to Bill Buyer at a price of $50 a table. Bill repudiates the contract, whereupon Sam sells the tables to Paula Purchaser at a price of $45 a table. Sam's action in selling the chairs to another buyer is known as:
a. liquidating damages.
b. specific performance.
c. mitigation of damages.
d. restitution.

_b_ 12. Carl Contractor has a contract to build an office complex for Big Bucks Inc. A clause in the contract calls for Carl to pay $2,000 a day for each day's delay after the date the contract is scheduled for completion.
a. This is a compensatory damages clause.
b. This is a liquidated damages clause that may be an unenforceable penalty clause.
c. Big Bucks will be given the benefit-of-the-bargain in calculating damages.
d. Big Bucks will only be allowed to recover nominal damages in the case of a breach.

13. Arthur, a world-famous rock star, has a contract to perform at the Superdome on New Year's Eve. However, he decides he would rather spend the night with his family and friends and so informs the owners of the Superdome.
    a. The owners of the Superdome are entitled to specific performances, because Arthur's services are unique.
    b. The owners of the Superdome will have to wait until after January 1 to sue for breach of contract.
    c. The owners of the Superdome are entitled to damages, but they are not entitled to specific performance.
    d. Because an adequate remedy at law is available here, a court would be unable to issue an injunction prohibiting Arthur from performing at Madison Square Garden on New Year's Eve if they gave him a better offer.

14. Sam Seller has a contract to provide 100 widgets to Bill Buyer at a price of $10 a widget. Delivery is due on October 1. Due to unanticipated delays, Sam is unable to get the widgets to Bill until October 2. Bill is not harmed by the delay but sues anyway, because he is angry at Sam.
    a. Sam's failure to deliver the goods on October 1 is a violation of the Code's perfect tender rule, even if it is not a material breach.
    b. Bill cannot sue, because this is not a materal breach.
    c. If Bill cannot establish any incidental or consequential damages as a result of the breach, he will only be able to recover nominal damages.
    d. Two of the above, (a) and (c).

15. Bill Businessman pays $500 down on a new computer to be used in the office. The salesman has told him the computer has a 100,000 megabyte memory. Bill learns from other sources that this is blatantly untrue and realizes now that the salesman induced him to enter into the contract based upon fraud in the inducement, but the company refuses to return the down payment. If Bill sues, an appropriate remedy would be:
    a. injunction.
    b. punitive damages.
    c. nominal damages.
    d. rescission and restitution.

SHORT ESSAY

1. Under what circumstances is a loss resulting from a breach of contract foreseeable and therefore recoverable by the injured party?

2. What is the doctrine of mitigation of damages? What will the effect be of the injured party's failure to take the appropriate steps?

3.   What are the two major types of equitable remedies? Discuss each type, including an explanation of
      when each is available. _____
      _____
      _____
      _____

4.   What is the remedy of restitution and when is it available? _____
      _____
      _____
      _____

PART II

SAMPLE EXAMINATION

_____ 1. Damages that are calculated by taking the difference between the value received and the value given are _____ damages.
a. reliance
b. nominal
c. out-of-pocket
d. benefit-of-the-bargain

_____ 2. A contract that involves the exchange of a promise for a promise is a/an _____ contract.
a. unilateral
b. bilateral
c. formal
d. informal

_____ 3. Article 2 of the Uniform Commercial Code applies to sales of:
a. real property.
b. intangible personal property.
c. goods.
d. services.

_____ 4. A negotiable instrument such as a check is an example of a/an _____ contract.
a. formal
b. unilateral
c. implied
d. informal

_____ 5. In consideration of $500 being paid to Amanda by Barbara, Amanda gives Barbara the right to purchase her house for a price of $85,000 any time within thirty days. This is an example of a/an:
a. firm offer.
b. option.
c. implied condition subsequent.
d. revocation.

_____ 6. David owes Charles an undisputed debt of $500. David writes a check for $400, and then puts "paid in full" in the notation section of the check. Charles cashes the check.
a. This is a valid accord and satisfaction.
b. David has a moral obligation to pay an additional $100, but there is no consideration for his obligation to do so.
c. Charles can still collect the $100, because there was no consideration given for accepting less than the full amount of the debt.
d. Two of the above, (a) and (b).

_____ 7. Which of the following will invalidate a contract?
a. Unilateral mistake.
b. A material misstatement of opinion.
c. Undue influence.
d. Failure to read a document.

_____ 8. An offer comes to an end by means of:
   a. rejection.
   b. counter-offer.
   c. destruction of the contract subject matter.
   d. rejection, counter-offer, and destruction of the contract subject matter.

_____ 9. Words such as "provided that," "on condition that," and "as soon as" usually precede a/an:
   a. express condition.
   b. implied in fact condition.
   c. implied in law condition.
   d. condition subsequent.

_____ 10. Which of the following is untrue regarding an enforceable restraint on trade?
   a. The purpose must be to protect a property interest of the promisee.
   b. The restraint can be no more extensive than is reasonably necessary to protect the interest.
   c. The restraints frequently involve the sale of a business.
   d. The reasonableness of the restraint has no relationship to the geographic area covered.

_____ 11. Barbara owes Anita $1,000. On June 1, Anita for value assigns the debt to Carol. Thereafter, on June 15, Anita assigns the same right to Darla.
   a. Under the American rule, Carol will prevail over Darla.
   b. Under the English rule, the first assignee to notify Barbara will prevail.
   c. Under the Restatement, the first assignee to notify Barbara will prevail.
   d. Two of the above, (a) and (b).

_____ 12. A/an _____ has no right to enforce a contract.
   a. creditor beneficiary
   b. donee beneficiary
   c. incidental beneficiary
   d. donee beneficiary or incidental beneficiary

_____ 13. Ron Roadbuilder has a contract to build a highway for the State of Wisconsin. The contract requires that the highway be completed by September 15. If the highway is not completed by that date, the contract requires that Ron be assessed $200 per day in damages. The $200 per day is:
   a. punitive damages.
   b. liquidated damages.
   c. nominal damages.
   d. an illegal penalty.

_____ 14. Carl Contractor has a contract to build a house. He delegates the plumbing to Paul's Plumbing Company. Paul's Plumbing improperly performs the job.
   a. Carl remains responsible, even though he delegated the duty.
   b. Paul alone has responsibility for the improperly performed plumbing.
   c. Carl can assign his rights under the contract, but he cannot delegate his duties.
   d. Two of the above, (a) and (c).

_____ 15. Damages that arise directly out of the breach, such as the costs incurred to acquire the nondelivered performance from another source are known as _____ damages.
   a. consequential
   b. incidental
   c. nominal
   d. reliance

_____ 16. Sarah Student agrees to go to work for Big Bucks Inc. upon her graduation from Ivory Towers University on June 12. The contract is for one year, beginning on September 1. She agrees to the contract in a telephone conversation on May 1.
   a. Sarah needs a writing signed by Big Bucks in order to enforce the contract, because the contract cannot by its terms be performed within one year from her graduation on June 12.
   b. Sarah needs a writing signed by Big Bucks in order to enforce the contract, because the contract cannot by its terms be performed within one year from its making on May 1.
   c. Sarah does not need a writing to enforce this contract, because it can be enforced within one year of September 1.
   d. This is a contract between merchants, which requires no writing under the UCC Statute of Frauds.

_____ 17. The transfer of a contract right to a third person is generally known as a/an:
   a. novation.
   b. assignment.
   c. delegation.
   d. assumption.

_____ 18. Ron Roadbuilder pledges $150,000 to the building fund of the First Missionary Church. Based upon Ron's pledge, the church enters into a contract for the construction of a new building. Now Ron's company has missed getting three new jobs he had counted on getting for the year. Ron tells the church he has changed his mind and has no intention of paying his pledge.
   a. There is no consideration for Ron's pledge, and it is not enforceable.
   b. There is no consideration for Ron's pledge, but it is enforceable based upon promissory estoppel.
   c. Under the Restatement, the church's probable reliance upon Ron's pledge is sufficient to make it enforceable.
   d. Two of the above, (b) and (c).

_____ 19. Which of the following is/are enforceable without consideration?
   a. Mel Merchant sends a letter to Ralph Retailer offering to sell him widgets at $5 per widget and stating that the offer will continue for two weeks.
   b. Harold Homeowner makes a promise under seal to sell a used television to his neighbor for $50 and states that he will hold the offer open for two weeks.
   c. Arthur promises to pay a $100 debt which has been discharged in a bankruptcy proceeding. The promise is approved by the bankruptcy judge.
   d. Two of the aboe, (a) and (c).

_____ 20. Which of the following is/are equitable remedies?
   a. Liquidated damages.
   b. Specific performance.
   c. Consequential damages.
   d. Incidental damages.

CHAPTER 17

INTRODUCTION TO SALES

PURPOSE

The sale of goods is the most common of all business and legal transactions. The law of sales was originally part of the Law Merchant. It was eventually absorbed into the common law and then codified in Article 2 of the Uniform Commercial Code. Article 2 has been adopted in all States, except Louisiana, as well as in the District of Columbia and the Virgin Islands. In this chapter, you begin your study of Article 2 of the UCC, which governs the sale of goods and is a specialized branch of both the law of contracts and the law of personal property. Chapter 17 covers the basic definitions and the fundamental principles of Article 2 of the Code.

CHAPTER CHECKPOINTS

After reading and studying the chapter, you should be able to:

1. Define the terms "sale" and "goods" and distinguish a sale of goods from other types of transactions that affect goods.

2. List and discuss the fundamental principles of Article 2.

3. List and discuss the selected rules found in Article 2 that apply to merchants.

4. Summarize the UCC Battle of the Forms provision and discuss how it varies from the common law mirror image rule.

5. Compare the Article 2 parol evidence rule and Statute of Frauds provisions to the common law parol evidence rule and the general Statute of Frauds provisions discussed earlier in this text.

CHAPTER OUTLINE

I. Nature of Sales Contracts - The sales law found in Article 2 is a specialized branch of both the law of contracts and the law of personal property.
   A. Definition - The Code defines a sale as the transfer of title to goods from seller to buyer for a price. Goods are movable, tangible, personal property and include the unborn young of animals, growing crops, and other items attached to real property but removed by the seller.

1. Governing Law - Sales transactions are governed by Article 2 of the Code, but where general contract law has not been specifically modified by the Code, general contract law continues to apply. Transactions not within the scope of Article 2 include employment contracts, service contracts, insurance contracts, contracts involving real property and contracts for the sale of intangibles such as stocks, bonds, patents, and copyrights.

2. Non-sales Transactions in Goods - Some transactions that are not sales affect goods. These include bailments and leases. A bailment is the transfer of possession but not title of personal property by the owner or rightful possessor. The owner or person in rightful possession is the bailor; the person to whom the goods are transferred is the bailee. A lease is the transfer of possession but not title by the owner of the property. The owner is the lessor; the other person is the lessee. A gift is the transfer of ownership of property from one person to another without consideration. The maker of the gift is the donor; the recipient is the donee. The donor must have the intent to make a present transfer and the donee must accept the gift. A sale is distinguished from a security interest in that a sale transfers to the buyer all of the ownership rights of the seller, whereas under a security agreement both the creditor and the debtor have ownership rights in the goods. The secured creditor has the right to take possession of the goods in the event of default by the debtor. In 1987, the drafters of the Code approved Article 2A of the Code which deals with leases. Because it is new, it has not been as yet widely adopted by States.

B. Fundamental Principles of Article 2 - The purpose of Article 2 is to modernize, clarify, simplify, and make uniform the law of sales. The Article is to be interpreted according to these principles. The Code's open-ended drafting includes the following fundamental concepts.

1. Good Faith - All parties to contracts under the Code must perform their obligations in good faith. The Code defines good faith as honesty in fact in the conduct or transaction concerned. In the case of a merchant, it also includes the observance of reasonable commercial standards.

2. Unconscionability - Every contract under the Code may be scrutinized by the court to determine whether in its commercial setting, purpose, and effect, it is unconscionable, and the court may refuse to enforce an unconscionable contract or any part of a contract found to be unconscionable. Procedural unconscionability involves scrutiny for the presence of "bargaining naughtiness." In other words, it involves an analysis of the fairness of the bargaining process or the presence of procedural irregularities such as burying terms in the fine print of a contract. Substantive unconscionability deals with the actual terms of the contract and looks for oppressive or grossly unfair provisions such as an exorbitant price or an unfair exclusion or limitation of contractual remedies.

3. Expansion of Commercial Practices - The Code places great emphasis on course of dealing and usage of trade in interpreting agreements. A course of dealing is a sequence of previous conduct between the parties that may fairly be regarded as establishing a common basis of understanding for interpreting their expressions and agreements. A usage of trade is a practice or method of dealing regularly observed and followed in a place, vocation or trade.

4. Sales By and Between Merchants - A novel feature of the Code is the establishment of separate rules that apply to transactions between merchants or involving a merchant as a party. A merchant is a dealer in goods or a person who by his occupation holds himself out as having knowledge or skill peculiar to the goods or practices involved, or who employs an agent or broker whom he holds out as having such knowledge or skill. There are a number of Code sections that apply solely to transactions between merchants or involving a merchant as a party. These rules exact a higher standard of conduct from merchants, because of their knowledge of trade and commerce, and because merchants as a class generally set the standards.

5. Liberal Administration of Remedies - The Code provides that its remedies shall be liberally administered in order to place the aggrieved party in as good a position as if the defaulting party had fully performed. It also provides that where no specific remedy is expressly provided, the

courts should provide an appropriate remedy.

6. Freedom of Contract - Most Code provisions are not mandatory, but instead permit the parties to vary or displace them altogether. Provisions to the Code may be varied by agreement, except as otherwise provided and except that the obligations of good faith, diligence, reasonableness, and care may not be disclaimed by agreement.

7. Validation and Preservation of Sales Contracts - The Code reduces formal requisites to the bare minimum and attempts to preserve agreements whenever the parties manifest an intention to enter into a contract.

II. Formation of a Sales Contract - The Code's approach to validation is to recognize contracts whenever the parties manifest an intent to contract. The Code has modified the general law of contract formation in order to modernize contract law, to relax the validation requirements of contract formation, and to promote fairness.

A. Manifestation of Mutual Assent

1. Definiteness of an Offer - The Code provides that a contract does not fail for indefiniteness even though one or more terms may have been omitted. At common law, the terms of a contract were required to be definite and certain.

   a. Open Price - The parties may enter into a contract for the sale of goods even though they have no agreement on the price. The Code provides that the price is a reasonable one at the time for delivery where the agreement (1) says nothing as to price; (2) provides that the parties shall agree later as to the price and they fail to so agree; or (3) fixes the price in terms of some agreed market or other standard or as set by a third person or agency and the price is not so set.

   b. Open Delivery - Unless otherwise agreed, the place for delivery is the seller's place of business. If not specified otherwise, delivery must be made within a reasonable time and in a single delivery.

   c. Open Quantity - Output and requirement contracts, agreements for the entire output of a seller for a stated period, or for the seller to supply the buyer with all her requirements of certain goods are enforceable by the application of an objective standard based on the good faith of both parties. The quantities may not be disproportionate to any stated estimate or the prior output or requirements.

   d. Other Open Terms - Rules are provided as to the terms of payment, duration and performance.

2. Irrevocable Offers - A firm offer is a signed writing by a merchant to hold open an offer for the purchase or sale of goods. Such an offer is irrevocable for the stated period up to a maximum of three months even if no consideration is given to the merchant offeror for the promise. An option is a contract to hold open an offer; it is binding on the offeror.

3. Variant Acceptances - The Code modifies the common law "mirror image" rule under which an acceptance cannot vary from the terms of the offer. Under the common law rule where two businesses exchange pre-printed forms with varying terms, no contract exists, even if the parties intend that there be a contract. The Code addresses this battle of the forms problem by focusing on the intent of the parties. The issue then becomes whether the offeree's different terms become part of the contract. If both parties are merchants, the additional terms will be part of the contract if they do not materially alter the offer; if the additional terms do materially alter the offer, they are merely construed as proposals for addition to the contract. Different terms proposed by the offeree will not become part of the contract unless specifically accepted by the offeror. If the offeree expressly makes his acceptance conditioned upon assent to the additional or different terms, no contract is formed.

4. Manner of Acceptance - An offer to make a contract invites acceptance in any manner and by any medium reasonable under the circumstances unless clearly indicated otherwise. An offer to

buy goods may be accepted either by a prompt promise to ship or by prompt shipment.
5. Auctions - In an auction without reserve, the auctioneer may not withdraw the article put up for sale unless no bids are made. Unless the sale is advertised as being without reserve, it is with reserve and the auctioneer may withdraw the goods at any time. A bidder may retract her bid at any time prior to acceptance by the auctioneer. If the auctioneer knowingly receives a bid on behalf of the seller and notice has not been given that the seller reserves the right to bid, the bidder to whom the goods are sold can either take the goods at the price of the last good faith bid or avoid the sale.

B. Consideration
1. Contractual Modifications - The Code has abandoned the common law rule that a modification of an existing rule must be supported by consideration.
2. Discharge of Claim After Breach - A written waiver or renunciation signed and delivered by the aggrieved party discharges a claim of right arising out of a breach, even if there is no consideration.
3. Firm Offers - They are not revocable for lack of consideration.

C. Form of the Contract
1. Statute of Frauds - The original Statute of Frauds provision requiring a writing for the sale of goods costing $500 or more has been used as the prototype for the Article 2 Statute of Frauds.
   a. Modification of Contracts Within the Statute of Frauds - An agreement modifying a contract must be in writing if the resulting contract is within the Statute of Frauds. Conversely, a modification that takes a contract outside of the Statute of Frauds may be oral.
   b. Written Compliance - The Statute of Frauds compliance provisions under the Code are more liberal than the rules under general contract law. The Code requires some writing sufficient to indicate that a contract has been made between the parties signed by the party against whom enforcement is sought or by her authorized agent or broker and including a term specifying the quantity of goods. Under the Code a writing may be sufficient even if it omits or incorrectly states a term agreed upon.
   c. Alternative Methods of Compliance - An oral contract for the sale of goods is enforceable against a party who admits in his pleading, testimony or otherwise in court that a contract was made. Enforcement is limited to the quantity of goods admitted. An oral contract for specially manufactured goods is enforceable against the buyer who has received part delivery or against a seller who has received partial payment. Partial payment validates the contract only for the goods that have been delivered and accepted or for which payment has been accepted.
2. Parol Evidence - Contractual terms that are set forth in a writing intended by the parties as a final expression of their agreement may not be contradicted by evidence of any prior agreement or of a contemporaneous oral agreement, but under the Code they may be explained or supplemented by course of dealing, usage of trade or course of performance. Evidence of consistent additional terms may also be used.
3. Seal - Seals are inoperative under the Code with respect to contracts for the sale of goods.

DEFINITIONS

1. Sale

2. Goods

3. Bailment

4. Gift

5. Good faith

6. Unconscionability

7. Course of dealing

8. Usage of trade

9. Merchant

10. Firm offer

11. "Mirror image" rule

12. Auction without reserve

13. Parol evidence

TRUE/FALSE

_____ 1. A sale is defined as the transfer of title of goods from seller to buyer for a price.

_____ 2. Where general contract law has not been specifically modified by Article Two of the Code, principles of general conract law govern.

_____ 3. An employment contract is within the scope of Article Two.

_____ 4. The Code defines "unconscionability" as "fairness under the circumstances."

_____ 5. Most of the Code's provisions permit the parties to vary or displace them by agreement.

_____ 6. A merchant's firm offer is irrevocable for the stated period, not to exceed 3 months, even though no consideration is given to the merchant-offeror for that promise.

_____ 7. The Code has adopted the common law "mirror image" rule stating that an acceptance cannot deviate from the terms of the offer.

_____ 8. Under the Code, a unilateral offer must be accepted by a prompt shipment of the goods accompanied by notice to the buyer within a reasonable time.

_____ 9. Under the Code, a modification of an existing contract does not need to be supported by consideration to be binding.

_____ 10. A term specifying the quantity of goods sold is necessary for a writing to satisfy the Code's Statute of Fraud's compliance provision.

_____ 11. A farmer who grows corn is a merchant with respect to corn.

_____ 12. Most Code provisions are mandatory and allow no room for negotiation by the parties.

_____ 13. Firm offers are not revocable for lack of consideration.

_____ 14. When the Article 2 parol evidence rule applies, parol evidence may be used to establish a course of dealing.

_____ 15. Unless otherwise agreed, the place for delivery is the buyer's place of business.

MULTIPLE CHOICE

_____ 1. Which of the following transactions would be governed by Article 2 of the Uniform Commercial Code?
   a.   The sale of a house.
   b.   The sale of a typewriter.
   c.   The lease of a typewriter.
   d.   A contract of employment.

_____ 2. A transfer of possession of goods without a transfer of title to them is called:
   a.   a bailment.
   b.   a sale.
   c.   a gift.
   d.   a lease.

_____ 3. For a merchant, "good faith" requires:
   a.   "honesty in fact in the conduct or transaction concerned."
   b.   "reasonable commercial standards of fair dealing in the trade."
   c.   neither (a) nor (b).
   d.   both (a) and (b).

_____ 4. A "merchant" is defined by the Code as a person:
   a.   who is a dealer in the goods involved.
   b.   who by his occupation holds himself out as having knowledge or skill peculiar to the goods or practices involved.
   c.   who employs an agent or broker whom he holds out as having knowledge or skill peculiar to the goods or practices involved.
   d.   all of the above.

_____ 5. Most of the Code's provisions are not mandatory but instead permit the parties to vary or displace them, except:
   a.   price.
   b.   place of delivery.
   c.   good faith.
   d.   none of the above.

_____ 6. Under the Code, if a merchant-seller's acceptance contains a term in addition to those contained in the non-merchant buyer's offer, the additional term is:
    a.   ignored.
    b.   construed as a proposal for an addition to the contract.
    c.   construed as part of the contract even if it materially alters the agreement.
    d.   construed as part of the contract unless the buyer expressly objects to its inclusion.

_____ 7. Under the Code, which of the following requires consideration to be binding?
    a.   A modification of an existing contract.
    b.   A contract to sell goods.
    c.   A written discharge of a claim after a breach of contract.
    d.   A merchant's firm offer.

_____ 8. In order to comply with the Code's version of the Statute of Frauds, the party seeking to enforce the contract must have a writing that is:
    a.   notarized.
    b.   signed by the party against whom enforcement is sought or by his authorized agent or broker.
    c.   includes all material terms.
    d.   none of the above.

_____ 9. Under the Code, seals are effective with respect to:
    a.   contracts for the sale of goods.
    b.   offers to buy goods.
    c.   offers to sell goods.
    d.   none of the above.

_____ 10. A practice or method of dealing regularly observed and followed in a place, vocation, or trade describes:
    a.   a "usage of trade."
    b.   a "course of performance."
    c.   a "course of dealing."
    d.   an express term in a contract.

_____ 11. Every contract or duty under the UCC imposes an obligation of:
    a.   reasonableness.
    b.   good faith.
    c.   course of performance.
    d.   course of dealing.

_____ 12. Under the UCC Statute of Frauds, which of the following must be included in the required memoranda?
    a.   The signatures of both parties.
    b.   The shipment terms.
    c.   The quantity of goods sold.
    d.   The time for delivery.

_____ 13. The UCC Statute of Frauds applies to contracts for the sale of goods of a price of _____ or more.
     a. $100
     b. $300
     c. $500
     d. $5,000

_____ 14. Bill Buyer writes to Sam Seller and orders 100 tables.
     a. Sam can accept this offer by sending a confirmation of the order.
     b. Sam can accept this offer by shipping the tables.
     c. Sam must both send a confirmation and ship the tables to accept the offer.
     d. Sam can accept either by sending a confirmation of the order or by shipping the tables.

_____ 15. If no place for delivery of the goods is mentioned in the contract, what is the place of delivery?
     a. The buyer's place of business.
     b. The seller's place of business.
     c. The buyer's warehouse.
     d. There is none. The goods must be shipped.

SHORT ESSAY

1. When is Article 2 of the Uniform Commercial Code applicable? When is it inapplicable? _____
_____
_____
_____

2. Compare the Code's position with that of the common law of contracts regarding the requisites of an effective acceptance of an offer. _____
_____
_____
_____

3. Compare the obligation of "good faith" as imposed on merchants and non-merchants. _____
_____
_____
_____

4. What is a "firm offer?" What are its characteristics? _____
_____
_____
_____

CHAPTER 18

TRANSFER OF TITLE AND RISK OF LOSS

PURPOSE

The common law historically determined the rights and duties of the buyer and seller arising out of a sales contract based upon the principle of title. The Code has de-emphasized the significance of title in determining risk of loss and other rights and duties that arise under a sales contract. Under the Code, title retains some significance, but the Code approaches each legal issue arising in a sales contract on its own merits. It provides separate and specific rules to control various transaction situations. In this chapter, you study the Code rules governing risk of loss in shipping contracts and destination contracts. You also study the rules governing risk of loss where one of the parties is in breach of the contract and where there is no breach. The Code rules governing risk of loss are complex for the student studying them for the first time and must be carefully studied in order to be fully understood. In this chapter, you also study property rights other than title, including the special property right that the buyer obtains upon identification of existing goods to which the contract of sale refers. The chapter concludes with a section on bulk transfers, which are covered by Article 6 of the Code, and the requirements that must be met when a transfer is made that is not in the ordinary course of the transferor's business and that involves a major party of his inventory.

CHAPTER CHECKPOINTS

After reading and studying this chapter, you should be able to:

1. Distinguish between a shipment contract and a destination contract and give the Code rules for risk of loss for each type of contract.

2. Give the rules for passage of title and risk of loss in situations where there is no movement of the goods and (a) the seller is a merchant; (b) the seller is not a merchant; (c) there is a document of title; (d) there is no document of title.

3. Distinguish between a void title and a voidable title and discuss the Code rule that applies when the owner of goods entrusts them to a merchant who then sells them to a good faith purchaser in the ordinary course of business.

4. Distinguish between a sale on approval and a sale or return and give the Code rule for risk of loss in each situation.

5. Define the term "transfer in bulk" and summarize the requirements of Article 6.

CHAPTER OUTLINE

I.   Transfer of Title and Other Property Rights
    A. Passage of Title - A sale of goods is defined as the transfer of title from the seller to the buyer for a consideration known as the price. Title passes when the parties intend it to pass. Where there is no specific agreement of the parties, the Code provides rules to determine when title passes to the buyer.
        1. Physical Movement of the Goods - When delivery is to be made by moving the goods, title passes at the time and place where the seller completes his performance with reference to delivery. When and where delivery occurs depends upon whether the contract is a shipment contract or a destination contract. Tender means that the seller offers conforming goods to the buyer and gives the buyer notice that the goods are available.
            a. Shipment Contract - In a shipment contract, the seller is required to tender delivery of the goods to a carrier for delivery to the buyer who bears the expense and risk of loss. Title passes to the buyer at the time and place that the seller delivers the goods to the carrier for shipment to the buyer.
            b. Destination Contract - In a destination contract, the seller is required to tender delivery of the goods at a particular destination; the seller bears the expense and risk of loss. Title passes to the buyer on tender of the goods at the destination.
        2. No Movement of the Goods - When delivery is to be made without moving the goods, title passes either (a) on delivery of a document of title where the contract calls for delivery of such a document; or (b) at the time and place of contracting where the goods at that time have been identified either by the seller or the buyer as the goods to which the contract refers and no documents are to be delivered. Where the goods are not identified at the time of contracting, title passes when the goods are identified.
    B. Other Property Rights
        1. The Code created a new property interest in goods known as a "special property" right that the buyer obtains by the identification of existing goods as goods to which the contract of sale refers.
        2. Insurable Interest - For a contract or policy of insurance to be valid, the insured must have an insurable interest in the subject matter. The Code extends the right to a buyer's interest in goods that have been identified to the contract. Nothing prevents both seller and byer from both having an insurable interest nad simultaneously carrying insurance on the goods identified to the contract.
        3. Security Interest - The Code defines "security interest" as an interest in personal property or fixtures that ensures payment or performance of an obligation. Security interests are governed by Article 9 of the Code.
    C. Power to Transfer Title - In some situations non-owner sellers may have the power to transfer good title to certain buyers. In general, the purchaser of goods obtains such title as his transferor either has or had the power to transfer. A purported sale by a thief or finder or ordinary bailee of goods does not transfer title to the purchaser. However, to encourage and make secure good faith acquisitions of goods, it is necessary that bona fide (good faith) purchasers for value be protected under certain circumstances. A good faith purchaser is defined as one who acts honestly, gives value, and takes the goods without notice or knowledge of any defect in the title of his transferor.
        1. Void and Voidable Title to Goods - A void title is no title. A thief or finder of goods has no title and can transfer none. A voidable title is one acquired under circumstances that permit the former owner to rescind the transfer and revest herself with title, as in the case of mistake, ordinary duress, undue influence, or fraud in the inducement. If a buyer who has voidable title should resell the goods to a bona fide purchaser for value who has no notice of any infirmity of title, the bona fide purchaser acquires good title, and the original seller's right of rescission is cut

off.

2. **Entrusting of Goods to a Merchant** - The Code protects good faith purchasers in the ordinary course of business from merchants who deal in goods of the kind in situations where the owner has entrusted possession of the goods to a merchant. When a merchant wrongfully sells an item that has been entrusted to him, as between the good faith purchaser in the ordinary course of business and the owner who has entrusted the goods to the merchant, the good faith purchaser from the merchant is preferred. The original owner's recourse is against the merchant for money damages; he cannot get back the goods. However, the Code does not protect the bona fide purchaser from a merchant when the goods have been entrusted to the merchant by a thief or finder or by someone who is completely unauthorized to entrust the goods. A buyer in the ordinary course of business is defined as a person who buys in ordinary course, in good faith, and without knowledge that the sale to him is in violation of anyone's ownership rights.

II. **Risk of Loss** - This terms addresses the allocation of loss between seller and buyer where the goods have been damaged, destroyed or lost without the fault of either the seller or the buyer.
   A. Risk of Loss in Absence of a Breach
      1. **Agreement of the Parties** - The parties may by agreement shift the allocation of risk of loss or divide the risk between them.
      2. **Trial Sales** - Under the Code there are two types of trial sales: a sale on approval and a sale or return.
         a. **Sale on Approval** - In such a sale possession, but not title to the goods, is transferred to the buyer for a stated period of time or, if none is stated, for a reasonable time. Both title and risk of loss remain with the seller until "approval" or acceptance of the goods by the buyer.
         b. **Sale or Return** - In such a sale the goods are sold and delivered to the buyer with an option to return them to the seller. The risk of loss is on the buyer, who also has title until she revests it in the seller by a return of the goods. Unless otherwise agreed, if the goods are delivered primarily for the buyer's use, the transaction is a sale on approval; if they are delivered primarily for resale by the buyer, it is a sale or return.
      3. **Contracts Involving Carriers** - If the contract does not require the seller to deliver the goods at a particular destination but merely to the carrier (a shipment contract), risk of loss passes to the buyer when the goods are delivered to the common carrier. If the seller is required to deliver them to a particular destination (a destination contract), risk of loss passes to the buyer at the destination when the goods are tendered to the buyer.
         a. **Shipment Contracts** - F.O.B. means "free on board"; F.A.S. means "free alongside." If a contract is F.O.B. place of shipment or F.A.S. port of shipment, then the contract is a shipment contract. C.I.F. means "cost, insurance and freight"; C.&F. means "cost and freight." Under the code, both C.I.F. and C.&F. contacts are regarded as shipment contracts, not destination contracts. C.O.D. means "collect on delivery"; a C.O.D. contract is generally a shipment contract.
         b. **Destination Contracts** - Where the contract is F.O.B. place of destination, the seller must at his own risk and expense transport the goods to the place of destination and there tender delivery of them to the buyer. A contract for delivery, "ex-ship," or "from the ship," is a destination contract. A contract "no arrival, no sale," is a destination contract.
      4. **Goods in Possession of Bailee** - When goods are held by a bailee, the risk of loss passes to the buyer (1) if a negotiable document of title is involved, when the buyer receives the document; (2) if a non-negotiable document of title is involved, when the document is tendered to the buyer; (3) if no documents of title are used, either (a) when the seller tenders to the buyer written directions or (b) when the bailee acknowledges the buyer's right to possession of the goods.
      5. **All Other Sales** - If the seller is a merchant, risk of loss passes to the buyer on the buyer's receipt of the goods. If the seller is not a merchant, it passes on tender of the goods from the seller to

the buyer.

B. Risk of Loss Where There is a Breach
   1. Breach by the Seller - If the seller ships goods to the buyer that do not conform to the contract, the risk of loss remains on the seller until the buyer has accepted the goods or the seller has remedied the defect.
   2. Breach by the Buyer - Where conforming goods have been identified to the contract that the buyer repudiates or breaches before risk of loss has passed to him, the seller may treat the risk of loss as resting on the buyer "for a commercially reasonable time" to the extent of any deficiency in the seller's effective insurance coverage.

III. Sale of Goods in Bulk - A bulk transfer is a transfer not in the ordinary course of the transferor's business of a major part of his inventory.
  A. Requirements of Article 6 - a bulk transfer is ineffective against any creditor of the transferor, unless the following four requirements are met:
    1. The transferor must furnish to the transferee a sworn list of his existing creditors.
    2. The transferor and the transferee must prepare a schedule or list of property being transferred.
    3. The transferee must preserve the list of creditors and schedule of property for six months and permit inspection by any creditor of the transferor.
    4. The transferee must give the notice of the proposed transfer in bulk to each creditor of the transferor at least ten days before the transferee takes possession of the goods or makes payment of them.
  B. Exempted Bulk Transfers - The following transfers need not comply with Article 6:
    1. Transfers by way of security.
    2. General assignments for the benefit of all the creditors of the transferor in bulk.
    3. Transfers in settlement or realization of a lien or security interest.
    4. Sales by executors, administrators, receivers, trustees in bankruptcy, or any public officer under judicial process.
    5. Sales in the course of proceedings for the dissolution or reorganization of a corporation.
    6. Transfers to a person who maintains a known place of business in the State and who agrees to become bound to pay in full the debts of the transferor in bulk, gives notice of that fact, and who is solvent after becoming so bound.
    7. Transfers to a new business enterprise organized to take over and continue the business of the transferor in bulk.
    8. Transfers of property that is exempt from execution under exemption statutes.
  C. Effect of Failure to Comply with Article 6 - Failure to comply means that the goods in the possession of the transferee continue to be subject to the claims of unpaid creditors of the transferor. A bona fide purchaser of the goods from the transferee who pays value in good faith and takes the property without notice of such defect acquires the goods free of any claim of creditors of the transferor.
  D. Application of the Proceeds - In an optional section the Code imposes a personal duty on the transferee to apply the new consideration to the payment of the debts of the transferor and if it is insufficient to pay them in full, to make a proportional distribution to the creditors.

DEFINITIONS

1. Shipment contract

2. Destination contract

3. Special property

4. Bona fide purchaser

5. Entrustment

6. "Buyer in ordinary course of business"

7. Risk of loss

8. Sale on approval

9. Sale or return

10. Consignment

11. C.I.F.

12. C & F

13. C.O.D.

14. F.O.B.

15. Ex-ship

16. "No arrival, no sale"

17. Bulk transfer

TRUE/FALSE

_____ 1. A transfer of title from seller to buyer is fundamental to the existence of a sale of goods.

_____ 2. Under a destination contract, title to the goods passes to the buyer at the time and place that the seller delivers the goods to the carrier.

_____ 3. Under the Code, only those persons with title to or a lien on goods have an insurable interest in those goods.

_____ 4. Any reservation by the seller of title to goods delivered to the buyer is the reservation of a security interest in those goods.

_____ 5. A seller may have the power but not the right to sell goods in his possession to certain buyers.

_____ 6. If a buyer with void title resells the goods to a bona fide purchaser for value and without notice of any flaw in his title, the bona fide purchaser acquires good title.

_____ 7. A "buyer in the ordinary course of business" is defined by the Code as one who acts honestly, gives value, and takes without notice or knowledge of any defect in the title of his transferor.

_____ 8. If risk of loss is placed on the seller, then he has no right to recover the purchase price for lost or damaged goods from the buyer.

_____ 9. Under both the common law and the Code, risk of loss is determined by ownership of the goods and whether title has been transferred.

_____ 10. Under the Code, risk of loss is allocated by the Code and an agreement by the parties to shift or divide the risk is not controlling.

_____ 11. In a sale on approval, risk of loss immediately passes to the buyer who retains title until he revests it in the seler by returning the goods.

_____ 12. Under the Code, a sale on consignment is regarded as a sale or return.

_____ 13. In a shipment contract, risk of loss passes to the buyer upon delivery of the goods to the carrier.

_____ 14. If a seller breaches a contract by shipping non-conforming goods to the buyer, risk of loss remains on the buyer until the buyer properly returns the goods to the seller.

_____ 15. A bulk transfer includes the sale of a merchant's inventory in the ordinary course of his business.

_____ 16. A transfer in bulk by way of security is exempt from the requirements of Article 6 of the Code.

MULTIPLE CHOICE

_____ 1. A "destination contract" requires the seller to deliver the goods to a particular destination and title passes to the buyer:
   a. at the time and place that the seller delivers the goods to the carrier for shipment to the buyer's place of business.
   b. upon tender of the goods to the buyer at that destination.
   c. upon delivery of a document of title.
   d. at the time and place that the contract is entered into.

_____ 2. A seller has an insurable interest in goods if:
   a. the goods have been identified as the goods to which the contract of sale refers.
   b. the seller has title to the goods.
   c. the seller has a security interest in the goods.
   d. all of the above.

_____ 3. An interest in personal property or fixtures that secures payment or performance of an obligation is called:
   a. a security interest.
   b. a consignment.
   c. a bailment.
   d. title to the goods.

_____ 4. In order to acquire good title to goods, a subsequent purchaser of goods from a transferee with voidable title must meet all of the following qualifications except:
   a. he must purchase the goods in good faith.
   b. he must purchase the goods after the original transferor rescinds the first transfer.
   c. he must purchase the goods for value.
   d. he must purchase the goods without notice of any infirmity of his title.

_____ 5. Under the Code, a merchant entrusted with the possession of goods has the power to transfer good title to a buyer in the ordinary course of business if the entruster is:
   a. a thief.
   b. the owner of the goods.
   c. one who found the goods.
   d. all of the above.

_____ 6. A transaction in which goods are sold and delivered to the buyer with an option to return them to the seller is called:
   a. a sale on approval.
   b. a sale or return.
   c. a bailment.
   d. a consignment.

_____ 7. In a sale on approval, risk of loss passes to the buyer when:
   a. the contract is entered into by the parties.
   b. the goods are sent by the seller.
   c. the goods are received by the buyer.
   d. the goods are accepted by the buyer.

_____ 8. In a shipment contract, risk of loss passes to the buyer when:
   a. the parties enter into the contract.
   b. the goods leave the seller's business.
   c. the goods are delivered to a carrier.
   d. the goods are received by the buyer.

_____ 9. Which, if any, of the following designations indicate that the contract is a shipment contract?
   a. F.O.B. place of shipment.
   b. F.A.S. port of shipment.
   c. C.I.F.
   d. All of the above.

_____ 10. In an ordinary contract in which the merchant-seller is required to tender or deliver the goods to a non-merchant buyer, risk of loss passes to the buyer:
   a. when the parties enter into the contract.
   b. upon the seller's tender of the goods to the buyer.
   c. when the buyer receives the goods.
   d. none of the above.

____ 11. If the seller ships non-conforming goods to the buyer, the risk of loss remains on the seller until:
   a.   the buyer accepts the goods.
   b.   the seller remedies the defect in the goods.
   c.   either (a) or (b).
   d.   both (a) and (b).

____ 12. A transfer in bulk is exempt from the requirements of Article 6 of the Code if:
   a.   it is a transfer by way of security.
   b.   it is a general assignment for the benefit of the creditors of the seller.
   c.   it is a sale in the course of proceedings for the reorganization of a corporation in a court proceeding where notice is given to creditors.
   d.   all of the above.

____ 13. Before title to goods can pass:
   a.   the goods must be in existence, but need not be identified.
   b.   the goods must be identified.
   c.   the goods must be included in inventory.
   d.   the goods must be represented by a document of title.

____ 14. Which of the following is true regarding a sale or return?
   a.   Title remains with the seller.
   b.   The buyer's creditors can attach the goods.
   c.   There is no sale until the buyer returns the unsold goods.
   d.   The seller bears the expense of return of the goods.

____ 15. A sale of a business, including its inventory and fixtures would be called a/an
   _____.
   a.   C.I.F. sale
   b.   sale on approval
   c.   sale or return
   d.   bulk transfer

SHORT ESSAY

1. Compare the significance of the concept of title under the common law with its role under the Code in allocating risk of loss. _____
_____
_____
_____

2. What is the difference between a shipment and a destination contract? When does risk of loss pass to the buyer under each? _____
_____
_____
_____

3.   What is the difference between void and voidable title?   Of what significance is this difference in determining the rights of subsequent purchasers of the goods. _____

_____

_____

_____

4.   When does risk of loss pass to the buyer if the goods are held by a bailee and are to be delivered without being moved? _____

_____

_____

_____

CHAPTER 19

PRODUCTS LIABILITY: WARRANTIES AND STRICT LIABILITY

PURPOSE

In this chapter you study the liability of manufacturers and sellers of goods to buyers, users, consumers, and bystanders for damages caused by defective products. The buyer of goods expects that his purchase will meet certain standards. If these standards are not met, then there is a breach of warranty. The breach may be one of title or of quality; and the seller will have liability for damages caused by such breach.

Traditionally, the law followed the concept of caveat emptor -- or " let the buyer beware." This rule was premised upon the principle that the buyer and the seller had equal bargaining power. That is not the case today when the consumer generally possesses far less bargaining power than the seller. Consequently, the law of sales has abandoned the concept of caveat emptor and employs warranties to protect the buyer. In this chapter, you study the various kinds of liability that a manufacturer or seller of goods may have for a defective product, or for its failure to perform adequately. In previous chapters you have studied negligence, misrepresentation, and violation of statutory duty. In this chapter, you study warranty and strict liability. The liability of manufacturers and sellers under these last two legal theories has expanded so much in recent years that product liability is now considered to be a separate and distinct field of law that combines and enforces rules and principles of contracts, sales negligence, strict liability and statutory law.

CHAPTER CHECKPOINTS

After reading and studying this chapter, you should be able to:
1. Identify and describe the warranties found in Article 2 of the Code.

2. List and discuss the defenses that may be raised by the seller in an action based on warranty and compare the defenses to an action based on warranty of merchantability to those to an action based upon 402A of the Restatement of Torts.

3. List and describe the elements of an action based upon strict liability in tort under 402A of the Restatement of Torts.

4. Discuss the concept of privity of contract and how the Code approaches the issue of horizontal privity.

5. Compare the provisions of the Code's warranty of merchantability to the provisions found in 402A of the Restatement of Torts.

CHAPTER OUTLINE

I. Warranties - Historically, the liability of a seller for breach of warranty was an action in tort for deceit. Today it is contractual and has been codified in the UCC. A warranty is an obligation of the seller to the buyer concerning title, quality, characteristics or condition of goods. A seller is not required to warrant goods, but when the warranties are prescribed by the Code, he must act affirmatively in tha manner prescribed by the Code to effectively disclaim liability for these implied warranties.

    A. Types of Warranties

        1. Express Warranties - An express warranty is an affirmation of fact or promise about the goods or a description, including a sample, of the goods which becomes part of the basis of the bargain. The seller does not need to use formal works such as "warrant" or "guarantee". Moreover, it is not necessary that the seller have knowledge of the falsity of a statement in order to be liable for breach of an express warranty. Statements or promises made by the seller to the buyer before the sale may become express warranties, because they may form a basis of the bargain. Statements or promises made by the seller to the buyer after the sale may become express warranties even though no new consideration is given. A statement of the value of the goods or a statement purporting merely to be the seller's opinion does not create a warranty. Such statements are considered to be accepted puffery. A statement of opinion by a seller is not a warranty, unless the seller is an expert, in which case, it may constitute a warranty.

        2. Warranty of Title - The warranty of title is the obligation of the seller to convey the right to ownership without any lien. Under the Code, the seller implicitly warrants that (1) the title conveyed is good and its transfer rightful; and (2) the goods have no security interest or other lien against them to the knowledge of the seller at the time of contracting. The Code does not label the warranty of the title an implied warranty even though it arises out of the sale and not from any particular words or conduct of the seller.

        3. Implied Warranties - An implied warranty is a contractual obligation arising out of certain circumstances of the sale. It exists by operation of law and is not found in the language of the sales contract. Implied warranties are a departure from the early rule of caveat emptor.

            a. Merchantability - At early common law a seller was not held to any implied warranty. However, under the Code a merchant seller makes an implied warranty of the merchantability of goods that are of the kind in which he deals. The warranty is an obligation of the merchant seller that the goods be reasonably fit for the ordinary purpose for which they are manufactured or sold, and that they be of fair, average quality. A contract for the sale of secondhand goods includes a warranty of merchantability that considers the price, age, and condition of the goods being sold.

            b. Fitness for Particular Purpose - Any seller, whether or not he is a merchant, makes an implied warrantly that the goods are reasonably fit for the particular purpose of the buyer, if at the time of contracting, the seller had reason to know the buyer's particular purpose and that the buyer was relying on the seller's skill and judgment to furnish suitable goods. This warranty pertains to a specific purpose, rather than the ordinary purpose, of the goods. A seller's conduct may involve both the implied warranty of merchantability and the implied warranty of fitness for a particular purpose.

    B. Obstacles to Warranty Actions

        1. Disclaimer or Modification of Warranties - A disclaimer is a negation of a warranty. The Code calls for a reasonable construction of words or conduct to negate or limit warranties. To be effective, disclaimers should be positive, explicit, unequivocal and conspicuous.

            a. Express Exclusions - A warranty of title may be excluded or modified only by specific language or by certain circumstances, including judicial sale or a sale by a sheriff, executor, or foreclosing lienor. In such cases the seller is clearly selling only such title as he or a third person has in the goods. A seller can avoid making an express warranty by carefully refraining from making any promise or affirmation of fact relating to the goods, and refraining from describing the goods or using a sample or model in a sale. The seller can also negate an express warranty by clear, specific, unambiguous language. A negation or limitation has no effect if it is unreasonable. A general disclaimer attempting to negate "all express warranties" is ineffective against the specific express warranty that an item is free of all defects. Oral warranties made before the execution of a written agreement that contains an express disclaimer are subject to the parol evidence rule. The language of a disclaimer or modification of an implied warranty of merchantability must mention "merchantability" and, in the case of a writing, it must be conspicuous. A disclaimer of an implied warranty of fitness for the particular purpose of the buyer must be in writing and conspicuous. Unless the circumstances indicate otherwise, all implied warranties are excluded by expressions like "as is," "with all faults," or other language calling the buyer's attention to the exclusion of warranties. Implied warranties may also be excluded by course of dealing, course of performance or usage of trade.

    b.   **Buyer's Examination or Refusal to Examine** - If the buyer inspects the goods, implied warranties do not apply to obvious defects that are apparent on examination. There are no implied warranties as to defects that an examination ought to have revealed where the buyer has examined as fully as she desires, or where the buyer has refused to examine the goods.

    c.   **Federal Legislation Relating to Warranties of Consumer Goods** - The Federal Trade Commission administers and enforces the Magnuson-Moss Warranty Act. The Act is designed to protect purchasers of consumer goods by providing that warranty information be clear and useful. The Act defines consumer goods as those which are primarily used for personal, family, or household purposes. It provides that a seller who makes a written warranty cannot disclaim any implied warranty.

2.   **Privity of Contract** - During the nineteenth century, the law became established that a plaintiff could not recover for breach of warranty unless he was in a contractual relationship with the defendant. This relationship is known as privity of contract.

    a.   **Horizontal Privity** - This pertains to noncontracting parties who are injured by the defective goods. Persons who are likely to be in horizontal privity today include users, consumers, and bystanders who are not the contracting purchaser. These persons may ordinarily bring an action for breach of warranty if they are injured by a defective good. The Code contains three alternatives which state different limits for horizontal privity. The least comprehensive and most widely adopted of these legistative alternatives provides that a seller's warranty, whether express or implied, extends to any natural person who is in the family or household of the buyer or who is a guest in his home if it is reasonable to expect that such a person may use, consume, or be affected by the goods. A seller may not exclude or limit the operation of this section except for injury other than to the person. Alternative B extends Alternative A to "any natural person who may reasonably be expected to use, consume or be affected by the goods." Alternative C further expands the coverage of the section to any person, not just natural persons. The Code was not intended to establish outer boundaries as to which third parties may recover for injuries caused by defective goods. Rather it sets minimum standards that may be expanded.

3.   **Notice of Breach** - If the buyer fails to notify the seller of any breach within a reasonable time, she is barred from any remedy against the seller. The purpose of the reasonable notice requirement is (1) to enable the seller to cure the defect or to minimize the buyer's loss; (2) to provide the seller an opportunity to prepare for conflict resolution and litigation; and (3) to provide the seller with an end point to liability. Consumers are given more sympathetic treatment for delay than are commercial entities.

4.   **Plaintiff's Conduct** - Contributory negligence of the buyer is to a defense to an action against the

seller for breach of warranty. However, if a buyer discovers a defect in the goods that may cause an injury and nevertheless proceeds to make use of them, he will not be permitted to recover damages from the seller. This is the voluntary assumption of a known risk.

II. Strict Liability in Tort
   A. Nature - Section 402A of the Restatement of Torts imposes liability on merchant sellers for both personal injuries and property damage for selling the product in a defective condition, unreasonably dangerous to the user or consumer. Negligence is not the basis for liability; it applies even though a seller has exercised all possible care in the preparation and sale of his product. The essential requirements for this type of liability are: (1) that the defendant sold the product in a defective condition; (2) that the defendant was engaged in the business of selling such a product; (3) that the defective condition made the product unreasonably dangerous to the user or consumer or to his property; (4) that the defect in the product existed at the time it left the hands of the defendant; (5) that the plaintiff sustained physical harm or property damage by use or consumption of the product; and (6) that the defective condition was the proximate cause of this injury or the defective condition was attributable to the defendant. Liability based on 402A is tort liability and arises out of the common law, not out of the Uniform Commercial Code.
      1. Defective Condition - In an action against a manufacturer or seller under the rule of strict liability in tort, the plaintiff must prove a defective condition in the product. However, she need not prove the reason or cause of the defect. Defects may arise through faulty manufacture, faulty product design, or by the failure to adequately label the package, instruct the user, or warn of possible harm resulting from use of the product.
         a. Manufacturing Defect - A defect of this kind occurs when the product is not properly made. Thus, it fails to meet its own manufacturing specifications. A chair that was missing screws would constitute a manufacturing defect.
         b. Design Defect - A defect of this kind occurs when the product is made as designed, but when the product is dangerous or hazardous, because the design is inadequate. Design defects result from poor engineering, poor choice of materials, and poor packaging. The Ford Pinto contained a design defect, because the fuel tank was placed too close to its rear axle, causing fuel tank explosions when the car was hit from the rear.
         c. Inadequate Warning or Instructions - A seller has a duty to provide adequate warning of possible danger and to provide appropriate direction for use of a product. In addition to warning of dangers, the seller must provide adequate directions for the safe and efficient use of the product. The product mut also be adequately packaged.
      2. Unreasonably Dangerous - Section 402A liability only applies if the defective product is unreasonably dangerous. An unreasonably dangerous product is one that contains a danger beyond that which would be contemplated by the ordinary consumer who purchases it with the common knowledge of its characteristics. Godd tobacco is not unreasonably dangerous, because smoking may be harmful; but tobacco containing a foreign substance may be unreasonably dangerous. Most courts let the jury decide what a consumer would reasonably expect.
   B. Obstacles to Recovery
      1. Disclaimers and Notice - Strict liability is based on tort law and therefore is not subject to contractual defenses. It is not affected by contractual limitations or disclaimers, and it is not subject to any requirement that notice be given to the seller by the injured party within a reasonable time. However, in commercial transactions, most courts have allowed enforcement of clear and specific disclaimers of Section 402A liability.
      2. Privity
         a. Horizontal Privity - Strict liability in tort protection extends not only to buyers, users, and consumers, but also to injured bystanders.
         b. Vertical Privity - Liability extends to any seller who is in the business of selling the product,

including a wholesaler or distributor as well as the manufacturer and the retailer. The manufacturer of the finished product is liable for damages caused by a defective component part even if that part was manufactured by someone else. Some jurisdictions extend strict liability in tort to merchant sellers of used goods.

3. Plaintiff's Conduct

    a. Contributory Negligence – This defense is immaterial in an action based on strict liability in tort, although a few States have held contributory negligence to be a valid defense.

    b. Comparative Negligence – Many states have adopted the rule of comparative negligence in negligence actions, and have also applied the principle to strict liability in tort.

    c. Voluntary Assumption of the Risk – This is a defense in an action based on strict liability in tort. A user or consumer who voluntarily uses the goods in an unusual, inappropriate or improper manner for which they were not intended, and that under the circumstances is unreasonable, assumes the risk of any injury resulting from the use. The burden of proof of this defense is on the defendant.

    d. Misuse or Abuse of the Product – This is a defense to a strict liability case. The major difference between misuse or abuse includes actions that the injured party does not know to be dangerous, whereas assumption of the risk does not include such conduct. A manufacturer will not avoid liability using this defense if the misuse of the product was foreseeable.

4. Subsequent Alteration – 402A provides that liability only exists if the product reaches "the user or consumer without substantial change in the condition in which it is sold." Alteration of the product is a defense that can be raised by the seller.

5. Statute of Repose – Lawsuits have frequently been brought against manufacturers many years after the product has been sold. In response to this threat of continued liability, many States have adopted statutes of repose. These laws limit the time period for which a manufacturer is liable for injury caused by its product. After a statutory time period has elapsed, a manufacturer ceases to be liable for harm caused by its defective products.

DEFINITIONS

1. Warranty

2. Caveat emptor

3. Express warranty

4. Implied warranties

5. Warranty of title

6. Implied warranty of mercantability

7. Implied warranty of fitness for particular purpose

8. Disclaimer of warranties

9. Privity of conduct

10. Strict liability in tort

11. Basis of the bargain

12. Consumer goods

13. State of the art

14. Statute of repose

TRUE/FALSE

_____ 1.   A warranty may arise out of a seller's affirmation of fact, her promise, or from the circumstances under which the sale is made.

_____ 2.   The Code requires that a seller's promise or affirmation of fact be relied upon by the buyer in order for it to constitute a warranty.

_____ 3.   The Code's implied warranty of merchantability is applicable to all sales made by merchants.

_____ 4.   Application of the implied warranty of fitness for a particular purpose does not depend on whether the seller is a merchant.

_____ 5.   The expression "as is" will only disclaim the implied warranty of merchantability if it is in writing and conspicuous.

_____ 6.   Most States have eliminated the requirements of horizontal and vertical privity in warranty actions.

_____ 7.   Strict liability in tort generally is not subject to disclaimer, exclusion, or modifications by contractual agreement.

_____ 8.   Strict liability in tort may arise from a manufacturing defect in the product but not from a mere defective design.

_____ 9.   The strict liability in tort of manufacturers and other sellers extends only to buyers and their families.

_____ 10. The doctrine of strict liability in tort may be held to be applicable to merchant sellers of used goods.

_____ 11. Misuse or abuse of the product is an effective defense to a claim of strict liability in tort only if the misuse or abuse was not foreseeable by the seller.

_____ 12. Under the Magnuson-Moss Act, no seller providing a written warranty can effectively disclaim any implied warranty.

_____ 13. Contributory negligence by the user of a defective product that is unreasonably dangerous will prevent the user from pursuing a claim based on 402A.

_____ 14. Any seller can make an implied warranty of fitness for a particular purpose, but only a merchant can make a warranty of merchantability.

_____ 15. Harold Homeowner buys a defective toaster at a neighborhood garage sale and is injured slightly when it explodes. Harold can sue his neighbor for breach of warranty of merchantability.

MULTIPLE CHOICE

_____ 1. A promise made by the seller constitutes an express warranty provided:
   a. the buyer relied upon the promise.
   b. the promise constitutes a part of the basis of the bargain.
   c. either (a) or (b).
   d. both (a) and (b).

_____ 2. An express warranty generally can arise from all of the following EXCEPT:
   a. a model of the product shown to the buyer by the seller.
   b. a seller's promise as to the quality of the goods.
   c. an opinion as to the quality of the goods given by a non-expert seller.
   d. a seller's affirmation of fact as to specifications of the goods.

_____ 3. In order for the implied warranty of fitness for a particular purpose to apply:
   a. the seller must, at the time of contracting, have reason to know of the particular purpose.
   b. the buyer must actually rely on the seller's skill and judgment to furnish suitable goods.
   c. either (a) or (b).
   d. both (a) and (b).

_____ 4. Which of the following will NOT bar an injured buyer from recovering in an action against the seller for breach of warranty:
   a. The buyer's failure to notify the seller of any breach of warranty within a reasonable time after he discovered it or should have discovered it.
   b. The buyer's contributory negligence.
   c. The buyer's voluntary assumption of the known risk.
   d. None of the above.

_____ 5. The doctrine of strict liability in tort applies only if:
   a. the seller is engaged in the business of selling the product that caused the harm.
   b. the product was sold was in a defective condition unreasonably dangerous to the user or consumer.
   c. the product reaches the user or consumer without substantial change.
   d. all of the above.

_____ 6. A party injured by a defective product can establish that it was defective by showing that the product had any of the following:
   a. a manufacturing defect.
   b. a design defect.
   c. inadequate instructions enclosed.
   d. all of the above.

_____ 7. Strict liability in tort is applicable only if the product is:
   a. defective.
   b. somewhat dangerous to the user or consumer.
   c. either (a) or (b).
   d. both (a) and (b).

_____ 8. An injured party's recovery under the doctrine of strict liability in tort will be barred by:
   a. a valid disclaimer of liablity included in the contract of sale.
   b. the failure of the injured party to give notice to the seller within a reasonable time.
   c. subsequent alteration of the product.
   d. the lack of privity between the injured party and the seller.

_____ 9. A party injured by a product that is defective because of a defective component can bring an action under the doctrine of strict liability in tort against all of the following EXCEPT:
   a. the seller of the finished product.
   b. the assembler of the finished product.
   c. the manufacturer of a non-defective chassis to which the assembler attached the defective component.
   d. the manufacturer of the defective component used without essential change in the final product.

_____ 10. Which of the following, even if properly shown, is NOT a complete defense to a claim of strict liability in tort?
   a. Comparative negligence.
   b. Voluntary assumption of the risk.
   c. Product misuse.
   d. All of the above.

_____ 11. Mel Merchant sells lawnmowers at his retail store. Mel impliedly warrants:
   a. that the mowers are the best available.
   b. that the mowers are fit for lawnmowing and are of fair, average quality.
   c. that all possible safety devices have been incorporated into the design.
   d. that the mowers will last at least two years.

_____ 12. Which of the following need NOT be proved by the plaintiff in a strict liability case?
   a. That the product was defective.
   b. That the plaintiff suffered damages.
   c. How the product became defective.
   d. That the plaintiff was someone who could reasonably have been expected to have been in contact with the product in some manner.

_____ 13. Which of the following would constitute an express warranty?
   a. Sam Seller shows a sample to Bill Buyer and says the product in the box is just like it.
   b. Sam Seller says the VCR Bill Buyer wants to buy is "the best around."
   c. Sam Seller says the VCR Bill wants to buy will give him many hours of enjoyment.
   d. Sam Seller tells Bill Buyer that he rally likes the RCA VCR better than the Sharpe one.

_____ 14. Which of the following defenses can be used against the plaintiff in a strict liability case?
   a. Voluntary assumption of the risk.
   b. Misuse of the product.
   c. Subsequent alteration of the product.
   d. All of the above can be used.

_____ 15. Which of the following would be considered to be a defect in a product?
   a. A container for paint which has a leak.
   b. Paint which contains a chemical that burns skin when spilled or dripped.
   c. Placing the fuel tank of an automobile too close to the rear axle.
   d. All of the above are defects.

SHORT ESSAY

1. Under what circumstances does an opinion constitute an express warranty? Why? _____
   _____
   _____
   _____

2. Compare and contrast the implied warranties of merchantability and fitness for a particular purpose. Can either be disclaimed? How? _____
   _____
   _____
   _____

3. What must an injured party show to recover under a theory of strict liability in tort? What obstacles, if any, will bar his recovery and what traditional defenses will not? _____
   _____
   _____
   _____

4. List and discuss the kinds of defects which can give rise to a defective condition in a product. _____
   _____
   _____
   _____

CHAPTER 20

PERFORMANCE

PURPOSE

In a sales contract as in other contracts, the obligations of the parties are determined by their contractual agreement. The contract may expressly state whether the seller must deliver the goods prior to the buyer's payment of the price, or whether the seller must pay the price before the seller must deliver the goods. However, if there is no specific agreement of the parties on this or other such items, they will be supplied by the Code, common law, course of dealing, usage of trade, and course of performance.

Performance is the carrying out of contractual obligations according to the terms of the contract so that the obligations are discharged. The basic obligation of the seller is to transfer and deliver the goods. The basic obligation of the buyer is to accept and pay for the goods in accordance with the contract. Unless the parties have agreed otherwise, the Code is explicit in requiring performance or tender of performance by one party as a condition to performance by the other party. In this chapter, you study the Code provisions that apply to the performance by the buyer and by the seller in a sales contract. These provisions vary depending upon the shipment terms of the contract and whether there has been a breach by one of the parties. You also study the circumstances under which the buyer or the seller may be excused from contractual obligations.

CHAPTER CHECKPOINTS

After reading and studying the chapter, you should be able to:

1. Distinguish a shipment contract from a destination contract and discuss the Code provisions regarding tender in each type of contract.

2. Explain the perfect tender rule and the three limitations upon it.

3. Distinguish between rejection and revocation of acceptance by the buyer and discuss the circumstances under which the buyer may exercise each of these rights.

4. Identify and discuss the excuses for nonperformance.

5. Discuss how a breach by one of the parties affects the obligations of performance by the other in various fact situations.

CHAPTER OUTLINE

I. Performance by the Seller - Unless the parties have agreed otherwise, the Code requires performance or tender of performance by one party as a condition to performance by the other party. Tender of delivery requires that the seller put and hold goods that conform to the contract at the buyer's disposition and that he give the buyer reasonable notification to enable him to take delivery. Tender must be made at a reasonable time and kept open for a reasonable period of time.

A. Time and Manner of Delivery - If no definite time for delivery is fixed by the terms of the contract, the seller is allowed a reasonable time after the making of the contract within which to deliver the goods to the buyer. The buyer has a reasonable time within which to accept delivery. A contract is not performable piecemeal or in installments unless the parties to agree.

B. Place of Tender - If no place is specified in the contract, the place for delivery is the seller's place of business, or if he has none, his residence. If the contract is for the sale of identified goods that the parties know at the time of making the contract are located elsewhere than the seller's place of business or residence, the location of the goods is the place for delivery. Any agreements by the parties by use of delivery terms determines the place where the seller must tender delivery of the goods.
   1. Shipment Contracts - The delivery terms "F.O.B. place of shipment," "F.A.S. seller's port," C.I.F.," "C. & F.," and "C.O.D." are all shipment contracts. In these cases the seller's tender of performance occurs at the point of shipment, provided the seller meets certain specified conditions designed to protect the interests of the absent buyer. The seller is required to: (1) deliver the goods to a carrier; (2) make a contract for their transportation that is reasonable according to the nature of the goods and the other circumstances; (3) obtain and promptly deliver or tender to the buyer any documents necessary to enable the buyer to obtain possession of the goods from the carrier; and (4) promptly notify the buyer of the shipment.
   2. Destination Contracts - The terms "F.O.B. city of buyer," "ex-ship," and "no arrival, no sale" all indicate a destination contract. A destination contract requires the seller to tender delivery of conforming goods at a specified destination. The seller must place the goods at the buyer's disposition and give the buyer reasonable notice to enable him to take delivery. He must also tender any necessary documents of title.
   3. Goods Held by Bailee - The seller may either tender a document of title or obtain an acknowledgement by the bailee of the buyer's right to possess the goods.

C. Quality of Tender
   1. Perfect Tender Rule - Under this rule, the seller's tender of performance must conform exactly to the contract. If the goods or the tender fail in any respect to conform to the contract, the buyer may (1) reject the whole lot; (2) accept the whole lot; or (c) accept any commercial unit or units and reject the rest.
   2. Agreement by the Parties - The parties may limit the operation of the perfect tender rule.
   3. Cure by the Seller - When the time for performance under the contract has not expired or when the seller has shipped non-conforming goods in the belief that the non-conforming tender would be acceptable, the Code recognizes that a seller may cure or correct his non-conforming tender.
   4. Installment Contracts - Unless the parties have agreed otherwise, the buyer does not have to pay any part of the price of the goods until the entire quantity specified in the contract has been delivered or tendered to her. If the contract is silent as to payment, the seller may demand payment for each lot if the price can be apportioned. The buyer may reject a nonconforming installment if it substantially impairs the value of that installment and cannot be cured. When the nonconformity of default of one or more of the installments substantially impairs the value of the whole contract, the buyer can treat the breach as a breach of the whole contract.

II. Performance by the Buyer - A buyer is obligated to accept conforming goods and to pay for them according to the contract terms. Unless otherwise agreed, tender of payment by the buyer is a condition to the seller's duty to tender and to complete any delivery.

    A. Inspection - Unless otherwise agreed, the buyer has a right to inspect the goods before payment or acceptance. In a C.O.D. contract, payment must be made prior to inspection, but payment in such cases is not acceptance of the goods. The buyer is allowed a reasonable time to inspect the goods and may lose his right to reject them or to revoke his acceptance if he fails to inspect the goods within a reasonable time.

    B. Rejection - This is a manifestation by the buyer of his unwillingness to become the owner of the goods. It must be made within a reasonable time after the goods have been tendered or delivered. It is not effective unless the buyer seasonably notifies the seller. A merchant buyer who has rightfully rejected goods is obligated to follow reasonable instructions from the seller about disposing of the goods, when the seller has no agent at the place of rejection. If the rejected goods are perishable or threaten to decline in value speedily, the buyer is obligated to make reasonable efforts to sell them for the seller's account.

    C. Acceptance - This means the buyer is willing to become the owner of the goods tendered or delivered to him by the seller. Acceptance precludes any rejection of the goods accepted. Acceptance may be express orimplied. It occurs when (1) the buyer signifies to the seller that the goods conform to the contract; (2) the buyer signifies to the seller that he will take the goods in spite of their nonconformity; or (3) the buyer fails to make an effective rejection of the goods. Acceptance of any part of a commercial unit is acceptance of the entire unit.

    D. Revocation of Acceptance - The buyer may rescind his acceptance of the goods based upon their nonconformity if the nonconformity substantially impairs their value. Revocation is not effective until notice is given to the seller. Notice must be given within a reasonable time after the buyer discovers or should have discovered the grounds for revocation and before the goods have undergone any substantial change not caused by their own defects. If the buyer revokes acceptance, he is in the same position as if he had rejected them.

    E. Obligation of Payment - In the absence of an agreement, payment is due at the time and place where the buyer is to receive the goods even though the place of shipment is the place of delivery.

III. Excuses for Nonperformance

    A. Casualty to Identified Goods - If the contract is for goods that are identified when the contract was made, and those goods are totally lost or damaged without fault of either party and before the risk of loss has passed to the buyer, the contract is avoided. Each party is excused from his performance obligation under the contract. Where the goods are partially destroyed, the buyer has the option to avoid the contract or to accept the goods with due allowance for the deterioration or destruction.

    B. Non-Happening of Presupposed Condition - The seller is excused from her duty of performance on the nonoccurence of presupposed conditions that were a basic assumption of the contract, unless the seller has expressly assumed the risk. The Code excuses performance when performance may not be literally impossible, but where it is commercially impracticable. This requires more than mere hardship. The impractiability must be a result of an unforeseen supervening event not within the contemplation of the parties at the time of contracting.

C. Substituted Performance - Where neither party is at fault and the agreed manner of delivery of goods becomes commercially impracticable, a substituted manner of performance must be tendered and accepted. If the means or manner in which the buyer is to make payment becomes impossible, the seller may withhold or stop delivery unless the buyer provides payment that is commercially a substantial equivalent to that required by the contract.

DEFINITIONS

1. Perfect tender rule

2. Cure

3. Inspection

4. Rejection

5. Acceptance

6. Revocation of acceptance

7. Substituted performance

TRUE/FALSE

_____   1.   In order for either party to a contract to maintain an action against the other party for non-performance of his contractual obligations, he must first put the other party into default.

_____   2.   Tender of delivery requires that the seller delivers the goods to the buyer's place of business.

_____   3.   Under the Code, the seller must tender all of the goods purchased under the contract in a single delivery and payment by the buyer is due on such tender, unless the parties specify otherwise in the contract.

_____   4.   If a contract does not identify the place for delivery of the goods, the place of delivery is the buyer's place of business; or if he has none, then the buyer's residence.

_____   5.   Under a shipment contract, the seller need only deliver the goods to a carrier and make a reasonable contract for their shipment.

_____   6.   Under the Code, the operation of the Perfect Tender Rule may not be limited by agreement of the parties to the contract.

_____   7.   If a buyer refuses a tender of non-conforming goods without informing the seller of the nature of the defect, he cannot then assert that defect as a breach of contract by the seller if the defect was curable.

_____   8.   If a non-conforming installment of goods substantially impairs the value of the whole contract, then the buyer can treat the breach of the installment as a breach of the whole contract.

_____ 9. Acceptance of any part of a commercial unit of goods operates as an acceptance of the entire unit.

_____ 10. If goods that were identified when the contract was made are totally or partially lost or damaged without fault of either party and before risk of loss passes to the buyer, the contract is avoided.

_____ 11. A party is not excused from his duty of performance under a contract upon the non-occurrence of a presupposed condition unless that condition was a basic assumption unerlying the contract.

_____ 12. A buyer's basic obligation under a sales contract is to accept and pay for the goods.

_____ 13. Under a shipment contract, a seller is required to tender delivery of the goods to a carrier for delivery to the buyer.

_____ 14. The delivery terms "F.O.B. city of buyer," "ex-ship," and "no arrival, no sale" indicate that the contract is a shipment contract.

_____ 15. Tender can be at any hour of the day or night regardless of what is reasonable.

MULTIPLE CHOICE

_____ 1. A party may fulfill her contractual duty of performance and place the other party in default by all of the following except by:
   a. performing according to the contract.
   b. tendering her performance according to the contract.
   c. assuming that the other party will not perform according to the contract.
   d. being excused from tender of performance under the contract.

_____ 2. Tender of conforming goods by the seller entitles him to:
   a. acceptance of the goods by the buyer.
   b. payment of the contract price by the buyer.
   c. both acceptance of the goods and payment of the contract price by the buyer.
   d. neither acceptance of the goods nor payment of the contract price by the buyer.

_____ 3. Which of the following is not correct?
   a. The seller has a duty to keep goods tendered for a period reasonably necessary for the buyer to take possession of them.
   b. Unless otherwise agreed, the buyer must furnish facilities reasonably suited to the receipt of the goods.
   c. Unless otherwise agreed, a contract is performable in installments.
   d. None of the above is correct.

_____ 4. If the contract does not specify the place for delivery of the goods, the place for delivery is:
   a. the place of manufacture of the goods.
   b. the seller's place of business.
   c. the buyer's place of business.
   d. the carrier's place of business.

_____ 5. Under a destination contract, the seller must do all of the following except:
   a. place the goods at the buyer's disposition at the specified destination.
   b. give the buyer reasonable notice to enable him to take delivery.
   c. tender the necessary documents of title if such documents are involved in the transaction.
   d. inspect the goods upon arrival at the specified destination to ensure that they are conforming.

_____ 6. Under the Code, if the goods or the tender of delivery fail to conform to the contract in any respect, the buyer may do any of the following except:
   a. reject the whole shipment.
   b. accept the whole shipment.
   c. accept as many commercial units as desired and reject the rest.
   d. none of the above.

_____ 7. The buyer must reject non-conforming goods under the perfect tender rule except where:
   a. the parties agree to limit the buyer's right to reject non-conforming goods.
   b. the seller refuses to cure a non-conforming tender of delivery.
   c. the non-conformity of an installment does not substantially impair the value of the whole contract.
   d. all of the above.

_____ 8. Which of the following is an incorrect statement concerning a buyer's right to inspect goods upon delivery?
   a. Unless the parties agree otherwise, the buyer has the right to inspect the goods before payment or acceptance.
   b. If the contract requires payment for the goods before acceptance, payment is required before inspection and operates as an acceptance of the goods.
   c. The buyer may lose his right to reject or revoke acceptance of non-conforming goods if he fails to inspect them within a reasonable time.
   d. The buyer must bear the expenses of inspection, but he may recover those costs from the seller if the goods prove to be non-conforming and are rejected.

_____ 9. After rejection of non-perishable goods, a merchant buyer who has received no instructions from the seller within a reasonable time after notice of rejection may:
   a. store the goods for the seller's account.
   b. reship the goods to the seller.
   c. resell the goods for the seller's account.
   d. all of the above.

_____ 10. An effective acceptance occurs when the buyer:
   a. signifies to the seller that the goods conform to the contract.
   b. signifies to the seller that he will keep the goods.
   c. fails to make an effective rejection of the goods.
   d. all of the above.

_____ 11. Acceptance of the goods precludes a buyer from:
   a. rejecting the goods.
   b. revoking his acceptance.
   c. suing the seller for breach for any non-conformity that could not be reasonably discovered by inspection.
   d. all of the above.

_____ 12. If the goods contracted for are partially destroyed after risk of loss has passed to the buyer:
   a.   the contract is avoided.
   b.   the contract is voidable at the buyer's option.
   c.   the contract is voidable at the seller's option.
   d.   the contract is neither void nor voidable at either party's election.

_____ 13. If no place for delivery is stated in the contract, then the place for delivery is:
   a.   the buyer's place of business.
   b.   the seller's place of business.
   c.   to be negotiated at a later date.
   d.   the buyer's home.

_____ 14. The seller's right to repair, adjust, or replace defective or nonconforming goods is known as:
   a.   perfect tender.
   b.   rejection.
   c.   cure.
   d.   revoation of acceptance.

_____ 15. Which of the following is a reason why the shipping terms in a contract for the sale of goods are important?
   a.   They determine who must bear the risk of loss.
   b.   They determine who must pay the shipping costs.
   c.   They determine whether the buyer may inspect before payment.
   d.   All of the above are affected by the shipping terms of a contract.

SHORT ESSAY

1. What are the basic performance obligations of the seller and buyer? _____
   _____
   _____
   _____

2. What must a seller do to discharge her obligation to tender delivery of the goods under a shipment contract?
   _____
   _____
   _____
   _____

3. What is meant by the doctrine of "cure?" When may a seller "cure" his defective tender or performance? Must the buyer accept the seller's cure? _____
   _____
   _____
   _____

4. What is the difference between a rejection and a revocation of acceptance? What are the buyer's rights under each? _____

_____

_____

_____

5. Under what conditions can the parties to a contract be relieved of their obligations of full performance?

_____

_____

_____

_____

CHAPTER 21

REMEDIES

PURPOSE

Breach is the failure of a party to perform his obligations under the contract. In a sales contract, breach may consist of the seller's delivery of defective goods, too few goods, the wrong goods, or of the seller's failure to deliver any goods. The buyer may breach by failing to accept conforming goods or by failing to pay for conforming goods which he has accepted.

In this chapter, you study the remedies that are available to the buyer and the seller in the case of a breach by the other party. The Code provides separate and distinct remedies for the seller and for the buyer. Each of the remedies available is specifically keyed to the factual situation. The intent of the Code drafters in providing the remedies which they did was to put the aggrieved party in as good a position as if the other party had fully performed. The Code provides that its remedies should be liberally administered to accomplish this purpose. In providing its various remedies, the Code has rejected the doctrine of election of remedies by providing that the remedies for breach are cumulative. Whether one remedy bars another depends entirely on the facts of the individual case.

CHAPTER CHECKPOINTS

After reading and studying this chapter, you should be able to:

1. List and describe the remedies available to the seller under the Code.

2. List and describe the remedies available to the buyer under the Code.

3. Identify and discuss the various kinds of money damages available to the seller and the buyer.

4. Distinguish between specific performance and replevin and discuss under what circumstances each is available.

5. Identify and describe the basic types of contractual provisions that affect the remedies available in the event of a breach and the limitations that the Code imposes upon these provisions.

CHAPTER OUTLINE

A. Remedies of the Seller - When the buyer defaults, the seller has been deprived of the rights for which he bargained. The buyer's default may consist of (1) wrongfully rejecting the goods; (2) wrongfully revoking acceptance; (3) failing to make a payment due on or before delivery; or (4) repudiating the contract in whole or in part. Withholding delivery of the goods; stopping delivery of the goods by a carrier; identifying conforming goods to the contract not already identified; and reclaiming the goods on the buyer's insolvency are all goods oriented remedies. Reselling the goods and recovering damages; recovering damages for non-acceptance of the goods or repudiation of the contract; and recovering the price are all money oriented. Reclaiming the goods on the buyer's insolvency is obligation oriented. The Code's remedies are cumulative; more than one may be used by an aggrieved seller.

1. To Withhold Delivery of the Goods - A seller may withhold delivery of the goods to a buyer who has wrongfully rejected or revoked acceptance of the goods; who has failed to make a payment due on or before delivery; or who has repudiated the contract. Where the contract calls for installments, any breach of an installment that impairs the value of the whole contract will permit the seller to withhold the entire undelivered balance of the goods.

2. To Stop Delivery of the Goods - This remedy is an extension of the right to withhold delivery of the goods. The seller must timely notify the carrier or other baliee to stop delivery of the goods. After this notification, the carrier or bailee who holds the goods must deliver them in accordance with the directions of the seller. The seller must pay any charges or damages incurred by the carrier or bailee. If the buyer is insolvent, the seller may stop any delivery; if the buyer repudiates or otherwise breaches, the seller may stop carload, truckload, planeload or larger shipments. The right of the seller to stop delivery ceases when (1) the buyer receives the goods; (2) the bailee acknowledges that he holds them for the buyer; (3) or the carrier acknowledges to the buyer that he holds them for the buyer by reshipment or as a warehouser; or (4) a negotiable document of title covering the goods is negotiated to the buyer.

3. To Identify Goods to the Contract - On breach by the buyer, the seller may identify to the contract conforming goods in her possession or control that were not so identified at the time she learned of the breach. The seller may either complete the manufacture and resell the unfinished goods for scrap or salvage value. The seller must exercise reasonable judgment to minimize her loss.

4. To Resell the Goods and Recover Damages - In the case of wrongful rejection or revocation, repudiation, or failure to make timely payment, the seller may resell the goods concerned or the undelivered balance of the goods. If the resale is made in good faith and in a commercially reasonable manner, the seller may recover the difference between the resale price and the contract price, together with any incidental damages. The seller is not accountable to the buyer for any profit made on any resale of the goods. A bona fide purchaser at a resale takes the goods free of any rights of the original buyer.

5. To Recover Damages for Nonacceptance or Repudiation - In the event of the buyer's wrongful rejection or revocation, repudiation, or failure to make timely payment, the seller may recover damages from the buyer measured by the difference between the market price at the time and place of tender of the goods and the unpaid contract price, plus incidental damages, less expenses saved in consequence of the buyer's breach. This is an alternative to the remedy of reselling the goods.

6. To Recover the Price - The Code permits the seller to recover the price in three situations: (1) where the goods have been lost or damaged after the risk of loss has passed to the buyer; and (2) where the goods have been identified to the contract and there is no ready market available for their resale at a reasonable price.

7. To Recover Incidental Damages - In the same action in which the seller seeks damages for the difference between the resale price and the contract price or in cases to recover the price, the seller may recover incidental damages. Incidental damages include any commercially reasonable charges, expenses, or commissions resulting from the breach.

8. **To Cancel the Contract** - Where the buyer wrongfully rejects or revokes acceptance of the goods, or fails to make a payment due on or before delivery, or repudiates the contract in whole or in part, the seller may cancel the part of the contract that concerns the goods directly affected. If the breach is of an installment contract and it substantially impairs the whole contract, the seller may cancel the entire contract. The Code defines cancellation as putting an end to the contract by one party by reason of a breach by the other.

9. **To Reclaim the Goods upon the Buyer's Insolvency** - The unpaid seller may reclaim goods from an insolvent buyer by demand made to the buyer within ten days after the buyer has received the goods. If the buyer has committed fraud by a misrepresentation of her solvency made to the seller in writing within three months prior to delivery of the goods, the ten-day limitation does not apply. This right is subject to the rights of a purchaser of the goods from the buyer in the ordinary course of business or other good faith purchaser. Use of this remedy precludes the use of all other remedies.

B. **Remedies of the Buyer** - The remedy of cancellation of the contract is obligation oriented. The remedies of recovery of payments made; recovery of damages for breach of warranty; incidental damages; and consequential damages are all money oriented. Recovery of identified goods if the seller is insolvent; replevy of the goods; and specific performance are all goods oriented.

1. **To Cancel the Contract** - Where the seller fails to make delivery or repudiates the contract, or where the buyer rightfully rejects or justifiably revokes acceptance of goods tendered or delivered, the buyer may cancel the contract with respect to any goods involved. If the breach concerns the whole contract, the buyer may cancel the entire contract. The buyer must give notice of cancellation, but he is excused from further performance and may "cover" and have damages for nondelivery of the goods.

2. **To Recover Payments Made** - On the seller's breach, the buyer may recover as much of the price as he has paid.

3. **To Cover** - On the seller's breach, the buyer may obtain "cover." This means that the buyer may in good faith and without unreasonable delay proceed to purchase goods or make a contract to purchase goods in substitution for those due under the contract of the seller. The buyer may also recover the difference between the cost of cover and the contract price plus any incidental and consequential damages less expenses saved in consequence of the seller's breach. The buyer is not required to obtain cover, and his failure to do so does not bar him from any other remedy provided in the Code. However, the buyer may not recover consequential damages that could have been prevented by cover.

4. **To Recover Damages for Nondelivery or Repudiation** - If the seller repudiates the contract or fails to deliver the goods, or if the buyer rightfully rejects or justiafiably revokes acceptance, the buyer is entitled to recover damages measured by the difference between the market price at the time when the buyer learned of the breach and the contract price, together with any incidental and consequential damages, less expenses saved in consequences of the seller's breach. This remedy is an alternative to cover and is available only to the extent the buyer has not covered. The buyer who elects this remedy may not recover those consequential damages that could have been avoided by cover.

5. **To Recover Identified Goods on the Seller's Insolvency** - Where existing goods are identified to the contract of sale, the buyer acquires a special property in the goods. This interest exists even though the goods are nonconforming, and the buyer has the right to return or reject them. Identification may be made by either the buyer or the seller. Under the Code the buyer has the right to recover from an insolvent buyer goods in which he has a special property interest. This right did not exist at common law; it applies where the seller, who is in possession or control of the goods, becomes insolvent within ten days after receipt of the first installment of the price. To exercise the right, the buyer must tender to the seller any unpaid portion of the price. If the buyer has identified the goods, he may recover the goods only if they conform to the contract.

6. **To Sue for Replevin** - Replevin is an action at law to recover specific goods in the possession of a defendant that are being unlawfully withheld from the plaintiff. The buyer may replevy goods where the seller has repudiated or breached the contract if (1) the buyer is unable to obtain cover; or (2) the

goods have been shipped under reservation of a security interest in the seller and satisfaction of this security interest has been made or tendered.

7. To Enforce a Security Interest in the Goods - A buyer who has rightfully rejected or justifiably revoked acceptance of goods that remain in her possession or control has a security interest in these goods to the extent of any payment of the price that she has made and for any expenses reasonably incurred in their inspection, receipt, transportation, care and custody. The buyer may hold such goods and resell them in the same manner as an aggrieved seller may resell the goods. The buyer must account to the seller for any excess of net proceeds of the resale over the amount of the security interest.

8. To Sue for Specific Performance - This is an equitable remedy compelling the party in breach to perform the contract according to its terms. At common law specific performance is available only if the legal remedies are inadequate. The Code continues the availability of specific performance and has sought to further a more liberal attitude towards its use. The Code says that "specific performance may be had where the goods are unique or in other proper circumstances."

9. To Recover Damages for Breach in Regard to Accepted Goods - Where the buyer has accepted nonconforming goods and has given timely notification to the seller of the breach of contract, the buyer is entitled to maintain an action at law to recover from the seller the damages resulting in the ordinary course of events from the seller's breach. Incidental and consequential damages may also be recovered. The contract price does not figure in this computation, because the buyer is entitled to the benefit of the bargain, which is to receive goods that are as warranted.

10. To Recover Incidental Damages - The buyer may recover incidental damages in addition to damages for non-delivery or repudiation, and breach of warranty. Incidental damages include expenses reasonably incurred in inspection, receipt, transportation, care and custody of goods rightfully rejected; any commercially reasonable expense connected to the delay or other breach.

11. To Recover Consequential Damages - In many cases the above remedies will not fully compensate the aggrieved buyer for her losses. Under the Code, the buyer has the opportunity to recover consequential damages resulting from the seller's breach, including (1) any loss resulting from the buyer's requirements and needs of which the seller at the time of contracting had reason to know and which could not reasonably be prevented by cover or otherwise; and (2) injury to person or property proximately resulting from any breach of warranty.

C. Contractual Provisions Affecting Remedies - The parties may modify, exclude, or limit by agreement the remedies or damages available for breach of that contract.

1. Liquidation or Limitation of Damages - The parties may specify the amount or measure of damages that either party may recover in the event of a breach by the other party. The amount of such damages must be reasonable and commensurate with the anticipated or actual loss resulting from a breach. A provision fixing unreasonably large liquidated damages is void as a penalty.

2. Modification or Limitation of Remedy by Agreement - The contract between the parties may expressly provide for remedies in addition to those in the Code. It may also limit or change the measure of damages recoverable for breach. A remedy in a contract is optional unless it is expressly agreed to be exclusive of other remedies. Where an exclusive remedy fails in its essential purpose, resort may be had to the remedies provided by the Code. The contract may limit or exclude consequential damages unless such limitation or exclusion would be unconscionable. Limitation of consequential damages for personal injury from breach of warranty in the sale of consumer goods is always unconscionable. This is not so where the loss is commercial.

DEFINITIONS

1. Insolvency

2. Incidental damages

3. Cancellation

4. Cover

5. Consequential damages

6. Specific performance

7. Replevin

8. Liquidated damages

TRUE/FALSE

_____ 1. The purpose of the Code's remedial provisions is to place the aggrieved party in as good a position as if the other party had fully performed.

_____ 2. An "obligation oriented" remedy is one that provides the aggrieved party with the opportunity to recover monetary damages.

_____ 3. The Code has adopted the common law principle of election of remedies.

_____ 4. The aggrieved seller's right to stop delivery of goods by a carrier or other bailee upon learning of the buyer's insolvency ceases when a negotiable document of title covering the goods is negotiated to the buyer.

_____ 5. If a seller in good faith and in a commercially reasonable manner resells goods which were wrongfully rejected by the buyer, the seller may recover from the buyer the difference between the resale price and the contract price, plus any incidental damages incurred.

_____ 6. Goods resold by an aggrieved seller must be sold at a public sale.

_____ 7. The Code permits an aggrieved seller to bring an action to recover the price where the goods have been identified to the contract and there is no ready market available for their resale.

_____ 8. If a buyer breaches an installment contract in a manner that substantially impairs the whole contract, the seller may cancel the entire contract.

_____ 9. An aggrieved buyer may make a reasonable contract of cover and then seek to recover from the seller the difference between the cost of cover and the market price, plus any incidental and consequential damages.

_____ 10. In the event of a breach of warranty, the measure of damages is the difference, at the time and place of the acceptance of the nonconforming goods, between the value of the accepted goods and the value of the goods as warranted.

_____ 11. A contract provision limiting consequential damages for commercial losses resulting from a breach of warranty in the sale of goods is on its face unconscionable.

_____ 12. An aggrieved seller may both identify the goods to the contract and withhold delivery.

_____ 13. The Code does away with the common law remedy of replevin.

_____ 14. The UCC gives the buyer the right to demand perfect tender of performance.

_____ 15. When a buyer covers, she may recover the difference between the cost of cover and the contract price plus any incidental and consequential damages less expenses saved in consequence of the seller's breach.

MULTIPLE CHOICE

_____ 1. Which of the following is not a money-oriented remedy?
   a. Cover or resale and recovery of damages.
   b. An action to recover market price damages.
   c. Cancellation.
   d. An action to recover damages for non-conformity.

_____ 2. Under the Code, the equity meaning of insolvency is:
   a. that a person has no assets.
   b. that a person is unable to pay her debts as they become due.
   c. that a person's total liabilities exceed the value of all her assets.
   d. none of the above.

_____ 3. A seller may withhold delivery of goods to a buyer who has breached their contract by:
   a. wrongfully rejecting the goods.
   b. failing to make a payment due on or before delivery.
   c. repudiating the contract.
   d. all of the above.

_____ 4. A seller may not recover market price damages if the buyer:
   a. wrongfully rejects the goods.
   b. wrongfully revokes his acceptance of the goods.
   c. fails to make a payment when due.
   d. none of the above.

_____ 5. In the event of the buyer's wrongful repudiation of the contract, the seller may recover damages measured by the difference between the unpaid contract price and the market price at the time and place:
   a. that the goods were tendered by the seller.
   b. that the buyer repudiated the contract.
   c. that the contract was entered into.
   d. none of the above.

_____ 6. The Code permits the seller to bring an action to recover the price in all of the following cases except:
   a.   where the buyer has accepted the goods but has failed to make a payment.
   b.   where the goods have been identified to the contract and a ready market is available for their resale at a reasonable price.
   c.   where conforming goods have been lost or damaged after risk of loss has passed to the buyer.
   d.   all of the above.

_____ 7. If an aggrieved party rightfully cancels a contract:
   a.   he discharges any obligation of future performance that he might have under the contract.
   b.   he retains any remedy for breach of the whole contract or of any unperformed balance.
   c.   neither (a) nor (b).
   d.   both (a) and (b).

_____ 8. Which of the following is not a correct statement concerning an unpaid seller's attempt to reclaim goods from an insolvent buyer?
   a.   The seller must demand that the goods be returned within twenty days after the buyer has received them unless the buyer has fraudulently misrepresented his solvency to the seller.
   b.   The seller, if successful in reclaiming the goods from an insolvent buyer, may not seek other remedies with respect to the goods.
   c.   The seller's right to reclaim the goods is subject to the rights of a buyer in the ordinary course of business or other good faith purchase.
   d.   All of the above.

_____ 9. If a seller tenders non-conforming goods and the buyer accepts them and then cannot justifiably revoke his acceptance, the buyer can still:
   a.   recover damages for non-conformity.
   b.   recover market price for damages.
   c.   neither (a) nor (b).
   d.   both (a) and (b).

_____ 10. If the buyer rightfully rejects the seller's tender of non-conforming goods, he may:
   a.   cover and recover damages.
   b.   recover payments made.
   c.   recover market price damages.
   d.   all of the above.

_____ 11. If the seller repudiates the contract, the buyer is entitled to recover damages from the seller in an amount equal to the difference between the contract price and the market price of goods when:
   a.   the parties entered into the contract.
   b.   the breach occured.
   c.   the buyer learned of the breach.
   d.   none of the above.

_____ 12. Bill Buyer contracted by buy 1000 widgets from Sam Seller for $5,000. Sam shipped defective widgets, but Bill accepted them and properly notified Sam of the breach. As warranted, the widgets were valued at $7,000, but as received they were worth $4,000. If Bill is successful in his suit for breach of warranty against Sam, he will be allowed to recover:
   a. $1,000.
   b. $2,000.
   c. $3,000.
   d. $7,000.

_____ 13. Sam Seller has shipped 100 widgets to Bill Buyer pursuant to a contract. The next day Sam discovers that Bill is insolvent. On learning this:
   a. Sam may stop delivery.
   b. Sam must cancel the contract.
   c. Sam has no recourse available under the Code.
   d. Sam may cover and sue for damages.

_____ 14. Which of the following would be recoverable as consequential damages?
   a. Expenses reasonably incurred in inspection, receipt, transportation, and care and custody of goods rightfully rejected.
   b. Expenses for injury or property proximately resulting from breach of warranty.
   c. Damages of $100 per day in accordance with a negotiated contractual provision.
   d. All of the above are recoverable as consequential damages.

_____ 15. Bill Businessman ordered 10 office chairs for his office. Two of the chairs delivered were defective.
   a. Bill must either send all of the chairs back or pay for all of them.
   b. Bill is entitled to ten new chairs.
   c. Bill can reject the two defective chairs and accept the others.
   d. Since Bill has already received the chairs, his only remedy is revocation of acceptance.

SHORT ESSAY

1. What remedies are available to a buyer who rightfully rejects a seller's tender of non-conforming goods?

   _____
   _____
   _____

2. What remedies are available to a buyer after the seller repudiates their contract? _____

   _____
   _____
   _____

3. What remedies are available to the seller after the buyer has wrongfully rejected a conforming tender of goods? _____

   _____
   _____
   _____

4. When is specific performance available under the Code? _____

_____

_____

_____

5. Under what conditions may the parties to a contract limit or modify remedies available for its breach?

_____

_____

_____

PART III

SAMPLE EXAMINATION

_____ 1. The UCC "battle of the forms" section is found in:
   a.   2-201.
   b.   2-205.
   c.   2-207.
   d.   2-314.

_____ 2. Mike Mechanic has a used car that he would like to sell. He puts an ad in the local newspaper. Bill Buyer comes to his house to look at the car and asks what kind of condition it is in. Mike says, "As a mechanic, I think the car is in good running order and should give you no problems for at least 60 days." Based on that statement, Bill purchases the car.
   a.   Mike's statement is an express warranty.
   b.   The sale by Mike gives rise to a warranty of merchantability.
   c.   Mike's statement gives rise to a warranty of fitness for a particular purpose.
   d.   Two of the above, (a) and (b).

_____ 3. Sam Seller agrees to sell 100 widgets to Bill Buyer at a price of $600. No mention is made of the time for delivery.
   a.   The goods must be delivered within two weeks.
   b.   The goods must be delivered within a reasonable time.
   c.   The goods must be delivered within thirty days.
   d.   There is no contract, because an essential term has been omitted.

_____ 4. Section(s) _____ impose(s) liability on sellers of defective products.
   a.   2-314 of the UCC
   b.   402A of the Restatement Second of Torts
   c.   2-201 of the UCC
   d.   2-314 of the UCC and 402A of the Restatement Second of Torts

_____ 5. Which of the following terms would indicate a destination contract?
   a.   C.I.F.
   b.   F.A.S. seller's port
   c.   F.O.B. city of buyer
   d.   F.O.B. city of seller

_____ 6. Sam Seller learns of Bill Buyer's insolvency while the goods are in transit.
   a.   Sam is out of luck and can't do much.
   b.   Sam can stop delivery.
   c.   If Sam stops delivery, he will be in breach of contract.
   d.   Sam will have to deliver the goods and then file a claim with the bankruptcy court.

_____ 7. A form of action at law that a party may use to recover specific goods that are in possession of the defendant is known as:
   a.   specific performance.
   b.   replevin.
   c.   stopping goods in transit.
   d.   reclaiming of the goods.

_____ 8. Happy Homemaker brings her VCR to Al's Quick Fix Repair Shop to have the head cleaned. While the VCR is in the shop, Carol Customer comes to the store and asks Al its price. Al says $50, so Carol pays him $50 cash and takes the VCR home. When Happy comes to the shop to pick up her VCR, it isn't there.
   a. Happy has entrusted the VCR to Al's Repair Shop.
   b. Al can transfer good title to the VCR to Carol.
   c. If Happy brings a replevin action against Carol, she will recover the goods.
   d. Two of the above, (a) and (b).

_____ 9. The buyer's remedy which allows him to in good faith and without unreasonable delay purchase goods in substitution of those due under the contract with the seller is known as:
   a. specific performance.
   b. replevin.
   c. cover.
   d. reclaiming the goods.

_____ 10. To protect purchasers of consumer goods, Congress enacted the:
   a. Statute of Frauds.
   b. Magnuson-Moss Warranty Act.
   c. UCC.
   d. Statute of Frauds, Magnuson-Moss Warranty Act, and the UCC.

_____ 11. In an action based upon 402A of the Restatement, the defendant manufacturer can raise the defense(s) of:
   a. misuse or abuse of the product.
   b. voluntary assumption of the risk.
   c. contributory negligence.
   d. misuse or abuse of the product, voluntary assumption of the risk, and contributory negligence.

_____ 12. Bill Buyer accepts 1,000 widgets from Sam Seller, and then discovers a latent defect in them that could not have been found earlier by a reasonable inspection.
   a. Bill must keep the goods, because he has already accepted them.
   b. Bill may revoke his acceptance.
   c. Bill is entitled to the difference between the value of the goods which have been accepted and the value that the goods would have had if they had been as warranted.
   d. Two of the above, (b) and (c).

_____ 13. Harold Homeowner used his lawnmower to trim his hedges. In the process he severely injured his hand. In a lawsuit against the manufacturer, the manufacturer is likely to raise the defense of:
   a. comparative negligence.
   b. assumption of the risk.
   c. misuse of the product.
   d. subsequent alteration.

_____ 14. Unless otherwise agreed by the parties, transfer of title in a shipment contract occurs when:
   a. the documents of title are delivered.
   b. payment is received.
   c. the seller delivers the goods to the carrier for shipment to the buyer.
   d. the goods are delivered to the buyer.

_____ 15. Sam Seller, who is located in New York, has a contract to sell 1,000 widgets to Bill Buyer, who is located in San Francisco. The contract is a shipment contract. Sam delivers the goods to Downs Transport for delivery. En route to San Francisco, the goods are destroyed.
   a. Bill bears the risk of loss.
   b. Sam bears the risk of loss.
   c. Bill and Sam will each share half of the loss.
   d. Bill has no interest in the goods, because he has not yet accepted them.

_____ 16. Sam Seller ships non-conforming goods to Bill Buyer. The risk of loss remains on Sam until:
   a. the goods are delivered to the carrier.
   b. Bill has had an opportunity to inspect the goods.
   c. Sam corrects the defect in the goods.
   d. Bill pays for the goods.

_____ 17. Bulk transfers that are exempted from Article 6 of the UCC include:
   a. transfers by way of security.
   b. sales by executors, administrators or receivers.
   c. sales by a trustee in bankruptcy.
   d. all of the above are exempt from Article 6.

_____ 18. Under a sale on approval, if the buyer fails to reasonably notify the seller of an election to return the goods, there is a/an:
   a. ratification.
   b. identification.
   c. acceptance.
   d. breach.

_____ 19. Under a _____ contract, the buyer must pay for the goods before he can exercise his right to inspect.
   a. C.I.F.
   b. C.O.D.
   c. F.O.B.
   d. F.O.S.

_____ 20. Mel Merchant sells all of his inventory at an auction. This is a/an:
   a. bulk transfer.
   b. sale on approval.
   c. exempt transfer.
   d. sale or return.

CHAPTER 22

FORM AND CONTENT

PURPOSE

Modern business could not be conducted without the use of checks, drafts, promissory notes, and certificates of deposit, all of which are commercial paper. Checks are a specialized form of draft, which provide an important monetary and credit function in the business world. Promissory notes serve consumers and small businesspeople as well as large corporations. In recent years, individuals have increasingly relied upon certificates of deposit instead of savings accounts. All of these forms of commercial paper are negotiable instruments. In this chapter, you study the concept of negotiability and the form necessary for an instrument to qualify as a "negotiable instrument." Negotiability invests commercial paper with a high degree of marketability and commercial utility. It allows commercial paper to be freely transferable and enforceable by a person with the rights of a holder in due course against any person obligated on the paper, subject only to a limited number of defenses.

CHAPTER CHECKPOINTS

After reading and studying this chapter, you should be able to:

1. Discuss the concept and importance of negotiability.

2. Identify the payee, drawee, maker, drawer and holder of a check, draft, note and certificate of deposit.

3. Identify and discuss the types of commercial paper that are promises to pay and those that are orders to pay.

4. List and discuss the formal requirements that an instrument must meet in order to qualify as a negotiable instrument.

5. Discuss the effect of the following on negotiability: (1) the absence of a statement of consideration; (2) the absence of a statement of where the instrument is drawn or payable; (3) the presence or absence of a seal; (4) postdating, antedating or not dating an instrument; (5) an incomplete instrument; and (6) an ambiguity within an instrument.

CHAPTER OUTLINE

A. Negotiability - This is a legal concept that makes written instruments a readily accepted form of payment in substitution for money. The concept of negotiability was devised to meet the needs of traders, merchants, and businesspeople who wanted promises and orders to pay money to circulate freely in the marketplace as a substitute for money. The concept of negotiability applies to commercial paper, which is governed by Article 3 of the Code, to documents of title, which are governed by Article 7, and to investment securities, which are governed by Article 8. Negotiability invests commercial paper with a high degree of marketability and commercial utility. It allows commercial paper to be freely transferable and enforceable by a person with the rights of a holder in due course against any person obligated on the paper, subject only to a limited number of defenses. To have the full benefits of negotiability, commercial paper must not only meet the requirements of negotiability, but it must also be acquired by a "holder in due course."

B. Types of Commercial Paper - There are four types of commercial paper. Drafts and checks are orders or directions to pay money. Notes and certificates of deposit are promises to pay.
   1. Drafts - A draft involves three parties. The drawer orders the drawee to pay a sum certain in money to the payee. The same party may appear in more than one capacity; for instance, the drawer may also be the payee. A time draft is one payable at a specified future date. A sight draft is payable immediately upon presentation to the drawee.
   2. Checks - A check is a specialized form of draft, namely an order to pay money drawn on a bank and payable on demand. There are three parties involved who are also known as the drawer, the drawee and the payee. The drawer is the holder of the account; the drawee is the bank on which the check is drawn; the payee is the person to whom payment is supposed to be made. A cashier's check is a check drawn by a bank on itself to the order of a named payee.
   3. Notes - A promissory note involves two parties. One party, the maker, promises to pay to the order of a second party, the payee, a stated sum of money, either on demand or at a stated future date.
   4. Certificates of Deposit - A certificate of deposit is a specialized form of promise to pay money that is given by a bank. The bank is the maker and promises to pay the payee, who is named in the C.D.

C. Form of Commercial Paper - Negotiability is wholly a matter of form. All of the information required to determine whether an instrument is negotiable must be found within the four corners of the instrument. No reference to any other source is required or permitted. That is why a negotiable instrument is sometimes called a "courier without luggage." To be negotiable an instrument must be (1) in writing; (2) signed; (3) must contain a promise or order to pay; (4) must be unconditional; (5) for a sum certain in money; (6) must contain no other promise or order; (7) it must be payable on demand or at a definite time; and (8) must be payable to order or to bearer.
   1. Writing - The writing requirement is broadly construed. Any tangible expression is sufficient to satisfy the requirement. Most negotiable instruments are written on paper, but this is not required.
   2. Signed - A note or certificate of deposit must be signed by the maker; a draft or check must be signed by the drawer. A signature is any symbol executed or adopted by a party with the intention to validate a writing. An X, a thumb print, initials, or a pre-printed trade name will suffice. Normally, a maker or drawer signs in the lower right-hand corner of the instrument, but this is not required.
   3. Promise or Order to Pay - A negotiable instrument must contain a promise or order to pay money in the case of a note or certificate of deposit, or an order to pay in the case of a draft or check. A promise must be more than a mere acknowledgement of indebtedness. An "I.O.U." is not a promise to pay. An order is a direction or command to pay. It must be more than an authorization or request. The usual way to express an order is by the use of the word "pay" or the phrases "Pay to the order of," or "Pay bearer."
   4. Unconditional - This requirement is to prevent the inclusion of any term that could reduce the promised obligation. The issue is whether there is an absolute promise to pay, that is, one which is not

subject to any contingencies or qualification. An instrument that states that "ABC Corp. promises to pay $100,000 to the order of Johnson provided the helicopter meets all contractual specifications" would not be negotiable. A promise or order is conditional if (a) the instrument states that it is subject to or governed by any other agreement, or (b) the instrument states that it is to be paid only out of a particular fund or source.

    a.   **Reference to Other Agreements** - The restriction against reference to another agreement is to enable any person to determine the right to payment provided by the instrument without having to look beyond its four corners. If such right is made subject to the terms of another agreement, the instrument is non-negotiable. A distinction is made between a mere recital that makes the instrument subject to the terms of another agreement, because such a recital does not destroy negotiability. The following statement is permissible: "This note is given in partial payment for a color TV set to be delivered in two weeks from date in accordance with a contract of this date between the payee and the maker." However, the addition of the following words would destroy negotiability: "and the seller is subject to all of the terms of said agreement."

    b.   **The Particular Fund Doctrine** - An order or promise to pay only out of a particular fund is conditional and destroys negotiability, because payment depends on the existence and sufficiency of the particular fund. However, a promise or order to pay, coupled with a mere indication of a particular fund out of which reimbursement is to be made or a particular account to be debited with the amount, does not impair negotiability, because the drawer's or the maker's general credit is relied on and charging a particular account is merely a bookkeeping entry to be followed after payment. There is a difference between "Sixty days after date pay to the order of John Jones $500 out of the proceeds of the sale of the contents of freight car No. 1234" and "Sixty days after date pay to the order of John Jones $500 and charge the proceeds of sale of contents of freight car No. 1234." The first is non-negotiable; the second is negotiable.

5.   **Sum Certain in Money**

    a.   **Money** - This term means a legal tender authorized or adopted by a sovereign government as part of its currency. It must have government sanction. A sum certain in French francs, German marks, Italian lira, Japanese yen, or other foreign currency is negotiable.

    b.   **Sum Certain** - This requirement must be considered from the point of view of the holder, not the maker or drawer. The holder must be assured of a determinable minimum payment. A frequent provision that is permissible is a provision in a note that the maker will pay, in addition to the face amount and specified interest, costs of collection and attorney's fees on default in payment. Such a provision is intended to make the paper more attractive without lessening the certainty of the amount due. An instrument payable with a stated rate of interest is an obligation for a sum certain. Rates may be different before and after default, or before and after a specified date. A sum payable is a sum certain even though it is payable in installments, or with a fixed discount if paid before maturity, or a fixed addition if paid after maturity. This is so, because it is always possible to make the necessary computations from the face of the instrument to determine the amount due at any given time.

6.   **No Other Promise or Order** - An instrument that contains a promise or order to do an act in addition to the payment of money, is not negotiable. For example, a promise to pay $100 "and a ton of coal" is non-negotiable.

7.   **Payable on Demand or at a Definite Time** - This requirement is intended to promote certainty in determining the present value of a negotiable instrument. Demand paper has always been considered sufficiently certain as to time of payment, because it is the holder who makes the demand and thus sets the time for payment. An instrument payable upon demand means that the money owed under the instrument must be paid upon the holder's request. An instrument qualifies as being payable on demand if it is payable "at sight" or "on presentation." Instruments payable at a definite time are called time paper. An instrument that by its terms is payable only on an act or event whose time of occurrence is uncertain is not payable at a definite time, even though the act or event has occurred.

Examples include instruments providing for payment to the payee or order "thirty days after my marriage" or "when the payee is twenty-one years old." Such promises destroy negotiability. Negotiability is determined from the face of the instrument.

    a. "On or Before" Clauses - An instrument is payable at a definite time if it is payable "on or before a stated date." The holder is thus assured that she will have her money by the maturity date, although she may receive it sooner. Even though the obligor may pay before the stated maturity date at his option, there is sufficient certainty so as not to impair negotiability.

    b. At a Fixed Period after a Stated Date - An instrument may be made payable "thirty days after a stated date." This means it is payable thirty days after the date of issuance given on the instrument. Such an instrument is payable at a definite time, because its exact maturity date can be determined by simple arithmetic. An undated instrument payable "thirty days after date" is not payable at a definite time, because the date of payment cannot be determined from its face. It is non-negotiable until a date is added.

    c. At a Fixed Period after Sight - This clause is frequently used in drafts. Such an instrument is negotiable, because the clause means a fixed period after acceptance. A slight mathematical calculation makes the maturity date certain.

    d. At a Definite Time Subject to Acceleration - If the instrument is payable at a fixed time, subject to acceleration by the holder, it satisfies the requirement of being payable at a definite time. Such an instrument has more certainty than a demand instrument, because it states a definite maturity date. Acceleration may be upon the happening of an event without impairing negotiability.

8. Payable to Order or to Bearer - A negotiable instrument must contain words indicating that the maker or drawer intends that it pass into the hands of someone other than the payee. The magic words of negotiability are "to the order of" or "to bearer." The use of synonyms invites trouble. An "order instrument" refers to the transferability of the instrument. It should not be confused with an order to pay.

    a. Payable to Order - The following are correct forms for order instruments: "Pay to the order of Jane Jones," "Pay to Jane Jones or her order," and "Pay to Jane Jones or her assigns." The person to whose order the instrument is payable must be designated with reasonable certainty. The payee may be an individual, the maker or drawer, the drawee, two or more payees, an office, an estate, a trust, a partnership or unincorporated association, or a corporation.

    b. Payable to Bearer - A bearer instrument is payable (1) to bearer or the order of bearer; (2) to a specified person or to bearer; or (3) to "cash" or to the order of "cash."

9. Terms and Omissions and Their Effect on Negotiability

    a. Absence of Statement of Consideration - Consideration is required to support a contract, but the negotiability of an instrument is not affected by the omission of a statement of consideration.

    b. Absence of Statement of Where the Instrument is Drawn or Payable - The place of issue must be known in order to know what law applies. Likewise the place of payment must be known to determine the law regarding payment. However, the omission of either of these facts on the face of the instrument does not affect negotiability.

    c. Sealed Instruments - A seal has no effect on an instrument's negotiability.

    d. Dating of the Instrument - In general, the negotiability of an instrument is not affected by the fact that it is undated, antedated, or postdated. An antedated instrument is due and payable the day before its issue. A postdated instrument is a time instrument. If a check is issued on January 2, 1989 and postdated to January 21, 1989, then the drawer's bank is not authorized to pay the instrument until January 21, 1989.

    e. Incomplete Instruments - If an essential term such as a promise or order, the designation of the payee, the amount payable, or the time for payment is omitted, the instrument is not negotiable until it is completed.

    f. Ambiguous Instruments - The Code establishes rules to resolve common ambiguities. This promotes negotiability by providing a degree of certainty to the holder. If it is unclear whether an instrument is a draft or a note, the holder may treat it as either and present it for payment to the drawee or the person signing it. Handwritten words control typewritten words, and typewritten words control printed words. If the amount payable is set forth on the face of instrument in both figures and words, and the amounts differ, the words control the figures. It is presumed that the maker or drawer would be more careful with words.

DEFINITIONS

1. Commercial paper

2. Check

3. Draft

4. Promissory note

5. Certificate of deposit

6. Negotiability

7. Drawer

8. Drawee

9. Payee

10. Maker

11. Order paper

12. Bearer paper

TRUE/FALSE

_____ 1. A draft may be handwritten on a napkin.

_____ 2. An instrument is non-negotiable if it is payable in a foreign currency.

_____ 3. An instrument in which no time for payment is stated is payable on demand.

_____ 4. An instrument is non-negotiable if the obligor may extend the maturity of the instrument for a definite period of time.

_____ 5. An instrument is non-negotiable if the holder may extend the maturity of the instrument for an indefinite period of time.

_____ 6. An instrument may be payable to two or more payees.

_____ 7. An instrument, otherwise negotiable, is negotiable bearer paper if by its terms it is payable to "cash."

_____ 8. An instrument is non-negotiable if it is complete.

_____ 9. An instrument may be payable to the maker or drawer.

_____ 10. In resolving ambiguities, printed words control typewritten and handwritten words, and typewritten words control handwritten words.

_____ 11. A cashier's check is a check drawn by a bank on itself to the order of a named payee.

_____ 12. A draft involves three parties.

_____ 13. An order or promise to pay only out of a particular fund is negotiable.

_____ 14. The sum certain requirement must be considered from the viewpoint of the holder.

_____ 15. The treasurer of Big Bucks Inc. uses a stamp to sign checks drawn on the corporate account. This meets the signature requirement of negotiability.

MULTIPLE CHOICE

_____ 1. If a negotiable instrument is not payable on demand, it cannot be:
    a. a draft.
    b. a check.
    c. a promissory note.
    d. a certificate of deposit.

_____ 2. A check must be signed by:
    a. the drawer.
    b. the drawee.
    c. the payee.
    d. the maker.

_____ 3. A promissory note must be signed by:
    a. the drawer.
    b. the drawee.
    c. the payee.
    d. the maker.

_____ 4. A signature on an instrument may:
    a. appear in the upper right hand corner.
    b. be a thumbprint.
    c. be an assumed name.
    d. all of the above.

_____ 5. An instrument is non-negotiable if it:
    a. refers to the existence of a separate agreement.
    b. states that it is subject to the terms of a separate agreement.
    c. is attached to a separate agreement.
    d. is made payable to the "assigns of Richard Roe."

_____ 6. An instrument is non-negotiable if it:
    a. relies upon the general credit of the drawer or maker.
    b. directs that a particular account be debited after payment.
    c. directs that payment be made out of a prticular fund.
    d. states that it is given in consideration for the purchase of a blue suit.

_____ 7. An instrument is non-negotiable if it:
    a. is payable with interest "at current rate."
    b. provides for the recovery of costs and attorney's fees upon default.
    c. is payable with a fixed addition if paid after maturity.
    d. is payable at a stated rate of interest which will increase by 2% upon default.

_____ 8. An instrument is non-negotiable if it:
    a. contains a promise or order to pay 800 French francs.
    b. provides that the payee, by cashing it, acknowledges full satisfaction of an obligation of the drawer.
    c. contains a promise to deliver goods.
    d. contains a promise to maintain collateral in case of a default in payment.

_____ 9. An instrument is non-negotiable if:
    a. it is payable upon an event uncertain as to time of occurrence.
    b. it is undated and payable 90 days after date.
    c. the obligor may extend the maturity of the instrument for an indefinite period of time.
    d. all of the above.

_____ 10. An instrument is non-negotiable if it is payable:
    a. to bearer.
    b. to Richard Roberts.
    c. to the order of Richard Roberts.
    d. to the order of Richard Roberts or bearer.

_____ 11. A negotiable promissory note must have:
    a. an endorser.
    b. a drawee.
    c. a payee.
    d. a holder in due course.

_____ 12. First Bank is the holder of a note which states that it is secured by a mortgage.
    a. The note is non-negotiable, because it refers to another agreement.
    b. The note is non-negotiable, because it is subject to another agreement.
    c. The note is non-negotiable, because it violates the particular fund doctrine.
    d. The note is negotiable.

_____ 13. Carol Customer deposits $10,000 at First Bank and gets a certificate of deposit from the bank.
   a. Carol is the maker of the certificate.
   b. First Bank is the maker of the certificate.
   c. Carol is the drawer of the certificate.
   d. First Bank is the drawer of the certificate.

_____ 14. Which of the following would create a bearer instrument?
   a. "Pay to the order of cash."
   b. "Pay to the order of Jane Smith or bearer."
   c. "Pay to the order of bearer."
   d. All of the above would create bearer paper.

_____ 15. Which of the following would be non-negotiable based upon a failure to meet the "unconditional promise or order to pay" requirement of negotiability?
   a. "I.O.U. $100."
   b. "Pay Jane Smith."
   c. "Please pay Jane Smith."
   d. "I promise to pay $100."

SHORT ESSAY

1. Can a check be converted to a time instrument? Explain. _____
   _____
   _____
   _____

2. Is the following instrument "I.O.U., Adam Brown $100, /s/ Joe Green" negotiable? Explain. _____
   _____
   _____
   _____

3. List the 8 requisites for an instrument to be negotiable. _____
   _____
   _____
   _____

4. Carol Contractor is the holder of an otherwise negotiable draft that contains the following notation: "Charge this against Construction Account 7890." What effect does this notation have upon the negotiability of the instrument? Explain. _____
   _____
   _____
   _____

CHAPTER 23

TRANSFER

PURPOSE

The primary advantage of commercial paper is the ease with which it can be transferred. In this chapter, you study the requirements that must be met in order for the transfer to be a negotiation such that the transferee can become a holder of the instrument. This concept is important, because only a holder of an instrument can become a holder in due course and thus be entitled to greater rights than the transferor may have possessed. The rights of a holder in due course are the reason why negotiable instruments move easily in the marketplace. In this chapter you study the methods by which commercial paper may be transferred. You should be especially concerned about the requirements of negotiation and the methods by which bearer paper and order paper may be negotiated.

CHAPTER CHECKPOINTS

After reading and studying this chapter, you should be able to:
1. Distinguish a transfer by negotiation from a transfer by assignment and discuss the ramifications of the distinction.

2. Define the term "holder" and discuss how a person becomes a holder of bearer paper in contrast to how a person becomes the holder of order paper.

3. Distinguish between a blank indorsement and a special indorsement and give an example of each.

4. Distinguish between a qualified indorsement and an unqualified indorsement and give an example of each.

5. List the various types of restrictive indorsements and give an example of each.

CHAPTER OUTLINE

A. Transfer and Negotiation - Whether a transfer is by "assignment" or "negotiation," the transferee acquires the rights that his transferor had. *Negotiation* is the transfer of a negotiable instrument in such a manner that the transferee becomes a holder. A *holder* is defined as "a person who is in possession of an instrument drawn, issued or indorsed to him or to his order or to bearer or in blank. If a transfer is by negotiation and the person to whom it is negotiated is a holder in due course, then the transferee may acquire more rights than his transferor had. A *bearer instrument* is negotiated by mere possession and is therefore similar to cash. To transfer an order instrument by negotiation, the transferor must both deliver possession of the instrument and supply the proper indorsements for the transferee to become a holder. Unless the parties otherwise agree, when a transferor transfers an order instrument for value, the transferee hs the enforceable right to have the unqualified indorsement of the transferor. Where a transfer is not for value, the transaction is normally not commercial and courts do not make such a presumption. When order paper is transferred without the proper indorsements, the transferee becomes an assignee, but it is not until the proper indorsement is made that the person in possession becomes a holder.

B.   Indorsements - An indorsement is the signature of a payee, drawee, accommodation indorser, or holder of an instrument. An indorsement must be written on the instrument or on a paper, called an allonge, so firmly affixed to the instrument as to become a part of it. An *allonge* is used when there is no room for additional signatures or when the indorsement is too lengthy to fit on the instrument. A purported indorsement on a separate piece of paper that is clipped or pinned is generally not valid. However, a piece of paper stapled to the instrument is generally valid. Indorsements are made on the back or reverse side of the instrument. The order of the indorsement and the liability of the indorsers is presumed to be the order in which their signatures appear. An indorsement showing that the signer is not in the chain or title is notice of its accommodation character. An *accommodation indorser* signs to add her liability to the instrument and thereby to accommodate another party who might otherwise be unable to obtain funds. An indorsement conveying less than the entire instrument is not a negotiation, but operates as a partial assignment. If it is unclear in what capacity a person has signed an instrument, the signature is treated as being an indorsement and the person is presumed to be an indorser. Parol evidence cannot be used to establish otherwise. The type of indorsement used affects its subsequent negotiation. Every indorsement is either (1) blank or special; (2) restrictive or nonrestrictive; and (3) qualified or unqualified, but these indorsements are not mutually exclusive. An indorser who merely signs her name on the back of an instrument makes a blank, nonrestrictive, unqualified indorsement.

1.   Blank Indorsements - A blank indorsement specifies no indorsee and may consist of merely the signature of the indorser or her authorized agent. A blank indorsement converts order paper into bearer paper. The holder of an instrument indorsed in blank should treat it with the same care as cash.

2.   Special Indorsements - A special indorsement specifically designates the person to whom or to whose order the instrument is to be payable (order paper). An indorsement reading "Pay Edward" is interpreted as meaning "Pay to the order of Edward." Any further negotiation would require Edward's indorsement. A holder of an instrument with a blank indorsement may protect himself by converting the blank indorsement to a special indorsement by writing over the signature of the indorser any contract consistent with the character of the indorsement. For example, if the instrument is indorsed in blank, the holder may convert the bearer instrument into order paper by inserting above the blank indorsement, "Pay Harry Holder" or similar words.

3.   Restrictive Indorsements - A restrictive indorsement attempts to restrict the rights of the indorsee in some fashion. The UCC defines four types of restrictive indorsements: conditional indorsements; indorsements prohibiting further transfer; indorsements for deposit or collection; and indorsements in trust. An unrestrictive indorsement does not attempt to restrict the rights of the indorsee.

   a.   Conditional Indorsements - In a conditional indorsement, the indorser makes the rights of the indorsee subject to the happening or nonhappening of a specified event. Example: "Pay Adam, but only if the good ship Jolly Jack arrives in Chicago harbor by November 15, 1989." In the instrument itself this language would make it non-negotiable. But indorsers are permitted to condition the rights of their indorsees without destroying negotiability.

   b.   Indorsements Prohibiting Further Transfer - An instrument that reads "Pay A" is not negotiable. However, an indorsement reading "Pay A" is interpreted as meaning "Pay to the order of A." Such indorsements are designed to prohibit further transfer; they are designed to be a restriction on the rights of the indorsee. The Code provides that no restrictive indorsement prevents further transfer or negotiation of the instrument. In effect, an indorsement that purports to prohibit further transfer of the instrument operates the same as an unrestricted indorsement.

    c.   Indorsements for Deposit or Collection - These are the most frequently used restrictive indorsements. They are designed to lodge the instrument in the banking system for deposit or collection. Examples include: "for collection," "for deposit," and "pay the bank." Such indorsements effectively limit further negotiation to those consistent with the limitation and put all nonbanking persons on notice as to who has a valid interest in the paper.

    d.   Indorsements in Trust - In this type of indorsement the indorser creates a trust for the benefit of himself or others. Examples are: "Pay Trish in trust for Boris," "Pay Trish for Boris," "Pay Trish for the account of Boris," and "Pay Trish as agent for Boris." In these indorsements, Trish is a fiduciary subject to liability for any breach of her obligation.

4.   Qualified Indorsements - Unqualified indorsers guarantee payment of the instrument if certain conditions are met. An indorser may disclaim liability on the contract of indorsement, but only if the indorsement so declares and the disclaimer is written on the instrument. The customary manner of disclaiming an indorser's liability is by adding the words "without recourse," either before or after his signature. A "without recourse" indorsement is called a *qualified* indorsement. A qualified indorsement does not eliminate all liability of an indorser, only the contractual liability of the indorser on the instrument. The qualified indorser remains liable for the indorser's warranties. A qualified indorsement does not destroy negotiability or prevent further negotiation of the instrument.

5.   Negotiations Subject to Rescission - A negotiation is valid even though the transaction in which it occurs is void or even voidable. If it conforms to the requirements previously discussed, it is effective to transfer the instrument even if it is (1) made by an infant, a corporation exceeding its power, or by any person without capacity; or (2) whether it is obtained by fraud, duress or mistake of any kind; or (3) part of an illegal transaction; or (4) made in breach of a duty. In such cases, the transferor loses all rights in the instrument until he regains possession of it. The transferor's right to regain possession is determined by State law, and is valid against the immediate transferee and all subsequent holders. However, it is not valid against a subsequent holder in due course.

DEFINITIONS

1.   Holder

2.   Negotiation

3.   Assignment

4.   Indorsement

5.   Qualified indorsement

6.   Blank indorsement

7.   Special indorsement

8.   Restrictive indorsement

TRUE/FALSE

_____ 1. A non-negotiable instrument is not transferable.

_____ 2. An indorsement written on a piece of paper clipped to the instrument is not negotiable.

_____ 3. An instrument may have no "holder."

_____ 4. A negotiable instrument may only be transferred by negotiation.

_____ 5. A negotiable instrument may only be negotiated by a holder.

_____ 6. Forging the signature of an accommodation indorser breaks the chain of title to the instrument.

_____ 7. Forging the signature of an indorsee breaks the chain of title to the instrument.

_____ 8. A qualified indorsement destroys the instrument's negotiability.

_____ 9. An instrument may have more than one holder at a time.

_____ 10. A restrictive indorsement prevents further negotiation of the instrument.

_____ 11. A check which is "payable to cash" requires an appropriate indorsement for further negotiations.

_____ 12. A thief or finder of order paper which has been indorsed in blank can transfer good title to a subsequent holder who may qualify as a holder in due course.

_____ 13. An indorser who has indorsed a negotiable instrument with a qualified indorsement stating that it is "without recourse" has absolutely no liability of any kind to subsequent holders.

_____ 14. A blank indorsement can be converted into a special indorsement.

_____ 15. An indorsement may be both blank and qualified.

MULTIPLE CHOICE

_____ 1. Indorsement by the appropriate parties is necessary to:
   a. transfer an instrument by assignment.
   b. negotiate a bearer instrument.
   c. negotiate an order instrument.
   d. (a) and (c) but not (b).

_____ 2. To be a holder of a bearer instrument requires:
   a. a transfer for value.
   b. possession of the instrument.
   c. the indorsement of the transferor.
   d. all of the above.

_____ 3. Order paper may be converted into bearer paper by:
    a.   a blank indorsement.
    b.   a special indorsement.
    c.   a restrictive indorsement.
    d.   a qualified indorsement.

_____ 4. Negotiability is destroyed if an instrument is indorsed with the words:
    a.   "pay to A only."
    b.   "pay to the order of A."
    c.   "pay to A or his order."
    d.   none of the above.

_____ 5. An indorsement is ineffective as a negotiation if it:
    a.   is not dated.
    b.   conveys only the unpaid balance on the instrument.
    c.   is forged.
    d.   (b) and (c) but not (a).

_____ 6. Bearer paper may be converted into order paper by:
    a.   a blank indorsement.
    b.   a special indorsement.
    c.   a restrictive indorsement.
    d.   a qualified indorsement.

_____ 7. If H, the holder of a note, indorses it, "Pay A, but only if P is elected President in November," the indorsement is:
    a.   blank, restrictive, qualified.
    b.   special, non-restrictive, qualified.
    c.   blank, non-restrictive, unqualified.
    d.   special, restrictive, unqualified.

_____ 8. An indorsement which reads "Pay only if the goods are delivered by December 1, without recourse, Jane Jones" is:
    a.   blank, non-restrictive, qualified.
    b.   blank, restrictive, unqualified.
    c.   blank, restrictive, qualified.
    d.   special, restrictive, unqualified.

_____ 9. Which of the following is an example of an effective restrictive indorsement?
    a.   "Pay A only."
    b.   "Pay any bank."
    c.   "Pay XYZ bank."
    d.   "Pay A, without recourse."

_____ 10. If a note is conditionally indorsed, then the indorsee:
     a.   is entitled to payment unless the condition fails.
     b.   has no rights in the instrument regardless of the outcome, because a promise to pay must be unconditional.
     c.   is entitled to payment, regardless of the outcome, because a promise to pay must be unconditional.
     d.   none of the above.

_____ 11. First Bank issued a certificate of deposit to Harold Homeowner. At Harold's request, the instrument was made payable to bearer.
     a.   A thief could never redeem the certificate.
     b.   The instrument needs a blank indorsement to be redeemed.
     c.   If Harold places a special, qualified indorsement on the instrument, he will avoid making a guarantee of its payment.
     d.   None of the above.

_____ 12. Sarah Salesclerk indorsed her paycheck with her signature and the words "for deposit only." This is indorsement is a:
     a.   blank indorsement.
     b.   special indorsement.
     c.   restrictive indorsement.
     d.   blank, restrictive indorsement.

_____ 13. Order paper is negotiated by:
     a.   delivery alone.
     b.   indorsement alone.
     c.   delivery and indorsement.
     d.   delivery or indorsement.

_____ 14. Harold Homeowner writes a check payable to Tim Teenager or his sister Tina Teenager in the alternative. This check requires the indorsement of:
     a.   both Tim and Tina.
     b.   either Tim or Tina.
     c.   either Harold or Tim.
     d.   Harold, Tim and Tina.

_____ 15. If there is no more room on an instrument, further indorsements can be written on a separate piece of paper firmly affixed to the instrument. This piece of paper is known as a/an:
     a.   amendment.
     b.   fixture.
     c.   allonge.
     d.   attachment.

SHORT ESSAY

1. Is it a good idea to send bearer paper by mail? Explain.

2. List and describe the various types of indorsements. _____
_____
_____
_____

3. When does the transferee become an assignee rather than a holder of an instrument? _____
_____
_____
_____

4. Can a negotiation be set aside if the underlying transaction is void or voidable? In your opinion, why is this rule followed? Explain. _____
_____
_____
_____

CHAPTER 24

HOLDER IN DUE COURSE

PURPOSE

The concept of holder in due course is the most significant aspect of negotiability; it is a concept that is unique to negotiable instruments. A mere holder of an instrument acquires it subject to all claims and defenses against it. However, a holder in due course in a nonconsumer credit transaction takes the instrument free of all claims of other parties and free of all defenses to the instrument except for a very limited number of claims that are specifically set forth in the Code. The holder in due course has a preferred position in the law, because such a position encourages the free negotiability of commercial paper by minimizing the risks that are assumed by an innocent purchaser of the instrument. A holder is a person in possession of an instrument that contains all necessary indorsements. However, not every holder is a holder in due course. In addition to being a holder, a holder in due course must have taken the instrument for value, in good faith, without notice that it is overdue or dishonored, and without notice of any defense or claim to it on the part of any person. In this chapter, you study how a transferee becomes a holder in due course and the advantages of being a holder in due course.

CHAPTER CHECKPOINTS

After reading and studying this chapter, you should be able to:

1. List and discuss the requirements for becoming a holder in due course.

2. Discuss why the holder in due course status is a preferential one and recognize fact situations which contain a holder in due course.

3. Explain the shelter rule and why the Code follows a rule that allows a person who is not a holder in due course to have the rights of one.

4. Distinguish between a real defense and a personal defense and identify the most common examples of each.

5. Discuss the Federal Trade Commission's holder in due course rule and its effect upon the status of a holder in due course who takes an instrument that is subject it.

CHAPTER OUTLINE

A. **Requirements of Holder in Due Course** - To acquire the preferential rights of a holder in due course, a person must meet the requirements of the Code or must "inherit" these rights under the shelter rule.

1. **Holder** - A holder is a person who has both possession of an instrument and all necessary indorsements. A holder is a person who is in possession of a negotiable instrument (1) issued to his order; (2) issued to bearer; (3) indorsed to him; or (4) indorsed in blank. A forged indorsement is not valid, so that a person who takes an instrument with a forged indorsement cannot be either a holder or a holder in due course. However, a thief or finder who is in possession of a bearer instrument is a holder, so that a person who takes a bearer instrument from a thief will be a holder and may be a holder in due course.

2. **Value** - A holder in due course must have given value. A holder who was given an instrument as a gift cannot be a holder in due course, because she has not given value. Value in the law of commercial paper is not the same as consideration under the law of contracts. An executory promise will support a contract, but it is not sufficient to constitute value for purposes of being a holder in due course. Value is the performance of legal consideration; the forgiveness of an antecedent debt; the giving of a negotiable instrument; or the giving of an irrevocable commitment to a third party. The giving of a negotiable instrument and the making of an irrevocable commitment to a third party are two situations that the Code provides to the general rule that an executory promise is not the giving of value. Where an instrument is given as security for an obligation, the lender is regarded as giving value to the extent of his security interest. Under general contract law an antecedent debt is not sufficient consideration to support a promise to pay the debt or a lesser amount in full satisfaction of it. However, under the Code a holder gives value when she takes an instrument in payment of or as security for an antecedent debt. A bank gives value when it allows a depositor to withdraw funds against a deposited item. If a number of checks have been deposited, and some but not all of the funds have been withdrawn, the Code traces the deposit by following the "FIFO" or or "first-in, first-out" method of accounting.

3. **Good Faith** - The Code defines good faith as "honesty in fact in the conduct or transaction concerned." The test is subjective; it measures good faith by what the purchaser knows or believes. It does not measure honesty by what a prudent man under the circumstances would have known.

4. **Lack of Notice** - To become a holder in due course, a holder must take the instrument without notice that it is (1) overdue; (2) dishonored; or (3) subject to any defense or claim.

   a. **Notice of Claim or Defense** - A person has "notice" of a fact when (a) he has actual knowledge of it; or (b) he has received a notice or notification of it; or (c) from all the facts and circumstances known to him at the time in question he has reason to know that it exists. Since the applicable standard is "actual notice," "notice received," or "reason to know," constructive notice through public filing or recording is not of itself sufficient notice to prevent a person from becoming a holder in due course. Although buying an instrument at an unusually large discount may indicate notice of a defense or claim, the mere fact that an instrument is purchased at less than face value does not mean that the buyer had notice or a claim or defense against it. Neither does it indicate lack of good faith. A defense to the instrument is a justification or shield protecting a person for liability, whereas a claim to the instrument is an assertion of ownership of it. Claims may be made against thieves, finders, or possessors with voidable or void title. If an instrument is irregular or an alteration is obvious, a person may be held to have notice of it, because a material alteration generally gives notice of a defense or claim.

   b. **Notice an Instrument is Overdue** - To be a holder in due course, the purchaser must take the instrument without notice that it is overdue. This requirement is based on the idea that overdue paper conveys a suspicion that something is wrong. Demand paper is not overdue for purposes of holder in due course status unless the purchaser has notice that she is taking it after demand has been made, or until it has been outstanding for a reasonable length of time. For checks, a reasonable period of time is presumed to be thirty days. However, business custom, the particular situation and other relevant factors are considered.

    c.   **Notice an Instrument Has Been Dishonored** - Dishonor is the refusal to pay or accept an instrument when it becomes due. If a transferee has notice that an instrument has been dishonored, he cannot become a holder in due course, because he knows the instrument may not be paid.

B.   Holder in Due Course Status

    1.   **A Payee May Be a Holder in Due Course** - This does not mean that he will always be a holder in due course. It only means that he may be one if he satisfies the holder in due course requirements. Usually, a payee will not be a holder in due course, because he will have notice of any claim or defense that is good against the instrument, but this is not always the case. Where the payee is not an immediate party to the transaction and therefore will not be subject to any claims and most defenses, he will usually meet the requirements of a holder in due course.

    2.   **The Shelter Rule** - The transferee of an instrument acquires the same rights in the instrument that the transferor had. Therefore, even if a holder does not qualify to be a holder in due course, he acquires all the rights of that status if some previous holder of the instrument has been a holder in due course. However, a person who is not a holder in due course may not obtain the rights of one by reacquiring the instrument from a subsequent holder who is either a holder in due course or who has the rights of one. In other words, he cannot improve his position by reacquiring the instrument.

C.   The Preferred Position of a Holder in Due Course - Only real defenses may be used against a holder in due course. Personal defenses cannot be used against him. Since the most common defenses asserted are personal ones, the holder in due course has a preferred position in the law.

    1.   **Real Defenses** - Real defenses are available against *all* holders, including holders in due course. The real defenses are as follows:

        a.   **Minority** - The Code does not state when minority is available as a defense or the conditions under which it may be asserted. Rather, it provides that minority is a defense available against a holder in due course to the extent that it is a defense to a simple contract under the laws of the State involved.

        b.   **Void Obligations** - When the obligation on an instrument originates in such a way that under the law of the State involved it is void, the Code authorizes the use of this defense against a holder in due course. To the extent that the underlying transaction is voidable only, the defense is not effective against a holder in due course. In most instances where a defense can be raised, the transaction will be voidable rather than void, and thus the defense cannot be used against a holder in due course.

        c.   **Fraud in the Execution** - Fraud in the execution of an instrument renders the instrument void and therefore is a valid defense against a holder in due course. The Code defines fraud in the execution as misrepresentation that induced the party to sign the instrument with neither knowledge of nor a reasonable opportunity to obtain knowledge of its character or its essential terms. This type of fraud is very rare. It must be of the kind that precludes the deceived party from knowing or having a reasonable opportunity to know what she was signing.

        d.   **Discharge in Insolvency Proceedings** - If a party's obligation on an instrument is discharged in a bankruptcy proceeding, he has a valid defense in any action brought against him on the instrument, including one by a holder in due course.

        e.   **Discharge of Which the Holder Has Notice** - Any holder, including a holder in due course, takes the instrument subject to any discharge of which he has notice. If a holder acquires an instrument with notice that all prior parties have been discharged, he cannot become a holder in due course.

        f.   **Forgery and Unauthorized Signature** - A person's signature on an instrument is unauthorized when it is made without authority. A person whose signature has been forged cannot be held liable on the instrument in the absence of estoppel or ratification, even if the instrument is negotiated to a holder in due course. Any unauthorized signature is totally invalid as that of the person whose name is signed unless he ratifies it or is precluded from denying it. The signature operates only as the signature of the unauthorized signer. A party may be estopped from asserting a defense because his conduct in the matter caused reliance by a third party to his loss or damage. Similarly, a party is precluded from denying the validity of his signature if his negligence substantially contributed to the making of the unauthorized signature. An unauthorized signature may be ratified and thereby become valid as a signature.

g.   Material Alteration - Any alteration that changes the contract of any party to the instrument in any way is material. An alteration by a holder that is both fraudulent and material discharges any party whose contract is thereby changed, unless that party assents to the change or is precluded from asserting the defense. An incomplete instrument may be enforced according to the authority given to the holder by the issuing party (e.g., an authorization to fill in an amount on a chck for the amount of a purchase). A subsequent holder in due course may always enforce the instrument according to its original tenor, and when an incomplete instrument has been completed, he may enforce it as completed. The addition or deletion of any words that do not in any way affect the contract of previous signers is not material. However, even a slight change in the contract of a party is material; the addition of one cent in the amount payable or the advancement of the day of payment by one day will operate as a discharge if it is fraudulent. A material alteration will not discharge a party unless it is made for a fraudulent purpose. Thus, there is no discharge when a blank is filled in the honest belief that it is authorized. Likewise, if the alteration is not material there is no discharge, and the instrument may be enforced according to its original tenor. A party will be discharged from liability on a negotiable instrument to any holder, other than a subsequent holder in due course, by an alteration if the alteration is (1) made by a holder; (2) with fraudulent intent; and (3) when the alteration is material. A holder in due course is given preferential treatment in that he can enforce any altered instrument according to its original terms or, if it was an incomplete instrument, as the instrument was completed. Any other holder would not be able to enforce the instrument at all, because the party whose contract was changed would be totally discharged from even his original agreement.

E.   Limitations on Rights of Holder in Due Course - The preferential position of a holder in due course has been severely limited by a Federal Trade Commission rule that applies to consumer credit contracts. The rule applies to sellers and lessors of consumer goods, which are defined to include goods for personal, family or household use. It also applies to lenders who advance money to finance the consumer's purchase of consumer goods or services. The rule is intended to prevent situations in which a consumer is required to make payments to a holder in due course when the product or services purchased are defective or when the transaction involves fraud in the inducement. This occurs when the purchaser executes and delivers to the seller a negotiable instrument (usually a note) which the seller then negotiates to a holder in due course with whom he has a business relationship. Under the law of commercial paper, the buyer's defense that the goods were defective or that the seller committed fraud in the inducement, even if valid against the seller, cannot be raised against a holder in due course of the instrument. The FTC rule preserves the claims and defenses of consumers by requiring that a conspicuous notice be included in the consumer credit contract. The purpose of this notice is to inform a subsequent holder that he takes the instrument subject to all claims and defenses which the buyer could assert against the seller. In effect, when the rule applies, it places the holder in due course in the position of an assignee of the original holder.

DEFINITIONS

1.   Holder in due course

2. Value

3. Material alteration

4. Notice

5. Shelter rule

6. Real defense

7. Personal defense

TRUE/FALSE

_____ 1. A transferee of a negotiable instrument may acquire greater rights than his transferor had.

_____ 2. A person may acquire the rights of a holder in due course even though he does not take the instrument for value.

_____ 3. A holder takes an instrument for value only when he pays the face amount of the instrument.

_____ 4. A check is presumed overdue if it has been outstanding more than 30 days.

_____ 5. A payee may be a holder in due course.

_____ 6. Real defenses may not be asserted against a holder in due course.

_____ 7. A person may be a holder in due course even if he takes the instrument after all of the parties to the instrument have been discharged regardless of whether or not he has notice of the discharge.

_____ 8. When an incomplete instrument has been complete in an unauthorized manner, a subsequent holder may enforce the instrument according to the authority actually given, even though the completion has the effect of changing the contract of the previous signers.

_____ 9. When an incomplete instrument has been completed in an authorized manner, a subsequent holder in due course may enforce the instrument as completed.

_____ 10. Under the FTC's holder in due course rule, the buyer may have a defense against the holder even though the buyer has no defense against the seller.

_____ 11. Failure of consideration is a real defense.

_____ 12. Bill Buyer issued a note to Sam Seller in return for goods to be used as inventory. Bill's customers later complained that the goods were defective, so Bill dishonored the note. Sam can assert holder in due course status to enforce the note against Bill.

_____ 13. A thief can transfer a bearer instrument to a holder in due course.

_____ 14. Happy Homemaker issues a $25 check to her niece for graduation. The niece is a holder in due course.

_____ 15. Hal Hoodlum holds a gun to Bill Buyer's head and forces him to sign a note for $5,000. Hal then transfers the note to First Bank who now wants to collect $5,000 from Bill. Bill can assert the defense of duress against First Bank in order to avoid payment.

MULTIPLE CHOICE

_____ 1. A person may be a holder in due course if he takes the instrument:
   a. for value.
   b. in bad faith.
   c. with notice that it has been dishonored.
   d. all of the above.

_____ 2. A person may acquire the rights of a holder in due course if he takes the instrument:
   a. for value.
   b. in bad faith.
   c. with notice that it has been dishonored.
   d. all of the above.

_____ 3. A holder takes an instrument for value when he:
   a. makes an irrevocable commitment to his transferor.
   b. promises to pay the agreed consideration.
   c. takes the instrument as security for an antecedent debt.
   d. (a) and (c) but not (b).

_____ 4. A purchaser takes an instrument in good faith if:
   a. he believes there is nothing wrong with it.
   b. he knows there is something wrong with it.
   c. a prudent man under the circumstances would not have known that something was wrong with it, but the purchaser in fact knows something is wrong with it.
   d. (a) and (c) but not (b).

_____ 5. A holder has knowledge of a claim or defense if:
   a. the instrument has been undetectably altered.
   b. he knows that one or more of the parties to the instrument have been discharged.
   c. he knows that all the parties to the instrument have been discharged.
   d. all of the above.

_____ 6. Assume M issues a note to P which is successively negotiated to A, B, C, and H. If H is a holder in due course with respect to all the parties to the instrument, then H is subject to the personal defenses of:
   a. A only.
   b. B only.
   c. C only.
   d. none of the above.

_____ 7. Assume M issues a note to P which is successively negotiated to A, B, C, and H. If H is a holder in due course with respect to all the parties to the instrument, then H is subject to the real defenses of:
   a. A only.
   b. B only.
   c. C only.
   d. all of the above.

_____ 8. A party to an instrument has a real defense if his obligation on the instrument:
   a. is void.
   b. is voidable.
   c. has been discharged.
   d. is the result of fraud in the inducement.

_____ 9. A forged signature operates as the signature of:
   a. the person whose name is forged.
   b. the forger.
   c. any person who takes the instrument with notice that the signature has been forged.
   d. none of the above.

_____ 10. Under the FTC's holder in due course rule, the consumer buyer may successfully assert:
   a. real defenses.
   b. personal defenses.
   c. real and personal defenses.
   d. none of the above.

_____ 11. Which of the following constitutes value for purposes of holder in due course status?
   a. An antecedent debt.
   b. An executory promise.
   c. A depositor withdraws funds against a deposited item at a bank.
   d. Two of the above, (a) and (c).

_____ 12. Michael Maker signs a note for $500 to Consumer Credit Company, which then alters the note to read $5,000.
   a. Michael must pay $500 to CCC.
   b. Michael must pay $5,000 to CCC.
   c. Michael is discharged from his obligation.
   d. Michael has no defenses against CCC, because it is a holder in due course.

_____ 13. Which of the following is a correct statement with regard to the shelter rule?
   a. It permits a holder who cannot be a holder in due course to better his position by reacquiring it from a later holder.
   b. It permits a transferee of a holder in due course to gain holder in due course status.
   c. It shelters a maker or drawer from potential liability.
   d. All of the above are correct.

_____ 14. Paula Payee by means of fraud in the inducement induces Michael Maker to sign an instrument payable to her. Paula subsequently negotiates the instrument to Harry Holder, a holder in due course. Paula later reacquires the note from Harry.
   a. Paula can invoke the shelter rule.
   b. Paula is a holder in due course if she gave value to Harry.
   c. Paula remains subject to the defense of fraud and cannot invoke the shelter rule.
   d. Paula can invoke the shelter rule and may be a holder in due course if she gave value to Harry.

_____ 15. Carol Customer has a checking account with First Bank. She deposits a $300 check in her account and then writes a check to Marlin's Department Store in the amount of $100 which First Bank then pays from her account.
   a. First Bank is a holder in due course in the amount of $300.
   b. First Bank is a holder in due course in the amount of $100.
   c. First Bank is not a holder in due course, because it has not given value.
   d. First Bank is not a holder in due course, because it has a customer relationship with Carol.

SHORT ESSAY

1. Who may be a holder in due course? _____
_____
_____
_____

2. Why is it so important to be considered a holder in due course? _____
_____
_____
_____

3. Most payees do not enjoy the rights of a holder in due course. Why? _____
_____
_____
_____

4. Suppose you are on your way out to do some shopping when your roommate hands you a list of a few things she would like you to pick up. She gives you a blank check to pay for them. Can you legally spend that check? _____
_____
_____
_____

LIABILITY OF PARTIES

PURPOSE

In this chapter, you study the liability scheme that is used in Article 3. This liability scheme is complex. You will have to study the chapter carefully and think about what you read in order to fully understand the material. There are two types of liability: (1) liability on the instrument, which is also called contractual liability and may be either primary liability on the instrument or secondary liability on the instrument; and (2) warranty liability, which may be based upon having transferred an instrument or may be based upon either having received payment or having had an instrument accepted. Liability on the instrument is only imposed upon persons who have signed the instrument. However, warranty liability is not based upon having signed the instrument; it is imposed upon both signers and nonsigners of an instrument. Study this chapter carefully, because it is one of the most difficult ones in the text.

CHAPTER CHECKPOINTS

After reading and studying this chapter, you should be able to:

1. Distinguish among and discuss contractual liability, warranty liability and liability for conversion.

2. Discuss the liability for authorized signatures and for unauthorized signatures.

3. Summarize the liability of makers, acceptors, drawees, drawers, indorsers and accommodation parties.

4. Compare the warranties on transfer with those on presentment.

CHAPTER OUTLINE

I. Contractual Liability - All parties whose signatures appear on a negotiable instrument incur certain contractual liabilities, unless they disclaim liability. The maker of a promissory note and the acceptor of a draft assume an absolute obligation (primary liability). Drawers of drafts and checks, and indorsers of all instruments incur secondary liability if the instrument is not paid.
   A. Signature - Signature is broadly defined to include any name, word, or mark, whether handwritten, typed, or printed so long as it is made with the intention of authenticating the instrument. It may be made by the individual or the individual's agent.

1. Authorized Signatures - An agent who executes a negotiable instrument on behalf of his principal is not liable if the instrument is executed properly. The correct form to avoid liability is "P, principal, by A, agent." If Adams, the agent of Prince, signs a note made on behalf of Prince with just "Adams," the signature does not indicate that he has signed the instrument on behalf of Prince. In this case, only Adams is liable. Prince is not liable on the instrument, because his signature does not appear on it. Prince may have liability to Adams based on the contract between them or under agency law, but he is not liable on the instrument under commercial law. If Adams in executing an instrument on behalf of Prince signs it "Adams, agent," he does not disclose the name of the principal. In this situation, Prince is liable to an immediate party, but not to subsequent ones. Adams alone is liable, because Prince's name does not appear on the instrument. If Adams signs an instrument on behalf of Prince, "Adams and Prince," a subsequent holder might reasonably believe that Adams and Prince are co-makers. Adams may prove his agency relationship by parol evidence to avoid liability.

2. Unauthorized Signatures - This includes both forgeries and signatures made by an agent without proper power to do so. An unauthorized signature is generally not binding on the person whose name appears on the instrument, but it is binding on the unauthorized signer whether or not her own name appears on the instrument. An important exception to this rule is that an unauthorized signature does bind the person whose name is signed if that person by his negligence substantially contributes to the making of the unauthorized signature. For example, Jones uses a signature stamp to sign his checks and carelessly leaves it accessible to third parties. Brown discovers the stamp and uses it to write checks with the unauthorized signature of Jones as the drawer. Howard, a subsequent holder in due course, will not be subject to Jones' defense of the unauthorized signature, because Jones substantially contributed to the forgery by his negligence.

B. Liability of Primary Parties
1. Makers - The maker of a note is the primary party. The maker guarantees that he will pay the note according to its original terms.
2. Acceptors - Unlike a note, there is no one primarily liable on a draft until the drawee (bank) accepts it. A bank does not have to pay any check drawn on it; however, if the drawer has an account with sufficient funds in it, the drawee's refusal to pay a check would constitute a breach of the drawee's contract with the drawer. When the drawee refuses to accept a draft, the drawer becomes liable on the instrument upon receiving notice of dishonor. If the drawee accepts the draft, then the drawee becomes primarily liable on it. Certification of a check is acceptance; it is the drawee's signed promise to pay the draft as presented. A bank is not obligated to certify a check. When a check is certified at the request of a holder, the drawer and all prior indorsers are discharged. Certification at the request of the drawer makes the bank primarily liable, but it does not relieve the drawer of secondary liability.

C. Liability of Secondary Parties - The drawer and indorsers (including a payee who indorses) are secondarily liable.
1. Indorsers and Drawers - If the instrument is not paid by a primary party and the conditions precedent to the liability of secondary parties are satisfied, then a secondary party is liable unless he has disclaimed his liability.
2. Conditions Precedent to Liability - The conditions precedent to liability are presentment, dishonor, notice of dishonor, and in some situations, protest.
    a. Presentment - Presentment is a demand for acceptance of payment made by the holder on the maker, acceptor or drawee. Presentment may be made in any reasonable manner. An instrument with a specified maturity date is due for presentment on that date. In any other case, presentment is due within "a reasonable time." A delay in presentment discharges the indorsers; however, it only discharges the drawer to the extent of any loss suffered because of

the delay.

b. Dishonor - An instrument is dishonored when (1) presentment has been made, and acceptance or payment is refused or cannot be obtained. Presentment may be for acceptance or for payment.

c. Notice of Dishonor - Notice of dishonor is necessary to charge any indorser. Notice must also be made to the drawer, the acceptor of a draft payable at a bank, or the maker of a note payable at a bank, but failure to give such notice discharges these parties only if the bank is insolvent. It is advisable for a holder to notify all prior parties, because if only one party is notified, he may fail to notify prior parties. Notice of dishonor is frequently given by returning the unpaid instrument with a stamp, ticket or memorandum attached stating that the item was not paid and requesting that the recipient make good on it. Notice may be given in any reasonable manner.

d. Protest - A protest is required only if the draft is drawn or payable outside the United States. A protest is a certificate of dishonor made under the hand and seal of a United States counsul or vice-counsul or a notary public or other person authorized to certify to a dishonor by the law of the place where the dishonor occurred.

e. Delay in Presentment, Notice, or Protest Excused - The Code excuses delay in two situations. The first is where the holder does not have notice that the instrument is due, such as when the maturity is accelerated. The second is where delay is caused by circumstances beyond the holder's control.

f. Presentment, Notice, or Protst Excused - The Code entirely excuses the holder from presentment, notice or protest if the party to be charged has himself dishonored the instrument or has countermanded payment, or if the holder has no reason to expect the instrument to be paid or accepted. The Code also excuses presentment, notice or protest if they cannot be accomplished by due diligence.

g. Presentment Excused - Presentment, but not notice or protest is excused when (1) the maker, acceptor, or drawee is dead or in insolvency proceedings; (2) payment or acceptance is refused for reasons not relating to proper presentment, making it clear that presentment would be useless.

h. Waiver of Presentment, Notice or Protest - Presentment, notice or protest may be expressly or impliedly waived.

3. Disclaimer by Secondary Parties - A qualified ("without recourse") indorsement may be used to disclaim secondary liability on the instrument, but the person who disclaims secondary liability may nonetheless be liable for breach of warranty.

D. Liability of Accommodation Parties - Accommodation parties sign a negotiable instrument for the purpose of lending their credit to another party. Accommodation parties have liability based upon the manner in which they sign. If they sign as makers, they have primary liability; if they as indorsers, they have secondary liability. The law of suretyship applies to accommodation parties.

E. Special Situations Affecting Liability
1. The Imposter Rule - The Code provides that the indorsement of an imposter who impersonates a person (usually a respected citizen) and thereby deceives a party into delivering a negotiable instrument to the imposter in the name of the imposter is effective if the imposter has induced the maker or drawer to issue the instrument to him using the name of the payee. The Code treats this situation as if the named payee had indorsed the instrument in order to hold the drawer or maker responsible for failing to detect the impersonation by the imposter.

2. The Fictitious Payee Rule - When a faithless agent or employee issues an instrument to a fictitious payee (usually so that he himself can have the money) and the drawee bank pays the instrument, the Code says that the indorsement by any person in the name of the named payee is effective.

The risk of employee fraud is placed upon the employer.

II. Liability Based Upon Warranty - There are two types of warranties: transferor's warranties and presenter's warranties. The warranties may be disclaimed by agreement between the immediate parties, but they are effective otherwise whether or not the transferor or presenter signs the instrument.

  A. Warranties on Transfer - These warranties are given by any person who transfers an instrument and receives consideration. If the transfer is by delivery, the warranties run only to the immediate transferee. If the transfer is by indorsement (either qualified or unqualified) the warranties run to "any subsequent holder who takes the instrument in good faith." The warranties of the transferor are as follows:
    1. Good Title - The transferor warrants that he has good title to the instrument or is authorized to obtain payment or acceptance on behalf of one who has good title, and that the transfer is otherwise rightful.
    2. Signatures Genuine - The transferor warrants that the signatures are genuine or authorized.
    3. No Material Alteration - The transferor warrants that the instrument has not been materially altered.
    4. No Defenses - The transferor warrants that no defense of any party is good against the transferor. A transferor who indorses "without recourse" warrants only that he has no knowledge of any such defense.
    5. No Knowledge of Insolvency - The transferor warrants that he has no knowledge of any insolvency proceedings instituted by the maker, acceptor, or drawer of an unaccepted instrument.

  B. Warranties on Presentment - If a drawee (bank) pays an instrument that has been forged or altered, it has the initial loss, because it cannot charge this amount to the drawer's account. The warranties of presentment allow the drawee to shift the loss to whom it made payment. Presenter's warranties run not only from the person who obtains payment or acceptance, but from all prior transferors. The presentment warranties are as follows:
    1. Good Title - The presenter's warranty of good title is essentially the same as the transferor's warranty of good title. It extends to the genuineness of the indorser's signatures, but not to the signature of the maker or drawer.
    2. Genuineness of Signature of Maker and Drawer - The presenter warrants that he has no knowledge that the signature of the maker or drawer is unauthorized. There are exceptions to this available only to a holder in due couse.
    3. No Material Alteration - The presenter, except for a holder in due course acting in good faith to a maker or drawer, warrants against material alteration.

III. Termination of Liability - The Code specifies the methods by and extent to which the liability of a party is discharged.

  A. Discharge by Performance - Payment to the holder discharges liability.

  B. Tender of Payment - Any party liable on an instrument who makes tender of full payment to a holder when or after payment is due is discharged from all subsequent liability for interest, costs, and attorney's fees, but does not relieve her of liability for the face amount of the instrument or any interest.

  C. Cancellation and Renunciation - Intentional cancellation of the instrument by the holder results in a discharge of all parties. Accidental destruction or cancellation by someone other than the holder does not have such an effect.

D. Impairment of Recourse or Collateral - A holder discharges any party to the instrument to the extent any of the party's rights are adversely affected by any of several acts listed in the Code.

E. Other Methods of Discharge - Other methods by which a party's liability may be discharged include: (1) fraudulent and material alteration; (2) discharge of the drawer and prior indorsers by certification of a check procured by the holder; and (3) unexcused delay in presentment, notice of dishonor, or protest. A party may also be discharged by agreeing to pay money for discharge.

DEFINITIONS

1. Acceptance

2. Certification

3. Presentment

4. Dishonor

5. Protest

6. Secondary liability

7. Discharge

8. Accommodation party

9. Conversion

10. Transferor's warranty

11. Presenter's warranty

12. Primary liability

TRUE/FALSE

_____ 1. A person may be liable on a negotiable instrument even if he doesn't sign it.

_____ 2. A forger will be liable on an instrument even though he signs someone else's name and not his own.

_____ 3. A bank must honor a check drawn upon it.

_____ 4. A delay in presentment of a check discharges the drawer, irrespective of any showing of loss.

_____ 5. The holder of a dishonored check may not sue the drawer if it involves skipping intermediate indorsers.

_____ 6. A bank that pays an instrument on a forged indorsement will not be liable for conversion if it acted in good faith.

_____ 7. Under the imposter rule, the indorsement of any person in the name of the named payee is effective as the indorsement of the named payee.

_____ 8. An indorser may disclaim warranty liability.

_____ 9. If an instrument is transferred by delivery alone (without indorsement) warranties in transfer run to the immediate transferee only.

_____ 10. An unreasonable delay in presentment of a check discharges an indorser, irrespective of any showing of loss.

_____ 11. A maker may be liable on a note even though he has already paid the holder.

_____ 12. Andrew is the indorser of a note for $1,000 on which Michael is the maker. Andrew becomes immediately liable for the face amount when the note becomes due.

_____ 13. David Drawer wrote a check for $1,000 payable to Paul Payee. Paul altered the check to read $11,000 and negotiated the check to Harold, a holder in due course. Harold can recover $1,000 from David.

_____ 14. David Drawer wrote a check for $1,000 payable to Paul Payee. Paul altered the check to read $11,000 and negotiated the check to Harold, a holder in due course. Paul is liable to Harold under the transferor's warranties.

_____ 15. Arthur brings a check to First Bank for certification and First Bank duly stamps the face of the check "Certified." One week later the bank dishonors the check. Arthur must now notify the drawer and seek payment from him.

MULTIPLE CHOICE

_____ 1. A signature may be:
   a. printed.
   b. made by an authorized agent.
   c. typed.
   d. all of the above.

_____ 2. A drawee bank becomes liable on a check when:
   a. the check is written.
   b. the drawer issues the check.
   c. the payee indorses the check.
   d. the bank accepts the check.

_____ 3. An indorser may disclaim contractual liability on an instrument if his indorsement contains the words:
   a. "time is of the essence."
   b. "Caveat Emptor."
   c. "without recourse."
   d. "notice of dishonor."

_____ 4. The holder of an instrument has an immediate right of recourse against drawers and indorsers upon:
   a. proper presentment.
   b. dishonor.
   c. proper presentment and dishonor.
   d. proper presentment, dishonor, and notice of dishonor.

_____ 5. Presentment and notice may be excused where the party to be charged:
   a. has himself dishonored the instrument.
   b. has himself counteracted payment.
   c. has no reason to expect the instrument to be accepted or paid.
   d. all of the above.

_____ 6. If A, B, and C indorse a note, in that order, as accommodation parties for the same individual, who will ultimately bear the loss upon the maker's default?
   a. A only.
   b. B only.
   c. C only.
   d. A, B, and C will share the loss equally.

_____ 7. Which of the following is not a warranty of transfer?
   a. No material alteration.
   b. Maker is solvent.
   c. Good title.
   d. Signatures genuine.

_____ 8. A drawee bank can recover from the person who obtains payment of a check if:
   a. the drawer's signature is forged.
   b. the payee's signature is forged.
   c. the amount is raised after the check has been certified.
   d. none of the above.

_____ 9. Which of the following is not an example of conversion?
   a. A drawee to whom a draft is delivered for acceptance refuses to return it on demand.
   b. An instrument is paid on a forged indorsement.
   c. A holder unjustifiably impairs any collateral given on an instrument by a party to that instrument.
   d. A drawee to whom an instrument is delivered for payment refuses on demand either to pay or to return it.

_____ 10. A holder who strikes out an indorser's signature:
   a. has discharged that indorser.
   b. is liable for conversion.
   c. has broken the chain of title.
   d. is not entitled to payment.

_____ 11. An indorser who is required to pay an instrument has no right of recourse against:
   a. subsequent indorsers.
   b. prior indorsers.
   c. makers and acceptors.
   d. any party.

_____ 12. Susan Kalinowsky owns a business and is known for business purposes as Susan Monroe. She signs her business checks and notes as Susan Monroe.
   a. Susan is liable on these checks and notes, because her signature is valid.
   b. Susan has no liability, because her signature is under an assumed name.
   c. Susan is a fictitious payee.
   d. Susan has secondary liability because the business has primary liability.

_____ 13. A presenter warrants:
   a. that all signatures are genuine and authorized.
   b. that there are no defenses against the instrument.
   c. that he has good title.
   d. that no defenses are good against him.

_____ 14. Harold is the holder of a check that has been dishonored by First Bank. Harold may seek payment:
   a. from the drawee.
   b. from the drawer.
   c. from the indorsers.
   d. from either the drawer or the indorsers.

_____ 15. Betty Bookkeeper is overworked and underpaid. To supplement her income she draws a check on her employer's account at First Bank made payable to Cathy Carson. Betty then indorses the check in Cathy's name and deposits the check in a savings account that she has opened in the name of Cathy Carson. When the employer discovers the scheme, it denies liability and asserts that the bank should bear liability for the checks which have been cashed.
   a. First Bank is liable under the fictitious payee rule.
   b. The employer is liable under the fictitious payee rule.
   c. Cathy Carson is liable under the fictitious payee rule.
   d. The employer is liable under the imposter rule.

SHORT ESSAY

1. Can a drawee bank recover payments made on some forged or altered instruments? Explain. _____
_____
_____
_____

2. If your roommate writes you a check for his or her share of the onthly telephone bill, and it is dishonored by the bank, how concerned should you be about giving the required notice of dishonor? Is your roommate discharged if you unreasonably delay in giving the notice? _____
_____
_____
_____

3. What are the differences between primary and secondary liability? _____
_____
_____
_____

4. When is a drawee liable? _____
_____
_____

BANK DEPOSITS AND COLLECTIONS

PURPOSE

In this chapter you study the process by which a check travels from the payee or holder back to the drawee bank so that the check can be charged to the drawer's account. You study the terminology and liability scheme involving the depositary bank and the intermediary banks and the payor bank. You also study the relationship between the maker of a check and the bank where he has his account. The material covered in this chapter is based upon Article 4 of the Uniform Commercial Code. Many of the concepts in this chapter are similar to those in Article 3 and also to those in Article 8, which deals with investment securities.

CHAPTER CHECKPOINTS

After reading and studying this chapter, you should be able to:

1. Define and distinguish among the depositary, payor, intermediary and collecting banks.

2. Define provisional credit, and discus the 48 hour rule and how and when credit becomes final.

3. Discuss the relationship and duties of the depositary, intermediary, collection and payor banks.

4. Discuss the obligations imposed on the customer and upon the drawee bank as part of their relationship.

5. Define electronic fund transfer, compare it to the check collection process of Article 4 and outline the major provisions of the Electronic Fund Transfer Act.

CHAPTER OUTLINE

A. Collection of Items - The depositary bank is the bank in which the payee or holder deposits a check for credit. Provisional credit is tentative credit for the deposit of an instrument until final credit is given. If the bank permits a customer to draw funds against provisional credit, the bank has given value and is a holder in due course. When the amount of the check has been collected from the payor bank, which is also the drawee banks, the credit becomes final. If the payor bank does not pay the check for some reason, the depositary bank reverses the provisional credit to the customer's account, debits his account, and returns the check to him with a statement of the reason for nonpayment. If he has been allowed to draw against the provisional credit, the customer must provide payment.   The Competitive Equality Banking Act has expedited the availability of funds to depositors. A bank may be both the depositary bank and the payor bank; however, in most cases they are different banks. When the two are different banks, a check must pass from one bank to the other, either directly, or through a clearinghouse or through one or more intermediary banks.   An intermediary bank is a bank involved in the collection process other than the depositary or payor bank. A clearinghouse is an association of banks for the purpose of settling accounts on a daily basis.

1.   Collecting Banks - A collecting bank is any bank that handles an item for payment except for the payor bank.   In the usual situation where the depositary bank and the payor banks are different, the depositary bank gives a provisional credit to its customer, transfers the item to the next bank in the chain, receiving a provisional credit or "settlement" from it, and so on to the payor bank, which then debits the drawer's account.   When the check is paid, the provisional settlements become final. If the payor bank does not pay the item, the process must be reversed so that ultimately the depositary bank charges the account of the customer who deposited the check.   He must then seek recovery from the drawer or indorsers. A collecting bank is an agent of the owner of the check until settlement becomes final.   Any credit provided is provisional until settlement becomes final at which time the depositary collecting bank changes from an agent of the depositor to a debtor of the depositor. The effect of this agency rule is to place the risk of loss on the owner depositor and not on the depositary collecting bank.

   a.   Duty of Care - A collecting bank must use ordinary care in handling an item transferred to it for collection.   It must act within a reasonable time after receipt of the item and must choose a reasonable method of forwarding the item for presentment. A collecting bank acts seasonably if it acts within the midnight deadline.   The midnight deadline means midnight of the banking day following the banking day on which the bank receives the item or notice of its dishonor. If a bank receives a check on Monday, it must take proper action by midnight on Tuesday. The Code allows banks to fix an afternoon hour of 2:00 P.M. or later as a cutoff hour for bookkeeping purposes in order to meet the midnight deadline.

   b.   Indorsements - When an item is restrictvely indorsed with words such as "pay any bank," it is locked into the bank collection system.   When a bank forwards an item for collection, it normally indorses it "pay any bank." This protects the bank by making it impossible for the item to go outside regular banking channels.   The depositary bank may supply any indorsement of its customer that is required unless the item contains the words "payee's indorsement required."

   c.   Warranties - Customers and collecting banks give basically the same warranties as those given by parties under Article 3 of the Code on presentment and transfer.

   d.   Final Payment - A critical issue is at what point in time the item has been paid by the payor bank.   Under the Code, final payment occurs when the payor bank does any of the following, whichever happens first: (1) pays an item in cash; (2) settles and does not reserve the right to revoke the settlement, or does not have such right through agreement, statute, or clearinghouse rule; (3) makes a provisional settlement and does not revoke it in the time and manner permitted by statute, clearinghouse rule, or agreement; or (4) completes the process of posting the item to the account of the drawer.   Posting is normally completed after: (a) verifying any signature; (b) ascertaining that sufficient funds are available; (c) affixing a "paid" or other stamp; (d) entering a charge or entry to a customer's account; and (e) correcting or reversing an entry or erroneous action on the item.

2.   Payor Banks - Under its contract with the drawer, the payor or drawee bank agrees to pay to the payee or his order checks that are issued by the drawer, provided the order is not countermanded by a stop payment order and provided there are sufficient funds in the drawer's account.   Banks have adopted production-line methods for handling checks in order to assure an even flow of items on a day-to-day basis.

B. **Relationship Between Payor Bank and Its Customer** - The relationship between a payor bank and its checking account customer is primarily the product of their contractual arrangement. A bank may not (1) disclaim responsibility for its lack of good faith; (2) disclaim responsibility for its failure to exercise ordinary care; or (3) limit its damages for breach of such lack or failure.

1. **Payment of an Item** - When a payor receives an item for which there are insufficient funds in the account, but which is otherwise properly payable, the bank may either (1) dishonor the item and return it; or (2) pay the item and charge the customer's account even though an overdraft is created as a result. The customer may be liable to pay a service charge and interest on the overdraft. The drawee is not liable on a check until it accepts the item. However, if a bank improperly refuses payment, it will incur liability to its customer from whose account the item should have been paid. If the customer has enough money in his account, the item is less than six months old, and it is in regular form, the bank is liable to the customer for any dishonor, because there is no basis for it to refuse payment. If a wrongful dishonor occurs through mistake, the bank's liability is limited to actual damaged proved, including damages for arrest or other consequential damages. A bank is under no obligation to pay an uncertified check that is over six months old. However, a bank is not obligated to dishonor such a check.

2. **Stop Payment Orders** - The drawer of a check may issue a stop payment order. To be effective, a stop payment order must be received by the bank in time to give it a reasonable opportunity to act on it. An oral stop payment order is binding on the bank for fourteen calendar days. The normal practice is for a customer to confirm an oral stop payment order in writing. The written order is effective for six months and may be renewed in writing. It is possible that when the check is dishonored by the bank, the drawer may incur liability to the holder, particularly if the holder is a holder in due course against whom personal defenses are not effective.

3. **Bank's Right to Subrogation on Improper Payment** - If a payor bank pays an item over a stop payment order or otherwise in violation of its contract with the drawer or maker, the payor bank is subrogated to the rights of (a) any holder in due course on the item against the drawer or maker; (b) the payee or any other holder against the drawer or maker; and (c) the drawer or maker against the payee or any other holder. This allows a bank to pay a holder in due course when the drawer's defense is a personal one notwithstanding the fact that the drawer has issued a valid stop payment order.

4. **Customer's Duties** - The Code imposes affirmative duties on bank customers and fixes time limits within which they must assert their rights. The customer is required to exercise reasonable care and promptness to examine the bank statement and items to discover an unauthorized signature or an alteration; he must notify the bank promptly. The customer must examine the statement and items within a reasonable time, which in no event may exceed fourteen days and must notify the bank of unauthorized signatures and alterations. Any alterations or unauthorized signatures on instruments by the same wrongdoer and paid by the bank during that period will still be the responsibility of the bank, but any paid thereafter but before the customer notifies the bank may not be asserted against it. The customer must always report an alteration or unauthorized signature within one year from the time the statement or items were made available to him or be barred from asserting them against the bank. Any unauthorized indorsement must be asserted within three years from the time the bank statements and items containing such indorsements are made available to the customer.

C. **Electronic Fund Transfers** - Financial institutions seek to substitute EFTs for checks (1) to eliminate the paperwork involved in processing checks; and (2) to eliminate the "float" that a drawer of a check enjoys as a result of having the use of his funds during the check processing period between issuing the check and final payment. An electronic fund transfer has been defined as "any transfer of funds, other than a transaction originated by check, draft, or similar paper instrument, which is initiated through an electronic terminal, telephonic instrument, or computer or magnetic tape so as to order, instruct or authorize a financial institution to debit or credit an account." EFTs have brought about considerable confusion concerning the legal rights of customers and financial institutions. A partial solution has been the enactment of the Electronic Fund Transfer Act, but important legal problems remain.

1. Types of Electronic Fund Transfers - At the moment there are principally four EFTs in use.

    a. Automatic Teller Machines - ATMs permit customers to conduct various transactions with their bank through the use of electronic terminals. After activating an ATM with a plastic identification card and a secret number, customers can deposit and withdraw funds from their accounts, transfer funds between accounts, obtain cash advances from bank credit card accounts and make payments on loans.

    b. Point-of-Sale Systems - Point-of-sale (POS) systems permit consumers to transfer funds from their bank account to a merchant automatically. The POS machines are located within the merchant's store and are activated by the consumer's identification card and code.

    c. Direct Deposits and Withdrawals - Direct deposits of payroll, Social Security and other payments can be made through an electronic terminal. Automatic withdrawals to pay insurance premiums, utility bills, or automobile loan payments are common examples of this type of EFT.

    d. Pay-by-Phone Systems - These permit customers to pay bills by telephoning the bank's computer system and directly transferring funds to a designated third party.

2. Electronic Fund Transfer Act - This act "provides a basic framework establishing the rights, liabilities, and responsibilities of participants in electronic fund transfers" with primary emphasis on "the provision of individual consumer rights." The act does not govern electronic transfers between financial institutions, between financial institutions and businesses, and between businesses. The Act is similar in many respects to the Fair Credit Billing Act, which applies to credit card transactions. It is administered by the Board of Governors of the Federal Reserve System.

    a. Disclosure - The terms and conditions of electronic fund transfers involving a consumer's account must be disclosed in readily understandable language at the time the consumer contracts for such services.

    b. Documentation and Periodic Statements - The financial institution must provide the consumer with written documentation of each transfer made from an electronic terminal at the time of the transfer. The documentation must clearly state the amount involved, the identity of any third party involved, and the location of the terminal. The institution must also provide periodic statements for each account of the consumer.

    c. Preauthorized Transfers - A preauthorized transfer from a consumer's account must be authorized in advance by the consumer in writing, and a copy of the authorization must be provided to the consumer when made. A consumer may stop payment of any preauthorized EFT by notifying the financial institution orally or in writing and up to three business days before the scheduled transfer.

    d. Error Resolution - The consumer has sixty days after the financial institution sends a periodic statement in which to notify the financial institution of any errors that appear on the statement. The financial institution is required to investigate and report the results within ten business days. If it determines that an error did occur, it must properly correct it. Failure to investigate in good faith makes the financial institution liable for treble damages.

    e. Consumer Liability - A consumer's liability is limited to a maximum of $500 if the consumer notifies the financial institution within two days after he learns of the loss or theft. If the consumer does not report the unauthorized use within two days, he is liable for losses up to $500. If the consumer fails to report the unauthorized use within sixty days, he is liable for losses resulting from any unauthorized use that would not have occurred but for the failure of the consumer to report the loss within sixty days.

    f. Liability of Financial Institutions - A financial institution is liable to a consumer for all damages proximately caused by its failure to make an EFT according to the terms and conditions of an account. It will not be liable if:

        1. the consumer's account has insufficient funds through no fault of the financial institution;

        2. the funds are subject to legal process;

3. such transfer would exceed an established credit limit;
4. an electronic terminal has insufficient cash; or
5. circumstances beyond the institution's control prevent the transfer.

The institution is also liable for failure to stop payment of a preauthorized transfer.

DEFINITIONS

1. Depositary bank

2. Payor bank

3. Intermediary banks

4. Collecting bank

5. Provisional credit

6. Final payment

7. Midnight deadline

8. Stop payment order

9. Automated teller machines

10. Point-of-sale systems

11. Preauthorized transfer

TRUE/FALSE

_____ 1. A provisional credit becomes final when the amount of the check has been paid by the drawee.

_____ 2. A collecting bank is strictly liable for mishandling an item transferred to it for collection.

_____ 3. Once a check is restrictively indorsed, only a bank may acquire the rights of a holder.

_____ 4. A payor bank which dishonors an item must either return the item or send written notice of dishonor before midnight of the banking day on which the item is received.

_____ 5. A bank may pay its customer's check and charge her account for the full amount even though there are insufficient funds in her account to cover the check.

_____ 6. A bank may refuse to pay its customer's check even though there are sufficient funds in his account to cover the check.

_____ 7. A bank is required to dishonor its customer's check if the check is over six months old.

_____ 8. A bank may pay a check drawn by its customer even though the bank knows of the death of the customer.

_____ 9. A consumer's liability for unauthorized electronic fund transfer is limited to $100 if the consumer notifies the financial institution within two days after she learns of the loss.

_____ 10. Point-of-sale systems enable a consumer automatically to transfer funds from his bank to a merchant seller.

_____ 11. The payor bank and the drawee bank are the same bank.

_____ 12. The first bank to receive a check fo rpayment is the depositary bank.

_____ 13. When a bank certifies a check, it becomes primarily liable on it.

_____ 14. Banks like electronic funds transfer because it eliminates paperwork.

_____ 15. Pending final payment, various banks in the collection process make a series of provisional settlements.

MULTIPLE CHOICE

_____ 1. If a check is not paid for any reason, the payor bank should:
   a. return it to the drawer.
   b. return it to the drawee.
   c. return it to its transferor.
   d. throw it away.

_____ 2. A depositary bank may treat a check as having been received on Monday if the check was actually received late in the afternoon on:
   a. Tuesday.
   b. Wednesday.
   c. Thursday.
   d. Friday.

_____ 3. In presenting an item for payment, a collecting bank may delay presentment for up to:
   a. one calendar day.
   b. one banking day.
   c. three banking days.
   d. one week.

_____ 4. Which of the following is responsible for examining a check for prior restrictive indorsements?
   a. The depositary bank.
   b. The intermediary bank.
   c. The payor bank.
   d. All of the above must examine it for restrictive indorsements.

_____ 5. Final payment of an item occurs during the processing of the item by:
    a. the depositary bank.
    b. the intermediary banks.
    c. the payor bank.
    d. none of the above.

_____ 6. Assume D issues several checks which are received by the payor bank on the same day. If there are insufficient funds in D's account to cover all the checks, the bank must pay the checks:
    a. in any order it deems convenient.
    b. in the order they were issued.
    c. in the order they were received.
    d. in the order specified by the drawer.

_____ 7. A bank may dishonor a check without incurring a liability to its customer from whose account the item should have been paid if:
    a. payment of the check has been stopped by the drawer.
    b. the check is over six months old.
    c. the signature on the check is forged.
    d. all of the above.

_____ 8. An oral stop payment order:
    a. is not valid.
    b. is valid for 7 days.
    c. is valid for 14 days.
    d. is valid for 6 months.

_____ 9. A written stop payment order:
    a. is valid for 60 days.
    b. is valid for 90 days.
    c. may be renewed in writing.
    d. (a) and (c) but not (b).

_____ 10. If a consumer does not report the loss of theft of his electronic fund transfer card within two days he is liable for losses up to:
    a. $500.
    b. $250.
    c. $50.
    d. any unauthorized use.

_____ 11. The Electronic Funds Transfer Act imposes liability on a customer for unauthorized transfers in the maximum amount of:
    a. $50 in most circumstances.
    b. $100 in most circumstances.
    c. $500 if the consumer fails to notify the financial institution within two days after learning of the loss or theft.
    d. two of the above, (a) and (c).

_____ 12. Any bank to which an item is transferred in the course of collection, other than the depositary or payor banks, is a/an _____ bank.
   a. drawee
   b. intermediary
   c. clearinghouse
   d. federal

_____ 13. First Bank pays a check over a stop payment order of its customer.
   a. First Bank is subrogated to the rights of any holder in due course on the item against the drawer or maker.
   b. First Bank is subrogated to the payee or any other holder against the drawer or maker.
   c. First Bank is subrogated to the rights of the drawer or maker against the payee or any other holder.
   d. All of the above are correct.

_____ 14. A/an _____ permits a consumer to transfer funds from his bank account to a merchant automatically. With this system, machines are located within the merchant's store and are activated by the consumer's identification card and code.
   a. automatic teller machine
   b. point-of-sale system
   c. direct deposit and withdrawal
   d. pay by phone system

_____ 15. When a customer has a checking account at a bank where he deposits funds, the customer is in the role of:
   a. creditor-agent.
   b. debtor-principal.
   c. creditor-principal.
   d. debtor-agent.

SHORT ESSAY

1. Suppose your roommate writes you a chck for his or her share of the monthly phone bill. Do you have to indorse the check when you deposit it? Explain. _____
   _____
   _____
   _____

2. If a bank honors its customer's stop payment order, is he automatically relieved of liability on the check? Explain. _____
   _____
   _____
   _____

3. Arthur issued a check to Brad. Carl stole the check, forged Brad's indorsement, and cashed the check at Arthur's bank. What are the rights of Arthur and of the bank? _____
   _____
   _____

4. David had a bank card that he used for EFT transactions with First Bank. On Tuesday, a thief stole David's wallet, including the bank card. David immediately notified the bank. Nevertheless, the thief withdrew $1,000 from David's account on Wednesday using the card. Discuss David's liability under this fact situation.

PART IV

SAMPLE EXAMINATION

_____ 1. Carl Criminal breaks into Brenda's apartment, steals her checkbook, then makes a check for $100 payable to "cash" and signs Brenda's name in the lower right hand corner of the check. Which of the following is correct regarding this instrument?
   a. Carl is the drawer of the check.
   b. Brenda is the drawer of the check.
   c. The instrument is non-negotiable.
   d. Carl is a fictitious payee.

_____ 2. Bill Businessman has a bearer instrument for $200. He transfers it to Acme Corporation, but does not indorse it. Which of the following is correct regarding this transaction?
   a. Bill incurs contract liability, but not warranty liability by transferring this bearer instrument.
   b. Bill incurs warranty liability, but not contract liability by transferring this bearer instrument.
   c. Bill incurs both contract and warranty liability by transferring this bearer instrument.
   d. Bill incurs neither contract nor warranty liability by transferring this bearer instrument.

_____ 3. First Bank pays an instrument with a forged indorsement which is drawn on the account of Big Bucks, Inc.
   a. First Bank may charge the account of Big Bucks.
   b. First Bank has no recourse against the person from whom it received the check.
   c. First Bank is liable to the named payee for conversion.
   d. None of the above is correct.

_____ 4. First Bank receives a check drawn on one of its accounts from American Bank, an intermediary collecting bank, at 10:00 a.m. Monday during banking hours. When must First Bank either pay or dishonor the item?
   a. Immediately.
   b. By midnight on Monday.
   c. By midnight on Tuesday.
   d. By 3:00 p.m. on Tuesday.

_____ 5. Harold Homeowner calls First Bank to issue a stop payment order on a check he has issued to a door to door salesman selling magazines.
   a. The stop payment order is binding on the bank for 10 days.
   b. The stop payment order is binding on the bank for 14 days.
   c. The stop payment order is binding on the bank for six months.
   d. Oral stop payment orders have no validity under the Code.

_____ 6. First Bank pays the check Harold Homeowner has issued over his oral stop payment order. First Bank has liability to Harold, but its rights are subrogated to the rights of:
   a. the payee against Harold.
   b. Harold against the payee.
   c. any holder in due course against Harold.
   d. Harold against the drawee.

_____ 7. In order to be negotiable under Article 3, an instrument must:
   a.   be signed by the maker or drawer.
   b.   contain an unconditional promise or order to pay a sum certain in money.
   c.   be payable on demand or at a definite time.
   d.   be signed by the maker or drawer, contain an unconditional promise or order to pay a sum certain in money, and be payable on demand or at a definite time.

_____ 8. After a busy day of running errands, Happy Homemaker stops at the grocery store, writes a check for groceries, but fails to insert the date. The instrument as issued by Happy is:
   a.   a negotiable demand instrument.
   b.   a negotiable time instrument.
   c.   non-negotiable.
   d.   an assignment of funds to the grocery store.

_____ 9. Sarah Student indorses a check "For deposit only." This is a _____ indorsement.
   a.   qualified
   b.   restrictive
   c.   special
   d.   blank

_____ 10. Sarah Student has a check that is payable to her order. She indorses it in blank. The insrument is now:
   a.   non-negotiable.
   b.   bearer paper.
   c.   an incomplete instrument.
   d.   a demand instrument.

_____ 11. Bill Businessman signs a blank check and then leaves it on his desk. His son Junior picks it up, and then uses it to buy a $500 VCR from the local electronic store by completing the instrument and making it payable to the store. As the drawer of the check, Bill:
   a.   has no liability on the instrument because it was an incomplete instrument when he signed it.
   b.   has no liability, because it was not completed according to his authorization.
   c.   will be liable since his negligence in leaving the blank check on his desk contributed to the unauthorized completion of the check.
   d.   can sue the bank if they pay the check from Bill's account.

_____ 12. The first bank where a check is deposited for collection is the:
   a.   drawee bank.
   b.   collecting bank.
   c.   presenting bank.
   d.   depositary bank.

_____ 13. Harold is a holder in due course of a negotiable instrument. He takes it:
   a.   free from all defenses.
   b.   subject to real defenses.
   c.   subject to personal defenses.
   d.   subject to all defenses.

_____ 14. Bill Buyer issues a check for $500 payable to the order of Sam Seller and drawn on First Bank.
   a.   First Bank is the drawer; Sam is the drawee; and Bill is the payee.
   b.   Bill is the drawer; Sam is the payee; and First Bank is the drawee.
   c.   Bill is the drawer; Sam is the drawee; and First Bank is the payee.
   d.   First Bank is the holder; Sam is the payor; and Bill is the drawee.

_____ 15. Sam Seller accepted a $400 negotiable demand note from Bill Buyer for goods he sold to him. Sam then negotiated the note to Carl Contractor who qualified as a holder in due course. Carl later indorsed the note to his son Junior as a gift. Unfortunately, Sam had misrepresented the goods to Bill and Bill now wants to dishonor the note based upon fraud in the inducement. Junior, of course, knew nothing about the dealings between Sam and Bill when he accepted the $400 note as a gift from his father.
   a.   Junior is a holder in due course.
   b.   The defense of fraud in the inducement can be asserted against Junior, because he is not a holder in due course.
   c.   Junior is not a holder in due course, but under the shelter rule he has the rights of one. The defense of fraud in the inducement cannot be asserted against him.
   d.   Junior is a mere assignee and has no right to collect the note.

_____ 16. In order for a transferee of a negotiable instrument to become a holder, the transfer must be made by:
   a.   negotiation.
   b.   indorsement.
   c.   assignment.
   d.   delivery.

_____ 17. An indorsement which includes a signature and the words "without recourse" is a/an _____ indorsement.
   a.   blank
   b.   special
   c.   qualified
   d.   restrictive

_____ 18. In what way is a note distinguishable from a draft?
   a.   A note contains an order to pay.
   b.   A draft contains an order to pay.
   c.   A draft is a two party instrument.
   d.   A note is a three party instrument.

_____ 19. Which of the following is "money" for purposes of negotiability?
   a.   Americal dollars.
   b.   French francs.
   c.   Mexican pesos.
   d.   American dollars, French francs and Mexican pesos.

_____ 20. Which of the following is not value for purposes of holder in due course status?
   a.   An executory promise.
   b.   The forgiveness of an antecedent debt.
   c.   The extension of credit by a bank.
   d.   The loan of money in return for security interest in an item.

RELATIONSHIP OF PRINCIPAL AND AGENT

PURPOSE

The law of agency is essential to business, because almost every type of contract or business transaction can be conducted through an agent. Agency is especially important in the case of partnerships and corporations. Partnership law is founded on the agency of the partners; each partner is an agent of the partnership. Each partner has the authority to bind the partnership in transactions pertaining to partnership business. Sole proprietors may, and often do, employ agents to work for them. The manager of a store and outside salesmen are common examples of persons who are agents. Because a corporation is an artificial entity, it can only act through agents. There are two main parts of agency law: (1) the internal part or the relationship between the principal and the agent; and (2) the external part or the relationship between the agent and the principal with third parties. In this chapter, you study the nature and function of agency, as well as other topics involving the internal part of agency law. Agency is primarily governed by State common law, which is presented in an orderly fashion in the Restatements of the Law of Agency.

CHAPTER CHECKPOINTS

After reading and studying this chapter, you should be able to:

1. Distinguish among (a) an agency relationship; (b) an employment relationship; and (c) an independent contractor relationship.

2. Discuss how an agency relationship comes into existence.

3. List and discuss the duties owed by an agent to her principal.

4. List and discuss the duties owed by a principal to his agent.

5. Identify the ways in which an agency relationship comes to an end.

CHAPTER OUTLINE

A. Nature of Agency - Business is very largely conducted, not by the proprietors of businesses, but by their representatives or agents. Agency is the relationship existing between two persons known as the principal and the agent. The agent acts on behalf of and as the business representative of the principal. An agent is not a party but simply an intermediary.

1. Scope of Agency Purposes
   a. The agent may negotiate the terms of contracts with others and bind her principal to such contracts.
   b. Qui facet per alium, facet per se means who acts through another, acts himself.
2. Other Legal Relations
   a. The employment relationship is one in which employer has right of control of the physical conduct if employee.
   b. Independent contractor is a person who contracts with another to do a particular job and is not subject to the control of the other.

B. Creation of Agency - Agency is a consensual relationship that may be formed by contract or agreement between the principal and agent.
   1. Formalities
      a. A power of attorney is a written, formal appointment of an agent.
      b. No particular formality is required in a contract of agency.
   2. Capacity
      a. Contracts entered into by a minor or an incompetent under a guardianship are voidable.
      b. Minors and incompetents not under guardianship can act as agents. The contract of agency may be voidable, but the contract with the principal and the third party is still valid.

C. Duties of Agent to Principal - An agent is liable for any loss caused to the principal for breach of any of these duties.
   1. Duty of Obedience - The duty of obedience requires the agent to act in the principal's affairs only as authorized by the principal and to obey all reasonable instructions and directions.
   2. Duty of Diligence - An agent must act with reasonable care and skill in performing the work for which he is employed.
   3. Duty to Inform - An agent must use reasonable efforts to give the principal information that is relevant to the affairs entrusted to her and that, as the agent knows or should know, the principal would desire to have.
   4. Duty to Account - The agent is under a duty to maintain nd provide the principal with a true and complete account of money or other property that the agent has received or expended on behalf of the principal.
   5. Fiduciary Duty - A fiduciary duty is imposed by law and is owed by a trustee to beneficiary of a trust. It is a duty of utmost loyalty and good faith owed by agent to principal.

D. Duties of Principal to Agent - More emphasis is placed on the duties of the agent than on those of the principal.
   1. Contractual Duty
      a. Compensation - The most important duty of the principal is to compensate the agent as specified in the contract.
      b. Reimbursement - It is the duty owed by principal to pay back authorized payments agent has made on principal's behalf.
      c. Indemnification - It is the duty owed by principal to agent to pay agent for losses incurred while acting, as directed by principal.
   2. Tort Duties - Among these is the duty to provide an employee with reasonably safe conditions of employment and to warn the employee of any unreasonable risk involved in the employment.

E. Termination of Agency - The power of the agent to bind the principal to contracts with third persons with whom the agent has previously dealt will continue until such persons have been notified or have knowledge of the revocation.

1. Acts of Parties - Termination by acts of the parties may be acts of both principal and agent or by the act of either one.
   a. Lapse of Time - Authority conferred upon an agent for a specified time terminates at the end of that period.
   b. Mutual Agreement of the Parties - The agency relationship is created by agreement and may be terminated at any time by mutual agreement of the principal and the agent.
   c. Fulfillment of Purpose
   d. Revocation of Authority - A principal may revoke an agent's authority at any time.
   e. Renunciation by the Agent - The agent has the power to put an end to the agency by notice to the principal that she renounces the authority given her by the principal.
2. Operation of Law - As a matter of law, an agency relationship is terminated by the following events.
   a. Bankruptcy - Bankruptcy is a proceeding in a Federal court affording relief to financially troubled debtors. If the credit standing of the agent is important to the agency relationship, then it will be terminated by the bankruptcy of the agent.
   b. Death - The death of the principal terminates the authority of the agent. The authority given to an agent by a principal is strictly personal, and the agent's death terminates the agency.
   c. Incapacity - Incapacity of the principal that occurs after the formation of the agency terminates the agent's authority. Subsequent incapacity of an agent to perform the acts authorized by the principal terminates the agent's authority.
   d. Change in Business Conditions - The authority of an agent is terminated by notice or knowledge of a change in the value of the subject matter or of a change in business conditions from which the agent should reasonably infer that the principal would not consent to an exercise of the authority given to them.
   e. Loss or Destruction of the Subject Matter - Where the authority of the agent relates to a specific subject matter that becomes lost or destroyed, her authority is thereby terminated.
   f. Loss of Qualification of Principal or Agent - When the authority given the agent relates to the conduct of a certain business for which a license from the government or regulatory agency is required the failure to acquire or the authority of the agent.
   g. Disloyalty of Agent - If an agent, without the knowledge of her principal, acquires interests that are adverse to those of the principal or otherwise breaches her duty of loyalty to the principal, her authority to act on behalf of the principal is terminated.
   h. Change of Law - A change in the law that takes effect after the employment of the agent may cause the performance of the authorized act to be illegal, or criminal. A change in the law terminates the agency relationship.
   i. Outbreak of War - Where the outbreak of war places the principal and agent in the position of alien enemies, the authority of the agent is terminated because its exercise is illegal. When the exercise may be hazardous, the agency is terminated.
3. Irrevocable Agencies - When agency is coupled with an interest, it is an irrevocable agency. This occurs where the agent has a security interest in the subject matter of the agency. The death of the principal will not terminate the agency unless the duty for which the security was given terminates with the death of the principal.

DEFINITIONS

1. Agent

2. Principal

3. Employee

4. Independent contractor

5. Diligence

6. Fiduciary duty

7. Reimbursement

8. Indemnification

9. Irrevocable agency

TRUE/FALSE

_____ 1. An agency relationship may only be created by contract.

_____ 2. An agent who is incompetent to bind himself by contract may not make a contract which is binding on his principal.

_____ 3. An agent is under a duty to keep her principal's property separate from her own.

_____ 4. A principal is under no duty to reimburse his agent for unauthorized expenses incurred by the agent.

_____ 5. An agent may make a contract which is binding on his principal even though the principal has terminated the agent's authority.

_____ 6. A person who engages an independent contractor to do a specific job has a right to control the conduct and activities of the independent contractor in the performance of his contract.

_____ 7. An independent contractor cannot be an agent.

_____ 8. A power of attorney is a formal appointment of an agent.

_____ 9. An agent has no duty to account for property or gifts received.

_____ 10. An agency contract must be in writing.

_____ 11. The principal-agent relationship is a fiduciary relationship.

_____ 12. A principal may revoke an agent's authority at any time, but if he does, he may be in breach of his contract with the agent.

_____ 13. Brian is appointed an agent for Independent Investors, Inc. Two months later, Brian files for bankruptcy because of personal debts arising prior to beginning work for III. Brian's agency is terminated by the bankruptcy.

_____ 14. An agency coupled with an interest can be revoked at any time.

_____ 15. A principal has no duty to compensate his agent.

MULTIPLE CHOICE

_____ 1. A person may ordinarily appoint an agent to:
   a. perform a contract for personal services.
   b. commit an illegal act.
   c. negotiate the terms of a contract for personal services.
   d. (a) and (c) but not (b).

_____ 2. Any contracts resulting from the appointment of an agent by a minor are:
   a. void.
   b. voidable.
   c. unenforceable.
   d. none of the above.

_____ 3. An agent may not ordinarily represent her principal in a transaction in which:
   a. she has a personal interest.
   b. she is acting on behalf of a competitor of her principal.
   c. she is acting on behalf of anyone whose interests conflict with those of her principal.
   d. all of the above.

_____ 4. Assume that S wants to sell his house and B is interested in buying it. If A is an agent who normally handles such transactions, A may represent:
   a. S or B, but not both.
   b. S and B, but only with the informed consent of S.
   c. S and B, but only with the informed consent of B.
   d. S and B, but only with the informed consent of S and B.

_____ 5. Where the agent has an interest in the subject matter of the agency, the agent's authority is terminated by:
   a. the death of the principal.
   b. the bankruptcy of the principal.
   c. a revocation of authority.
   d. the mutual agreement of the parties.

_____ 6. Mel Merchant owns a retail store. Sarah Salesclerk works for Mel in the store. The relationship between Sarah and Mel is an example of:
   a. employer and independent contractor.
   b. master and servant.
   c. principal and agent.
   d. either master and servant or principal and agent.

_____ 7. Bill Businessman hires Andrew Attorney to represent him in a lawsuit. The relationship between Bill and Andrew is an example of:
   a. employer and independent contractor.
   b. master and servant.
   c. principal and agent.
   d. both employer and independent contractor and principal and agent.

_____ 8. In modern terminology, a master-servant relationship is most synonymous with:
   a. employer and independent contractor.
   b. employer and employee.
   c. agent and principal.
   d. employer and agent.

_____ 9. Peter Principal listed a parcel of real estate with Ron Realtor. Two months later, Peter decides not to sell the property and revokes Ron's authority.
   a. Peter cannot revoke Ron's authority.
   b. Peter has the power to revoke Ron's authority, but does not have the right to revoke it.
   c. Peter may be liable to Ron for damages for breach of contract.
   d. Two of the above, (b) and (c).

_____ 10. A principal owes an agent a duty of:
   a. loyalty.
   b. care.
   c. compensation.
   d. loyalty, care and compensation.

SHORT ESSAY

1. What is an agent's fiduciary duty? _____
_____
_____
_____

2. What are the practical consequences of an agent's fiduciary duty? _____
_____
_____
_____

3. Distinguish between an employer-employee relationship and an employer-independent contractor relationship. Give an example of each. _____
_____
_____
_____

4. Under what circumstances does an employer have an obligation to reimburse an employee? _____
_____
_____
_____

RELATIONSHIP WITH THIRD PARTIES

PURPOSE

In this chapter, you study the external part of agency involving the relationship between the agent and third parties with reference to the liability of the agent and of the principal to those third parties. In general with regard to contracts, so long as the agent operates within his actual or apparent authority, the principal and the third party acquire contractual rights and liabilities to each other, but the agent has neither. However, in some situations, the agent will assume either rights or liabilities as a result of his actions. In addition to studying the contractual liability of the principal and agent, you also study the liability of the principal and agent for torts committed by the agent.

CHAPTER CHECKPOINTS

After reading and studying this chapter, you should be able to:

1. Distinguish between and identify actual authority and apparent authority.

2. Discuss the liability of principal and the agent to third parties upon termination of the agency relationship.

3. Distinguish between a disclosed principal, an undisclosed principal and a partially disclosed principal and discuss the liability of each with respect to third parties.

4. Define the doctrine of respondeat superior and discuss when a principal will be liable for the torts of his agent under the doctrine.

5. Discuss when an agent will be liable for the commission of authorized and unauthorized torts.

CHAPTER OUTLINE

I. Relationship of Principal and Third Persons - The purpose of an agency relationship is to allow the principal to extend his business activities by authorizing agents to enter into contracts with third persons on the principal's behalf.
    A. Contract Liability of the Principal - Authority is the power of an agent to change the legal status of his principal. The authority of an agent to act for his principal in business transactions is the basis of

agency.
1. Types of Authority
   a. Actual authority is the power conferred upon agent by actual consent given by principal.
   b. Apparent authority is power conferred upon agent by acts or conducts of principal that reasonably lead a third party to believe that agent has such powers.
   c. Express authority is the actual authority derived from written or spoken words of principal.
   d. Implied authority is the actual authority inferred from words or conduct manifested to agent by principals.
2. Fundamental Rules of Contractual Liability
   a. A disclosed principal and the third party are contractually bound if the agent acts within her actual or apparent authority in making the contract.
   b. A partially disclosed principal and the third party are contractually bound if the agent acts within her actual or apparent authority in making the contract.
   c. An undisclosed principal and the third party are contractually bound if the agent acts within her actual authority in making the contract unless (a) the principal is excluded by the terms of the contract; or (b) his existence is fraudulently concealed.
3. Delegation of Authority - A subagent is a person appointed by agent to perform agent's duties.
4. Effect of Termination of Agency Upon Authority
   a. Actual notice is the knowledge actually and expressly communicated.
   b. Constructive notice is knowledge imputed by law.
5. Ratification - Ratification is the affirmation by one person of a prior act that another, without authority, has done as his agent.

B. Tort Liability of the Principal - Tort liability may arise directly or indirectly vicariously from authorized or unauthorized acts of the agent.
1. Direct Liability of Principal - A principal may be held liable in damages for his own negligence or recklessness in carrying out an activity through employees or agents.
2. Vicarious Liability of Principal for Authorized Act of Agent - A vicarious liability is indirect legal responsibility for the act of another.
3. Vicarious Liability of Principal for Unauthorized Acts of Agent
   a. The liability of a principal for unauthorized torts by an agent depends primarily on whether the agent is an employee or not.
   b. A respondeat superior lets the superior (employer) respond.
   c. An independent contractor is not the employee of the person for whom he is performing work or rendering services.

C. Criminal Liability of the Principal - A principal is liable for the authorized criminal acts of his agents only if the principal directed, participated in or approved of the act.

II. Relationship of Agent and Third Persons - The function of an agent is to assist in the conduct of the principal's business by carrying out his orders.
A. Contract Liability of Agent - The agent is not normally a party to the contract he makes with a third person.
1. Disclosed Principals - A disclosed principal is one whose existence and identity are known.
2. Unauthorized Contracts - If an agent exceeds his actual and apparent authority, the principal is not bound.
3. Agent Assumes Liability - An agent may agree to become liable on a contract between the principal and the third party.
4. Partially Disclosed Principal - An agent acts for a partially disclosed principal if the third party has noticed that the agent is acting for a principal but has no notice of the principal's identity.

5. Undisclosed Principals - An agent acts for an undisclosed principal when she appears to be acting in her own behalf and the third person with whom she is dealing has no knowledge that she is acting as an agent.

6. Nonexistent or Incompetent Principal - A person who purports to act as agent for a principal, whom both the agent and the third party know to be nonexistent or incompetent, is personally liable on a contract entered into with a third person on behalf of such a principal.

B. Tort Liability of Agent - An agent is personally liable for his tortious acts that injure third persons, whether or not such acts are authorized by the principals and whether or not the principal may also be liable.

C. Rights of Agent Against Third Persons - An agent who makes a contract with a third person on behalf of a disclosed principal usually has no right of action against the third person for breach of contract.

DEFINITIONS

1. Actual express authority

2. Actual implied authority

3. Apparent authority

4. Actual notice

5. Constructive notice

6. Ratification

7. Vicarious liability

8. Respondeat superior

9. Non-delegable duty

10. Implied warranty of authority

11. Undisclosed principal

12. Partially disclosed principal

13. Disclosed principal

14. Non-existent principal

TRUE/FALSE

_____ 1. An agent who has express authority to sell his principal's car ordinarily has implied authority to do whatever is reasonably necessary to sell the car.

_____ 2. An agent has no apparent authority to bind her principal in any transaction in which the identity of the principal is not disclosed.

_____ 3. An agent may not ordinarily appoint a subagent to perform the agent's duties.

_____ 4. An agent's actual authority is terminated by a revocation of authority.

_____ 5. An agent's apparent authority is terminated by a renunciation of authority.

_____ 6. A principal may not be held liable for the wrongful acts of his agent if the agent acted in flagrant disobedience of the principal's instructions.

_____ 7. Under the doctrine of respondeat superior, a principal may be held liable for the torts of her agent even though the agent is sufficiently solvent to pay for the damage himself.

_____ 8. A principal is ordinarily liable for the unauthorized criminal acts of his agents.

_____ 9. An agent who knowingly enters into a contract on behalf of a nonexistent principal is personally liable on the contract.

_____ 10. An agent who is personally liable on a contract has no right of action against the third person for breach of the contract.

MULTIPLE CHOICE

_____ 1. An agent may bind her principal by acts which are within the scope of her:
   a. express authority.
   b. implied authority.
   c. apparent authority.
   d. all of the above.

_____ 2. An agent may be liable to his principal for exceeding his actual authority even though his acts are within the scope of his:
   a. express authority.
   b. implied authority.
   c. apparent authority.
   d. none of the above.

_____ 3. An agent has apparent authority to bind her principal in any transaction in which:
   a. third persons have no knowledge of the agency relationship.
   b. the existence and identity of the principal are undisclosed.
   c. third persons reasonably rely upon the existence of actual authority as indicated by the principal's conduct.
   d. none of the above.

_____ 4. When an agency is terminated by operation of law, the agent's apparent authority continues with respect to third parties with whom the agent had previously dealt until they:
  a. receive actual notice of the termination.
  b. receive constructive notice of the termination.
  c. read of the termination in a newspaper of general circulation.
  d. none of the above.

_____ 5. An agent who, without authority, enters into a contract with a third person on behalf of his principal binds:
  a. his principal but not the third person.
  b. the third person but not his principal.
  c. neither his principal nor the third person.
  d. both his principal and the third person.

_____ 6. Ratification of an unauthorized contract is effective to bind the principal and a third person to the contract even though:
  a. the principal does not ratify the entire contract.
  b. the principal does not ratify the third person of his intent to ratify the contract.
  c. the third person has already notified the principal of his withdrawal from the contract.
  d. the agent failed to indicate to the third person that his acts were on behalf of the principal.

_____ 7. If P directs his agent, A, to slash the tires on competitor C's car, who is liable to C for the damage?
  a. P only.
  b. A only.
  c. Both P and A.
  d. Neither P nor A.

_____ 8. The doctrine of respondeat superior imposes liability upon:
  a. an employer.
  b. an employee.
  c. an independent contractor.
  d. a fellow servant.

_____ 9. Assume that A enters into a contract with T on behalf of A's undisclosed principal, P. If T fails to discover the existence of P, whom may T hold to performance of the contract?
  a. A only.
  b. P only.
  c. A or P but not both.
  d. Neither A nor P.

_____ 10. Assume that A enters into a contract with T on behalf of A's undisclosed principal, P. If T discovers the existence and identity of P, whom may T hold to performance of the contract?
  a. A only.
  b. P only.
  c. A or P but not both.
  d. Neither A nor P.

SHORT ESSAY

1. What is the difference between actual authority and apparent authority? _____
    _____
    _____
    _____

2. What is the difference between having the power to bind one's principal and having the right to bind him?
    _____
    _____
    _____

3. Under respondeat superior, who ultimately foots the bill for an employee's tortious conduct? _____
    _____
    _____
    _____

4. When is an agent liable for the torts he commits? When is the principal liable for the torts of his agent?
    _____
    _____
    _____

PART V

SAMPLE EXAMINATION

TRUE/FALSE

_____ 1. Historically the employment relationship has been referred to as a master-servant relationship.

_____ 2. An agency relationship always requires a formal written contract.

_____ 3. The principal generally retains the power to revoke the agent's authority, even though he may be liable for resulting damage to the agent.

_____ 4. An employer has a duty to provide an employee with reasonably safe conditions of employment and to warn the employee of any unreasonable risk involved in the employment.

_____ 5. Martin is the manager of the Paymark Discount Store. He has implied authority to hire and fire salesclerks to work in the store.

_____ 6. The principle of respondeat superior applies to independent contractors.

_____ 7. Carl Contractor hires Andrew Attorney to negotiate a contract on his behalf. Andrew is both an independent contractor and an agent acting on behalf of Carl.

_____ 8. A master is never liable for intentional torts committed by his servants.

_____ 9. Although the agent has duties to the principal, the principal has no duties to the agent.

_____ 10. Ron Realtor is hired by Lyle Landowner to find a purchaser for a 10 acre hobby farm he owns in the country. Two days later, Paula Purchaser comes to Ron and asks him whether he would be willing to be her agent in finding a small acreage in the country for her to buy. Ron agrees. Ron can serve as agent to both Lyle and Paula in arranging a deal between them without violating any of his duties as an agent.

MULTIPLE CHOICE

_____ 11. The Individual Indemnity Insurance company hires Audrey Agent to sell insurance for it. Audrey makes her own hours and drives her own automobile to see prospects. While hurrying to see a customer, Audrey drives a little too fast for the weather conditions and negligently injures a pedestrian. The pedestrian sues Individual Indemnity for his injuries.
   a. The pedestrian can recover from Individual Indemnity.
   b. Audrey was an independent contractor for whose physical acts Individual Indemnity was not liable.
   c. Audrey's authority to sell insurance policies means that Individual Indemnity will be liable for policies which Audrey sells on its behalf.
   d. Two of the above, (b) and (c).

_____ 12. Ratification by a principal of an unauthorized act may occur by:
   a. silence that indicates consent.
   b. express statements.
   c. acceptance of the benefits of the contract.
   d. silence indicating consent, express statements, and acceptance of the benefits of the contract.

_____ 13. When a principal terminates an agent who has dealt with third parties and has collected accounts on the principal's behalf, the principal must give the third parties _____ notice of the termination of the agent's authority.
   a. constructive
   b. actual
   c. no
   d. written

_____ 14. Power conferred upon an agent by acts or conduct of the principal that reasonably lead a third party to believe that the agent has such power is known as:
   a. actual authority.
   b. apparent authority.
   c. implied authority.
   d. constructive authority.

_____ 15. Sam is a salesman at the Paymart Discount Store. He inadvertently misrepresents the capabilities of a computer which he sells to Thomas. Thomas is upset and sues the Paymart Store for breach of an express warranty.
   a. Paymart has no liability, because it did not authorize the misrepresentation.
   b. Paymart has no liability, because Sam's misrepresentation was not a tort.
   c. Paymart is responsible for Sam's unauthorized misrepresentations.
   d. Paymart has no liability, because it did not authorize Sam to make the misrepresentation.

_____ 16. The powers specifically granted by a principal to his agent constitute:
   a. express authority.
   b. implied authority.
   c. apparent authority.
   d. customary authority.

_____ 17. When a principal's existence is known but his identity is not known, the principal is known as a:
   a. disclosed principal.
   b. undisclosed principal.
   c. partially disclosed principal.
   d. fiduciary.

_____ 18. A principal is generally liable for the torts committed by a/an _____ within the scope of his employment but not for the torts of a/an _____.
   a. employee, servant
   b. employee, independent contractor
   c. independent contractor, servant
   d. independent contractor, agent

_____ 19. Duties that are owed by the agent to the principal include:
   a.   the duty of obedience.
   b.   the duty of diligence.
   c.   the duty to inform.
   d.   the duties of obedience and diligence, and the duty to inform.

_____ 20. Arthur authorizes Bob to sell his eighty acres of farm land for $800 per acre. Subsequently, oil is discovered on the neighboring land and Arthur's land greatly increases in value. Bob is aware of this, but Arthur is not.
   a.   Bob can sell the land to his brother for $800 per acre.
   b.   Bob can sell the land to a stranger for $800 per acre, but not to his brother.
   c.   Bob's authority to sell the land is terminated by operation of law.
   d.   Bob's authority to sell the land is terminated by the acts of the parties.

NATURE AND FORMATION

PURPOSE

This is the first of four chapters dealing with partnerships and the first of three chapters dealing with general partnerships, which are frequently referred to simply as partnerships. The fourth chapter deals with limited partnerships, which are a special form of partnership. The law of partnerships is uniform throughout the United States, because most States have adopted the Uniform Partnership Act with only a few variations. Partnerships are an important form of business organization in that they allow individuals with different expertise, backgrounds, resources and interests to bring their various skills together to form a more competitive enterprise. Partnerships are relatively easy to form. However, there can be disadvantages to the partnership form of business, and as you study the chapters in this section, you should note the disadvantages as well as the advantages of the partnership form of business organization.

CHAPTER CHECKPOINTS

After reading and studying this chapter, you should be able to:

1. Identify and discuss the situations when a partnership is treated as a legal entity and those situations for which it is treated as an aggregate.

2. List the main provisions which should be included in a partnership agreement and discuss the legal reasons for the inclusion of these provisions.

3. Give the UPA definition of a partnership and discuss the tests for the existence of a partnership.

4. Distinguish between partnership capital and partnership property.

5. Discuss the rights that a partner has in partnership property in contrast to the rights that a partner has in the partnership itself.

CHAPTER OUTLINE

A. Nature of Partnership
   1. Definition of Partnership - The partnership form of business organization is an extremely old form of

business association. Today the law governing partnerships is the Uniform Partnership Act, which has been adopted in all States except Louisiana as well as the District of Columbia, the Virgin Islands, and Guam. Areas not provided for by the Act are governed by the rules of the common law and equity. The UPA defines a partnership as "an association of two or more persons to carry on as co-owners of a business for profit."

2. Entity Theory - A legal entity is an organization having a separate legal existence from its members. It is a unit with the capacity of possessing legal rights and being subject to legal duties. A legal entity may acquire, own, and dispose of property. It may also enter into contracts, sue and be sued. At common law, a partnership was regarded as a legal aggregate. The UPA treats a partnership as a legal entity for some purposes. Specifically, a partnership is considered as separate and distinct from its members in that (1) partnership assets are treated as those of a business and are considered separate and distinct from the assets of its members; (2) title to real estate may be acquired by a partnership in the partnership name; (3) a partner is accountable as a fiduciary to the partnership; (4) every partner is considered an agent of the partnership; and (5) under the doctrine of marshaling of assets, partnership creditors have a prior right to partnership assets while creditors of the individual members have a prior right to the separate assets of their individual debtors. Some States and some courts have extended entity treatment to other matters also.

3. Partnership as Legal Aggregate - A partnership is considered an aggregate for some purposes. It can neither sue nor be sued in the firm name unless a statute specifically so allows. The debts of the partnership are ultimately the debts of the individual partners. In addition, a partnership generally lacks continuity of existence. The Internal Revenue Code treats a partnership as an aggregate. The partnership must file an information return, but the individual partners and not the partnership pay the taxes. Partnership income is taxed to the individual partners regardless of whether the income is actually distributed.

4. Types of Partners - A general partner is a member of either a general or limited partnership with unlimited liability for its debts, full management powers and a right to share in the profits. A limited partner is a member of a limited partnership with liability for its debts only to the extent of his capital contribution. A secret partner is one whose membership in the firm is not disclosed to the public. A dormant partner is one who is both a silent and secret partner.

B. Formation of Partnership - Partnership formation is simple and may be done consciously or unconsciously. A partnership may be formed from an oral or written agreement, an informal arrangement, or from the conduct of the partners. A partnership of only general partners is referred to as a "general partnership." A silent partner is one who has no voice and elects to take no part in the partnership business. The legal existence of a partnership depends upon the explicit or implicit agreement of the parties and the existence of (1) common ownership in a business; (2) the sharing of profits and losses; and (3) the right to manage the business.

1. Articles of Partnership - It is preferable but not required that the partners put their agreement in writing. A written agreement creating a partnership is referred to as the partnership agreement or the articles of partnership. It should include: (1) the firm name and the identity of the partners; (2) the nature and scope of the partnership business; (3) the duration of the partnership; (4) the capital contribution of each partner; (5) the division of profits and the sharing of losses; (6) the duties of each partner in the management; (7) a provision for salaries (optional); (8) restrictions on the authority of partners to bind the firm; (9) provisions on the withdrawal of a partner; and (10) a provision for continuation of the business by the remaining partners.

a. Statute of Frauds - A writing is not required for the formation of a partnership. However, a contract to form a partnership to continue for a specified period longer than one year is within the statute and requires a writing to be enforceable.

b. Firm Name - The name selected should not be identical with or deceptively similar to any other existing business concern. The name of the partners may be used, or they may use a fictitious or assumed name. A partnership may not use a name that would be likely to indicate to the public that it is a corporation. Nearly all States have statutes that require that any person transacting business under an assumed or fictitious name file a certificate setting forth the real names and addresses of all persons conducting business as partners or proprietors under an assumed or fictitious name.

2. Tests of Partnership Existence - Partnerships can be created without the slightest formality. There are three components to the UPA definition, all of which have to be met to have a partnership: (1) an association of two or more persons; (2) conducting a business for profit; (3) which they co-own.

    a. Association - A partnership must have two or more persons who agree to become partners. Any natural person having full capacity may enter into a partnership. No person may become a member of a partnership without the consent of all the partners. A minor may become a partner, but he has the right to disaffirm the partnership agreement at any time in order to avoid personal liability. A nonadjudicated incompetent may become a partner, although incompetency affords the co-partners a ground for seeking dissolution by court decree. An adjudicated incompetent lacks contractual capacity and may not become a partner. A corporation is a "person" within the meaning of the UPA and may enter into a partnership; a partnership may also be a member of another partnership.

    b. Business for Profit - Co-ownership does not of itself establish a partnership, even though the co-owners share the profits derived from use of the property. Social clubs, fraternal orders, civic societies, and charitable organizations cannot be partnerships. Co-ownership of the means or instrumentality of accomplishing a single business transaction or a limited series of transactions may result in a joint venture but not a general partnership.

    c. Co-ownership - Although co-ownership of property used in business is not sufficient for the existence of a partnership, the co-ownership of a business is essential. In determining whether co-ownership of a business exists, the sharing of profits, the sharing of losses, and the right to manage and control the business are important. The receipt of profits of a business is a prima facie evidence that a person is a partner in a business unless the profits are received in payment of (1) a debt; (2) wages of an employee or rent to a landlord; (3) an annuity to a widow or representative of a deceased partner; (4) interest on a loan; or (5) as consideration for the sale of the good will of a business. The sharing of gross returns, in contrast to profits, does not of itself establish a partnership. Nor does participation in the management or control of a business furnish conclusive proof of a partnership relation. However, an agreement to share losses furnishes strong evidence of an ownership interest.

3. Partnership Capital and Property - The total money and property contributed by the partners and dedicated to the permanent use in the enterprise is the partnership capital. Partnership property is the sum of all of the partnership assets (including capital contributions). It may vary in amount, whereas partnership capital is a fixed amount, changed only by an amendment to the articles of partnership. By the terms of the agreement, a partner may contribute no capital but only his skill and services, or a partner may contribute the use of certain property rather than the property itself. A loan by a partner should be distinguished from capital. A clear differentiation should be made between capital and profits.

4. Rights in Specific Partnership Property - A partner's ownership interest in any specific item of partnership property is that of a tenant in partnership. Tenancy in partnership is equal among the co-partners, but gives no right to possess the property for any other purpose; a partner may not make an assignment of his right in specific partnership property; the partner's interest in specific property is not subject to attachment or execution by his individual creditors; and upon the death of a partner, his right in specific partnership property vests in the surviving partner or partners.

5. Partner's Interest in the Partnership - In addition to owning an interest in every specific item of partnership property, each partner has an interest in the partnership that is defined as his share of the profits and surplus and is stated to be personal property.

a. Assignability - A partner may sell or assign his interest in the partnership. The new owner does not become a partner, does not succeed to the right to participate in management, and does not have access to the information available to a partner as a matter of right. He is merely entitled to receive the share of profits and rights on liquidation to which the assigning partner would be entitled.

b. Creditors' Rights - A partner's interest is subject to the claims of creditors who may obtain a charging order against the partner's interest. A creditor who has charged the interest of a partner with a judgment debt may apply for the appointment of a receiver who when appointed by the court will receive and hold for the creditor a portion of the profits that would ordinarily be paid to the partner, but who does not become a partner himself.

DEFINITIONS

1. Partnership

2. Person

3. Legal entity

4. Aggregate

5. General partner

6. Limited partner

7. Silent partner

8. Secret partner

9. Dormant partner

10. Articles of partnership

11. Joint venture

12. Capital contribution

13. Partnership capital

14. Partnership property

TRUE/FALSE

_____ 1. Every partner is considered an agent of the partnership.

_____ 2. Any one partner may be held liable for the entire indebtedness of the partnership.

_____ 3. A partnership is required to pay Federal income tax on its income.

_____ 4. A partnership agreement must be in writing.

_____ 5. A partnership may use the name of an existing corporation as long as no other partnership is using that name.

_____ 6. A person may be a partner even though he has no authority to conduct the ordinary activities of the business.

_____ 7. A partnership relation exists whenever a person has any right to manage and control the business.

_____ 8. A partner may not ordinarily withdraw his capital contribution without the consent of all the partners.

_____ 9. Upon dissolution, a debt owing to a partner has priority over debts owing to creditors.

_____ 10. Partners may agree to share the profits and losses of the business unequally.

_____ 11. The UPA is a "gap-filler" in that the partners can agree to provisions in their partnership agreement that are different from those in the UPA.

_____ 12. Areas not covered by the UPA are governed by the rules of the common law and equity.

_____ 13. The sharing of losses has no relevance as to the existence of a partnership.

_____ 14. A partner may not sell or assign his interest in the partnership.

_____ 15. A creditor who has obtained a charging order becomes a partner in the partnership.

MULTIPLE CHOICE

_____ 1. Under the UPA, a partnership may be formed by two or more:
       a. individuals.
       b. partnerships.
       c. corporations
       d. all of the above.

_____ 2. A general partner is one:
       a. who is liable for partnership indebtedness only to the extent of the capital which he has contributed.
       b. who has full management power.
       c. whose membership in the firm is disclosed to the public.
       d. none of the above.

_____ 3. No person may become the member of a partnership without the consent of:
       a. at least one partner.
       b. two or more partners.
       c. a majority of the partners.
       d. all of the partners.

Chapter 29

_____ 4. A partnership agreement entered into by an adjudicated incompetent is:
   a. void.
   b. voidable.
   c. unenforceable.
   d. none of the above.

_____ 5. A minor partner who disaffirms the partnership agreement is personally liable to partnership creditors to the extent of:
   a. his capital contribution.
   b. his accrued and unpaid share of the profits.
   c. the entire indebtedness of the partnership.
   d. (a) and (b) but not (c).

_____ 6. No writing is required in order to enforce:
   a. a contract for the transfer of interest in land to or by a partnership.
   b. a contract to form a partnership for a period longer than one year.
   c. the promise of an incoming partner to assume existing debts incurred in the prior operations of the business.
   d. all of the above.

_____ 7. The name of a partnership should not be:
   a. a fictitious or assumed name.
   b. deceptively similar to the name of any other existing business concern.
   c. the name of only one of the partners.
   d. all of the above.

_____ 8. A partnership agreement which restricts the authority of particular partners to bind the partnership is:
   a. void.
   b. voidable.
   c. unenforceable.
   d. none of the above.

_____ 9. A person who is entitled to receive a share of the profits of a partnership is prima facie a partner unless the payment is of:
   a. a debt to a creditor.
   b. rent to a landlord.
   c. wages to an employee.
   d. all of the above.

_____ 10. Title to real estate which is purchased with partnership funds may stand in the name of:
   a. the partnership.
   b. an individual partner.
   c. a third partner.
   d. all of the above.

_____ 11. Partnership property is held by the partners as:
    a. tenants in partnership.
    b. tenants in common.
    c. joint tenants.
    d. trust property for creditors.

_____ 12. Which of the following is necessary to establish the existence of a partnership?
    a. The partners must have a formal written agreement.
    b. The partners must all be above the age of majority.
    c. The partnership must follow all rules set forth in the UPA.
    d. The partnership must carry on a business for profit.

_____ 13. Arthur, Betty and Christopher are partners in a business that owns an apartment building in the firm's name. Upon Arthur's death, Arthur's ownership interest in the specific partnership property:
    a. vests in the remaining partners.
    b. vests in the remaining partners and Arthur's estate.
    c. must be divided among the two remaining partners and Arthur's heirs.
    d. vests in Arthur's estate.

_____ 14. A partner that is both silent and secret is a:
    a. limited partner.
    b. dormant partner.
    c. general partner.
    d. creditor with a charging order.

_____ 15. Every partner is a/an _____ of the partnership.
    a. employee
    b. employer
    c. agent
    d. creditor

SHORT ESSAY

1. What are the factors considered by a court in determining whether a partnership relation exists? _____
_____
_____
_____

2. Why would anyone want to prove the existence of a partnership relation? _____
_____
_____
_____

3. Is a partnership a legal entity? Explain. _____
_____
_____
_____

4.   Two sisters have inherited an apartment building from their parents. They agree that one sister will live in the building and manage it as she sees fit and will pay the other sister 1/3 of the profits from the building. Is this a partnership? Explain. _____

_____

_____

_____

CHAPTER 30

RIGHTS AND DUTIES

PURPOSE

In this chapter, you study the interactions among the partners as well as with third persons in the operation and management of a partnership. In the first part of the chapter, you study the relationship of the partners to one another. The duties and rights of the partners among themselves are determined by the partnership agreement, the common law, and the Uniform Partnership Act. In the second part of the chapter, you study the relations of partners to third persons who deal with the partnership. The rights and duties of the parties in these relationships are governed by the law of agency, contracts, and torts as well as the law of the UPA.

CHAPTER CHECKPOINTS

After reading and studying this chapter, you should be able to:
1. List and discuss the three principal duties owed by a partner to her co-partners.

2. List and discuss the principal rights of a partner.

3. Discuss the contract liability of a partner and of the partnership.

4. Discuss under what circumstances the partnership and the partners will have tort liability.

CHAPTER OUTLINE

I. Relationship of Partners to One Another - The law imposes certain obligations on the parties to a partnership and also gives them specific rights. The parties may by agreement vary these rights and obligations so long as standards of fairness are met and so long as the rights of third parties are not affected.
    A. Duties Among Partners - The legal duties imposed upon partners in their relationship are (1) the fiduciary duty (duty of loyalty), (2) the duty of obedience, and (3) the duty of care. Each partner also has a duty to inform his co-partners and a duty to account to the partnership.
        1. Fiduciary Duty - Each partner owes a duty of absolute and utmost good faith and loyalty to his partners. As part of the fiduciary duty, partnership law states that a partner shall not make a profit other than his agreed compensation, shall not compete with the partnership, and shall not otherwise profit from the relationship at the expense of the partnership. Every partner must hold

234

as trustee for the firm any profits he made without the consent of the other partners from any transaction connected with the formation, conduct, or liquidation of the partnership or from use by him of its property. He may not prefer himself over the firm and may not even deal at arm's length with his partners. A partner's duty is one of undivided and continuous loyalty to his partners. A partner cannot acquire for himself a partnership asset or opportunity without the consent of all of the partners. Partners must disclose fully and accurately all material facts to the other partners.

2. Duty of Obedience - A partner must act in obedience to the partnership agreement and to any business decisions properly made by the partnership. A partner who violates this duty is individually liable for any resulting loss.

3. Duty of Care - A partner must manage the partnership affairs without culpable negligence. Culpable negligence is something more than ordinary negligence, yet short of gross negligence. Honest errors of judgment or the failure to use ordinary skill in transacting business are not culpable negligence.

B. Rights Among Partners - Partners have certain rights which include: (1) rights in specific partnership property; (2) an interest in the partnership; (3) the right to share in distributions; (4) the right to participate in management; (5) the right to choose associates; and (6) the right of enforcement. The first two were covered in the last chapter; the remaining ones are covered in this chapter.

1. Right to Share in Distributions - A distribution is a transfer of partnership property from the partnership to a partner. Distributions include a division of profits; a return of capital contributions; a repayment of a loan or advance made by a partner to the partnership; and a payment made to compensate a partner for services rendered to the partnership.

   a. Right to Share in Profits - Each partner is entitled, unless otherwise agreed, to a share in the profits. Conversely, each partner must contribute toward any loss sustained by the partnership. If there is no agreement about dividing the profits, the partners share profits equally, regardless of the ratio of their financial contribution. Unless otherwise agreed, the partners bear losses in the same proportion in which they share profits. Partners may agree otherwise, however.

   b. Right to Return of Capital - After all partnership creditors have been paid, each partner is entitled to be repaid his capital contribution when the firm is terminated. Unless otherwise agreed, a partner is not entitled to interest on his capital contribution, unless there is a delay in the return of it. In such case, he is entitled to the legal rate of interest.

   c. Right to Return of Advances - If a partner makes advances (loans) to the firm over and above his capital contribution, he is a creditor of the firm and is entitled to repayment of the advances plus interest. However, his position as a creditor is subordinate to nonpartner creditors. His right to repayment is superior to the other partners' right to return of capital. A partner who has incurred personal liability on behalf of the partnership is entitled to indemnification or repayment.

   d. Right to Compensation - The UPA provides that, unless otherwise agreed, no partner is entitled to remuneration for acting in the partnership business. Even if one partner performs a disproportionate share of the work in conducting the business, he is not entitled to a salary. He is only entitled to a share of the profits, unless the partnership agreement provides otherwise. A surviving partner is entitled to reasonable compensation for services in winding up the partnership affairs.

2. Right to Participate in Management - Unless otherwise agreed, each partner has an equal voice in management, even if each partner has responsibility for a certain area of the business. Accounting and law firms frequently have two classes of partners (junior and senior partners) or three classes of partners (junior, senior, and managing partners) and to concentrate most or all management authority in a committee of a few partners or even in just one partner.

3. Right to Choose Associates - Because of the fiduciary relationship between partners and because each partner has a right to participate in management and to act as an agent of the partnership, no partner may be forced to accept a person as a partner whom he does not choose. *Delectus personae* is the term which refers to a partner's right to choose who may become a member of the partnership; it is a term which literally means "choice of the person." The UPA provides that "No person can become a member of a partnership without the consent of all the partners." That is why the purchaser of a partner's interest in the partnership does not become a partner.

4. Enforcement Rights - Each partner is allowed by law to have access to all information concerning the partnership and its books. Under certain circumstances, a partner may obtain a judicially ordered accounting in an action brought in a court of equity against the partnership or his partners.

    a. Right to Information and Inspection of the Books - Each partner may demand full information about all partnership matters and each partner has a duty to supply other partners with full and accurate information on all things affecting the partnership. This right extends to the legal representative of a deceased partner. Unless otherwise agreed, the books of the partnership are to be kept at the principal place of business and each partner has the right to inspect them and to copy any of them.

    b. Right to an Accounting - At common law and under the UPA, a partner is entitled to an accounting. An accounting is an equitable proceeding for a complete settlement of all partnership affairs. A partner may seek an accounting whenever (1) he is wrongfully excluded from the partnership business or property by his co-partners; (2) the partnership agreement allows an accounting; (3) a partner makes a profit in violation of his fiduciary duty; or (4) other circumstances render it just and reasonable. A partner is not allowed to sue the partnership at law; however, he may sue in equity for an accounting.

II. Relationship Between Partners and Third Parties - Under agency law a principal is liable on contracts made on his behalf by his duly authorized agents and is liable in tort for the wrongful acts his employees commit in the course of their employment. The UPA states, "The law of agency shall apply under this act" and "Every partner is an agent of the partnership for the purpose of its business."

    A. Contracts of Partnership - The act of every partner binds the partnership on transactions within the scope of partnership business unless the partner does not have actual or apparent authority to so act. If the partnership is bound, each partner has unlimited personal liability. The UPA states that partners are jointly liable on all debts and contract obligations of the partnership. Joint liability means that a creditor must bring suit against all of the partners as a group.

    1. Authority to Bind Partnership - A partner may bind the partnership (a) if she has actual authority, express or iplied to perform the act, or (b) if she has apparent authority to perform the act. Where there is no actual or apparent authority, the partnership is bound only if it ratifies the act.

        a. Actual Express Authority - The actual express authority of the partners may be set forth in the partnership agreement or in additional oral or written agreements between the partners. The UPA provides that the partnership is not bound unless they are authorized by all of the partners: (1) assignment of partnership property for the benefit of its creditors; (2) disposal of the good will of the business; (3) any act that would make it impossible to carry on the ordinary business of the partnership; (4) confession of a judgment; (5) submission of a partnership claim or liability to arbitration. A confession of judgment is a written agreement by a debtor authorizing a creditor to obtain a court judgment in the event the debtor defaults. A partner who does not have actual authority may not bind the partnership by any act which does not appear to be for the carrying on of the business in the usual way. This includes (1) execution of contracts of guaranty and suretyship in the firm name; (2) sale of partnership property not held for sale in the usual course of business; and (3) payment of individual debts out of partnership assets.

      b.   Actual Implied Authority - This is authority that is neither expressly granted nor expressly denied, but which is reasonably deduced from the nature of the partnership, the terms of the partnership agreement, or the relations of the partners. Examples include hiring and firing employees and purchasing property necessary for the business.

      c.   Apparent Authority - Apparent authority may or may not be actual. It is authority that a third person in light of the circumstances and the conduct of the parties may reasonable assume to exist when that third person has no knowledge or notice of the lack of actual authority. A partner has apparent authority to indorse checks and notes, make warranties in selling goods and enter into contracts to advertise the business.

  2. Partnership by Estoppel - Partnership by estoppel imposes partnership duties and liabilities on a non-partner who has either represented himself or consented to be represented as a partner.

B.   Torts of Partnership - A partnership is liable for loss or injury caused by any wrongful act or omission of any partner while acting within the ordinary course of the business of the partnership or with the authority of his co-partners. If the partnership is liable, then each partner has unlimited personal liability for the partnership obligation. Partners are jointly and severally liable for a tort or breach of trust committed by any partner or by an employee of the firm in the course of partnership business. Joint and several liability is liability where a creditor may sue the partners jointly as a group or separately as individuals. If more than one judgment is received, payment of any one of the judgments satisfies all of them. This liability is comparable to the liability of a principal under respondeat superior. The partner who commits the tort is directly liable to the third party and must also indemnify the partnership for damages it pays to the third party.

C.   Admissions of and Notice to a Partner - An admission by one partner may be used against the partnership. A partnership is bound by (1) notice to any partner of any matter relating to partnership affairs; (2) the knowledge of the partner acting in a particular matter acquired while he was a partner; and (3) the knowledge of any other partner who reasonably could and should have communicated it to the acting partner. A demand on one partner as a representative of the firm is a demand on the partnership.

D.   Liability of Incoming Partner - A person admitted as a partner into an existing partnership is liable for all of the obligations of the partnership arising before his admission as though he had been a partner when such obligations were incurred, although this liability may be satisfied of an incoming partner for pre-existing debts and obligations of the firm is limited to his capital contribution. His liability for obligations that arise after his admission into the partnership is unlimited.

DEFINITIONS

1.   Partner's interest in partnership

2.   Tenancy in partnership

3.   Charging order

4.   Delectus personae

5.   Actual express authority

6.   Actual implied authority

7. Apparent authority

8. Partnership by estoppel

9. Vicarious liability

10. Joint liability

11. Several liability

12. Accounting

TRUE/FALSE

_____ 1. A partner may not ordinarily use partnership property for his own purposes.

_____ 2. A partner who fails to use ordinary care and skill in discharging his assigned duties will be personally liable to his partners for any resulting loss.

_____ 3. A partner's interest in specific partnership property is not subject to attachment by his individual creditors.

_____ 4. A partner who sells his interest in the partnership remains a partner with all the usual rights and duties.

_____ 5. A partner's interest in the partnership is not subject to the claims of his individual creditors.

_____ 6. Unless otherwise agreed, partners bear losses in the same proportion in which they share profits.

_____ 7. A partner who performs a disproportionate share of the partnership duties is entitled to a salary in addition to his share of the profits.

_____ 8. A partner may not ordinarily inspect the books of the partnership after business hours.

_____ 9. The majority generally governs the actions and decisions of the partnership.

_____ 10. A partner who commits a tort in the ordinary course of the business of the partnership must indemnify the partnership for any damages it pays to the third party.

_____ 11. A partner's right to participate in the management of the partnership depends upon the size of his capital contribution.

_____ 12. Partners have joint liability on contracts and joint and several liability on torts.

_____ 13. An incoming partner's capital contribution can be taken to pay previous partnership debts.

_____ 14. A majority vote of the partners is sufficient to admit a new partner into the partnership.

_____ 15. A partner may deal at arms length with his co-partners.

MULTIPLE CHOICE

_____ 1. The rights and duties of the partners **among** themselves are determined by:
   a. the partnership agreement.
   b. the common law.
   c. the Uniform Partnership Act.
   d. all of the above.

_____ 2. The rights and duties of the partners with respect to the third persons with whom the partnership deals are determined by:
   a. the partnership agreement.
   b. the Uniform Third Persons Act.
   c. the Uniform Partnership Act.
   d. none of the above.

_____ 3. A partner may make an individual assignment of:
   a. his rights in specific partnership property.
   b. his share of the profits of the partnership.
   c. his right to participate in the assets upon liquidation of the partnership.
   d. (b) and (c) but not (a).

_____ 4. A person who is entitled to participate in the management of a partnership is generally:
   a. an individual partner's assignee.
   b. an individual partner's judgment creditor.
   c. a receiver for an individual partner's interest.
   d. none of the above.

_____ 5. A partner is entitled to receive interest on:
   a. his capital contributions to the partnership.
   b. his advancements to the partnership over and above his agreed capital contributions.
   c. both of the above.
   d. none of the above.

_____ 6. A partner may bind the partnership by an act which is not apparently within the scope of the partnership busines if he has:
   a. express authority to perform the act.
   b. implied authority to perform the act.
   c. either (a) or (b).
   d. neither (a) nor (b).

_____ 7. A partner who has actual authority from a majority of his co-partners may bind the partnership to:
   a. an assignment of partnership property for the benefit of its creditors.
   b. a sale of partnership property held for sale in the usual course of business.
   c. a sale of partnership property not held for sale in the usual course of busienss.
   d. a contract of suretyship in the firm name.

_____ 8. The liability of an incoming partner upon antecedent debts and obligations of the firm is:
   a. unlimited.
   b. limited to his capital contribution.
   c. limited to his accrued and unpaid share of the profits.
   d. none of the above.

_____ 9. The books of the partnership may be:
   a. kept at the home of one of the partners.
   b. inspected by the legal representative of a deceased partner at any time.
   c. inspected by any certified accountant on behalf of a creditor.
   d. none of the above.

_____ 10. An action for an accounting may be brought:
   a. at law.
   b. in equity.
   c. at law or in equity.
   d. none of the above.

_____ 11. When a partner commits a tort in the course of partnership business:
   a. only the tortfeasor is liable.
   b. the partnership has no liability.
   c. the rules of agency apply.
   d. the partnership will only have liability for intentional torts.

_____ 12. Ann and Betty were partners in a business. They represented to First Bank that Carl was a partner with them. When contacted by First Bank, Carl did not deny the representation, because he was seriously considering the possibility of joining the business. First Bank loaned the money, but Ann and Betty defaulted. First Bank is entitled to collect from:
   a. Carl only.
   b. Ann, Betty and Carl jointly.
   c. Ann, Betty or Carl severally.
   d. Ann and Betty jointly but not from Carl.

_____ 13. A partner may seek an accounting whenever:
   a. the partnership agreement allows one.
   b. he is wrongfully excluded from the partnership business.
   c. circumstances render it just and reasonable.
   d. the partnership agreement allows one, the partner is wrongfully excluded from the partnership business, or circumstances render it just and reasonable.

_____ 14. Arthur breaches his fiduciary duty to the Main Street Partnership by usurping a partnership opportunity. As a result of his breach of this duty, the partnership suffered a loss of $10,000 and Arthur made a secret profit of $20,000.
   a. Arthur must pay the firm triple damages.
   b. Arthur must pay the firm $10,000.
   c. Arthur must pay the firm the $20,000 secret profit and the $10,000 loss.
   d. Arthur need not pay the firm anything.

_____ 15. Which of the following acts can be done with the consent of only a majority of the firm members?
   a. Submission of a partnership claim to arbitration.
   b. Confession of judgment.
   c. Any sale of partnership property.
   d. Submission of a partnership claim to arbitration, confession of judgment and any sale of partnership property.

SHORT ESSAY

1. What standard is applied to determine whether partners may by agreement vary their legal rights and obligations? _____
_____
_____
_____

2. List five specific instances in which partners may by agreement vary their legal rights and obligations. ____
_____
_____
_____

3. List six specific instances in which a partner may have actual implied authority to bind the partnership. ___
_____
_____
_____

4. Arthur, Bob and Clark have a partnership, but their agreement is silent as to the sharing of profits and losses. Arthur's capital contribution is $12,000; Bob's capital contribution is $6,000; Clark's contribution is a computer and other equipment valued at $3,400. How would the partners divide a $36,000 profit? _____
_____
_____
_____
_____

DISSOLUTION, WINDING UP, AND TERMINATION

PURPOSE

In this chapter you study the three stages that lead to the extinguishment of a partnership. Dissolution is a change in the relationship of the partners caused by any partner's ceasing to be associated in the carrying on of the business. The business is not terminated by dissolution but continues until the winding up of the partnership affairs is completed. During the winding up stage, receivables are collected, payments are made to creditors, and the remaining assets are distributed to the partners. When the winding up has been completed, the partnership is terminated.

CHAPTER CHECKPOINTS

After reading and studying this chapter, you should be able to:

1. Identify when dissolution occurs by act of the partners, by operation of law and by court order.

2. Explain the effect of dissolution upon the authority and liability of the partners.

3. List the order in which the assets of a partnershp are distributed to creditors and partners and be able to properly distribute the assets of a partnership in chapter problems.

4. Compare and distinguish the rights of partnership creditors and creditors of the partners under the UPA and the Bankruptcy Act.

5. Identify and discuss the situations in which a partnership may continue to do business after dissolution.

CHAPTER OUTLINE

A. Dissolution - The Uniform Partnership Act defines dissolution as a change in the relation of the partners caused by any partner's ceasing to be associated in the carrying on of the business. Three stages lead to the extinguishment of a partnership: (1) dissolution; (2) winding up or liquidation; and (3) termination. During winding up, receivables are collected, payments are made to creditors, and distribution of the remaining assets is made to the partners. Termination occurs when the process of winding up has been completed.
   1. Causes of Dissolution - Dissolution may be brought about by (1) an act of the partners; (2) operation of

law; or (3) court order. Under the UPA, the assignment of a partner's interest, a creditor's charging order on a partner's interest, and an accounting are not cause for dissolution, although they were at common law.

    a.   **Dissolution by Act of the Partners** - A partner always has the power to dissolve a partnership, but whether he has the right to do so is determined by the partnership agreement. A partner who wrongfully dissolves a partnership may have liability to the remaining partners. A partnership is rightfully dissolved by act of the partners when (1) they specifically agree to dissolve the partnership; (2) the period of time provided in the agreement has ended or the purpose for which the partnership was formed has been accomplished; (3) a partner withdraws from a partnership at will (one with no definite term or specific undertaking); or (4) a partner is expelled in accordance with a power to expel conferred by the partnership agreement.

    b.   **Dissolution by Operation of Law** - A partnership is dissolved by operation of law upon: (1) the death of a partner; (2) the bankruptcy of a partner or of the partnership; or (3) the subsequent illegality of the partnership. A partnership engaged in the practice of a profession would be dissolved if one of its members lost his license.

    c.   **Dissolution by Court Order** - A court will order dissolution of a partnership if it finds that: (1) a partner is incompetent or suffers some other incapacity that prevents him from functioning as a partner; (2) a partner is guilty of conduct prejudicial to the business or has willfully and persistently breached the partnership agreement; (3) the partnership business can only be carried on at a loss; or (4) other circumstances render a dissolution equitable. An assignee of a partner's interest or a partner's personal creditor who has obtained a charging order or judicial lien against the partner's interest is entitled to a dissolution by court decree, but if the partnership is other than an at will partnership, the dissolution will not be effective until after the agreed upon term or undertaking has occurred.

2.   **Effects of Dissolution** - A partnership is not terminated, but continues until the winding up is completed. Dissolution brings about restrictions on the authority of partners to act for the partnership.

    a.   **Authority** - A partner's actual authority to act for the partnership terminates, except so far as may be necessary to wind up partnership affairs. Actual authority includes completing existing contracts, reducing partnership assets to cash, and paying partnership obligations. Apparent authority persists and binds the partnership for acts within the scope of the partnership business unless notice of the dissolution is given to the third party. A third party who extends credit to the partnership before dissolution may hold the partnership liable for any transaction that would bind the partnership before dissolution, unless the third party has actual notice (actual knowledge expressly communicated) of the dissolution. A third party who had not extended credit to the partnership before dissolution can hold the partnership liable unless actual or constructive notice (knowledge imputed by law) of the dissolution. An ad in a newspaper is constructive notice. No notice need be given to third parties who had no knowledge of the partnership before its dissolution.

    b.   **Existing Liability** - Dissolution does not by itself discharge the existing liability of any partner. In some instances, dissolution may result in discharging an executory contract, such as where a contract calls for the personal services of a partner who dies. A novation may discharge a retiring partner from his existing liabilities.

B.   **Winding Up** - The process of liquidation is called winding up and consists of completing unfinished business, collecting debts, reducing assets to cash, taking inventory, auditing the partnership books, paying creditors, and distributing the remaining assets to the partners. Fiduciary duties of the partners continue during winding up.

1.   **The Right to Wind Up** - On dissolution any partner has the right to insist on the winding up of the partnership unless the partnership agreement provides otherwise. A partner who has wrongfully dissolved the partnership or who has been expelled according to the terms of the partnership

agreement, however, cannot force the liquidation of the partnership. All nonbankrupt partners who have not wrongfully dissolved the partnership have the right to wind up a partnership. On petition of a partner, a court may appoint a receiver who has authority to operate the business under the court's direction for such time as may be reasonably necessary. Reasons for which a court might appoint a receiver include dissension among the partners, waste, fraud, mental incompetence, misconduct, or other breach of duty by a partner.

2. Distribution of Assets - When the partnership has been profitable, the order of distribution is not critical; however, when liabilities exceed assets, the order of distribution is of great importance. Under the UPA, the liabilities of a partnership are to be paid out of partnership assets in the following order: (1) amounts owed to creditors other than partners; (2) amounts owing to partners other than for capital and profits; (3) amounts owing to partners for capital contributions; and (4) amounts owing to partners for profits. The partners may by agreement change the internal priorities (2, 3 and 4), but they may not change the preferred position of third parties. The proportion in which the partners bear losses, whether capital or otherwise, does not depend on their relative contributions, but on the terms of their agreement, and if there is none, losses are borne in the same proportion in which profits are shared. If the partnership is insolvent, the partners individually must contribute their respective share of the losses in order to pay the creditors. If one partner is insolvent or bankrupt, the other partners must contribute the additional amount necessary to pay the firm's liabilities. Any partner who pays more than his proper share of the losses has the right of contribution against the other partners who have not paid their share.

    a. Solvent Partnership - A, B, and C form the ABC Company partnership. A contributes $6,000 capital; B contributes $4,000 capital, and C contributes services but no capital. A loans the partnership $3,000. There is no agreement as to the proportions for sharing profits and losses. At liquidation the assets are $54,000, and liabilities to creditors are $26,000. The partnership is solvent and has a profit of $15,000 ($54,000 - $39,000 = $15,000). The partners share the profits equally, with each receiving $5,000. After the outside creditors have been paid, A will receive $14,000, because he is entitled to $3,000 for repayment of the loan, $6,000 for capital and $5,000 for his share of the profits. B will receive $9,000, because he is entitled to $4,000 for capital and $55,000 for his share of the profits. C will receive $5,000 for his share of the profits.

    b. Insolvent Partnership - If the same partnership still owed creditors $26,000, but had assets of only $112,000, the partnership would have sustained a loss of $27,000. This is calculated by subtracting the total liabilities from the total assets ($39,000 - $12,000 = $27,000). Each partner's share of the loss will be $9,000. A will receive nothing. ($3,000 for the loan plus $6,000 for capital minus $9,000 for his share of the losses). B must make an additional contribution of $5,000 to cover his share of the loss ($4,000 minus $9,000 equals a negative $5,000). C must contribute $9,000 to cover his share of the loss.

    c. Contribution of Partner Upon Insolvency - If A and B were solvent and C were individually insolvent, C would be unable to pay any of his share of the loss. A and B must then contribute equally in order to make good the amount of C's share. Each would have to contribute an additional $4,500. Thus, A would have to contribute $4,500 and B would have to contribute $9,500 in order to satisfy the unpaid claims of partnership creditors. If A and C were individually insolvent and B was solvent, B would be required to pay the entire balance of $14,000 due to partnership creditors plus a contribution of the full amount of C's unpaid share of the loss.

3. Marshaling of Assets - This doctrine only applies when the assets of a partnership and of its members are administered by a court of equity. Marshaling means segregating and considering the assets and liabilities of the partnership separately from the respective assets and liabilities of the individual partners. Partnership creditors are entitled to be satisfied first out of partnership assets. They have a right to recover any deficiency out of the individually owned assets of the partners, subordinate however to the rights of the nonpartnership creditors to those assets. Nonpartnership creditors have first claim to the individually owned assets of their respective debtors and their claims to partnership

assets are subordinate to claims of partnership creditors. If the Bankruptcy Act applies, this rule is no longer followed. The Bankruptcy Act directs the trustee to administer the estate of the debtor. If the partnership property is insufficient to pay all the claims against the partnership, then the trustee is directed to seek recovery of the deficiency first from the general partners who are not bankrupt, then against the estates of bankrupt partners on the same basis as other creditors of the bankrupt partner.

C. Continuation After Dissolution - After dissolution, the partnership must either be liquidated or the remaining partners must continue the partnership. The UPA gives each partner the right to have the partnership liquidated except in a limited number of instances where the partners may continue the business.

1. Right to Continue Partnership - The remaining partners have the right to continue the partnership (1) when the partnership has been dissolved in violation of the partnership agreement; (2) when a partner has been expelled in accordance with the partnership agreement; or (3) when all the partners agree to continue the business.

   a. Continuation After Wrongful Dissolution - Courts will not decree specific performance of a partnership agreement, because of the personal element in a partnership. However, a partner who wrongfully withdraws cannot force the liquidation of the firm. The aggrieved partners can either liquidate the firm and recover damages for the breach or continue the firm by buying out the withdrawing partner less the amount of damages they have sustained as a result of the breach. The interest of the withdrawing partner is calculated without considering the good will of the business; the remaining partners have the right to use the capital contribution of the withdrawing partner for the unexpired period of any agreement. They must, however, indemnify him against present and future partnership liabilities.

   b. Continuation After Expulsion - A partner expelled according to the partnership agreement cannot force liquidation of the partnership. He is entitled to discharge from partnership liabilities and to receive in cash the net amount due him from the partnership.

   c. Continuation Agreement of the Partners - The most reliable way of assuring the preservation of a partnership business after dissolution is a continuation agreement. Such an agreement permits the remaining partners to keep partnership property, carry on its business, and provides a specified settlement to the departing partner.

2. Rights of Creditors - Whenever a partnership is continued after dissolution, a new partnership is formed even though a majority of the old partners are present in the new combination. The creditors of the old partnership have claims against the new partnership and may also proceed against all the members of the dissolved partnership, all of whom have personal liability. Even if a withdrawing partner has made arrangements with the remaining partners to have them assume obligations, creditors whose claims arose rior to dissolution may proceed against the withdrawing partner. A withdrawing partner may protect herself by giving notice to creditors that she is no longer a member of the firm. Actual notice must be given to creditors who extended credit to the partnership prior to its dissolution. Constructive notice may be given to those who knew of the partnership but had not extended credit to it before its dissolution.

DEFINITIONS

1. Dissolution

2. Winding up

3. Liquidation

4. Termination

5. Rightful dissolution

6. Actual notice

7. Constructive notice

8. Solvent partnership

9. Insolvent partnership

10. Marshaling of assets

11. Continuation

12. Wrongful dissolution

13. Continuation agreement

14. Partnership at will

TRUE/FALSE

_____ 1. A partnership is dissolved whenever it undergoes any change in membership.

_____ 2. A partner always has the power to dissolve the partnership.

_____ 3. A partner who withdraws in violation of the partnership agreement remains a partner with all the usual rights and duties.

_____ 4. Dissolution terminates the actual authority of a partner to complete existing contracts.

_____ 5. Dissolution discharges the existing liability of each partner.

_____ 6. A retiring partner will be discharged from his existing liabilities by entering into a novation with the continuing partners.

_____ 7. The proportion in which the partners bear losses depends upon their relative capital contributions.

_____ 8. A partnership is liable for the personal obligations of its partners.

_____ 9. A partner who wrongfully withdraws from the partnership is liable to the remaining partners for damages resulting from the breach of the partnership agreement.

_____ 10. A retiring partner is ordinarily entitled to be paid the value of his interest as of the date of the dissolution.

_____ 11. A retiring partner may be liable upon contracts which are entered into by the partnership subsequent to his withdrawal.

_____ 12. A partner expelled according to the partnership agreement can force liquidation of the partnership.

_____ 13. Once the outside creditors have been paid, the next priority is return of partners' capital.

_____ 14. The doctrine of marshaling of assets applies in every dissolution of a partnership.

_____ 15. Courts will decree specific performance of a partnership agreement.

MULTIPLE CHOICE

_____ 1. Dissolution is brought about by:
   a.   the assignment of a partner's interest.
   b.   the bankruptcy of a partner.
   c.   a creditor's charging order on a partner's interest.
   d.   all of the above.

_____ 2. Dissolution will not be brought about by:
   a.   the death of a partner.
   b.   the bankruptcy of a partner.
   c.   an action for an accounting.
   d.   a withdrawal in violation of the partnership agreement.

_____ 3. A court will order a dissolution if it finds that:
   a.   a partner is insane.
   b.   a partner has breached the partnership agreement.
   c.   the business has been losing money.
   d.   all of the above.

_____ 4. Ashley, Barbara, and Clarence form a partnership to erect an office building. If Ashley assigns his interest to Terrance, Terrance may petition the court to dissolve the partnership:
   a.   at any time.
   b.   as soon as partnership liabilities exceed partnership assets.
   c.   as soon as the building is completed.
   d.   none of the above.

_____ 5. Apparent authority is not sufficient to bind the partnership after dissolution if:
   a.   the third party extended credit to the partnership prior to dissolution.
   b.   the third party never extended credit to the partnership prior to dissolution but nevertheless knew of the partnership.
   c.   the third party never extended credit to the partnership prior to dissolution nor knew of the partnership.
   d.   (b) and (c) but not (a).

_____ 6. A partner cannot force the liquidation of the partnership if:
   a. he has wrongfully dissolved the partnership.
   b. he has been expelled pursuant to the partnership agreement.
   c. the partnership agreement provides for the continuation of the partnership.
   d. all of the above.

_____ 7. In a liquidation of a general partnership, the last items to be paid are amounts owing:
   a. to partners in respect of profits.
   b. to partners in respect of capital.
   c. to partners other than for capital and profits.
   d. to creditors who are not also partners.

_____ 8. Ashley, Barbara, and Clarence form a partnership with Ashley contributing $1,000 capital, Barbara contributing $5,000 capital, and Clarence contributing $10,000 capital. Each partner has also loaned the partnership $2,000 which has not been repaid. When the partnership is liquidated, its assets are $550,000 and its liabilities to creditors are $25,000. How much will Ashley receive?
   a. $1,000
   b. $2,000
   c. $4,000
   d. None of the above.

_____ 9. Ashley, Barbara, and Clarence form a partnership with Ashley contributing $2,000 capital, Barbara contributing $10,000 capital, and Clarence contributing $16,000 capital. Each partner has also loaned the partnership $2,000 which has not been repaid. When the partnership is liquidated, its assets are $50,000 and its liabilities to creditors are $25,000. How much will Barbara receive?
   a. $4,000
   b. $8,000
   c. $12,000
   d. None of the above.

_____ 10. Ashley, Barbara, and Clarence form a partnership with A contributing $6,000 capital, Barbara contributing $10,000 capital, and Clarence contributing $14,000 capital. Each partner has also loaned the partnership $5,000 which has not been repaid. When the partnership is liquidated, its assets are $50,000, its liabilities to creditors are $50,000, and Ashley is insolvent. How much will Clarence receive?
   a. $1,000
   b. $2,000
   c. $4,000
   d. None of the above.

_____ 11. Ashley and Barbara are partners in a partnership in which no fixed duration has been specified.
   a. This is a partnership at will.
   b. This is a partnership by estoppel.
   c. This is a partnership in perpetuity.
   d. This is a limited partnership.

_____ 12. David, Elvis and Fred are partners in the DEF Company. David causes a dissolution of the partnership in breach of the partnership agreement and is expelled in accordance with the agreement.
   a.   David can compel the liquidation of the partnership.
   b.   David is liable to Elvis and Fred for damages caused by the breach.
   c.   Elvis and Fred can continue in business, but they must pay David for his interest in the firm less damages and any amount attributable to the firm good will.
   d.   Two of the above, (b) and (c).

_____ 13. David, Elvis and Fred are partners in the DEF Company. David retires from the partnership.
   a.   David has no further liability to partnership creditors.
   b.   David has liability to creditors whose claims arose prior to dissolution.
   c.   To protect himself, David should give actual notice of his leaving the firm to creditors who extended credit to the firm while he was a member.
   d.   Two of the above, (b) and (c).

_____ 14. The process of liquidating a partnership is known as:
   a.   marshaling of assets.
   b.   dissolution.
   c.   winding up.
   d.   termination.

_____ 15. If one partner is _____ or _____, the other partners must contribute the additional amount necessary to pay the firm's liabilities.
   a.   incompetent or incapacitated
   b.   insolvent or bankrupt
   c.   in violation of the partnership agreement or planning to retire
   d.   incompetent or insolvent.

SHORT ESSAY

1.   What steps are usually taken in winding up the affairs of a partnership? _____
   _____
   _____
   _____

2.   What are the three major causes of dissolution? _____
   _____
   _____
   _____

3.   What is the order of distribution of an insolvent partner's assets under the UPA? _____
   _____
   _____
   _____

4. In 1986, David, Elvis and Fred formed a partnership to practice tax accounting. Each contributed $15,000 in capital. In 1987, David loaned the partnership $5,000. In 1988, Elvis loaned the firm $10,000. In early 1989, the partnership was dissolved and Fred agreed to do the winding up with the agreement that he be paid $2,000 for his services. The firm has assets of $123,000 and debts to outside creditors of $40,000. How will the $123,000 be distributed? _____

    _____

    _____

    _____

LIMITED PARTNERSHIPS

PURPOSE

In this chapter, you study limited partnership and other types of unincorporated business associations, such as joint ventures and business trusts. Although these forms of business associations are not as common as general partnerships, sole proprietorships and corporations, they do meet special business and investment purposes that make each appropriate in certain circumstances. In recent years, limited partnerships have become more common as investment vehicles similar to owning stock in a corporation. The limited partnership has limited liability for limited partners and has had certain tax advantages that have made it an attractive vehicle for a variety of investments.

CHAPTER CHECKPOINTS

After reading and studying this chapter, you should be able to:

1. Compare a limited partnership to a general partnership with respect to creation, liability of the partners, management, and duration of existence.

2. Compare the liability of the general partner to that of the limited partner under both the ULPA and the RULPA.

3. List and discuss the activities in which a limited partner may engage without forfeiting limited liability under both the ULPA and RULPA.

4. List the order in which the assets of a limited partnership are distributed to creditors, limited partners, and general partners and be able to correctly work through distribution problems.

5. List the main characteristics of and distinguish among joint ventures, joint stock companies, mining partnerships, limited partnerships, limited partnership associations, and business trusts.

CHAPTER OUTLINE

A. Limited Partnerships - The limited partnership has proved itself to be an attractive vehicle for a variety of investments, because of its tax advantages and the limited liability it confers upon the limited partners.

Limited partnerships are statutory creations. There are many variations in the law of limited partnerships from State to State. Before 1976 all States except Louisiana followed the Uniform Limited Partnership Act (ULPA) in their governing statute. In 1976 the National Conference of Commissioners on Uniform State Laws developed the Revised Uniform Limited Partnership Act (RULPA) to overcome some of the shortcomings inherent in the ULPA for the large scale and multistate limited partnerships that were beginning to develop and which were severely burdened by the framework established in the ULPA. More than forty States have adopted the 1976 version of the RULPA. In 1985 the National Conference revised the RULPA. The 1985 Act makes almost no changes in the basic structure of the 1976 RULPA and does not alter the underlying philosophy of that Act. However, it does make some changes with respect to the activities in which a limited partner may engage without incurring the liability of a general partner. The ULPA, RULPA and the 1985 Act are supplemented by the Uniform Partnership Act, which applies to limited partnerships also except where it is inconsistent with the Limited Partnership Act. Limited partnerships are almost always considered to be securities, and their sale is therefore subject to the State and Federal securities laws.

1. **Definition** - A limited partnership is a partnership formed by two or more persons under the laws of a State and having one or more general partners and one or more limited partners. A person includes a natural person, partnership, limited partnership, trust, estate, association, or corporation. A limited partnership differs from a general partnership in that (1) there must be a statute providing for such a partnership; (2) the limited partnership must substantially comply with the requirements of such statute; and (3) the liability of a limited partner for debts or obligations is limited to the extent of the capital which he has contributed.

2. **Formation** - Although a general partnership may be formed without special procedures, a limited partnership can only be formed in compliance with the limited partnership statute of a State. When a limited partnership does not substantially conform to the State statute in its formation, the limited partners may lose their limited liability.

   a. **Filing of Certificate** - To form a limited partnership under the RULPA, two or more persons must file a signed certificate in the office of the Secretary of State of the State in which the limited partnership has its principal office. The certificate must be amended if there are certain changes in the partnership. The 1985 Act requires fewer matters in the certificate than does the original RULPA. Under the RULPA the certificate must include the following information:

      1) The name of the limited partnership.
      2) The general character of the partnership business.
      3) The address of the office and the name and address of the agent for service of process.
      4) The name and the business address of each partner listing general partners and limited partners separately.
      5) The amount of cash, and a description and statement of the value of the other property or services contributed by each partner.
      6) The times at which, or events on the happening of which, additional contributions are to be made by each partner.
      7) Any power of a limited partner to make an assignee of his partnership interest a limited partner.
      8) The events permitting a partner to withdraw from the partnership.
      9) The rights of partners to receive distributions of limited partnership property.
      10) The rights of partners to receive a return of their capital contributions.
      11) The time or events upon which the limited partnership is to be dissolved.

   b. **Name** - The surname of a limited partner may not be included in the name of the partnership unless it is also the surname of a general partner, or unless the business had been carried on under that name before the admission of the limited partner. Inclusion of a limited partner's surname in the partnership name in violation of this provision will result in the loss of the limited partner's limited liability. The name may not be deceptively similar to that of any corporation or other limited partnership. The name must also contain without abbreviation the words "limited partnership."

c. Contributions - The contribution of a partner may be cash, property, services, or a promissory note to contribute cash, property or services. A partner is liable to the partnership for the difference between the contribution actually made and the amount stated in the certificate. Under the 1985 Act a promise by a limited partner to contribute to the limited partnership is enforceable only if it is in a signed writing.

d. Defective Formation - The limited partnership is formed when the certificate is filed, if it substantially complies with the requirements of the statute. If there is no certificate filed or if one is filed but does not substantially meet the statutory requirements, the formation is defective. Where formation is defective, the limited liability of the limited partners is jeopardized. The 1985 Act greatly reduces the risk that a limited partner will be exposed to liability because of an inadvertent omission from the certificate.

e. Foreign Limited Partnerships - A limited partnership is considered "foreign" in any State in which it has not been formed. Under the RULPA the laws of the State under which a foreign limited partnership is organized govern its organization, internal affairs, and the liability of its limited partners. However, all foreign limited partnerships must register with the Secretary of State. A partnership that fails to register may not bring enforcement actions in the State's courts, although it may defend itself if sued.

3. Rights - The rights of the parties are usually set forth in the articles of limited partnership. A general partner has all the rights and powers of a partner in a general partnership.

a. Control - The general partners have almost exclusive control and management of the limited partnership. If a limited partner shares in the management or control of the association, he forfeits his limited liability. A limited partner who exercises the powers of a general partner has the liability of a general partner to all third parties who transact business with the partnership. If the limited partner's participation in control of the business is not substantially the same as the exercise of the powers of a general partner, he is liable as a general partner to only those persons who transact business with the limited partnership with actual knowledge of his participation in control. Under the 1985 Act, a limited partner who participates in the control of the business is liable only to those persons who transact business with the limited partnership reasonably believing, based upon the limited partner's conduct, that the limited partner is a general partner. The RULPA enumerates certain activities in which a limited partner may engage without being deemed to have taken part in control of the business. Under the RULPA this list is not exclusive. Activities that are permitted are as follows:

1) Being a contractor for, an agent or employee of the limited partnership or of a general partner.

2) Consulting with and advising a general partner with respect to the business of the limited partnership.

3) Acting as surety for the limited partnership.

4) Approving or disapproving an amendment to the partnership agreement.

5) Voting on one or more of the following matters:

a) The dissolution and winding up of the partnership.

b) The sale, exchange, lease, mortgage, pledge, or other transfer of all or substantially all of the assets of the limited partnership other than in the ordinary course of its business.

c) The incurrence of indebtedness by the limited partnership other than in the ordinary course of its business.

d) The removal of a general partner.

Under the 1985 Amendments, the following have been added to the safe harbor list given above:

6) Winding up the partnership.

7) Exercising any right or power granted by the Act.

8)   Voting on the admission of a general partner.
9)   Voting on the admission or removal of a limited partner.
10) Voting on any matter relating to the business of the limited partnership which the partnership agreement makes subject to the approval or disapproval of the limited partners.

b.   Choice of Associates - No person may be added as a general partner or a limited partner without the consent of all partners.   Once the limited partnership is formed, the admission of additional limited partners requires the written consent of all partners unless the partnership agreement provides otherwise.   After the formation of a limited partnership, new general partners may be admitted only with the specific written consent of all partners.   Under the 1985 Act, the written partnership agreement determines the procedure for authorizing the admission of additional general partners, and the written consent of all partners is required only if the partnership agreement fails to deal with this issue.

c.   Withdrawal - A general partner may withdraw from a limited partnership at any time by giving written notice to the other partners.   If the withdrawal violates the partnership agreement, the limited partnership may recover damages from the withdrawing general partner.   A limited partner may withdraw as provided in the limited partnership certificate or, under the 1985 Act, the written partnership agreement.   Upon withdrawal, a withdrawing partner is entitled to receive any distribution to which she is entitled under the partnership agreement, subject to the restrictions discussed below.   If the partnership agreement makes no provision, the partner is entitled to receive the fair value of her interest in the limited partnership as of the date of withdrawal based upon her right to share in distributions from the limited partnerships.

d.   Assignment of Partnership Interest - A partnership interest is a partner's share of the profits and losses of a limited partnership and the right to receive distributions of partnership assets.   It is considered to be personal property.   Unless otherwise provided in the partnership agreement, a partner may assign his partnership interest without dissolving the limited partnership, although the assignee does not become a partner and may not exercise the rights of a partner.   An assignee may become a substituted limited partner if all other partners consent.   Upon the death of a partner, the executor or administrator has all the rights of the partner for purposes of settling the estate.

e.   Profit and Loss Sharing - The profits and losses are allocated among the partners as provided in the partnership agreement.   If the partnership agreement has no such provision, then the profits and losses are allocated on the basis of the value of contributions actually made by each partner.   Limited partners are not liable for losses beyond their capital contribution.   Under the 1985 Act, the agreement sharing profits and losses must be in writing.

f.   Distributions - The partners share distributions of cash or other assets of a limited partnership as provided in the partnership agreement.   The 1985 Act requires such an agreement to be written.   The RULPA allows partners to share in distributions in a proportion different than they share in profits.   In the absence of an agreement, the distributions are made on the basis of the value of the contribution actually made by each partner.   Unless otherwise provided, distributions are made in cash.   A partner who is entitled to a distribution has the status of a creditor, but a partner may not receive a distribution unless there are sufficient assets after the distribution to pay all liabilities other than those owing to partners on account of their partnership interests.

g.   Loans - Both general and limited partners may be secured or unsecured creditors of the partnership.   This right is subject to applicable State and Federal bankruptcy and fraudulent conveyance statutes.

h.   Information - The RULPA requires that the partnership maintain within the State an office at which basic organizational and financial records are kept.   Each limited partner has the right to inspect and copy any of the partnership records.   The limited partner is also entitled to copies of tax returns and any other reasonable information regarding the affairs of the limited partnership.

i.   Derivative Actions - The RULPA recognizes the right of the limited partner to bring an action on behalf of a limited partnership to recover a judgment in its favor if the general partners have refused to bring the action. Standing and pleading requirements similar to those in a shareholder derivative action are established by the RULPA.

4. Duties and Liabilities - The duties and liabilities of general partners are quite different from those of limited partners.

    a. Duties - A general partner has a fiduciary relationship to the limited partners. It remains unclear whether a limited partner is a fiduciary to the general partners or to the partnership. The law does not distinguish between the duty of care owed by a general partner to a general partnership and that owed by a general partner to a limited partnership. A limited partner owes no duty of care to a limited partnership as long as he remains a limited partner.

    b. Liabilities - The limited personal liability offered to limited partners is one of the most appealing features of a limited partnership. Limited liability means that one has a limited partner who has paid her contribution and has no further liability to the limited partnership or its creditors. The general partners have unlimited external liability. Any general partner who knew or should have known that the limited partnership certificate contained a false statement is liable to anyone who suffers loss by reason of that false statement.

5. Dissolution - As with a general partnership, the three stages are (1) dissolution; (2) winding up or liquidation; and (3) termination. The causes of dissolution are different from those of a general partnership.

    a. Causes - The limited partners do not have the right or the power to dissolve the partnership, except by decree of the court. Under the RULPA the following events trigger a dissolution after which the partnership must be liquidated:

        1) The expiration of the time period, or the happening of the events specified in the certificate.
        2) The unanimous written consent of all the partners.
        3) The withdrawal of a general partner, unless all partners agree to continue the business.
        4) A decree of judicial dissolution which may be granted whenever it is not reasonably practicable to carry on the business in conformity with the partnership agreement.

    b. Winding Up - Unless otherwise provided in the partnership agreement, the general partners who have not wrongfully dissolved the partnership may wind up its affairs. Under certain circumstances, the limited partner may wind up the affairs.

    c. Distribution of Assets - The priorities for distribution are as follows: (1) creditors including partners who are creditors, except in respect to liabilities for distribution; (2) partners and ex-partners in satisfaction of liabilities for unpaid distributions; (3) partners for the return of contributions except as otherwise agreed; and (4) partners for their partnership interests in the proportions in which they share in distributions, except as otherwise agreed.

B. Other Types of Unincorporated Business Associations

    1. Joint Ventures - A joint venture is a form of temporary partnership organized to carry out a particular business enterprise for profit. Examples include a securities underwriting syndicate, a syndicate formed to acquire a certain tract of land for subdivision and resale, joint research by corporations, and the manufacturing and sale of goods in a foreign country. Unlike a partner, a joint venturer is not an agent of her co-venturers and does not have authority to bind them. The death of a joint adventurer does not necessarily dissolve the venture. A court of law will allow a joint venturer to sue his co-venturers, but it will not allow a partner to sue his partners.

    2. Joint Stock Company - A joint stock company is a form of general partnership that has some characteristics of a corporation and differs from an ordinary partnership in the following respects: (1) its capital is divided into shares with transferable certificates; (2) it is managed by directors or managers elected by the members; (3) its members are not its agents; and (4) a transfer of shares by a member, or the death, insanity or other incapacity of a partner does not dissolve it.

    3. Mining Partnerships - A mining partnership is a specific type of partnership for the purpose of

extracting raw minerals. A mining partner has the right to sell his interest in the partnership. The death of a partner does not dissolve the partnership.

4. Limited Partnership Associations - A limited partnership association is a partnership which closely resembles a corporation.

5. Business Trusts - A business trust is managed by a trustee for the benefit of a beneficiary; it is established to conduct a business for profit. The business trust is also known as a Massachusetts trust. It was devised to avoid the burdens of corporate regulation. Like an ordinary trust between natural persons, a business trust may be created by a voluntary agreement without authorization or consent of the State. It has three distinguishing characteristics: (1) the trust estate is devoted to the conduct of business; (2) each beneficiary is entitled to a certificate evidencing his ownership of a beneficial interest that he is free to sell or transfer; and (3) the trustees must have the exclusive right to manage and control the business free from control by the beneficiaries.

DEFINITIONS

1. Limited partnership

2. Equity participant

3. Foreign limited partnership

4. Substituted limited partner

5. Certificate of limited partnership

6. Joint stock company

7. Joint venture

8. Mining partnership

9. Limited partnership association

10. Business trust

11. Unincorporated association

TRUE/FALSE

_____ 1. The liability of a limited partner for partnership debts or obligations is usually limited to his capital contribution.

_____ 2. Under the RULPA, a certificate of limited partnership must be filed in the office of the Attorney General of the State in which the limited partnership has its principal office.

_____ 3. A limited partner is liable to the partnership for the difference between what he has actually contributed and what he agreed to contribute.

_____ 4. An equity participant who erroneously believes that he has become a limited partner in a limited partnership will be liable as a general partner to any third party who transacts business with the enterprise.

_____ 5. A general partner of a limited partnership has all the rights of a partner in a partnership without limited partners.

_____ 6. A limited partner may not assign his interest without the consent of all of the partners.

_____ 7. Unless otherwise agreed, under the RULPA the profits of a limited partnership are allocated on the basis of the value of contributions actually made by each partner.

_____ 8. A limited partner owes a fiduciary duty to his general partners.

_____ 9. A general partner owes a fiduciary duty to his limited partners.

_____ 10. The liability of a general partner in a limited partnership for partnership debts or obligations is limited to his capital contribution.

_____ 11. A limited partner has the same power to dissolve the partnership that a general partner has.

_____ 12. A limited partnership may be created by either an oral or written agreement.

_____ 13. The Revised Uniform Limited Partnership Act has been adopted by all fifty States.

_____ 14. In general, the surname of a limited partner cannot be included in the partnership name.

_____ 15. Under the 1985 RULPA, a limited partner is less likely to incur the liability of a general partner by participating in management.

MULTIPLE CHOICE

_____ 1. A limited partnership may be composed of:
  a. one general partner and one limited partner.
  b. two limited partners.
  c. one general partner and two limited partners.
  d. (a) and (c) but not (b).

_____ 2. The names of all limited partners should be included in:
  a. the certificate of limited partnership.
  b. the name of the partnership.
  c. each partner's income tax return.
  d. all of the above.

_____ 3. Under the ULPA, the capital contribution of a limited partner may not be made in:
  a. cash.
  b. services.
  c. real property.
  d. personal property.

_____ 4. Under the RULPA, if a limited partnership transacts business in a foreign State without first registering to transact business in that State:
    a.   its limited partners will be liable as general partners in the foreign State's courts.
    b.   it may not defend itself in the foreign State's courts.
    c.   it may not bring enforcement actions in the foreign State's courts.
    d.   (b) and (c) but not (a).

_____ 5. Under the RULPA, a limited partner forfeits his limited liability if he:
    a.   becomes an agent of the limited partnership.
    b.   advises a general partner with respect to the business of the limited partnership.
    c.   votes on a change in the nature of the business.
    d.   none of the above.

_____ 6. If a limited partner makes a loan to the partnership, he is entitled to repayment of the loan:
    a.   before general creditors of the partnership are repaid.
    b.   on a pro rata basis with general creditors of the partnership.
    c.   after general creditors of the partnership are repaid.
    d.   none of the above.

_____ 7. A limited partnership is dissolved upon:
    a.   the death of a limited partner.
    b.   the bankruptcy of a limited partner.
    c.   the withdrawal of a general partner.
    d.   all of the above.

_____ 8. Under the RULPA, unless otherwise agreed, a limited partner is entitled to repayment of his capital contribution:
    a.   before general partners are repaid their capital contributions.
    b.   on a pro rata basis with general partners.
    c.   after general partners are repaid their capital contributions.
    d.   none of the above.

_____ 9. Which of the following unincorporated business associations is dissolved by the death of a member?
    a.   A joint stock company.
    b.   A mining partnership.
    c.   A limited partnership association.
    d.   None of the above.

_____ 10. Which of the following unincorporated business associations may be formed without the authorization or consent of the State?
    a.   A joint stock company.
    b.   A business trust.
    c.   A joint venture.
    d.   All of the above.

_____ 11. A _____ is a form of general partnership that has some characteristics of a corporation and differs from an ordinary partnership in that its shares are divided into shares with transferable certificates.
   a. mining partnership
   b. business trust
   c. limited partnership
   d. joint stock company

_____ 12. The _____ was devised to avoid the burdens of corporate regulation, particularly the formerly widespread prohibition denying corporations the power to deal in real estate.
   a. mining partnership
   b. Massachusetts trust
   c. limited partnership
   d. joint stock company

_____ 13. In a limited partnership, the general partner has:
   a. unlimited liability.
   b. liability to $500.
   c. liability to $5,000.
   d. liability to the extent of his capital contribution.

_____ 14. Bill Businessman is a limited partner in the Hickory Street Limited Partnership. With regard to liability for the debts and obligations of the Hickory Street Limited Partnership, Bill will generally have:
   a. no liability.
   b. unlimited personal liability.
   c. limited personal liability.
   d. absolute liability.

_____ 15. With regard to voting rights, a limited partner has:
   a. no voting rights.
   b. no right to vote on the admission of a new general partner.
   c. no right to vote on the dissolution of the partnership.
   d. the right to vote on any matter if it is so provided in the partnership agreement.

SHORT ESSAY

1. When may a limited partner rightfully demand the return of his contributions? _____
   _____
   _____
   _____

2. When may a limited partner be subject to unlimited personal liability for the debts and obligations of the partnership? _____
   _____
   _____
   _____

3. According to the RULPA, when may a limited partnership be dissolved? _____

_____

_____

_____

4. What are the duties owed by a general partner to the limited partnership? _____

_____

_____

_____

PART VI

SAMPLE EXAMINATION

_____ 1. A general partner may do which of the following without the consent or ratification of the limited partners?
   a. Admit a general partner.
   b. Act as an agent for the partnership.
   c. Dissolve the partnership and wind up the business.
   d. A general partner may do all of the above without the consent of the limited partners.

_____ 2. The last amendments to the RULPA were made in _____.
   a. 1950
   b. 1965
   c. 1970
   d. 1985

_____ 3. The process of liquidating a partnership is known as _____.
   a. dissolution
   b. liquidation
   c. marshaling
   d. bankruptcy

_____ 4. Arthur and Byron agree to form a partnership. Arthur contributes $3,000 in assets and agrees to devote full time to the partnership. Byron contributes $1,000 and agrees to devote full time to the partnership. How will Arthur and Byron share their profits and losses?
   a. Arthur will get 3/4 and Byron 1/4.
   b. Arthur will get 2/3 and Byron 1/3.
   c. Arthur and Byron will share profits and losses equally.
   d. Arthur will get 1/3 and Byron will get 2/3.

_____ 5. A _____ is a form of temporary partnership organized to carry out a particular business enterprise for profit.
   a. joint venture
   b. Massachusetts trust
   c. mining partnership
   d. joint stock company

_____ 6. Which of the following is correct regarding a limited partnership?
   a. Limited partners cannot have voting rights.
   b. The limited partner may not participate in management in any form without losing his limited liability.
   c. It can only be created pursuant to statutory provisions.
   d. A general partner cannot be named in the partnership name.

_____ 7. The death of a partner will dissolve a:
   a. limited partnership.
   b. mining partnership.
   c. general partnership.
   d. limited partnership, mining partnership or a general partnership.

_____ 8. In order to _____ a foreign limited partnership must register with the office of the Secretary of State.
   a. do business in Canada
   b. defend the partnership in a lawsuit
   c. bring an enforcement action in the State's courts
   d. solicit capital contributions from new limited partners

_____ 9. The _____ manage(s) a business trust.
   a. general partner
   b. trustee
   c. managing partner
   d. beneficiaries

_____ 10. Paul Partner is a partner in the Elm Street Partnership which owns the office building where its headquarters are located. Paul's interest in the building is that of a:
   a. joint tenant.
   b. tenant in the entirety.
   c. tenant in common.
   d. tenant in partnership.

_____ 11. Anita and Melva form an organization to collect donations and establish a food shelf for needy people. They raise money through a series of activities and jointly manage the enterprise. Are they a partnership?
   a. Yes, because each has a voice in management.
   b. Yes, because they both contribute to the project.
   c. No, because they have no written partnership agreement.
   d. No, because they are not running a business for profit.

_____ 12. The UPA provides that partners are _____ liable on all debts and contract obligations of the partnership.
   a. jointly
   b. strictly
   c. partially
   d. not

_____ 13. Under the UPA, the principal test to determine the existence of a partnership is:
   a. whether there is a written partnership agreement.
   b. whether the partners share equally in management.
   c. whether there is a sharing of profits and losses among the partners.
   d. whether each of the partners contributes capital.

_____ 14. In which of the following situations may a partner invoke the power of a court of equity to decree an accounting of partnership affairs?
   a. A partner is wrongfully excluded from the partnership business.
   b. The partnership agreement provides for one.
   c. A partner makes a profit in violation of his fiduciary duty.
   d. A partner may seek an accounting in all of the above situations.

_____ 15. Which of the following is correct regarding the distribution of assets upon the termination of a partnership?
   a. A partner's capital is returned before partner creditors are paid.
   b. Profits are returned before capital contributions.
   c. Outside creditors are paid before partner creditors.
   d. Capital contributions are returned before outside creditors are paid.

_____ 16. Which of the following require a unanimous vote of the partners to a general partnership?
   a. Disposal of the good will of the business.
   b. Relocating the partnership office across the street.
   c. Submission of a partnership claim or liability to arbitration.
   d. Both disposal of the good will of the business and submission of a partnership claim or liability to arbitration.

_____ 17. In his relationship with other partners, a partner has a duty of:
   a. loyalty.
   b. obedience.
   c. care.
   d. loyalty, obedience and care.

_____ 18. In a general partnership, each partner is a/an _____ to every other partner.
   a. employee
   b. agent
   c. joint venturer
   d. master

_____ 19. When a tort action is brought against a partnership and it is found to be liable, the partners have:
   a. joint liability.
   b. joint and several liability.
   c. strict liability.
   d. no liability.

_____ 20. Which of the following can be done by a vote of the majority of the partners?
   a. Admit a new partner.
   b. Dispose of the partnership's good will.
   c. Hire an office manager.
   d. Assign the partnership property for the benefit of creditors.

CHAPTER 33

NATURE AND FORMATION

PURPOSE

A corporation is a separate entity from its shareholders that is created by a law and is distinct from the individuals who create it. The corporate form of doing business is more formal than the types of business organizations that you have already studied in the previous chapters. The business corporation today is a key institution in both the American economy and in the world. The use of the corporation as a means of doing business has allowed vast concentrations of wealth and capital that have transformed this country from an agrarian to an industrial economy. Corporate law differs slightly from State to State, because each State has its own business corporation statute. However, most statutes contain many of the provisions found in the Model Business Corporation Act. The MBCA sets a standard for the statutory law of business corporations that you should study carefully even though it has not been as widely adopted as the UPA or the UCC.

CHAPTER CHECKPOINTS

After reading and studying this chapter, you should be able to:

1. List the principal attributes of a corporation and compare the corporate form of organization to the partnership and limited partnership.

2. Discuss the liability of the promoter of a corporation and the fiduciary duty of a promoter.

3. Define a "de jure" corporation and a "de facto" corporation and compare the approach of the MBCA with regard to defective incorporation to that of the common law.

4. Define "piercing the corporate veil" and discuss the circumstances under which courts are likely to pierce a corporate veil.

5. Define the term "ultra vires" and discuss the common law and modern approaches to acts of a corporation that are ultra vires.

CHAPTER OUTLINE

I. Nature of Corporations
  A. Corporate Attributes
    1. Legal Entity - A corporation is a legal entity separate and apart from its shareholders, with rights and liabilities entirely distinct from theirs.
    2. Creature of the State - A corporation may be formed only by compliance with a State incorporation statute.
    3. Limited Liability - A corporation is a legal entity and is therefore liable out of its own assets for its debts. Generally, the shareholders have limited liability for the corporation's debts that does not extend beyond the amount of their investment.
    4. Free Transferability of Corporate Shares - In the absence of contractual restrictions, shares in a corporation may be freely transferred by sale, gift or pledge. Transfers of shares of stock are governed by Article 8 of the Uniform Commercial Code.
    5. Perpetual Existence - Unless otherwise stated in its articles of incorporation, a corporation has perpetual existence and does not terminate upon the death, withdrawal, or addition of a shareholder, director, or officer.
    6. Centralized Management - The shareholders of a corporation elect the board of directors, which manages the business affairs of the corporation.
    7. As a Person - A corporation is considered a person within the meaning of the due process clause of the Fifth and Fourteenth Amendments to the Federal Constitution and of the equal protection clause of the Fourteenth Amendment. A corporation also enjoys the right of a person to be secure against unreasonable searches and seizures, as provided for in the Fourth Amendment. However, a corporation is not a person within the meaning of the clause in the Fifth Amendment that protects a "person" against self-incrimination.
    8. As a Citizen - A corporation is a citizen for some purposes but not for others. It is not a citizen as the term is used in the Fourteenth Amendment privileges and immunities of citizenship clause. A corporation is regarded as a citizen of the State of its incorporation and of the State in which it has its principal office for the purpose of determining whether diversity of citizenship exists for diversity jurisdiction in the Federal courts.

  B. Classification of Corporations
    1. Public or Private - A public corporation is one that is created to administer a unit of local civil government or one created by the United States to conduct public business. A private corporation is one organized to conduct either a privately owned business enterprise for profit or a nonprofit corporation.
    2. Profit or Nonprofit - A profit corporation is one founded for the purpose of operating a business for profit. A nonprofit corporation is one whose profits must be used exclusively for the charitable, educational, or scientific purpose for which it was formed.
    3. Domestic or Foreign - A corporation is a domestic corporation in the State in which it is incorporated. It is a foreign corporation in every other State or jurisdiction. In States other than the State of incorporation, a corporation must obtain a certificate to do business. This involves filing certain information with the Secretary of State, the payment of prescribed fees, and the designation of a resident agent. In most States an unlicensed foreign corporation is not entitled to maintain a suit in the State courts until it has obtained a certificate of authority, but it may defend against an action brought against it. Many States impose fines on the corporation's officers and directors and hold them personally liable on contracts made within the State.
    4. Closely Held - A corporation is closely held when its outstanding shares of stock are held by a small number of persons, who frequently are relatives or friends. Shareholders are usually active in the management and control of the business. Generally, closely held corporations are subject to

the general incorporation statute that governs all corporations. Some States have enacted special legislation to accommodate the needs of closely held corporations. A Statutory Close Corporation Supplement to the MBCA has recently been promulgated.

5. Professional Corporations - All States have statutes that permit the practice of professions by duly licensed individuals who wish to do business in the corporate form. There is a Model Professional Corporation Supplement to the MBCA.

II. Formation of a Corporation - Incorporation involves greater expense and formality than the formation of a partnership or sole proprietorship. Under a general incorporation statute, the process requires the performance of several acts by various groups, individuals, and State officials.

A. Organizing the Corporation

1. Promoters - A promoter is a person who brings about the "birth" of a corporation. This person arranges for the capital and financing of the corporation; she assembles the necessary assets, equipment, licenses, personnel, leases and services.

a. Promoter's Contracts - Promoters enter into contracts in anticipation of the creation of the corporation. If these contracts are executed by the promoter in her own name and there is no further action, the promoter is liable on such contracts and the corporation, when it is created, is not automatically liable. The corporation is liable only if it adopts the contract.

b. Promoter's Fiduciary Duty - The promoters have a fiduciary duty among themselves, and with the corporation, its subscribers and its initial shareholders. This duty requires good faith, fair dealing, and full disclosure. Promoters must account for any secret profit; failure to do so may violate Federal or State securities laws.

2. Subscribers - A subscriber is a person who agrees to purchase initial stock in a corporation. A preincorporation subscription is an offer to purchase capital stock in a corporation yet to be formed. The majority of courts regard a subscription as a continuing offer to purchase stock from a nonexistent entity which is incapable of accepting the offer until created. Under this view, the subscription may be revoked at any time prior to its acceptance. A minority of jurisdictions treat a subscription as a contract among the various subscribers which is irrevocable except with the consent of all of them. The MBCA provides that a subscription is irrevocable for a period of six months, unless otherwise provided in the subscription agreement or unless all of the subscribers consent to the revocation of the subscription. If the corporation accepts during the period of irrevocability, a binding contract exists.

3. Selection of State for Incorporation - A corporation is usually incorporated in the State in which it intends to be located and to transact all or the principal part of its business. It may be formed in one State, however, and have its principal place of business in another.

B. Formalities of Incorporation - Typically, the incorporators execute and deliver to the Secretary of State the articles of incorporation in duplicate. Under the Model Act, once the certificate of incorporation (charter) is issued, the board of directors named in the articles of incorporation holds an organizational meeting. At this meeting they adopt bylaws, elect officers, and transact other business.

1. Selection of Name - Most incorporation laws required that the name contain a word or words such as "corporation," "Inc.," "Co.," or "Ltd." to clearly indicate the entity is a corporation. A name may not be deceptively similar to that of another domestic corporation or of a foreign corporation authorized to do business within the State.

2. Incorporators - The incorporators are the persons who sign the articles of incorporation that are filed with the Secretary of State of the State of incorporation.

3. Articles of Incorporation - The articles of incorporation (charter) generally include the corporation's name, address, purpose, period of duration, number of authorized shares and designations of classes of shares, the number and names of the initial directors, the name and address of each incorporator, the preemptive rights of shareholders, if any, and other provisions

consistent with the incorporation statute and other law.

4. Organizational Meeting - The Model Act requires that an organizational meeting be held to adopt bylaws, elect officers, and transact "such other business as may come before the meeting."

5. Bylaws - The bylaws of a corporation are the rules and regulations that govern its internal management. The bylaws may not contain anything contrary to or inconsistent with any provision in the incorporation statute or in the articles of incorporation. The bylaws do not have to be publicly filed. In many States they may be changed without shareholder approval. Under the Statutory Close Corporation Supplement, a close corporation may elect not to adopt any bylaws if there is a shareholder agreement or if the articles of incorporation contain all of the information required to be stated in the bylaws.

III. Recognition of Disregard of Corporateness - Because a corporation is a creature of the State, corporate attributes such as limited liability and perpetual existence are recognized when the enterprise complies with the State's requirements for incorporation.

A. Defective Incorporation - Simplified incorporation procedures have greatly reduced the frequency of defective incorporation. Possible consequences of defective incorporation include: (1) the State may bring an action for involuntary dissolution; (2) associates may be held personally liable on an obligation; (3) the association may assert that it is not liable on an obligation; or (4) a third party may assert that he is not liable to the association.

1. Common Law Approach - Under the common law, a defectively formed corporation was sometimes accorded corporate attributes.

a. Corporation de Jure - A corporation de jure is one that has been formed in substantial compliance with the incorporation statute and the organizational procedure. Such a corporation may not be challenged by anyone.

b. Corporation de Facto - A corporation de facto is one that is not de jure, because it has failed to substantially comply with the incorporation statute. Nevertheless, it is recognized for most purposes as a corporation. There must be a bona fide attempt to comply with the law organizing a corporation under a general incorporation statute and there must be the actual exercise of corporate power by conducting a business in the belief that a corporation has been formed. The State can challenge the existence of a de facto corporation in a quo warranto ("by what right") action.

c. Corporation by Estoppel - Estoppel does not create a corporation. It operates only to prevent a person or persons from raising the question of the corporation's existence where the necessary elements of holding out and reliance are present.

d. Defective Corporation - If the associates who purported to form a corporation have not formed either a de jure or a de facto corporation and the doctrine of estoppel does not apply, then the associates will be held unlimitedly liable as though they were partners.

2. Statutory Approach - The Model Act and many States provide that a "certificate of incorporation" shall be conclusive evidence that all conditions precedent required to be performed by the incorporators have been complied with and that the corporation has been incorporated under this Act, except as against this State." Some courts have interpreted this to mean that the Model Act has abolished the doctrines of de facto corporations by estoppel. Under the Revised Act, the filing of the articles of incorporation by the Secretary of State is conclusive proof that the incorporators have satisfied the conditions precedent to incorporation. The Revised Act imposes liability only on persons who purport to act as or on behalf of a corporation, knowing that there was no incorporation, a provision analogous to the RULPA.

B. Piercing the Corporate Veil - Courts will pierce the corporate veil of a properly formed corporation when it is used to defeat public convenience, commit wrongdoing, protect fraud, or circumvent the law. Courts have done so most frequently with closely held corporation in parent-subsidiary relationships.

1. Closely Held Corporations - Courts will pierce the corporate veil where shareholders have: (1) not conducted the business on a corporate basis; (2) not provided an adequate financial basis for the business; or (3) used the corporation to defraud. Under the Statutory Close Corporation Supplement, a court may pierce the corporate veil of a close corporation if the same circumstances would justify imposing personal liablity on the shareholders of a general business corporation, but a court may not pierce the corporate veil just because the corporation is a statutory close corporation.

2. Parent-Subsidiary - A subsidiary corporation is one in which another corporation, the parent corporation, owns at least a majority of the subsidiary's shares and therefore has control over it. Courts will pierce the corporate veil and hold the parent liable for the debts of the subsidiary if: (1) both corporations are not adequately capitalized; (2) the formalities of separate corporate procedures are not observed; (3) each corporation is not held out to the public as a separate enterprise; (4) the funds of the two corporations are commingled; or (5) the parent corporation completely dominates the operation of the subsidiary to advance only the parent's own interests.

IV. Corporate Powers - A corporation has only those powers that the State has conferred on it. These powers are those expressly set forth in the statute and in the articles of incorporation and those that may reasonably be implied from them.

A. Sources of Corporate Powers

1. Statutory Powers - The general powers of a corporation are typically set forth in the incorporation statute. Under the Model Act these include perpetual existence, the right to hold property, to sue, to make contracts, and to conduct its business.

2. Express Charter Powers - The objects or purposes for which a corporation is formed are stated in its articles of incorporation. These powers must relate to a legitimate business activity or industry within the purview of the general statute.

3. Implied Powers - A corporation has the authority to take any action that is necessary or convenient to and consistent with the execution of any of its express powers and the operation of the business that it was formed to conduct. Express powers may and should be stated in general language.

B. Ultra Vires Acts - Any action or contract made by a corporation that goes beyond its express and implied powers is ultra vires. This term means that the action is outside of the scope and type that the corporation is legally empowered to perform.

1. Effect of Ultra Vires Acts - Traditionally, ultra vires contracts were unenforceable as null and void. Under the modern approach, courts allow the ultra vires defense where the contract is wholly executory on both sides. An illegal contract, whether ultra vires or not, is unenforceable on the basis of illegality. Most statutes have now abolished the defense of ultra vires in an action by or against a corporation. The MBCA provides that "no act of a corporation and no conveyance or transfer of real or personal property to or by a corporation shall be invalid by reason of the fact that the corporation was without capacity or power to do such act or to make or receive such conveyance or transfer."

2. Remedies for Ultra Vires Acts - Although under modern statutes ultra vires may no longer be used defensively against liability, the following ways to redress ultra vires acts are provided by the Model Act: (1) an injunction may be issued; (2) a suit for damages may be brought by the corporation or through shareholders (derivatively) against officers or directors; (3) the attorney general of the State of incorporation may bring suit to dissolve the corporation or to enjoin it from transacting unauthorized business.

C. Liability for Torts and Crimes - A corporation is liable for the torts and crimes committed by its agents in the course of their employment. The doctrine of respondeat superior imposes full liability on a corporation for the torts committed by its agents and employees during the course of their employment. A corporation may be liable for violation of statutes imposing liability where the offense is perpetrated by a high corporate officer or the board of directors. Punishment of a corporation for crimes is by fine and not imprisonment.

DEFINITIONS

1. Corporation

2. Management

3. Public corporation

4. Private corporation

5. Profit corporation

6. Non-profit corporation

7. Domestic corporation

8. Foreign corporation

9. Closely-held corporation

10. Professional corporation

11. Promoter

12. Subscriber

13. Articles of incorporation

14. Incorporators

15. By-laws

16. Corporation de jure

17. Corporation de facto

18. Corporation by estoppel

19. Defective corporation

20. Piercing the corporate veil

21. Ultra vires

TRUE/FALSE

_____ 1. Shareholders are personally liable for the corporation's debts up to the amount of their investment.

_____ 2. A corporation is liable for the personal obligations of its shareholders.

_____ 3. A shareholder is neither a principal nor an agent of the corporation.

_____ 4. A non-profit corporation may make a profit.

_____ 5. A promoter who enters into a pre-incorporation contract in the name of the corporation is ordinarily personally liable on that contract.

_____ 6. Under the MBCA, a subscription may be revoked at any time prior to its acceptance.

_____ 7. A corporation must be incorporated in the State in which it has its principal place of business.

_____ 8. The by-laws of a corporation may not be changed without shareholder approval.

_____ 9. A corporation may be created by estoppel.

_____ 10. Under the MBCA, persons who assume to act as a corporation without authority to do so are subject to unlimited personal liability for the debts of the enterprise.

_____ 11. A general statement of corporate purpose is sufficient to give rise to all of the powers necessary to accomplish that purpose.

_____ 12. A corporation is liable for the torts and crimes committed by its agents in the course of their employment.

_____ 13. The Ajax Corporation is incorporated in the State of Wisconsin. If it wishes to do business in Minnesota, it must register as a foreign corporation.

_____ 14. The Model Business Corporation Act is the Federal statute governing corporations in the United States.

_____ 15. The United States Postal Service is a public corporation.

MULTIPLE CHOICE

_____ 1. A corporation:
   a. may sue or be sued by one of its shareholders.
   b. is dissolved by a transfer of its stock from one individual to another.
   c. may not own or deal in real property.
   d. all of the above.

_____ 2. A corporation is dissolved by:
  a.   the death of a director.
  b.   the withdrawal of an officer.
  c.   the bankruptcy of a shareholder.
  d.   none of the above.

_____ 3. The officers of a corporation:
  a.   must be shareholders of the corporation.
  b.   are elected by the shareholders of the corporation.
  c.   are appointed by the board of directors of the corporation.
  d.   (a) and (c) but not (b).

_____ 4. If a corporation transacts business in a foreign State without first qualifying to transact business in that State:
  a.   its contracts are invalid in the foreign State's courts.
  b.   it may not defend itself in the foreign State's courts.
  c.   it may not bring enforcement actions in the foreign State's courts.
  d.   (b) and (c) but not (a).

_____ 5. A corporation becomes liable on a pre-incorporation contract made by promoters in the name of the corporation and in its behalf when:
  a.   the contract is executed.
  b.   the corporation is formed.
  c.   the corporation adopts or ratifies the contract.
  d.   none of the above.

_____ 6. The promoters of a corporation owe a fiduciary duty to:
  a.   each other.
  b.   subscribers.
  c.   initial shareholders.
  d.   all of the above.

_____ 7. The existence of a *de facto* corporation can be challenged by:
  a.   the State.
  b.   creditors of the corporation.
  c.   debtors of the corporation.
  d.   none of the above.

_____ 8. Piercing the corporate veil:
  a.   invalidates the contracts of the corporation.
  b.   imposes personal liability upon the shareholders for the obligations of the corporation.
  c.   denies the corporation access to the State's courts.
  d.   (b) and (c) but not (a).

_____ 9. Under the MBCA, a corporation may:
  a.   lend money to its employees.
  b.   be a shareholder in other corporations.
  c.   make charitable contributions.
  d.   all of the above.

_____ 10. Under the MBCA, the defense of *ultra vires* in an action for breach of contract by or against a corporation:
   a.   is unavailable.
   b.   is available where the contract is wholly executory on both sides.
   c.   is available where the corporation has received full performance from the other party.
   d.   is available where the other party has received full performance from the corporation.

_____ 11. A corporation:
   a.   is not capable of committing a crime.
   b.   is capable of committing a crime but may not be punished by imprisonment.
   c.   is capable of committing a crime but may not be punished by fine.
   d.   none of the above.

_____ 12. The City of San Francisco would best be described as which of the following?
   a.   A public corporation.
   b.   A corporation formed pursuant to the Model Business Corporation Act.
   c.   A close corporation.
   d.   A domestic corporation.

_____ 13. Albert invested $500 in the stock of the Ajax Corporation. Six months later, Ajax filed for bankrupcty with debts of $50,000. What is the amount of Albert's liability?
   a. $500.
   b. $50,000.
   c.   Albert is liable for a portion of the debt based upon the ratio of the number of shares he held to the total number of shares outstanding and can be liable for more than his initial investment.
   d.   Albert has no liability, because he is a creditor of the corporation.

_____ 14. What do the initials "P.C." after a firm name indicate?
   a.   They indicate the firm is a public corporation.
   b.   They indicate the firm is a private corporation.
   c.   They indicate the firm is a for profit corporation.
   d.   They indicate the firm is a professional corporation.

_____ 15. Under the Model Business Corporation Act, which of the following corporate names would not be permissible?
   a.   Ajax Corporation.
   b.   Ajax Incorporated.
   c.   Ajax Limited.
   d.   Ajax.

SHORT ESSAY

1.   What distinguishes a corporation from a partnership? _____
   _____

2.   Under what conditions may a *de facto* corporation be formed? _____
   _____

3.   When is a court likely to pierce the corporate veil? _____
   _____

CHAPTER 34

FINANCIAL STRUCTURE

PURPOSE

In this chapter, you study debt and equity securities as a means of raising capital. Equity securities represent an ownership interest in the corporation and include both common and preferred stock. Bonds are debt securities and do not represent an ownership interest in the corporation. Instead, they create a debtor-creditor relationship between the corporation and the bondholder. Retained earnings are also essential to the financial structure of a corporation. In this chapter, you study the circumstances under which a corporation may use debt and equity securities and the various tests used for determining whether a corporation may pay a dividend.

CHAPTER CHECKPOINTS

After reading and studying this chapter, you should be able to:

1. Define the characteristics of and distinguish between debt securities and equity securities.

2. Identify and describe the principal types of debt and equity securities.

3. Give the MBCA definition of the term "distribution" and then list and summarize the various types of distributions.

4. List and discuss the legal restrictions upon the payment of dividends and other distributions. Compare the various tests for the legality of distributions that are commonly found in State corporate statutes.

5. Summarize the provisions of Article 8 with respect to the transfer of investment securities.

CHAPTER OUTLINE

I. Debt Securities - Two of the principal sources of capital formation in corporations involve debt and equity investment securities. Equity securities represent an ownership interest in the corporation which provides an initial and often continuing source of corporate funds. Debt securities do not represent an ownership interest in the corporation but create a debtor-creditor relationship. The third principal way a corporation may meet its financial needs is through retained earnings. Corporations frequently find it advantageous to use debt as a source of funds. Debt securities involve a promise to repay the principal amount of the loan at a stated time and to pay interest.

A. Authority to Issue Debt Securities - The Model Act provides that each corporation has power to issue their debt securities, and the board of directors may do so without the authorization or consent of the shareholders.

B. Types of Debt Securities - Debt securities are typically issued under an indenture or debt agreement which specifies the terms of the loan.
   1. Unsecured Bonds - Unsecured bonds are called debentures. Debenture holders are unsecured creditors who rank equally with other general creditors. To protect unsecured creditors, agreements impose limitations on the corporation's borrowing, payment of dividends, and redemption and reacquisition of its own shares. The agreements may also require minimum reserves.
   2. Secured Bonds - These are claims against a corporation's general assets and also a lien on specific property.
   3. Income Bonds - Income bonds condition the payment to some extent on corporate earnings.
   4. Convertible Bonds - These may be exchanged for other securities of the corporation at a specified ratio.
   5. Callable Bonds - Callable bonds are subject to a redemption provision that permits the corporation to redeem or call all or part of the issue before maturity at a specified redemption price.

II. Equity Securities - Shareholders as owners of the corporation occupy a position of greater financial risk than others. A share is a proportionate ownership interest in a corporation. A shareholder generally has the right to participate in control, participate in earnings, and participate in residual assets on dissolution.
   A. Issuance of Shares
      1. Authority to Issue - The initial amount of shares is determined by the promoters or incorporators. A corporation is limited to selling only the amount of shares that has been authorized in the articles of incorporation. Shareholders have the residual authority to change the amount of authorized capital stock. Unauthorized shares purportedly issued are void.
      2. Qualification of Stock - Blue sky laws are State laws regulating the issuance nad sale of securities. They all have provisions prohibiting fraud in the sale of securities. The 1933 Federal securities statute is often called the Truth in Securities Act and is administered by SEC. It requires a corporation to disclose certain information about the security.
      3. Pre-emptive Rights - Pre-emptive rights are a shareholder's right to purchase a pro rata share of new stock offerings in order to preserve his proportionate interest in the equity. They do not apply to the re-issue of previously issued shares, noncash consideration, or in connection with a merger or consolidation.
      4. Amount of Consideration for Shares - Shares are deemed fully paid and nonassessable when a corporation receives full payment of the lawful consideration for which the shares are issued.
         a. Par Value Stock - Par value shares may be issued for any amount, not less than par, set by board of directors or shareholders stated in charter. It indicates only the minimum price corporation must receive. Par value must be stated in the articles of incorporation. The consideration received constitutes stated capital to the extent of the par value. Any excess constitutes capital surplus. The 1979 MBCA eliminated the concept of par value.
         b. No Par Value Stock - Shares without par value may be issued for any amount set by the board of directors or shareholders. Directors are free to allocate any or all of the consideration received, unless the no par stock has a liquidation preference.
         c. Treasury Stock - Treasury stock are shares reacquired by a corporation. They are issued but not outstanding, and they do not have voting rights and pre-emptive rights. They are not entitled to the payment of dividends.
      5. Payment for Newly Issued Shares

     a.   Type of Consideration - Consideration is defined in a more limited fashion than under contract law. It includes cash, property and services actually rendered but not promissory notes and future services.

     b.   Valuation of Consideration - The determination of value is the responsibility of directors. In the absence of fraud, the judgment of the board as to the value of the consideration shall be conclusive.

6.   Liability for Shares - A corporation issues watered stock when it issues stock that is fully paid up and nonassessable consideration shares that are worth less than the full lawful consideration for the shares. The liability of shareholders on this is enforceable by both the corporation and its creditors. A transferee is also liable for the balance due on the stock until the par or stated value of the stock has been fully paid and without knowledge that the shares not fully paid or if shares are issued for promissory notes or for contracts for services to be performed. Transferor remains liable for the unpaid balance.

B.   Classes of Shares - Corporations are authorized by statute to issue two or more classes of stock.

1.   Common Stock - Common stock is stock not having any special contract rights. The greatest proportion of the corporation's capital structure is common stock. It bears the greatest risk of loss in the event of failure of the enterprise.

2.   Preferred Stock - Preferred stockholders have contractual rights superior to those of common stockholders.

     a.   Dividend Preferences - Shareholders of preferred stock receive full dividends before any dividend may be paid to holders of common stock. With cumulative preferred stock, if the board does not declare regular dividends on the preferred stock, such omitted dividends are cumulative, and no dividend may be declared on the common stock until all dividend arrearages on the preferred stock are declared and paid. With noncumulative stock, the regular dividends do not cumulate on failure of the board to declare them. With cumulative to the extent earned stock, cumulative unpaid dividends are payable only to the extent funds were legally available to pay. With participating preferred stock, payment of the prior preferred dividends and payment of dividends on the common stock is at a rate equal to the fixed rate of preferred.

     b.   Liquidation Preferences - The holders of preferred stock share pro rata with the common shareholders if the stock does not expressly provide for a prefernce of any kind on dissolution and liquidation. If a liquidation preference is provided, preferred stock has priority over common to the extent of the par value of the stock.

     c.   Additional Rights and Limitations - Preferred stock may have additional rights, designations and limitations, such as denial of voting rights or conertibility into shares of another class.

3.   Stock Rights and Options - A stock option is a contractual right to purchase stock from a corporation. One use of stock options is as incentive compensation for directors, officers and employees.

III. Dividends and Other Distributions - It is a fundamental desire of most shareholders to share in the profits through the receipt of distributions or dividends. Dividend payout depends on the contractual rights of the holders of the particular shares involved, the provisions in the charter and by-laws, and provisions of the State incorporation statute.

A.   Types of Dividends and Other Distributions - The Model Act defines a distribution as a direct or indirect transfer of money or other property or incurrence of indebtedness, by a corporation to or for benefit of any of its shareholders.

1.   Cash Dividends - These are the customary types of dividend. They are declared and paid at regular intervals from legally available funds.

2.   Property Dividends - The distribution of earnings can be made to shareholders in the form of

property. A distillary once paid each of its stockholders a dividend in whiskey.

3. Stock Dividends - These are a ratable distribution of additional shares of the capital stock of the corporation to its shareholders.

4. Stock Splits - In a stock split, each of the issued and outstanding shares is simply broken up into a greater number of shares, each representing a proportionately smaller interest in the corporation.

5. Liquidating Dividends - These are a distribution of capital assets to shareholders on termination of the business and is considered a form of dividend.

6. Redemption of Shares - The repurchase by the corporation of its own shares is a redemption. Preferred shares are frequently redeemable at a call price.

7. Acquisition of Shares - A corporation may acquire its own shares by purchase, gift or otherwise. Unless canceled, these shares are referred to as treasury shares.

B. Legal Restrictions on Dividends and Other Distributions - All States have statutes restricting the funds that are legally available for dividends and corporate assets. All States impose the equity insolvency test. Insolvent means the inability of a corporation to pay its debts as they become due in the usual course of its business.

1. Defintions
   a. Nimble Dividends - The nimble dividends test allows dividends to be paid from current earnings even when there is no surplus.
   b. Earned Surplus - Undistributed net profits, income, gains and losses from the date of incorporation are a corporation's earned surplus.
   c. Surplus - Excess of net assets of a corporation over its stated capital.
   d. Net Assets - Amount by which the total assets of a corporation exceed the total debts of the corporation.
   e. Stated Capital - Defined as the sum of the consideration received by the corporation for its issued stock capital surplus. The entire surplus of a corporation other than its earned surplus.

2. Legal Restrictions on Cash Dividends
   a. Earned Surplus Test - Unreserved and unrestricted earned surplus is available for dividend in all jurisdictions.
   b. Surplus Test - Some States permit dividends to be paid out of any surplus, earned or capital.
   c. Net Assets Test - The Model Act allows a dividend to be paid unless corporation's total assets after payment of the dividend would be less than the sum of its total liabilities.
   d. Nimble Dividends - The statutes of a number of States permit payment of dividends out of current earnings notwithstanding the existence of deficit.

3. Legal Restrictions on Liquidating Distributions - States usually will permit distribution, of dividends, in partial liquidation from capital surplus. A distribution paid out of such surplus is a return to the shareholders of a part of their investment. No such distribution may be made if the company is insolvent.

4. Legal Restrictions on Redemptions and Acquisition of Shares - To protect creditors and holders of preferred shares, in most States, a corporation may not redeem or purchase its redeemable shares when insolvent or when such redemption or purchase would render it insolvent or reduce its net assets below the aggregate amount payable.

C. Declaration and Payment of Dividends - Shareholder may not maintain an action at law against the corporation to recover a dividend until and unless the dividend has been formally declared by the board of directors. A dividend declared is a debt of the corporation and enforceable at law. Shareholders may bring a suit in equity against the board of directors and seeking a mandatory injunction requiring the director to declare a dividend.

D. Liability for Improper Dividends and Distributions - There is joint and several liability on the director of a corporation who votes for or assents to the declaration of a dividend or other distribution of corporate assets contrary to the incorporation statute, unless they rely in good faith on financial statements presented to them by the corporation's officers, public accountants, or finance committee. The liability of a director is to the corporation or creditors. Shareholders who receive illegal dividends as a result of their own fraudulent act or with knowledge of the unlawful character of the dividends are under a duty to refund them to the corporation.

IV. Transfer of Investment Securities - An investor has the right to transfer her securities by sale, gift, or pledge. The availability of a ready market for security affords liquidity and makes the security attractive and useful as collateral.
   A. Ownership of Securities
      1. Record Ownership - A security is intangible personal property and exists independently of a certificate. A certificated security is one represented by a certificate. An uncertificated security is not represented by a certificate.
      2. Duty of Issuer to Register Transfer of Security - It is the issuing corporation's duty to register transfer of its certificated securities and issue new certificates to the new owner.
      3. Lost, Destroyed, or Stolen Certificated Securities - The owner is entitled to a new certificate to replace the missing one, provided (a) he request it before the issuer has notice that the lost certificate has been acquired by bona fide purchaser; (b) he files a sufficient indemnity bond with the issuer; and (c) he satisfies other reasonable requirements. If these are not met, the shareholder may be deprived of the right to a replacement certificate by failing to notify the issuer within a reasonable time.

   B. Transfer of Securities
      1. Manner of Transfer - Under Article 8 of the Code, a transfer is made by delivery of the certificate if it is in bearer form or indorsed in blank, or if in registered form with either (a) indorsement on it by an appropriate person; or (b) a separate document of assignment and transfer signed by an appropriate person (person specified in the certificate or entitled to it by special indorsement).
      2. Bona Fide Purchaser - A bona fide purchaser is a purchaser for value in good faith and without notice of any adverse claim who takes delivery of a certificated security in bearer form or in registered form issued to her or indorsed to her in blank.
      3. Transfer Warranties - A person by transferring certificated securities warrants that (a) the transfer is effective and rightful; (b) the security is genuine and not materially altered; and (c) he knows of no fact that might impair the validity of the security.
      4. Forged or Unauthorized Indorsement - The owner of securities represented by a certificate is not deprived of his title by a transfer of the certificate bearing a forged or unauthorized indorsement. An issuer who registers an unauthorized indorsement is subject to liability for improper registration.

DEFINITIONS

1. Equity security

2. Debt security

3. Pre-emptive right

4. Par value stock

5. Stated capital

6. Capital surplus

7. No par value stock

8. Treasury stock

9. Common stock

10. Preferred stock

11. Cumulative dividend

12. Non-cumulative dividend

13. Liquidating dividend

14. Insolvency test

15. Nimble dividends

16. Earned surplus

17. Surplus

18. Net assets

19. Earned surplus test

20. Surplus test

21. Amended MBCA test

22. Uncertificated security

23. Certificated security

24. Indenture

25. Secured bond

26. Income bond

27. Convertible bond

28. Callable bond

TRUE/FALSE

_____ 1. Equity securities create a debtor-creditor relationship between the corporation and the shareholder.

_____ 2. The board of directors of a corporation may not issue bonds or other obligations in the name of the corporation without shareholder approval.

_____ 3. The amount of shares that a corporation is authorized to issue may not be changed without shareholder approval.

_____ 4. Shares without par value may be issued for any amount set by the board of directors.

_____ 5. The rights of preferred shareholders are subordinate to the rights of all of the creditors of the corporation.

_____ 6. No dividend is payable upon any class of stock unless duly declared by the board of directors.

_____ 7. Shares of common stock are frequently redeemable by the corporation at a call price stated in the stock certificate.

_____ 8. A corporation may not pay a dividend when the payment of the dividend would render the corporation insolvent.

_____ 9. Under the MBCA, a corporation may purchase its own shares only out of earned surplus.

_____ 10. Once properly declared, a cash dividend is considered a debt owing by the corporation to the shareholders.

_____ 11. In most States, an unsuspecting shareholder who receives an illegal dividend from an insolvent corporation cannot be compelled to make a refund.

_____ 12. Title to a certificated security cannot be transferred through a forged or unauthorized indorsement.

_____ 13. Under the earned surplus test, capital surplus may be used for the payment of dividends.

_____ 14. In most States, a corporation may not redeem shares when it is insolvent.

_____ 15. The Model Business Corporation Act requires that a par value be set for the stock of a corporation.

MULTIPLE CHOICE

_____ 1. The claim of a secured creditor is enforceable:
   a. only against the general assets of the corporation.
   b. only against specific property of the corporation.
   c. against both the general assets and specific property of the corporation.
   d. none of the above.

____ 2. A corporation that sells its shares of stock in violation of the applicable regulatory statutes is subject to:
   a. court injunction.
   b. possible criminal prosecution.
   c. civil liability in damages.
   d. all of the above.

____ 3. The par value of a share of stock must:
   a. be stated in the articles of incorporation.
   b. reflect the actual value of the share.
   c. reflect the actual price paid to the corporation.
   d. (b) and (c) but not (a).

____ 4. Treasury shares may be:
   a. voted.
   b. paid dividends.
   c. sold at less than par value.
   d. none of the above.

____ 5. Valid consideration for the issuance of capital stock includes:
   a. promissory notes.
   b. real property.
   c. future services.
   d. all of the above.

____ 6. Shares of stock which are redeemed by the corporation become:
   a. unauthorized shares.
   b. authorized but unissued shares.
   c. issued but not outstanding shares.
   d. treasury shares.

____ 7. Capital surplus may result from:
   a. an allocation of part of the consideration received for no-par shares.
   b. any consideration in excess of par value received for par shares.
   c. a reappraisal upward of certain corporate assets.
   d. all of the above.

____ 8. A shareholder may maintain an action at law against the corporation to recover a dividend whenever:
   a. unreserved and unrestricted earned surplus is available for payment of the dividend.
   b. the dividend may be paid out of capital surplus without impairing stated capital.
   c. the dividend has been formally declared by resolution of the board of directors.
   d. all of the above.

____ 9. A stock dividend:
   a. may be revoked unless actually distributed.
   b. cannot be rescinded as against non-assenting shareholders.
   c. is considered a debt owing by the corporation to the shareholders.
   d. (b) and (c) but not (a).

_____ 10. A purchaser for value and without notice of adverse claims who receives a re-registered certificated security on registration of transfer warrants that:
   a. the transfer is effective and rightful.
   b. he has no knowledge of any unauthorized signature in a necessary indorsement.
   c. the security has not been materially altered.
   d. all of the above.

_____ 11. An issuer who registers the transfer of a certificated security upon an unauthorized indorsement is subject to liability for:
   a. conversion.
   b. interference with contractual relations.
   c. improper registration.
   d. fraudulent misrepresentation.

_____ 12. Which of the following tests for the payment of dividends is the most restrictive?
   a. The surplus test.
   b. The earned surplus test.
   c. The net assets test.
   d. The nimble dividends test.

_____ 13. Which of the following tests for the payment of dividends is the least restrictive?
   a. The surplus test.
   b. The earned surplus test.
   c. The net assets test.
   d. The nimble dividends test.

_____ 14. Bonds that are subject to a redemption provision which permit the corporation to redeem or pay off all or a part of the issue before maturity at a specified redemption price are known as _____ bonds.
   a. secured
   b. income
   c. callable
   d. convertible

_____ 15. What law governs the transfer of securities?
   a. The Model Business Corporation Act.
   b. Article 9 of the UCC.
   c. Article 8 of the UCC.
   d. The Federal Securities and Exchange Act.

SHORT ESSAY

1. What are the rights of a shareholder?

2. Why is preferred stock usually issued with a par value?

_____

_____

3. When will a court of equity grant an injunction requiring the directors of a corporation to declare a
    dividend? _____

    _____

    _____

    _____

4. What warranties are given by a person who transfers certificated securities to a purchaser for value? _____

    _____

    _____

    _____

MANAGEMENT STRUCTURE

PURPOSE

In this chapter, you study the pyramidal corporate structure that is required by State incorporation statutes. Shareholders are the base of the pyramid as the residual owners of the corporation. Their role is to elect the board of directors who determine questions of operating policy. Directors have broad authority to delegate power to the officers and agents of the corporation. The directors appoint the officers who in turn hire and fire the personnel necessary to operate and run the day-to-day affairs of the corporation. In this chapter, you study the statutory provisions regarding the management structure.

CHAPTER CHECKPOINTS

After reading and studying this chapter, you should be able to:

1. Compare the statutory model of corporate governance to the actual governance of closely held corporations and publicly held corporations.

2. Compare straight and cumulative voting and discuss who benefits from cumulative voting.

3. Summarize the role of the board of directors in corporate governance and discuss the liability of directors under the business judgment rule.

4. Summarize the enforcement rights of shareholders.

5. List and discuss the duties of directors and officers.

CHAPTER OUTLINE

I. Role of Shareholders - Corporate management structure is pyramidal. Shareholders are residual owners of a corporation. The board of directors are the shareholders' elected representatives. They have been delegated the power to manage the business. The corporate officers hold office at the will of the board.
    A. Voting Rights of Shareholders - Shareholders are entitled to one vote for each share of stock that is owned. A shareholder may exercise voting rights at both annual and special shareholder meetings. Annual meetings are required and must be held at a time fixed in the by-laws. If none is held within a 13-month period, any shareholder may petition and obtain a court order requiring that a meeting be

held. The Revised Act modifies this slightly. Special meetings may be called by the board of directors, holders of at least 10% of the shares. Majority shares entitled to vote constitutes a quorum, but can't consist of less than 1/3 of shares entitled to vote.

1. Election and Removal of Directors - Directors are elected each year at the annual meeting of shareholders. If directors are divided into 2 classes, they are elected once a year in alternate years for a two-year term; if 3 classes, for three-year terms; to provide an element of continuity in membership of the board. Directors are elected by a plurality of the votes. Cumulative voting entitles each shareholder who has one vote for each share owned, to cumulate his votes and give one candidate as many votes as the number of directors to be elected multiplied by number of shares owned. Permits a minority group, acting together, to obtain representation on the board if they own a certain minimum number of shares. Shareholders may by majority vote remove, with or without cause, any director or entire board of directors in a meeting called for that purpose.

2. Approval of Fundamental Changes - Extraordinary matters require shareholder approval.

3. Concentrations of Voting Power
   a. Proxies - A proxy is an authorization to vote another's shares at a shareholder meeting. The duration is typically limited by statute to no more than 11 months.
   b. Voting Trusts - Transfer of corporate shares' voting rights to a trustee. Duration is limited to 10 years. Usually used in publicly held and closely held corporations.
   c. Shareholder Agreements - Are not limited in duration. Frequently used in closely held corporations in order to provide each of the shareholders with greater control and delectus personae.

B. Enforcement Rights of Shareholders - To protect a shareholder's interests in the corporation.

1. Right to Inspect Books and Records - Shareholder is entitled to examine specified corporate records upon prior written request if the demand is made in good faith and for a proper purpose. Proper purpose means a purpose that is reasonably relevant to that shareholder's interest in the corporation.

2. Shareholder Suits - The ultimate recourse of a shareholder.
   a. Direct Suits - Suit brought by a shareholder against the corporation based upon his ownership of shares.
   b. Derivative Suits - Suit brought by a shareholder on behalf of the corporation to enforce a right belonging to the corporation, to recover damages from an ultra vires act.

3. Shareholder's Right to Dissent - Includes most mergers, consolidations, compulsory share exchanges, and a sale or exchange of all or substantially all the assets of the corporation not in the usual and regular course of business.

C. Liability of Shareholders - Limited to his investment.

1. Defective Incorporation - Shareholders who actively participated may be personally liable for the enterprise's obligation.

2. Disregard of the Corporate Entity - Where justice requires, courts will pierce the corporate veil and impose liability on shareholders even though they have strictly complied with the required incorporation procedures.

3. Illegal Distributions - Shareholders who knowingly receive improperly declared dividends are liable to return them, if the corporation is insolvent.

4. Controlling Shareholders - Those who own a sufficient number of shares to have effective control over the corporation. Courts require sales of controlling shareholders' shares be made with due care.

II. Role of Management - The board of directors determines general corporate policy and appoints officer to execute that policy and to administer the day-to-day operation of the corporation.

A. Board of Directors - The directors are fiduciaries who must perform their duties in good faith, in the best interests of the corporation, and with due care.
   1. Selection and Removal of Officers - Directors have the responsibility to appoint the corporate officers and may remove any officer at any time.
   2. Capital structure - The directors determine the capital structure and financial policy of the corporation.
   3. Fundamental Changes - The power to make, alter, amend, or repeal the by-laws lies with the board of directors.
   4. Dividends - Directors declare the amount and type of dividends, subject to restrictions in the State incorporation statute and the articles of incorporation.
   5. Management Compensation - Directors determine the compensation of officers.

B. Qualification, Election and Tenure of Directors
   1. Qualifications of Directors - Stated in articles of incorporation or by-laws.
   2. Election, Number and Tenure of Directors - Elected at annual meetings of shareholders and hold office for one year or until their successors are duly elected and qualified.
   3. Vacancies and Removal of Directors - Vacancy in the board may be filled by the affirmative vote of a majority of the remaining directors. Removal of one or more of the directors or of the entire board by the shareholders, with or without cause, subject to cumulative voting rights.
   4. Compensation of Directors - Do not receive salaries for their services as directors, but are paid a fee or honorarium for attendance at meetings.

C. Exercise of Directors' Functions
   1. Meeting - Do not have the power to bind the corporation when acting individually but only when acting as a board. Meetings are held at a regular time and place fixed in the by-laws or at special times as they are called. Notice of meeting must be given.
   2. Quorum - A quorum is the minimum number necessary to be present at a meeting in order to transact business; may require a number greater tan a simple majority.
   3. Action Taken Without a Meeting - Any action required by the statute to be taken at a meeting of the board may be taken without a meeting if a consent in writing is signed by all of the directors.
   4. Delegation of Board Powers - Committees, all of whom must be directors, but does not relieve any board member of his duties to the corporation.
   5. Directors' Inspection Rights - So they can competently and fully perform their duties, directors have the right to inspect corporate books and records.

D. Officers - Officers are appointed by the board of directors. They consist of a president, one or more vice-presidents, a secretary and a treasurer. A person may hold more than one office.
   1. Selection and Removal of Officers - Officers may be removed by the board with or without cause.
   2. Role of Officers - Fiduciaries to the corporation, agents of the corporation.
      a. President - Principal executive officer, control of the board of directors, supervises and controls all of the business and affairs of the corporation.
      b. Vice-President - In the absence of the president, he shall perform the duties of the president.
      c. Secretary - Keeps the minutes of the proceedings of the shareholders and board of directors.
      d. Treasurer - Has charge and custody of and is responsible for all funds and securities of the corporation.
   3. Authority of Officers - Provided in the by-laws or determined by resolution of the board of directors.
      a. Actual Express Authority - Officer acts on the behalf of the corporation.
      b. Actual Implied Authority - To do what is reasonably necessary to perform their actual, delegated authority.

    c.   Apparent Authority - Acts of the principal that lead a third party to believe reasonably and in good faith that an officer has the required authority.

    d.   Ratification - A corporation may ratify the unauthorized acts of its officers. Ratification is equivalent to having granted the officer prior authority.

E.   Duties of Directors and Officers - A corporation may not recover damages from its directors and officers for losses resulting from their poor business judgment or honest mistake of judgment.
1.   Duty of Obedience - Must act within their respective authority.
2.   Duty of Diligence - Must exercise ordinary care and prudence, then the court will not substitute their judgment for the board's or officer's judgment called business judgment rule.
    a.   Reliance on Others - Permitted to entrust important work to others. Will be liable for losses resulting from an employee's carelessness if he knew or ought to have known. May also rely on information provided by employees of the corporation.
    b.   Business Judgment Rule - Precludes imposing liability on directors for honest mistake of judgment by exercising due care, acting in good faith, or acting in a manner reasonably believed to be best interests of the corporation.
3.   Duty of Loyalty - Requires undeviating loyalty on the part of officers and directors to the corporation. Required to make full disclosure to the corporation of any financial interest he may have in any contract or transaction.
    a.   Conflicts of Interest - Contracts between corporations having interlocking directorates, or having one or more person who are members of both boards of directors, the court subject the contract to be fair and entered into in good faith.
    b.   Loans to Directors - Does not permit a corporation to lend money to its directors without authorization in each instance by its shareholders, unless approved by majority of disinterested shareholders or by board of directors.
    c.   Corporate Opportunity - Directors and officers may not usurp any corporate opportunity that in all fairness should belong to the corporation.
    d.   Transaction in Shares - Prohibiting officers and directors from purchasing or selling shares of the corporation without adequate disclosure of all material facts in their possession that may affect the value or potential value of the stock. Statute requires insiders to give to the corporation any profit realized by their short swing speculation in its stock.
    e.   Duty Not to Compete - Court will closely scrutinize any interest that competes with the business of the corporation.

F.   Liabilities of Directors and Officers - Incur personal liability for breaching any of the duties they owe to the corporation and shareholders.
1.   Breach of Duties to Corporation - Whenever a director or officer breaches his fiduciary duty, he forfeits his rights to compensation during the period he engaged in the breach.
2.   Defective Incorporation - Impose joint and several liability who assume to act as a corporation without authority for all debts and liabilities.
3.   Contracts - Within his apparent but beyond his actual authority is liable to corporation for any resulting loss.
4.   Torts - Personal liability for their intentional wrongdoing or negligent conduct.
5.   Violation of State and Federal Statutes - Civic or criminal liability for violating State and Federal statutes.
6.   Illegal Distributions - Jointly and severally liable for issuing shares of the corporation at a discount and for declaring a dividend that is paid when corporation is insolvent or violation of the State incorporation statute.

DEFINITIONS

1. Pyramidal management structure

2. Quorum

3. Classification of directors

4. Cumulative voting

5. Proxy

6. Voting trust

7. Shareholder agreement

8. Direct suit

9. Derivative suit

10. Right to dissent

11. Controlling shareholder

12. Fundamental change

13. Business judgment rule

14. Corporate opportunity

TRUE/FALSE

_____ 1. A corporation may not issue non-voting stock.

_____ 2. A shareholder normally has one vote for each share owned.

_____ 3. Shareholders may not remove any director without just cause.

_____ 4. Any recovery in a shareholder's direct suit usually goes to the corporate treasury so that all shareholders can benefit proportionately.

_____ 5. A shareholder may not bring a derivative suit without first making demand upon the board of directors to enforce the corporate right.

_____ 6. A shareholder who has not fully paid the required consideration for his shares is liable for the deficiency.

_____ 7. Once established, the number of directors may not be increased or decreased.

_____ 8. Under the MBCA, each director is entitled to fix his own compensation.

_____ 9. Directors do not have the power to bind the corporation when acting individually.

_____ 10. Directors may not vote by proxy.

_____ 11. Officers may be removed by the board with or without cause.

_____ 12. Whenever an officer breaches his fiduciary duty, he forfeits his right to compensation during the period he engaged in the breach.

_____ 13. Directors like shareholders may vote by proxy.

_____ 14. Directors, but not officers, are fiduciaries of the corporation.

_____ 15. Shareholders, but not directors, are liable for shares issued when a corporation is insolvent.

MULTIPLE CHOICE

_____ 1. Special shareholder meetings may be called by:
   a. any member of the board of directors.
   b. any shareholder.
   c. any person so authorized in the articles of incorporation.
   d. all of the above.

_____ 2. The board of directors may be classified into:
   a. three groups.
   b. six groups.
   c. nine groups.
   d. none of the above.

_____ 3. Big Bucks, Inc. has two shareholders, Arthur and Brad, and 100 shares of voting stock. If Big Bucks, Inc. uses cumulative voting, how many shares would Arthur need to elect three of the five directors?
   a. 50
   b. 51
   c. 60
   d. 61

_____ 4. In general, a proxy:
   a. must be in writing to be effective.
   b. is not revocable unless coupled with an interest.
   c. transfers legal title to the stock.
   d. (a) and (b) but not (c).

_____ 5. Which of the following are agents of the corporation?
    a. Shareholders.
    b. Directors.
    c. Officers.
    d. (b and (c) but not (a).

_____ 6. Under the modern view, the board of directors must consist of at least:
    a. one member.
    b. three members.
    c. nine members.
    d. none of the above.

_____ 7. Assume that Big Bucks, Inc. has nine directors. What is the minimum number of directors that may bind the corporation?
    a. One.
    b. Three.
    c. Five.
    d. Nine.

_____ 8. An executive committee may be appointed by the board to:
    a. amend the by-laws.
    b. authorize the sale of stock.
    c. declare dividends.
    d. set management compensation.

_____ 9. The same person may not simultaneously hold the office of:
    a. president and vice-president.
    b. president and secretary.
    c. president and treasurer.
    d. secretary and treasurer.

_____ 10. A contract between a director and the corporation is neither void nor voidable, if:
    a. it is approved after full disclosure by the board of disinterested directors.
    b. it is fair and reasonable to the corporation.
    c. either (a) or (b).
    d. neither (a) nor (b).

_____ 11. A director can take personal advantage of an opportunity:
    a. in which the corporation has a property interest.
    b. which the corporation is financially unable to accept.
    c. which the corporation expressly accepts by a vote of disinterested directors after full disclosure.
    d. none of the above.

_____ 12. Which of the following is correct regarding the role of the shareholders of a corporation?
    a. They have no voice in policy matters.
    b. They exercise control over policy by electing directors.
    c. They are consulted regularly by management when decisions must be made on broad policy matters.
    d. Contracts which they make on behalf of the corporation are binding on it.

_____ 13. If four directors are to be elected, and a shareholder holds 300 shares of stock, how many votes does the shareholder normally have?

    a.   4

    b.   300

    c.   1200

    d.   None of the above is correct.

_____ 14. The Ajax Corporation has two shareholders -- Albert with 75 shares and Brad with 25 shares. The board of directors consists of four directors. Under cumulative voting, how many shares must Brad own in order to be assured of electing one director if all four directors come up for election at the same time?

    a.   20

    b.   21

    c.   24

    d.   25

_____ 15. Which of the following rights do shareholders normally have?

    a.   They may by a majority vote remove a director or the entire board of directors in a meeting called for that purpose.

    b.   They have an unqualified right to inspect the corporate books and records of the corporation.

    c.   They have the right to approve fundamental changes in the corporation.

    d.   Two of the above are correct, (a) and (c).

SHORT ESSAY

1. When may a shareholder be denied his right to inspect the books and records of the corporation? _____

_____

_____

_____

2. List five actions that may be initiated by the board of directors but require shareholder approval. _____

_____

_____

_____

3. List four actions that may be taken by the board of directors without shareholder approval. _____

_____

_____

_____

4. What are the duties of directors and officers? _____

_____

_____

_____

5. What is the standard of care imposed upon directors and officers? _____
_____
_____
_____

FUNDAMENTAL CHANGES

PURPOSE

Certain fundamental changes in a corporation require shareholder approval, because they are outside the authority of the board of directors of the corporation. These include charter amendments, the sale or lease of all or substantially all of the corporation's assets, and mergers and consolidations. Each of these is a fundamental change, because it alters the basic structure of the corporation. The approval of the shareholders does not need to be unanimous. This means that a minority of shareholders may oppose the change. In such cases, the minority shareholders have the right to recover the fair value of their shares if they follow the appraisal remedy procedure found in State statute. In this chapter, you study the legal aspects of the various fundamental changes in a corporation.

CHAPTER CHECKPOINTS

After reading and studying this chapter, you should be able to:

1. List and discuss the charter amendments which do not require shareholder approval and those which give disenting shareholders an appraisal remedy.

2. List and discuss the corporate combinations which do not require shareholder approval and those which give dissenting shareholders an appraisal remedy.

3. Define a cash-out combination and a management buyout and discuss the fairness of each to shareholders.

4. List and discuss the ways in which judicial and nonjudicial dissolutions may occur.

5. Discuss the relative rights of the shareholders and the board of directors in tender offers, going private transactions and in compulsory share exchanges.

CHAPTER OUTLINE

A. Charter Amendments - Modern statutes permit the articles of incorporation to be amended freely. Amendments may contain only those provisions that would be lawful in the original articles of incorporation. The Model Act is comprehensive in its authorization for amendments and includes very broad powers. The most common amendments today are to make changes in the capital structure of the corporation. The typical procedure for amending the articles of incorporation requires the board of directors to adopt a resolution setting forth the proposed amendment, which then must be approved by a majority vote of the shareholders. After approval, articles of amendment are filed with the Secretary of State. The amendments become effective upon the issuance of the certificate of amendment by the Secretary of State. The Revised Act permits the board to adopt certain amendments without shareholder action unless the articles of incorporation provide otherwise. Under the Model Act, disenting shareholders are given an appraisal remedy only if an amendment materially and adversely affects the shareholder's rights. Under the Revised Act the required shareholder approval must be by majority of all votes entitled to be cast on the amendment if the amendment would give rise to dissenters' rights. All other amendments must only be approved by a majority of the votes cast unless the Act or the charter requires a greater vote.

B. Combinations - It may be desirable and profitable for a corporation to acquire all or substantially all of the assets of another corporation or corporations. This may be accomplished by (1) purchase or lease of the assets; (2) purchase of a controlling stock interest in other corporations; (3) merger with other corporations; or (4) consolidation with other corporations. When any of these methods of combination involves the issuance of shares, proxy solicitations or tender offers, it may be subject to Federal securities regulation.

1. Purchase or Lease of All or Substantially All of the Assets - In this transaction, there is no change in the legal personality of either corporation. Each corporation continues its separate existence with only the form or extent of the assets altered. Generally, the purchaser does not assume the other's liabilities.

   a. Regular Course of Business - If the sale or lease of all or substantially all of its assets is in the usual and regular course of business of the selling or lessor corporation, approval by its board of directors is required, but shareholder authorization is not.

   b. Other Than in Regular Course of Business - Shareholder approval is necessary if such a sale or lease is not in the usual and regular course of business. In most States, dissenting shareholders of the selling corporation are given an appraisal remedy.

2. Purchase of Shares - The purchase of a corporation's stock is an alternative to the purchase of its assets. When one corporation acquires all or a controlling interest of the stock of another corporation, there is no change in the legal existence of either corporation. The acquiring corporation acts through its board of directors. The capital structure of the subsidiary remains unchanged. No formal shareholder approval of either corporation is required. No appraisal remedy is available.

   a. Sales of Control - A privately negotiated transaction is possible when a controlling interest is owned by one or a few shareholders. The sale must be made with due care. The controlling shareholders must take care to establish that the transfer is not being made to purchasers who plan to act contrary to the best interests of the corporation.

   b. Tender Offer - A tender offer is a general invitation to all of the shareholders of a target company to tender their shares for sale at a specified price. Tender offers for publicly held companies are frequently subject to Federal securities regulation.

3. Compulsory Share Exchange - A compulsory share exchange is a transaction by which a corporation becomes the owner of all the outstanding shares of one or more classes or stock of another corporation by an exchange that is compulsory on all owners of the acquires shares. Although they produce results similar to a merger, compulsory share exchanges are used instead of mergers where it is desirable that the acquired corporation does not go out of existence as in the formation of holding company systems for insurance companies and banks. The board of directors of each corporation and the shareholders of each must approve the compulsory share exchange. Dissenting shareholders are given an appraisal remedy.

4. Merger - A merger is the combination of the assets of two or more corporations into one of the corporations. One corporation, known as the surviving corporation, receives title to all of the assets. The other corporation, known as the merged corporation, ceases to exist as a separate entity. All debts and other liabilities of the merged corporation are assumed by the surviving corporation by operation

of law. The board of directors and the shareholders of each corporation must approve the merger by a majority vote of the shares entitled to vote. In a short-form merger, a corporation that owns at least 90% of the outstanding shares of a subsidiary may merge the subsidiary into itself without approval by the shareholders of either corporation. Dissenting shareholders of the subsidiary have the right to obtain payment from the parent for their shares, but the shareholders of the parent do not have an appraisal remedy.

5. Consolidation - A consolidation is the combination of two or more corporations into a new corporation which is known as the consolidated corporation. Each of the constituents ceases to exist, all of their debts and liabilities are assumed by the new corporation. A combination requires the approval of the boards of each constituent corporation and the affirmative vote of the holders of a majority of the shares entitled to vote. Dissenting shareholders have an appraisal remedy.

6. Going Private Transactions - Corporate combinations are sometimes used to take a publicly held corporation private in order to eliminate minority interests or to reduce the burdens of the Federal securities laws. One method of going private is for a majority shareholder to acquire the corporation's shares through purchases on the open market or through a tender offer. Cash out combinations are also possible.

7. Cash Out Combinations - These are used to eliminate minority shareholders by forcing them to accept cash or property for their shares. A cash out combination is often used after a person or company has acquired a large interest in a target company through a tender offer. The tender offeror then seeks to eliminate all other shareholders, thereby achieving complete control of the target company. Some States require that such cash out combinations have a valid business purpose and that they are fair to all concerned. Fairness includes fair dealing and a fair price.

8. Management Buyout - A management buyout is a transaction by which existing management increases its ownership of a corporation and eliminates its public shareholders. Because of the extensive use of borrowed funds, management buyouts are commonly called leveraged buyouts. In recent years, leveraged buyouts have become more frequent and some have involved large well-known companies. A critical issue raised by a management buyout is its fairness to the shareholders of the existing corporation that is purchased by the new corporation created by management and then issues bonds to institutional investors to raise cash to purchase the existing corporation.

9. Dissenting Shareholders - A dissenting shareholder is one who opposes a fundamental change and has the right to receive the fair value of her shares. If a shareholder dissents and strictly complies with the provisions of the statute, she is entitled to receive the fair value of her shares. A dissenting shareholder must: (1) file a written objection before the vote of the shareholders; (2) refrain from voting in favor of the proposed corporate action; (3) make a written demand on the corporation on a form provided by the corporation within the time period set, which may not be less than thirty days after the corporation mails the form. A dissenting shareholder is entitled to the fair value of her shares, which the Model Act defines to mean their value immediately before the corporate action to which the dissenter objects place, excluding any appreciation or depreciation in anticipation of such corporate action unless such exclusion would be inequitable.

C. Dissolution - Although a corporation may have perpetual existence, it may be terminated in a number of ways. Dissolution does not terminate the corporation's existence, but it does require that the corporation wind up its affairs and liquidate its assets.

1. Nonjudicial Dissolution - Nonjudicial dissolution may be brought about by: (a) act of the legislature of the State of incorporation; (b) expiration of the period of time provided for in the articles of incorporation; or (c) voluntary action by the corporation, pursuant to a resolution of the board of directors approved by the affirmative vote of the holders of a majority of the shares of the corporation entitled to vote at a meeting of the shareholders duly called for that purpose.

2. Judicial Dissolution - Involuntary dissolution may occur by: (a) court action taken at the insistance of the attorney general of the State of incorporation; (b) court action brought by shareholders when it is

established that the directors are deadlocked in the management; and (c) court action instituted by a creditor on a showing that the corporation has become unable to pay its debts and obligations as they mature in the regular course of its business.

3. Liquidation - A corporation must cease carrying on its business except as is necessary to wind up once dissolution has occurred. When a corporation is dissolved, its assets are liquidated and used first to pay the expenses of liquidation and its creditors according to their respective contract or lien rights. Any remainder is distributed to shareholders proportionately according to their respective contract rights. Stock with a liquidation preference has priority over common stock. If liquidation is voluntary, it is carried out by the board of directors, who serve as trustees. If involuntary, liquidation is conducted by a receiver.

4. Protection of Creditors - The statutory procedures usually prescribe procedures to safeguard the interests of creditors of the corporation. Typically, notice must be mailed to known creditors, and geneal publication of the notice must also be made. The Revised Act provides a five year period for: (a) a claimant who did not receive notice; (b) a claimant whose timely claim was not acted on; or (c) a claimant whose claim is contingent on an event occurring after dissolution. The Model Act gives protection for only two years.

DEFINITIONS

1. Fundamental change

2. Appraisal remedy

3. Articles of amendment

4. Combination

5. Merger

6. Surviving corporation

7. Consolidation

8. Dissenting shareholder

9. Fair value

10. Nonjudicial dissolution

11. Involuntary judicial dissolution

12. Liquidation

13. Compulsory Share Exchange

14. Tender offer

15. Cash out combination

16. Management buyout

TRUE/FALSE

_____ 1. Changes which alter the basic structure of the corporation require shareholder approval.

_____ 2. Shareholder approval for fundamental changes must be unanimous.

_____ 3. Under the MBCA, shareholders who dissent from some charter amendments are accorded the right to recover from the corporation the fair value of their shares.

_____ 4. Charter amendments do not affect the existing rights of non-shareholders.

_____ 5. All debts and other liabilities of a merged corporation are assumed by the surviving corporation.

_____ 6. In a consolidation of two or more corporations, each of the constituent corporations ceases to exist.

_____ 7. Nonjudicial dissolution may be brought about by voluntary action on the part of the holders of a majority of the outstanding shares of stock.

_____ 8. Involuntary dissolution by judicial proceeding may be instituted by the creditors of the corporation.

_____ 9. A corporation is subject to involuntary judicial dissolution if the shareholders are deadlocked and cannot elect directors.

_____ 10. When liquidation is involuntary, it is carried out by a court-appointed receiver.

_____ 11. When liquidation is voluntary, it is carried out by the board of directors.

_____ 12. Under a compulsory share exchange, approval of the shareholders of the acquiring corporation is required.

_____ 13. A shareholder who dissents and strictly complies with the provisions of the incorporating statute, is entitled to receive the fair value of her shares.

_____ 14. Management buyouts are always fair to the shareholders.

_____ 15. There are no statutory provisions to protect creditors upon the dissolution of a corporation.

MULTIPLE CHOICE

_____ 1. Under the MBCA, a corporation may amend its charter to:
   a. change its corporate name.
   b. change the preferential rights of shares.
   c. deny pre-emptive rights.
   d. all of the above.

_____ 2. Charter amendments become effective upon:
   a. adoption of a resolution by the board setting forth the proposed amendment.
   b. approval by a majority vote of the shareholders.
   c. execution and filing of articles of amendment with the Secretary of State.
   d. issuance of the certificate of amendment by the Secretary of State.

_____ 3. A corporation ceases to exist as a separate entity when:
   a. all or substantially all of its assets are purchased by another corporation.
   b. a controlling interest in its stock is purchased by another corporation.
   c. it is merged into another corporation.
   d. all of the above.

_____ 4. The sale or lease of all or substantially all of a corporation's assets in the usual course of its business requires approval by its:
   a. board of directors.
   b. shareholders.
   c. board of directors and shareholders.
   d. none of the above.

_____ 5. A corporation ceases to exist as a separate entity when:
   a. it purchases all or substantially all of the assets of another corporation.
   b. it purchases a controlling interest in the stock of another corporation.
   c. another corporation is merged into it.
   d. none of the above.

_____ 6. The sale or lease of all or substantially all of a corporation's assets not in the usual course of its business requires approval by its:
   a. board of directors.
   b. shareholders.
   c. board of directors and shareholders.
   d. none of the above.

_____ 7. A merger requires the approval of:
   a. the board of directors of each corporation.
   b. the board of directors and shareholders of each corporation.
   c. the board of directors and shareholders of the merged corporation.
   d. the shareholders of each corporation.

_____ 8. The merger of a wholly-owned subsidiary into its parent requires the approval of:
   a. the board of directors of the parent corporation.
   b. the board of directors and shareholders of the subsidiary corporation.
   c. the board of directors and shareholders of each corporation.
   d. the shareholders of the subsidiary corporation.

_____ 9. If a wholly-owned subsidiary is merged into its parent, an appraisal remedy is available to the shareholders of:
   a. the parent corporation.
   b. the subsidiary corporation.
   c. both the parent and the subsidiary.
   d. none of the above.

_____ 10. A consolidation requires the approval of:
   a. the board of directors of each constituent corporation.
   b. the shareholders of each constituent corporation.
   c. the board of directors and shareholders of each constituent corporation.
   d. none of the above.

_____ 11. The corporation may pay dissenting shareholders out of:
   a. earned surplus.
   b. capital surplus.
   c. stated capital.
   d. all of the above.

_____ 12. A _____ is a transaction by which existing management increases its ownership of a corporation and eliminates its public shareholders.
   a. short-form merger
   b. consolidation
   c. leveraged buyout
   d. compulsory share exchange

_____ 13. Who would have to approve a merger of the Ajax Corporation and the Borax Corporation?
   a. The boards of the two corporations.
   b. Ajax shareholders.
   c. Borax shareholders.
   d. All of the above would have to approve the merger.

_____ 14. Which of the following would not require a vote of the shareholders?
   a. A voluntary dissolution of the corporation.
   b. A merger with another corporation.
   c. Election of a Chief Executive Officer.
   d. An amendment to the corporate articles of incorporation adding two more directors to the board.

_____ 15. Which of the following is correct regarding shareholder approval of charter amendments?
   a. The Revised Act permits the board to adopt certain amendments without shareholder approval.
   b. Under the Model Act, a dissenting shareholder is given an appraisal remedy only if an amendment materially and adversely affects his rights.
   c. Under the Revised Act, if the amendment would give rise to dissenter's rights, it must be approved by a majority of all votes entitled to be cast on the amendment.
   d. All of the above are correct.

SHORT ESSAY

1. List five examples of fundamental changes. _____
   _____
   _____
   _____

2. Outline the procedure for amending the articles of incorporation. _____
   _____

_____

_____

3. By what methods may a corporation acquire all or substantially all of the assets of another corporation?

_____

_____

_____

4. What must a dissenting shareholder do to perfect his right to payment for his shares? _____

_____

_____

_____

PART VII

SAMPLE EXAMINATION

_____ 1. The legal document that the incorporators of a corporation prepare and submit to the State in order to establish a corporation is known as the:
   a. summons.
   b. articles of incorporation.
   c. certificate of registration.
   d. corporate by-laws.

_____ 2. Which of the following is correct regarding the by-laws of a corporation?
   a. They are inferior to the Articles of Incorporation and are adopted by the board of directors.
   b. They are adopted and amended by the shareholders.
   c. They must be filed with the Secretary of State of the State of incorporation in order to be effective.
   d. They must be approved by a two-thirds vote of the shareholders in order to become effective.

_____ 3. Acts of a corporation that are beyond the authority granted to it in its charter are known as _____ acts.
   a. proxy
   b. de jure
   c. de facto
   d. ultra vires

_____ 4. In which of the following situations will the directors of a corporation be liable?
   a. The directors refuse to declare dividends even though the corporation has retained earnings.
   b. Two directors miss a meeting, because they are ill and don't notify the others.
   c. The directors violate the business judgment rule in their corporate dealings.
   d. The directors make an honest mistake in judgment when they decide to move the corporate headquarters to a new location.

_____ 5. The amount by which the total assets of a corporation exceed the total debts of the corporation is referred to as the corporation's:
   a. earned surplus.
   b. surplus.
   c. net assets.
   d. stated capital.

_____ 6. The test which the MBCA now uses to determine whether a corporation can legally pay a dividend is known as the _____ test.
   a. surplus
   b. earned surplus
   c. net asset
   d. nimble dividends

_____ 7. The test used by the MBCA until 1979 and which states that a corporation may pay dividends only out of unreserved and unrestricted earned surplus is known as the _____ test.
   a. surplus
   b. earned surplus
   c. net asset
   d. nimble dividends

_____ 8. Which of the following is the least restrictive test used by States to determine the legality of a dividend payment?
   a. The earned surplus test.
   b. The surplus test.
   c. The net asset test.
   d. The nimble dividends test.

_____ 9. Under the Model Act, directors who vote for or assent to the payment of an illegal divident have liability to the:
   a. shareholders.
   b. corporation.
   c. creditors of the corporation.
   d. shareholders, the corporation and the creditors of the corporation.

_____ 10. Tel-Ko Corporation has two shareholders. Arthur has 64 shares and Bill has 36 shares. The board of directors consists of three directors. How many shares does Bill need to elect one director under cumulative voting?
   a. 26
   b. 36
   c. 40
   d. 51

_____ 11. In which of the following is shareholder approval required?
   a. A corporation sells substantially all of its assets outside of the regular course of business.
   b. There are amendments to the Articles of Incorporation.
   c. The board of directors has approved a merger of a corporation with another.
   d. All of the above situations require shareholder approval.

_____ 12. Bill Businessman sues the Tel-Ko Corporation in a stockholder derivative suit and wins the case. The judgment will be paid to:
   a. Bill personally.
   b. all of the shareholders as a dividend.
   c. the corporate treasury.
   d. the board of directors.

_____ 13. A shareholder normally has which of the following rights?
   a. The right to elect the corporate directors.
   b. The right to elect the corporate officers.
   c. The right to approve the sale of any real estate owned by the corporation.
   d. A shareholder normally has all of the above rights.

14. A corporation is considered to be a "person" for purposes of:
    a. the Fifth Amendment due process clause.
    b. the Fourteenth Amendment due process clause.
    c. the Fifth Amendment right against self-incrimination.
    d. the Fifth and Fourteenth Amendment due process clauses.

15. A corporation that is owned by a few shareholders and whose shares are not actively traded is known as a _____ corporation.
    a. closely held
    b. Subchapter S
    c. public
    d. nonprofit

16. The rules and regulations that govern the internal management of a corporation are normally found in the:
    a. articles of incorporation.
    b. corporate charter.
    c. corporate by-laws.
    d. State statute.

17. Which of the following are normally included in the Articles of Incorporation of a corporation?
    a. The location and address of a corporation.
    b. The period of duration of the corporation.
    c. The name and address of each incorporator.
    d. All of the above are normally included in the Articles of Incorporation.

18. A _____ is the combination of the assets of two or more corporations into one corporation.
    a. merger
    b. consolidation
    c. tender offer
    d. cash-out combination

19. A _____ is a transaction by which existing management increases its ownership of a corporation and eliminates its public shareholders.
    a. cash-out combination
    b. leveraged buyout
    c. tender offer
    d. consolidation

20. Bradley signed a five year lease for office space on behalf of the Ajax Corporation, which has not yet been formed, but which Bradley is promoting.
    a. Bradley is personally liable on the lease.
    b. Bradley is not liable, because he is an agent of the Ajax Corporation.
    c. The Ajax Corporation is liable on the lease.
    d. Two of the above, (b) and (c).

SECURED TRANSACTIONS AND SURETYSHIP

PURPOSE

A secured transaction includes two elements: (1) a debt or obligation to pay money; and (2) an interest of the creditor in specific property of the debtor that secures performance of the obligation. Transaction involving security in personal property are governed by Article 9 of the Uniform Commercial Code. Article 9 does not cover secured transactions involving real estate. Before you can completely understand the next chapter dealing with bankruptcy, you must thoroughly understand the concepts of attachment and perfection and how a perfected security interest is obtained. In this chapter, you also study the concept of suretyship. Sureties are frequently used in addition to a security interest in order to further reduce the risk of the creditor in extending credit. Sureties are also frequently used by employers to protect against losses caused by employees who embezzle or abscond with the employer's funds and are frequently required in construction contracts to assure the performance of the contractor.

CHAPTER CHECKPOINTS

After reading and studying this chapter, you should be able to:

1. Define the terms "attachment" and "perfection" and identify when a security interest attaches and when it becomes perfected.

2. List the five classes of collateral discussed in the chapter and explain how a security interest in each is perfected.

3. Distinguish between a purchase money security interest and a nonpurchase money security interest and explain the legal effect of each.

4. Explain what rights the creditor in a secured transaction has in the event of a default by the debtor.

5. Identify the parties to a surety agreement and explain how a surety contract is created.

CHAPTER OUTLINE

I. Secured Transactions in Personal Property - A secured transaction is an agreement by which one party gets a security interest in the personal property of another. It is governed by Article 9 if the debtor consents to provide a security interest in personal property to secure the payment of a debt. Debtor is a person who owes payment or obligation. Secured party is the creditor or lender, who possesses a security interest in collateral. Collateral is the property subject to security interest. Security agreement is an agreement that grants a security interest. Security interest is a right in personal property to insure payment of an obligation.

A. Classification of Collateral
    1. Goods - Tangible personal property that can be moved when the security interest becomes enforceable. It may fall into different classifications depending on its use or purpose.
        a. Consumer Goods - Goods bought primarily for personal, family or household purposes.
        b. Equipment - Used primarily in business, not included in the definition of inventory.
        c. Farm Products - Crops, or livestock and supplies used or produced in farming operations in their unmanufactured states.
        d. Inventory - Goods held for sale or lease and raw materials used or consumed in business.
        e. Fixtures - Goods that are so firmly attachd to real property that they are considered part of the real estate.
    2. Indispensable Paper
        a. Chattel Paper - Is written evidence stating both a monetary obligation and a security interest in or a lease of specific goods.
        b. Instrument - Is written evidence that a right to payment of money which includes negotiable instruments, stocks, bonds, and other investment securities.
        c. Documents - Includes documents of title, either negotiable or non-negotiable. Negotiable if by its terms the goods it covers are deliverable to bearer or to the order of a named person; any other documents are non-negotiable.
    3. Intangibles - Accounts and general intangibles are not evidenced by any indispensable paper.
        a. Accounts or Accounts Receivable - Refer to the right to payment for goods sold or leased or for services rendered that is not evidenced by an instrument.
        b. General Intangibles - Applies to any personal property other than goods. It includes goodwill to the extent thay are not regulated by Federal statute.

B. Attachment - Is a security interest enforceable against the debtor. Also a prerequisite to a security interest's enforceability against parties other than the debtor, called perfection.
    1. Value - Includes consideration under contract law, a binding commitment to extend redit and an antecedent debt.
    2. Debtor's Rights in Collateral - Personal property debtor owns, possesses, or in process of acquiring; illusive and not specifically defined by the Code.
    3. Security Agreement - Agreement which cannot secure unless there is an agreement between the debtor and creditor which must be in writing, signed by the debtor, and contain a reasonable description of the collateral.
        a. After-acquired Property - Property the debtor may acquire at some time in the future. Concept of a "continuing general lien" or a "floating lien" is accepted by Article 9. No security interest may attach under an after-acquired property clause to consumer goods.
            1) Proceeds - Consideration for the sale, exchange, or other disposition of the collateral.
            2) Future Advance - Debtor will obtain a line of credit from a creditor for advances to be made at some later time.

C. Perfection - Security interest enforceable against third party, is perfected when it has attached and when all the applicable steps required have been taken.
    1. Filing a Financing Statement - Document filed by the secured party to provide notice of the security interest. It will be effective for 5 years from the date of filing, and if a continuation

statement is filed by the secured party within 6 months prior to expiration, the effectiveness will be extended for another 5-year period. Security interest in motor vehicles must be perfected by a notation on the certificate of title.

    a.   Where to File - Three alternatives differ as to which types of collateral are to be filed locally or centrally.

        1) First Alternative - Fixtures or timber to be cut; minerals to be extracted should be filed locally and all other filing central.

        2) Second Alternative - Fixture, farm products, consumer goods, timber, minerals, and farming equipment should be filed locally and all other centrally.

        3) Third Alternative - Similar to second alternative with the exception of central filing required. The secured party must also file locally if debtor has a place of business in only one county or if debtor has no place of business in the State but resides in the States.

    b.   Improper Filing - Ineffective, subject to 2 exceptions. Filing is made in good faith and person who has knowledge of the contents of that financial statement.

  2. Possession - A pledge or possessory security interest is the delivery of personal property for a creditor, or to a third party acting as an agent for the creditor, as security for the payment of a debt cannot be used with items that are completely intangible. Possession is the only way to perfect a security interest in instruments.

    a.   Field Warehouse - Secured party takes possession of the goods while the pledgor has access to the goods.

  3. Automatic - Perfection upon attachment.

    a.   Purchase Money Security Interests in Consumer Goods - A seller of goods who retains a security interest in goods purchased or a lender who obtains a security interest in goods purchased with the loaned money has a purchase money security interest.

    b.   Temporary Perfection - A security interest in negotiable instrument is perfected without filing for 21 days from the time it attaches, to the extent that it arises for new value given under a written security agreement.

D. Priorities - Precedence in order of right.

  1. Against Unsecured Creditors - Once a security interest attaches, it has priority over chains of other creditors who do not have a security interest or a lien.

  2. Against Lien Creditors - A perfection security interest has priority over lien creditors who acquire their lien after perfection. Unperfected security interest is subordinate to the rights of a person who becomes a lien creditor before the security interest is perfected.

    a.   Lien Creditor - A creditor who has acquired a lien on the property by attachment.

    b.   Trustee in Bankruptcy - Representative of the estate in bankruptcy who is responsible for collecting, liquidating, and distributing the debtor's assets.

  3. Against Other Secured Creditors - Depend on which security interests are perfected, when and type of collateral.

    a.   Perfected vs. Unperfected - Perfected has greater rights in the collateral than unperfected.

    b.   Perfected vs. Perfected - They rank according topriority in time of filing of perfection. If there is a purchase money security interest in the collateral, depending on the collateral , is non-inventory or inventory.

        1) Non-inventory - Takes priority over a conflicting security interest if receives possession of collateral or within 10 days of receipt.

        2) Inventory - Has priority over conflicting security interest if the purchase money security holder has perfect perfect interest at the time the debtor receives the inventory and he must notify in writing all holders and give a description of secured inventory.

    c)   Unperfected vs. Unperfected - The first to attach has priority.

306   Chapter 37

4. **Against Buyers** - A security interest continues in collateral even though it is sold, unless the secured party authorizes the sale.
   a. **Buyers in the Ordinary Course of Business** - A person who buys in good faith, without knowledge that the sale violates a security interest, and from a merchant. It does not apply to farm products. It frequently applies to a store customer who purchases from inventory in which someone has a security interest.
   b. **Buyers of Consumer Goods** - A buyer who buys without knowledge of a security interest, for value, and for his own personal, famly or household use, takes the goods free of any purchase money security interest automatically perfected, but takes the goods subject to security interest perfected by filing.
   c. **Other Buyers** - An unperfected security interest is subordinate to the following rights: (1) goods, instruments, chattel paper, of a purchaser who gives value for the collateral, and takes it without knowledge; (2) accounts and general intangibles of a purchaser.

E. **Default** - The secured party may take possession of the collateral on default without judicial process. Unless the debtor has waived his rights in the collateral, he has a right of redemption at any time before the secured party has disposed of the collateral.
   1. **Sale of Collateral** - The secured party may sell, lease, or otherwise dispose of any collateral.
      a. Debtor is entitled to any surplus and is liable for any deficiency, except sale of account or chattel paper.
      b. May be disposed of at public or private sale if its disposition is commercially reasonable.
      c. Reasonable notice must be given to debtor of a public sale.
      d. Secured party may buy at a public or private sale.
   2. **Retention of Collateral** - May send written notice to the debtor that he proposes to retain the collateral in satisfaction of the obligation, if no objection within 21 says.
      a. Consumer goods, which the debtor has paid 60%, and has not signed a statement renouncing his rights, must dispose within 90 days. If not, debtor may receover not less than the credit service charge plus 10% of principal amount of debt.

II. **Suretyship** - Promise to pay the debt of another, if that other party fails to perform.
   A. **Nature and Formation** - A surety promises to answer for the payment of a debt or the performance of a duty owned to one person (creditor) by another (principal debtor) on the failure of the principal debtor to make payment. 1. Cosureties - More than one person bound for the same debt of a principal debtor.
      2. **Absolute Surety** - Creditor may hold the surety liable as soon as the principal debtor defaults.
      3. **Conditional Guarantor of Collection** - He is liable only when the creditor exhausts his legal remedies against the principal debtor.
      4. A surety who is required to pay creditor for principal debtor's obligation is entitled to be exonerated and reimbursed by the principal debtor.
      5. Surety is subrogated to the rights of creditor and has a right of contribution from cosureties.
      6. Surety is bound with the principal debtor as a primary obligor and guarantor is separately or collaterally bound to pay if the principal debtor does not.
      7. **Types of Sureties**
         a. A surety arrangement is used by creditors seeking to reduce the risk of default by their debtor.
         b. If purchaser assumes the mortgage, becomes the principal debtor and is personally liable unless the purchaser does not assume the mortgage but takes the property subject to the mortgage.
         c. **Fidelity Bonds** - Undertakings by a surety to protect an employer against the dishonesty of an employee.

      d. Performance Bonds - Guarantee the performance of the terms and conditions of a contract.
      e. Official Bonds - Statutes commonly require that a public officer furnish a bond for the faithful performance of her duties.
      f. Judicial Bonds - Provided on behalf of a party to a judicial proceeding to cover losses caused by delay or deprivation of use of property.
      g. Bail Bond - Is to assure the appearance of the defendant in court.
  8. Formation - The contractual promise of a surety to the creditor must be in writing to be enforceable under the Statute of Frauds. It is not binding without consideration.

B. Rights of Surety
  1. Exoneration - Relieved of liability, which is enforceable at equity.
  2. Reimbursement - Right of reimbursement against the principal debtor.
  3. Subrogation - Assumes the rights of the creditor.
  4. Contribution - Payment from cosureties of their proportionate share.

C. Defenses of Surety - The obligations owed to the creditor by the principal debtor and the surety both arise out of contracts.
  1. Personal Defenses of Principal Debtor - The principal debtor's incapacity due to infancy or mental incompetency is a defense for the principal debtor but may not be used by the surety. A discharge of principal debtor's obligation in bankruptcy also does not discharge the surety's liability.
  2. Personal Defense of Surety - May use his own incapacity as a defense as assert noncompliance with the Statute of Frauds or the absence of mutual assent and/or consideration. Fraud or duress practiced by the creditor on the surety is a defense for the surety. A surety may act off his claims against the creditor if the creditor is solvent. If principal debtor and creditor enter into a binding modification of contract, surety is discharged unless he assents to the modification.
  3. Defense of Both Surety and Principal Debtor - If the principal debtor's signature on an instrument is forged or the creditor has exerted fraud or duress on the principal debtor, neither the principal nor the surety are liable, or when the contract is fraudulently and materially altered.
      a. Absence of mutual assent or consideration to support debtor's obligation.
      b. Illegality and impossibility of performance of debtor's contract.
      c. Payment or performance of the debtor's obligation discharges both the debtor and surety. If the creditor releases the debtor, then the surety is also discharged. Creditor's refusal to accept tender of payment or performance by either debtor or surety completely discharges the surety.

DEFINITIONS

1. Secured transaction

2. Collateral

3. Security agreement

4. Security interest

5. Attachment

6. Perfection

7.   Financing statement

8.   Automatic perfection

9.   Consumer goods

10. Equipment

11. Farm products

12. Inventory

13. Fixtures

14. Chattel paper

15. Instrument.

16. Document

17. Account

18. General intangibles

19. Purchase money security interest

20. Surety

21. Absolute surety

22. Conditional guarantor

23. Exoneration

24. Reimbursement

25. Subrogation

TRUE/FALSE

_____   1.   A "secured party" may be either the seller of the goods or a third party creditor lender.

_____   2.   A security interest in property may continue even after the underlying debt is discharged.

_____   3.   A security interest can be perfected without attachment.

_____   4.   A security interest will be perfected if the interest has attached and the secured party files a financing statement signed by the creditor.

_____ 5. A purchase money security interest in consumer goods is perfected automatically upon attachment.

_____ 6. The Code's classification of collateral as equipment and farm products are not mutually exclusive.

_____ 7. Unless the parties agree otherwise, a security agreement covering the debtor's inventory does not give the secured party rights to the proceeds from the sale of that inventory.

_____ 8. The Code determines whether and when goods become fixtures.

_____ 9. A security interest in goods represented by a negotiable document is perfected by negotiation of the document.

_____ 10. If two parties have unperfected security interests in the same collateral, the first to attach has priority.

_____ 11. A buyer in the ordinary course of business takes free of any security interest created by any previous seller of the collateral.

_____ 12. Unless the parties have otherwise agreed, after default the secured party may take possession of the collateral without judicial process if it can be done without a breach of the peace.

_____ 13. Unless the debtor waived his rights in the collateral before default, he has a right of redemption at any time before the secured party disposes of the collateral or enters into a contract to dispose of it.

_____ 14. Fidelity bonds guarantee the performance of the terms and conditions of a contract.

_____ 15. The principal debtor's mental incompetency is a valid defense of the principal debtor but not the surety.

MULTIPLE CHOICE

_____ 1. Article 9 of the UCC governs financing transactions involving security in all of the following except:
   a. tangible consumer goods.
   b. stocks and securities.
   c. real property.
   d. accounts receivable.

_____ 2. A security interest "attaches" to the collateral in the security agreement only after:
   a. value is given to the debtor by the secured party.
   b. the debtor acquires rights in the collateral.
   c. the collateral is in the possession of the secured party or it is described in a security agreement signed by the debtor.
   d. all of the above.

____ 3. In general, a security interest in an intrument can be perfected by:
    a.   the secured party's taking or retaining possession of the instrument.
    b.   the secured party's filing a financing statement.
    c.   either (a) or (b).
    d.   both (a) and (b).

____ 4. Which of the following is not required for a financing statement to be effective?
    a.   the amount of the obligation secured.
    b.   the names and addresses of the secured party and the debtor.
    c.   a description of the collateral.
    d.   the signature of the debtor.

____ 5. A tractor used by a farmer to plow his land, if collateral in which a security interest is granted is classified as:
    a.   farm products.
    b.   equipment.
    c.   either (a) or (b).
    d.   both (a) and (b).

____ 6. The term "inventory" includes:
    a.   a retailer's merchandise.
    b.   a manufacturer's raw materials.
    c.   goods held for lease.
    d.   all of the above.

____ 7. A creditor with an unperfected, but attached security interest has greater rights in the collateral than:
    a.   the debtor's trustee in bankruptcy.
    b.   the debtor's secured creditors.
    c.   the debtor.
    d.   none of the above.

____ 8. As between two parties with continuously perfected security interests in the same collateral, the party with the superior interest is the one who:
    a.   first filed a financing statement covering the collateral.
    b.   first perfected his security interest.
    c.   first did (a) or (b), whichever first occurred.
    d.   first did (a) and (b), whichever first occurred.

____ 9. A perfected security interest has priority over claims of:
    a.   lien creditors of the debtor.
    b.   unsecured creditors of the debtor.
    c.   the debtor himself.
    d.   all of the above.

____ 10. On the debtor's default, the secured party may do all of the following except:
    a.   foreclose on his claim.
    b.   take possession of the collateral even if it requires a breach of the peace.
    c.   reduce his claim to judgment.
    d.   render the collateral useless on the debtor's premises.

_____ 11. Upon the surety's payment of the principal debtor's entire obligation, the surety obtains all the rights the creditor has against or through the principal debtor. This is the right of:
- a. exoneration.
- b. reimbursement.
- c. subrogation.
- d. contribution.

_____ 12. Which of the following is not a personal defense of the surety?
- a. The surety's incapacity.
- b. The Statute of Frauds.
- c. The principal debtor's bankruptcy.
- d. Fraud practiced by the creditor upon the surety.

_____ 13. Donald Debtor takes out a $2,000 loan from Consumer Credit Corporation on May 15 to buy a new video camcorder to record his brother's wedding. He buys the camcorder immediately and signs a financing agreement. On May 20, before Consumer Credit has had an opportunity to file the financing statement, Donald files for bankruptcy. Consumer Credit files the financing statement on May 22. It is now July and the trustee in bankruptcy claims that he is entitled to the camcorder to sell and use the proceeds to pay the expenses of administration and the general creditors of the estate. As between the trustee in bankruptcy and Consumer Credit, who is entitled to the video camcorder?
- a. Consumer Credit, because its security interest is a purchase money security interest in consumer goods that is thus automatically perfected.
- b. Consumer Credit, because it has a perfected security interest that it filed within ten days of the debtor's receipt of collateral.
- c. The trustee, because this was a preferential transfer.
- d. The trustee, because the trustee always has the power to invalidate a perfected security interest.

_____ 14. David loaned Elvis $1,000 to buy a big screen television for his business. Elvis signed a security agreement, which David filed in his personal files, but not with the County Recorder. A week later, Elvis used the big screen television as collateral on a loan from Consumer Credit, which filed its security interest with the County Recorder on the same day. A month later, David notices the financing agreement in his personal files and files it with the County Recorder. Who has priority?
- a. David, because his security interest was the first to attach.
- b. David, because he has a purchase money security interest.
- c. Consumer Credit, because it was the first to file.
- d. Consumer Credit, because it has the most recent security interest.

_____ 15. David loaned Elvis $1,000 to buy a big screen television for his business. Elvis signed a financing statement, which David filed in his personal files, but not with the County Recorder. A week later, Elvis used the big screen television as collateral on a loan from Consumer Credit. Elvis signed a financing statement, but the new manager had forgotten to study business law and didn't know that he was supposed to file it with the County Recorder. Who has priority?
- a. David, because his security interest was the first to attach.
- b. David, because he has a purchase money security interest.
- c. Consumer Credit, because it has the most recent security interest.
- d. Neither party, because neither has a perfected security interest.

SHORT ESSAY

1. Outline briefly the steps that a lender must go through to attain a perfected security interest in a boat as collateral for a loan. _____
    _____
    _____
    _____

2. Would your answer in (1) differ if the collateral was: (a) a house; (b) a sewing machine; (c) a car; (d) 100 shares of IBM Stock? How? _____
    _____
    _____
    _____

3. What is a purchase money security interest in consumer goods? How is it perfected? When is the perfection effective? _____
    _____
    _____
    _____

CHAPTER 38

BANKRUPTCY

PURPOSE

Various solutions to the conflict between creditor rights and relief for the overburdened debtor have developed. These include voluntary adjustments and compromises requiring payment in installments over time. Other voluntary methods include compositions and assignments of assets by a debtor to a trustee or assignee for the benefit of creditors. The most adaptable and frequently employed method of debtor relief and the one that also affords some relief to the creditor is a proceeding in a Federal court under the Bankruptcy Act. In this chapter, you study the various chapters of the Federal Bankruptcy Act. As you study this chapter, you should recall the previous chapter and apply the concepts learned there in working through problems that apply the priority scheme for payment of creditors in a bankruptcy liquidation.

CHAPTER CHECKPOINTS

After reading and studying this chapter, you should be able to:

1. List the various forms of non-bankruptcy debt resolution and distinguish them from the relief available under the Bankruptcy Act.

2. Distinguish between a Chapter 7 and a Chapter 11 Bankruptcy proceeding.

3. List the various debts that cannot be discharged in bankruptcy and identify the property of the debtor which is exempt from the bankruptcy estate and thus can be kept by the debtor under the Federal Bankruptcy Act.

4. Work through a problem involving a Chapter 7 bankruptcy and identify which assets are exempt and the priority in which the debtor's debts will be paid from the estate.

5. Distinguish between a fraudulent transfer and a voidable preference and identify each in case problems involving bankruptcy.

CHAPTER OUTLINE

I. Federal Bankruptcy Law - Bankruptcy law is the most adaptable and frequently used method of debtor relief. It is one that also affords protection to creditors by a proceeding in a Federal court under the Bankruptcy Act. Bankruptcy serves a dual purpose: (1) to bring about an equitable distribution of the debtor's property among her creditors; and (2) to discharge the debtor from her debts and enable her to rehabilitate herself and start afresh. The Bankruptcy Reform Act of 1978 which became effective on 10/1/1979 and consists of 8 odd-numbered chapters: (1) general provisions; (3) case administration; (5) creditors, the debtor and the estate; (7) liquidation; (9) adjustment of debts of a municipality; (11) reorganization; (13) adjustment of debts of an individual with regular income; and (15) United States trustees. Bankruptcy Amendments Act of 1984 grants to U.S. district courts original and exclusive jurisdiction over all bankruptcy cases and original, but not exclusive, jurisdiction over civil proceedings arising under bankruptcy cases.

A. Case Administration - Chapter 3
    1. Commencement of the Case - Jurisdiction of bankruptcy court and the operation of the bankruptcy laws are begun by the filing of a voluntary or involuntary petition.
        a. Voluntary Petitions - Any person eligible to be a debtor under a given bankruptcy proceeding may file a voluntary petition under that chapter. He need not be insolvent; constitutes an automatic order for relief.
        b. Involuntary Petitions - May be filed only under chapter 7 or 11. It may be filed: (1) by 3 or more creditors who have unsecured claims that total $5000 or more; or (2) if there are less than 12 creditors of the debtor, by one or more creditors whose total claims equal $5000 or more. May not be filed against a farmer or a banking, insurance, or nonprofit corporation. Court may enter an order of relief only if: (1) debtor generally not paying his debts as they become due; or (2) within 120 days before the filing of the petition.
    2. Automatic Stays - The filing of a petition is to prevent the attempts by creditors to begin or continue to recover claims against the debtor. Applies to both secured and unsecured creditors.
    3. Trustees - Selected by a vote of the creditors; responsible for collecting, liquidating, and distributing the debtor's estate. The duties and powers of the trustee include: (a) use, sell, lease property of the estate; (b) deposit or invest money of the estate; (c) employ attorneys, accountants, appraisers; and (d) assume or reject any executory contract or unexpired lease of the debtor.
    4. Meeting of Creditors - Within a reasonable time after relief is ordered. Debtor must appear and submit to an examination by creditors and the trustee of his financial situation.

B. Creditors, the Debtor and the Estate - Chapter 5
    1. Creditors - Any entity that has a claim against the debtor that arose at the time of or before the order of relief. Claim means a right to payment.
        a. Proof of Claims - Creditors may file a proof of claim. If not, debtor or trustee may file a proof of claim. Court will not allow any claim that: (1) is unenforceable against the debtor; (2) is for unmatured interest; (3) may be offset against a debt owing the debtor; or (4) is for services of an insider which includes a relative or general partner of a debtor.
        b. Secured Claims - Claim with a lien on property of the debtor.
        c. Unsecured Claims - The creditor's claim is unsecured to the extent that the value of his interest is less than the allowed amount of his claim.
        d. Priority of Claims - The right of a claim to be paid before claims of lesser rank: (1) expenses of administration; (2) unsecured claims in an involuntary case in ordinary course of the debtor's business - "gap" creditors; (3) allowed up to $2000 for wages, salaries, or commissions earned within 90 days; (4) employee benefit plans from services rendered within 180 days, but limited to $2000 multiplied by number of employees; (5) $2000 for grain or fish producers against a storage facility; (6) $900 for consumer deposits for the purchase, lease; and (7) specified amounts owed to governmental units or excise taxes.
        e. Subordinates of Claims - Even if 2 claims of equal statutory priority, the court declares that one claim must be paid in full before the other can be paid.

2. Debtors
    a. Debtor's Duties - The debtor must file a list of creditors, a schedule of asets and liabilities, and a statement of financial affairs. Must cooperate with the trustee and surrender to all property of the estate: (1) up to $7500 in equity used as a residence; (2) up to $1200 in equity in one motor vehicle; (3) $1200 for any item of household goods; (4) up to $500 in jewelry; (5) property up to $400 plus any unused amount of first exemption; (6) $750 in implements, professional books, or tools of debtor's trade; (7) unmatured life insurance; (8) professionally prescribed health aids; (9) social security, veterans, and disability benefits; (10) unemployment compensation; (11) alimony and support payment; (12) payment from pension; and (13) payment from an award under a crime victim's reparation.
    b. Debtor's Exemptions - Purpose of Bankruptcy Act is to bring about an equitable distribution of the debtor's assets and to provide a discharge to the debtor.
    c. Discharge - Termination of certain allowed claims against a debtor. No private employer may terminate the employment against an individual who is or has been a debtor under Bankruptcy Act. State law permits a discharge only if: (1) agreement was made before the discharge has been granted; (2) debtor has not rescinded the agreement within 30 days after it becomes enforceable; (3) court has informed the debtor he is not required to enter into agreement; of (4) court approves the agreement as not imposing an undue hardship.
3. The Estate - All legal and equitable interests of a debtor in nonexempt property.
    a. Trustee as Lien Creditor - Judicial lien is a charge or interest in property to secure payment of a debt or performance of an obligation that is obtained by judgment of court action. Trustee gains the rights and powers of any creditor.
    b. Voidable Preferences - Bankruptcy Act invalidates certain preferential transfers from the debtor to favored creditors before the date of bankruptcy.
    c. Insolvency - Financial condition where debts exceed fair value of assets. Debtor is insolvent on and during the 90 days immediately preceding the date of the filing of the petition. Trustee may not avoid a transfer made: (1) in payment of a debt incurred in the ordinary course of business of debtor and transferee; (2) not later than 45 days after the debt was incurred; or (3) according to ordinary business terms.
    d. Fraudulent Transfers - Trustee may avoid fraudulent transfers made on or within one year before the date of the filing of the petition.
    e. Statutory Liens - Interest in property to secure payment of a debt that arises solely by statute. Trustee may avoid a statutory lien on property of the debtor if the lien: (1) becomes effective when debtor becomes insolvent; or (2) not perfected or enforceable on the date of filing of petition against a bona fide purchaser.

C. Liquidation - Chapter 7 - Termination of the business of the debtor, distribution of his nonexempt assets, and usually a discharge of all dischargeable debts of the debtor.
    1. Proceedings - Except railroads, insurance companies, banks, savings and loan associations, homestead associations and credit unions. If an order is entered, the court appoints an interim trustee, who serves until a permanent trustee is selected by creditors.
    2. Distribution of the Estate - After the trustee has collected all the assets, he distributes them to creditors. If any remain, to debtor in the following order:
        a. Secured creditors.
        b. Creditors entitled to a priority.
        c. Payment is made to unsecured creditors who filed on time.
        d. Who file late.
        e. Claims for multiple, exemplary, punitive damages.
        f. Interest at the legal rate.
        g. Whatever remains is distributed to debtor.

3. Discharge - After the distribution of the estate, the court will grant the debtor a discharge.

D. Reorganization - Chapter 11 - A distressed business enterprise and its value as a going concern are preserved through the correction or elimination of the factors that brought about its distress.
    1. Proceedings - After the order for relief, the court will appoint a committee of unsecured creditors. Debtor will remain in possession and management of the property of the estate unless the court appoints a trustee who will operate the debtor's business.
    2. Plan - May file a plan at any time and has the exclusive right to file a plan during the 120 days after the order for relief, and a written disclosure statement approved by the court as containing adequate information must be transmitted to each holder of a claim before seeking acceptance or rejection of the plan.
    3. Acceptance of Plan - A class of claims has accepted a plan if it has been accepted by creditors that hold at least 2/3 in amount and more than 1/2 of the allowed claims of such class. Acceptance of a plan by a class of interests requires acceptance by holders of at least 2/3 in amount of the allowed interest. A class that is not impaired under a plan is deemed to have accepted the plan.
    4. Confirmation of Plan - A plan must be confirmed by the court before it is binding on any parties which required:
        a. Good faith.
        b. Feasibility.
        c. Cash payments.
        d. Acceptance by creditors.
    5. Effect of Reorganization - The new entity succeeding to debtor's properties emerges from the proceeding and begins life anew with only those obligations that are imposed on it by the plan. Debtor is discharged from all its debts and liabilities, except those that are not dischargeable.

E. Adjustment of Debts of Individuals - Chapter 13 - Permits an individual debtor to file a repayment plan that, if confirmed by the court, will discharge him from debts.
    1. Proceeding - May be initiated only by a voluntary petition.
    2. Plan - Debtor files the plan and may notify it at any time before confirmation which must meet 3 requirements: (a) submission of all or any portion of future earnings or income of the debtor; (b) full payment on a deferred basis of all claims entitled to a priority; and (c) must provide the same treatment for each claim in the same class.
    3. Confirmation - Confirmed by court if: (a) applicable law and proposed in good faith; (b) value of property must not be less than the amount that would be paid them under chapter 7; (c) secured creditors must accept the plan; or (d) debtor must be able to make all payments and comply with the plan.
    4. Discharge - After a debtor completes all payment under the plan, the court will grant him a discharge of all debt.

II. State Law - The rights and remedies of debtors and creditors outside of bankruptcy are principally governed by State law.
    A. Creditor's Rights - May file suit to collect the debt owed.
        1. Pre-judgment Remedies
            a. Attachment - Seizure of property to bring it under the custody of the court; is limited to situations in which: (1) defendant cannot be personally served; (2) claim is based upon fraud or the equivalent; or (3) defendant has or likely to transfer away his property.
            b. Garnishment - Proceeding by a creditor against a third person who owes money to debtor.
        2. Post-judgment Remedies - May proceed to trial and try to obtain a court judgment against the debtor. Writ of execution is an order served by sheriff upon debtor demanding payment of a

court judgment against debtor, but limited to property not exempt. Then order a levy on and sale of specified nonexempt property belonging to defendant. Supplementary proceeding if the proceeds of the sale do not produce sufficient funds and he may also proceed by garnishment.

B. Debtor's Relief - Resolving conflicts between creditors' rights and debtor relief involves a compromise under which the debtor will disclose and surrender all his assets to a trustee for the benefit of his creditors who will receive fair and equal treatment.

1. Compositions - Agreement between debtor and 2 or more of her creditors that each will take a portion of his claim as full payment.

2. Assignments for Benefit of Creditors - A voluntary transfer by the debtor of some or all of his property to a trustee, who applies the property to the payment of all of the debtor's debts. Advantage is that it prevents the debtor's assets from being attached or executed and halts the race of diligent creditors to attach.

3. Statutory Assignments - Combine the idea of the assignment with a corresponding benefit to debtor by discharging him from the balance of his debts.

4. Equity Receiverships - One of the oldest remedies in equity is the appointment of a receiver by the court. A receiver is a disinterested (unbiased) person appointed by the court who collects and preserves the debtor's assets and income and disposes of them at the direction of the court.

DEFINITIONS

1. Voluntary petition

2. Involuntary petition

3. Trustee

4. Claim

5. Secured claim

6. Unsecured claim

7. Discharge

8. Voidable preference

9. Insider

10. Transfer

11. Liquidation

12. Reorganization

13. Confirmation of plan

14. Adjustment of debts of individuals

15. Composition

16. Assignment for benefit of creditors

17. Receivership

18. Subordination of claims

19. Judicial lien

20. Insolvency

21. Statutory lien

TRUE/FALSE

F 1. Federal bankruptcy law is generally superseded by State insolvency laws.

T 2. Chapter 13 of the Bankruptcy Act applies to individuals with regular income who owe liquidated unsecured debts of less than $100,000 and secured debts of less than $350,000.

T 3. The jurisdiction of the bankruptcy court and the operation of the bankruptcy laws are commenced by the filing of a voluntary or involuntary petition.

F 4. A debtor must be insolvent before he can file a voluntary petition.

T 5. As the representative of the estate, the trustee in bankruptcy has the capacity to sue or to be sued.

F 6. A secured creditor's claim is secured to the extent of the allowed amount of his claim, even if that amount exceeds the value of his interest in the debtor's property.

T 7. After creditors with secured claims and creditors with claims having a priority have been satisfied, creditors with allowed, unsecured claims share proportionately in any remaining assets.

T 8. The debtor's estate in bankruptcy includes any property received by the debtor by inheritance or as a beneficiary of a life insurance policy within one year after commencement of the case.

F 9. All transfers made by the debtor within ninety days of bankruptcy are voidable.

F 10. Any person that may be a debtor under Chapter 7 and railroads may be a debtor under Chapter 11.

T 11. Under Chapter 11, the debtor will remain in possession of and management of the property of the estate unless the court appoints a trustee, who then may operate the debtor's business.

F 12. A plan of reorganization under Chapter 11 need not be confirmed by the court to be binding on the parties.

F 13. A composition is an alternative method of settling a debtor's estate under the Bankruptcy Act.

14. A plan under Chapter 13 will not be confirmed by the bankruptcy court if the value of the property to be distributed to unsecured creditors under the plan is less than they would receive under Chapter 7.

15. The trustee has the status of a lien creditor, which allows him to set aside a perfected security interest.

MULTIPLE CHOICE

1. The Chapter of the Bankruptcy Act containing the provisions dealing with case administration is:
   a. Chapter 1.
   b. Chapter 3.
   c. Chapter 4.
   d. Chapter 5.

2. Chapter 7 of the Bankruptcy Act is entitled:
   a. liquidation.
   b. adjustment of debts of a municipality.
   c. reorganization.
   d. adjustments of debts of an individual with regular income.

3. Chapter 7 of the Bankruptcy Act applies to all debtors except:
   a. railroads.
   b. insurance companies.
   c. homestead associations.
   d. all of the above.

4. Which of the following is not a duty or power of a trustee under the Bankruptcy Act?
   a. To use, sell or lease property of the estate.
   b. To deposit or invest money of the estate.
   c. To conduct the affairs of the debtor's estate for the trustee's own benefit.
   d. to assume or reject any executory contract or unexpired lease of the debtor.

5. The Bankruptcy Court will not allow a creditor's claim when the claim:
   a. is unenforceable against the debtor and his property.
   b. is for an interest that has not yet matured.
   c. may be offset against a debt owing the debtor.
   d. all of the above.

6. A creditor's claim will be denied by the Bankruptcy Court as that of an insider if the creditor is any of the following except:
   a. a general partner of the debtor.
   b. a partnership in which the debtor is a limited partner.
   c. a relative of the debtor.
   d. a corporation of which the debtor is a director.

b 7. Which of the following items of the debtor's property is not exempted from the bankruptcy proceedings by the Bankruptcy Act?
   a. Social security benefits.
   b. Future wages.
   c. Unemployment compensation.
   d. All of the above.

c 8. The following debts are not dischargeable in a bankruptcy proceeding except:
   a. alimony and support of a spouse or child.
   b. student loans that first become due less than five years before the filing of the bankruptcy petition.
   c. accounts payable due less than six months before the filing of the bankruptcy petition.
   d. none of the debts.

d 9. The estate in bankruptcy includes property that the trustee recovers under his powers:
   a. as a lien creditor.
   b. to avoid a voidable preference.
   c. to avoid a fraudulent transfer.
   d. all of the above.

d 10. The trustee may avoid a fraudulent transfer made by the debtor on or within _____ before the date of the filing of the petition.
   a. 60 days
   b. 90 days
   c. 180 days
   d. one year

d 11. Under Chapter 7 of the Bankruptcy Act, after secured creditors collect on their security interests, the next to receive assets from the estate in bankruptcy is/are:
   a. the debtor.
   b. unsecured creditors who file their claims on time.
   c. the trustee, for his services.
   d. creditors entitled to a priority.

a 12. A court will confirm a plan of reorganization under Chapter 11 of the Bankruptcy Act only if it meets all of the requirements of the Act, including all of the following except:
   a. the plan must be accepted by all of the creditors.
   b. certain classes of creditors must have their allowed claims paid in full in cash immediately, or in some instances, upon a deferred basis.
   c. the court must find that the plan is feasible.
   d. the plan must have been proposed in good faith.

d 13. Under the exemptions found in the Federal Bankruptcy Act, which of the following items may be kept by the debtor?
   a. $7,500 cash if the debtor does not have equity in a residence.
   b. A $500 diamond ring.
   c. A $400 VCR.
   d. All of the above can be exempt from the bankruptcy proceeding and may be kept by the debtor.

14. Which of the following is a correct statement regarding the automatic stay?
    a. It permanently discharges the debtor's obligation to pay.
    b. It is discretionary with the court.
    c. It automatically comes into existence when the debtor's petition is filed.
    d. It applies only to unsecured creditors.

15. Which of the following claims would be paid first by the trustee out of the debtor's estate?
    a. A perfected security interest secured by an item of personal property.
    b. The expenses of administering the estate.
    c. The unpaid wages of employees.
    d. Back taxes owed to the government.

SHORT ESSAY

1. Identify and describe briefly each of the steps involved in the administration of a case under Chapter 3 of the Bankruptcy Act. _____
_____
_____
_____

2. What is the effect of a discharge of a debt? When is an agreement to enforce a discharged debt enforceable? _____
_____
_____
_____

3. Describe briefly the role of a trustee in bankruptcy as a lien creditor. _____
_____
_____
_____

4. Under what conditions can a trustee recover a preferential transfer made to a creditor?_____
_____
_____
_____

5. Identify and discuss briefly three non-bankruptcy forms of compromises that have been developed to provide relief to debtors. _____
_____
_____
_____

PART VIII

SAMPLE EXAMINATION

_____ 1. Which of the following is covered by Article 9 of the UCC?
   a. A mortgage on an office building.
   b. A mechanic's lien on a house.
   c. A financing agreement on an office copier.
   d. The cash purchase of an automobile.

_____ 2. Andrew Attorney buys a set of tax books to include in his office library. He gives First Bank a security interest in the books in return for a $1,500 loan which he uses to purchase the books. Under Article 9 of the Code, the books would be classified as:
   a. consumer goods.
   b. equipment.
   c. inventory.
   d. fixtures.

_____ 3. Andrew Attorney buys a set of encyclopedias to include in his home library. He gives First Bank a security interest in the books in return for a $1,500 loan which he uses to purchase the books. Under Article 9 of the Code, the books would be classified as:
   a. consumer goods.
   b. equipment.
   c. inventory.
   d. fixtures.

_____ 4. Which of the following must be done in order for a security interest in goods to attach?
   a. The secured party must give value.
   b. The debtor must sign a security agreement which describes the goods.
   c. The debtor must retain possession of the goods.
   d. The secured party must properly file a financing statement.

_____ 5. The enforceability of a security agreement against third parties is called:
   a. security.
   b. attachment.
   c. perfection.
   d. value.

_____ 6. In which of the following situations is a security interest automatically perfected?
   a. First Bank loans $1,000 to Harold Homemaker so that Harold may purchase a gold necklace for his wife which Harold then gives to her on their anniversary.
   b. First Bank loans $1,000 to Harold Homemaker so that Harold may purchase a computer for his office which Harold then purchases and allows his secretary to use.
   c. First Bank files a financing statement covering the computer which Harold Homemaker purchased for his office.
   d. Harold Homemaker purchases a refrigerator and uses his bank credit card to finance it.

_____ 7. Bill Businessman grants a security interest in a Picasso painting to First Bank. In accordance with the loan agreement, the bank advances $5,000 to Bill. First Bank then files a financing statement. Six months later, Bill needs more money and goes to his friend David who owns an art gallery and

deals in art. David advances $2,000 to Bill based on Bill's pledge of the painting.
a. Both First Bank and David Dealer have a perfected security interest in the painting.
b. First Bank has a perfected security interest, but David does not, because he has not filed a financing statement.
c. The interest of First Bank has priority over that of David, because First Bank was the first to file or perfect its security interest.
d. Two of the above, (a) and (c) are correct.

8. First Bank loans Bill Businessman $1,500 so that Bill may purchase a personal computer and printed for his son Junior to use in writing term papers for school. Bill signs a financing statement which First Bank duly files. Junior never uses the computer so Bill puts an ad in the paper and sells it to Carol Consumer. If Bill defaults on the loan, which of the following is correct?
a. The bank has a perfected security interest, because it has filed a financing statement.
b. The bank has a perfected security interest, because it gave Bill the money to purchase an item of consumer goods, as a result of which its security interest is automatically perfected.
c. As between the bank and Carol, Carol will prevail, because she is a buyer in the ordinary course of business.
d. Two of the above, (a) and (c) are correct.

9. First Bank loans Bill Businessman, $1,500 so that Bill may purchase a personal computer for his office secretary. Bill signs a financing statement which First Bank duly files. His secretary never uses the computer, so Bill puts an ad in the paper and sells it to Carol Consumer. If Bill defaults on the loan, which of the following is correct?
a. The bank has a perfected security interest, because it has filed a financing statement.
b. The bank has a perfected security interest, because it gave Bill the money to purchase the item.
c. As between the bank and Carol, the bank will prevail and be able to repossess the computer, because it has a perfected security interest which it has filed, if it has not authorized the sale.
d. Two of the above, (a) and (c) are correct.

10. First Bank loans Bill Businessman $1,500 so that Bill may purchases a personal computer for his office secretary. Bill signs a financing statement which First Bank duly files within ten days. After Bill purchases the computer, he takes out a loan at Valley Bank, gives the computer as collateral and signs a financing statement, which Valley Bank then duly files. His secretary never uses the computer, so Bill puts an ad in the paper and sells it to Carol Consumer. If Bill defaults on the loans, which of the following is correct?
a. Both First Bank and Valley Bank have perfected security interests in the computer, which is classified as noninventory collateral.
b. First Bank has a perfected purchase money security interest while Valley Bank has only a perfected security interest.
c. Both First Bank and Valley Bank have rights in the computer that are superior to those of Carol Consumer even if she had no knowledge of the two security interests.
d. All of the above are correct.

11. First Bank loans Marlin, who is the owner of Marlin's Department Store, $15,000 so that he may purchase personal computers for the store's inventory. Marlin signs a financing statement which First Bank duly files before Marlin takes possession. After Marlin purchases the computers, he then goes to Valley Bank and takes out a loan for which he gives the computers as collateral. Marlin signs a financing agreement which Valley Bank then duly files. Later Carol Consumer comes into the store and purchases one of the computers. If Marlin defaults on the loans, which of the following is correct?

a. First Bank and Valley Bank both have perfected security interests in the computers.
b. First Bank has a purchase money security interest in inventory, which has priority over conflicting security interests if certain requirements have been met.
c. Carol is a buyer in the ordinary course of business whose interest in the computer she purchased is superior to that of both First Bank and Valley Bank.
d. All of the above are correct.
e. Only (a) and (b) are correct.

_____ 12. Which of the following claims are not dischargeable in bankruptcy?
a. Child support.
b. Claims of back taxes.
c. Claims for federally insured student loans that first became due last year.
d. All of the above are nondischargeable debts.

_____ 13. Which Chapter of the Federal Bankruptcy Act is sometimes referred to as "straight bankruptcy?"
a. Chapter 7.
b. Chapter 9.
c. Chapter 11.
d. Chapter 12.

_____ 14. Which of the following assets is exempt from claims by creditors in a bankruptcy proceeding?
a. Social Security benefits.
b. Unemployment compensation.
c. $500 in jewelry.
d. All of the above assets are exempt from claims by creditors.

_____ 15. If the only nonexempt asset in a bankruptcy estate is a piece of equipment valued at $25,000, which of the following claims will be paid first by the trustee in bankruptcy?
a. The wages, salaries and commissions earned by employees within ninety days before the filing of the petition and the cessation of a business.
b. The necessary expenses of the trustee in administering the estate.
c. Unsecured claims in the amount of $15,000.
d. A claim of $15,000 by a bank and secured by the piece of equipment where the bank has duly filed a financing statement.

_____ 16. If the only nonexempt asset in a bankruptcy estate is a piece of equipment valued at $25,000, which of the following claims will be paid second by the trustee in bankruptcy?
a. The wages, salaries and commissions earned by employees within ninety days before the filing of the petition and the cessation of the business.
b. The necessary expenses of the trustee in the administration of the estate.
c. Unsecured claims in the amount of $15,000.
d. A claim of $15,000 by a bank and secured by the piece of equipment where the bank has duly filed a financing statement.

_____ 17. A company files for bankruptcy. Its only non-exempt asset is a piece of equipment valued at $25,000. The claims that have been approved by the trustee for payment are as follows:
(1) $10,000 in wages, salaries and commissions earned by employees within ninety days before the filing of the petition and the cessation of the business.
(2) $3,000 in expenses of the trustee in the administration of the estate.
(3) Unsecured claims in the amount of $15,000.

(4) A claim of $15,000 by a bank and secured by the piece of equipment where the bank has duly filed a financing statement.

How much money will be available to pay the $10,000 claim of the employees?

a. $15,000

b. $10,000

c. $7,000

d. No money will be left to pay the employees.

_____ 18. A company files for bankruptcy. Its only non-exempt asset is a piece of equipment valued at $25,000. The claims that have been approved by the trustee are as follows:

(1) $10,000 in wages, salaries and commissions earned by employees within ninety days before the filing of the petition and the cessation of the business.

(2) $3,000 in expenses of the trustee in the administration of the estate.

(3) Unsecured claims in the amount of $15,000.

(4) A claim of $15,000 by a bank and secured by the piece of equipment where the bank has duly filed a financing statement.

How much money will be available to pay the unsecured creditors?

a. $25,000

b. $10,000

c. $7,000

d. No money will be available to pay the unsecured creditors.

_____ 19. Three months before filing for bankruptcy, Carol Consumer transferred title to her house to her father without any payment by him and with the understanding that he would reconvey the house to Carol after she receives her discharge from the bankruptcy court. The transfer of the house by Carol to her father is a/an:

a. voidable preference.

b. fraudulent transfer.

c. statutory lien.

d. exempt transfer.

_____ 20. Bill Businessman has an allowed claim of $5,000 against the bankruptcy estate of Donald Debtor. He has a valid security interest in a painting owned by Donald, which security interest is in the amount of $3,000 and which painting is valued by the trustee at $5,000.

a. Bill will probably receive nothing from the bankruptcy estate, because the priorities stated in the Bankruptcy Act will be paid before his claim.

b. Bill will probably receive the full $5,000 from the bankruptcy estate.

c. Bill will receive the $3,000 which is secured by the painting, but is a general creditor in the amount of $2,000 and may or may not receive that money from the estate.

d. Bill will probably receive nothing from the bankruptcy estate, because his claim is a voidable preference.

TRADE REGULATION

PURPOSE

Fair competition in industry and trade have historically been the backbone of our free enterprise system. However, with the concentration of economic power created by the combining of forces within the business world, the need for government regulation has become increasingly apparent. With the growth of big business in the last half of the nineteenth century, the Federal government came to the aid of State lawmakers in controlling business operations to assure free and fair competition. The Sherman Antitrust Act, enacted in 1890, was the first such legislative action taken by Congress. This act sought to control unfair competition by prohibiting contracts, combinations, and conspiracies that restrain trade as well as outlawing monopolies and any attempts to monopolize. Other statutes in the field followed, including the Clayton Act, the Robinson-Patman Act, and the Federal Trade Commission Act. These legislations further regulated unfair business practices. This chapter discusses these acts and their implications regarding business practice. You will examine the various rights protected by Federal legislation and the remedies provided upon infringement of fair competition.

CHAPTER CHECKPOINTS

After reading and studying this chapter, you should be able to:

1. Discuss the Sherman Antitrust Act and its rules governing trade restraints and monopolization.

2. Discuss the Clayton Act and its rules governing (a) tying contracts, (b) exclusive dealing, and (c) mergers.

3. Discuss the Robinson-Patman Act and the various defenses to it.

4. Explain what is protected by trade secrets and how they may be infringed.

5. Distinguish among the various types of trade symbols and distinguish between copyrights and patents.

CHAPTER OUTLINE

I. Antitrust - Antitrust laws emerged in the last half of the nineteenth century when Congress decided it had to intervene in order to balance the economic power of big business.
  A. Sherman Act - The Sherman Antitrust Act, enacted by Congress in 1890, has two sections. Section 1

prohibits contracts, combinations, and conspiracies that restrain trade while Section 2 outlaws monopolies and attempts to monopolize.

1. Restraints of Trade - Restraints are tested as to whether their imposition promotes or destroys fair competition.
   a. Rule of Reason - This is a standard that balances the anticompetitive effects against the procompetitive effects of the restraint.
   b. Per Se - A practice which is conclusively presumed unreasonable is considered illegal per se.
   c. Price Fixing - This is an agreement with the purpose or effect of inhibiting price competition.
   d. Marketing Allocation - Markets may be divided by customers, geographic locations, or products.
   e. Boycotts - This is an agreement among competitors not to deal with a supplier or customer.
   f. Tying arrangements - This involves conditioning a sale of a desired product on the buyer purchasing a second product.

B. Patents - A patent is the exclusive right to an invention.
   1. Patentability - The Patent Act specifies those inventions that may be patented. Generally, the invention must be new and useful.
   2. Procedure - A patent is issued by the United States Patent and Trademark Office. The applicant must be the inventor. The invention should have novelty, utility, and be nonobvious.
   3. Infringement - This occurs when anyone, without permission, is involved in making, using, or selling a patented invention.
   4. Remedies - The remedies for infringement under the Patent Act are: (a) injunctive relief, (b) adequate damages, (c) attorney's fees, and/or (d) costs.
   5. Trade Names - A trade name is any name used to identify a business, vocation, or occupation.

C. Copyrights - This is the exclusive right to original works of authorship.
   1. Procedure - Applications for copyright are filed with the Copyright Office in the Library of Congress. This registration is strongly advised, but not required.
   2. Rights - copyright protection subsists in most instances for the author's life plus 50 years. The owner of the copyright has the exclusive right to, and to authorize others to: (a) reproduce the copyrighted work, (b) prepare derivative works based on the copyright work, (c) distribute copies of the work, and (d) perform or display the work publicly.
   3. Ownership - The ownership of a copyright may be transferred in whole or in part by conveyance, will, or intestate succession.
   4. Infringement - This occurs when someone exercises the copyright owner's rights without authorization.
   5. Remedies - Available remedies are: (a) injunction, or (b) impoundment and possible destruction of infringing articles.
      a. Horizontal Merger - This is the acquisition by one company of a competing company.
      b. Vertical Merger - This is the acquisition by one company of its suppliers or customers.
      c. Conglomerate Merger - This is an acquisition not involving a competitor, customer or supplier.

II. Unfair Competition - The law of unfair competition has been developed to prevent businesses from taking unfair advantage of their competitors. An important part of this area of law is for the protection of intellectual property.
   A. Trade Secrets - Every business has secret information which can be commercially available. Lists of customers, contracts, suppliers, and customers and often secret formulas are vital and need to be protected.

B. Trade Symbols - Every product on the market has an origin, such as the manufacturer, which can and should be exclusively identified.
   1. Types of Trade Symbols - The Lanham Act recognizes four types of trade symbols which are all distinctive in their identification of a good or service.
      a. Trademark - This is a distinctive mark, word, letter, number, design, picture, or combination which is adopted by a person identifying goods he manufactures or sells.
      b. Service Mark - This is a distinctive symbol, word, or design that is used to identify the services of a provider.
      c. Certification Mark - This is a distinctive symbol, word, or design used with goods or services to certify specific characteristics.
      d. Collective Mark - This is a distinctive symbol used to indicate membership in an organization.
   2. Registration - To be accepted by the Lanham Act, a mark must be distinctive so that it identifies the origin of the goods or services.
   3. Infringement - This occurs when a person without authorization uses an identical or substantially indistinguishable mark that is likely to cause confusion, mistake, or deception.
   4. Monopolies - Monopolies will use their power tolimit production and increase prices.
      a. Monopolization - In order for the courts to rule against a monopoly, the market power must be either atained unfairly or abused.
      b. Attempts to monopolize - These can take many forms, but they generally involve controlling prices or excluding competitors from the marketplace.

C. Clayton Act - The major provisions of this act deal with price discrimination, tying contracts, exclusive dealing, and mergers.
   1. Tying Arrangements - A tying arrangement exists where a seller exploits its economic power in one market to expand its empire into another market.
   2. Exclusive Dealing - An exclusive dealing arrangement is one by which the seller or lessor of a product conditions an agreement on the buyer's or lessee's promise not to deal in the goods of competitor.
   3. Mergers - Mergers, which can be completely legal and good in business, involve the acquisition by a corporation of stock or assets in another corporation.

D. Robinson-Patman Act - This act amended the Clayton Act to prohibit buyers from inducing and sellers from granting.
   1. Cost Justification - If a seller can show that it costs less to sell a product to a particular buyer, the seller may lawfully pass along the cost savings.
   2. Meeting Competition - A seller may lower his price in a good faith attempt to meet competition.

E. FTC Act - The Federal Trade Commission Act, enacted by Congress in 1914, attempts to prevent unfair methods of competition in commerce, and unfair or deceptive acts or practices in commerce.

DEFINITIONS

1. Rule of reason test

2. Per se test

3. Horizontal restraint

4. Vertical restraint

5. Retail price maintenance

6. Tying arrangement

7. Monopoly

8. Attempt to monopolize

9. Interlocking directorate

10. Price discrimination

11. Trademark

12. Trade name

13. Copyright

14. Patent

TRUE/FALSE

_____ 1. State courts are empowered to issue injunctions restraining violations of the Sherman Act.

_____ 2. Under the Sherman Act, those restraints not characterized as *per se* illegal are judged by the Rule of Reason test.

_____ 3. The Sherman Act prohibits sellers' agreements not to advertise their prices.

_____ 4. While the Sherman Act prohibits sellers' agreements to establish minimum prices, sellers are free to agree to establish maximum prices.

_____ 5. Under the Sherman Act, the refusal of a seller to deal with any particular buyer is considered illegal *per se*.

_____ 6. Because of their tendency to exclude competitors from the market, all tying arrangements have been declared illegal *per se*.

_____ 7. Under the Robinson–Patman Act, liability may be imposed upon buyers as well as sellers.

_____ 8. Restrictive employment agreements are enforced by the courts if their time and area limitations are reasonable.

_____ 9. Under the Trademark Act of 1946, a trademark is required to be affixed to the goods it identifies.

_____ 10. The granting of a patent guarantees the patentee the exclusive right to make, use, or sell his invention.

_____ 11. Meeting competition is a defense to a charge of price discrimination under the Robinson-Patman Act.

_____ 12. A vertical merger occurs when a wholesale manufacturer acquires a retail outlet for its products by way of merger.

_____ 13. A patent like a copyright may be renewed when the initial period for which it was granted expires.

_____ 14. Tel-Ko computers has been having problems with its competitors copying its magazine ads. A magazine ad may be copyrighted.

_____ 15. Tel-Ko computers has been having problems with its competitors copying its computer software. Computer software may be copyrighted.

MULTIPLE CHOICE

_____ 1. Violators of the Sherman Act are subject to:
   a. fines and imprisonment.
   b. injunctions.
   c. civil actions for treble damages.
   d. all of the above.

_____ 2. The Rule of Reason test is used to determine the legality of:
   a. horizontal price fixing agreements.
   b. vertical territorial and customer restrictions.
   c. horizontal market allocation agreements.
   d. retail price maintenance agreements.

_____ 3. A company is not in possession of monopoly power if its share of the market is:
   a. 100%.
   b. 85%.
   c. 75%.
   d. 50%.

_____ 4. Labor unions are exempted from the antitrust laws by:
   a. the Sherman Act.
   b. the Clayton Act.
   c. the Robinson-Patman Act.
   d. The FTC Act.

_____ 5. A company which unilaterally fixes prices has violated:
   a. the Sherman Act.
   b. the Clayton Act.
   c. the FTC Act.
   d. none of the above.

_____ 6. A person who knowingly induces or receives an illegal discrimination in price as violated:
   a.   the Sherman Act.
   b.   the Clayton Act.
   c.   the Robinson–Patman Act.
   d.   none of the above.

_____ 7. A corporation which acquires the stock of another corporation where the effect may be substantially to lessen competition between the two corporations has violated:
   a.   the Sherman Act.
   b.   the Clayton Act.
   c.   the Robinson–Patman Act.
   d.   the FTC Act.

_____ 8. A company which engages in unfair methods of competition has violated:
   a.   the Sherman Act.
   b.   the Clayton Act.
   c.   the Robinson–Patman Act.
   d.   the FTC Act.

_____ 9. Membership in a trade union is generally indicated by:
   a.   a trademark.
   b.   a service mark.
   c.   a collective mark.
   d.   a certification mark.

_____ 10. A patent is valid for a period of:
   a.   17 years.
   b.   the inventor's life plus 17 years.
   c.   50 years.
   d.   the inventor's life plus 50 years.

_____ 11. "Kodak," "Nylon," and "Coke" are examples of:
   a.   trade names.
   b.   service marks.
   c.   trademarks.
   d.   copyrights.

_____ 12. Which one of the following is not a *per se* violation of the Sherman Act?
   a.   Price fixing.
   b.   Horizontal market allocation.
   c.   Vertical market allocation.
   d.   Group boycotts.

_____ 13. Which of the following is necessary for an item to be patentable?
   a.   Novelty.
   b.   Utility.
   c.   Nonobviousness.
   d.   Novelty, utility and nonobviousness are all required.

_____ 14. Which of the following items would not be patentable?
    a.   A computer.
    b.   A genetically engineered micro-oganism.
    c.   An idea such as Einstein's formula $E = mc^2$.
    d.   A process by which to manufacture a new product.

_____ 15. A _____ merger involves the acquisition by a company of all or substantially all or part of the stock or assets of a competing company.
    a.   horizontal
    b.   vertical
    c.   conglomerate
    d.   monopolistic

SHORT ESSAY

1. What is the purpose of the Federal and State antitrust statutes? _____

2. According to economic theory, how does a monopolistic market differ from a competitive market? _____

3. What must be shown to prove a company guilty of monopolization under Section 2 of the Sherman Act?

4. What must be shown to prove a company guilty of an attempt to monopolize under Section 2 of the Sherman Act? _____

CHAPTER 40

SECURITIES REGULATION

PURPOSE

The primary purpose of Federal securities regulation is to prevent fraudulent practices in the sale of securities and thereby to maintain public confidence in the securities market. Federal securities law consists principally of two statutes: (1) the Securities Act of 1933, which focuses on the issuance of securities; and (2) the Securities Act of 1934, which deals mainly with the trading of already issued securities. Both statutes are administered by the Securities and Exchange Commission (SEC), an independent, quasi-judicial agency. In addition to the Federal laws regulating the sale of securities, there are also State laws, commonly known as "Blue Sky" laws, which prohibit fraud in the sale of securities and sometimes require State registration.

CHAPTER CHECKPOINTS

After reading and studying this chapter, you should be able to:

1. Identify the scope and purpose of the 1933 and 1934 Federal Securities laws.

2. Define a security and recognize one in problems.

3. Summarize the requisites of Rule 10b-5 and define the terms "insider" and "tippee."

4. Summarize the requirements of Section 16(b) and differentiate between 16(b) and 10b-5.

5. Summarize the Federal securities provisions dealing with proxy solicitations.

CHAPTER OUTLINE

A. Securities Act of 1933 - Also called the Truth in Securities Act, it requires a registration statement be filed with the SEC before any securities may be offered for sale to the public unless they are exempt from the registration and disclosure requirement of the Act. Civil and criminal liability may be imposed for violations of the Act.
   1. Definition of a Security - Includes any note, stock, bond, debenture, evidence of indebtedness, preorganization certificate or subscription, investment contract, voting trust certificate, fractional undivided interest in oil, gas, or other mineral rights, or any interest or instrument.

2. Registration of Securities - The purpose of registration is to provide disclosure of financial and other information on which investors may judge the merits of the securities. However, the SEC does not make judgment on the financial merits or guarantee the accuracy of the facts presented. The effective date of a registration statement is the 20th day after filing.

    a. Rule 415 - Shelf registrations permit qualified issuers to register "off the shelf" on a delayed or continuous basis in the future.

3. Exempt Securities - The securities may be resold without registration.

    a. Regulation A - Permits an issuer to offer up to 1.5 million of securities in 12 month period without registering. The issuer must file a notification and an offering circular with SEC, offerees, and purchasers.

    b. Intrastate Issues - Exempted from registration if offered and sold only to persons who live in a single State where the issuer is resident and doing business. Rule 147 requires that: (1) issuer is incorporated in the State in which the issuance occurs; (2) issuer is principally doing business in that state (80% of gross revenue, assets and not proceeds); (3) all offerees and purchasers are residents of that State; (4) no resales to nonresidents during the period of sale and for 9 months after the last sale; and (5) precautions are taken.

    c. Short-term Commercial Paper - That issued for working capital with a maturity of not more than 9 months when issued.

    d. Other Exempt Securities - (1) domestic governments; (2) domestic banks and savings and loan associations; (3) nonprofit charitable organization; (4) where issuance is regulated by the Interstate Commerce Commission; (5) issued by a receiver or trustee in bankruptcy with court approval; (6) insurance policies and annuity contracts issued by regulated insurance companies; (7) issued solely for exchange with existing security holders where no commission is paid; and (8) reorganization securities and exchanged with court or other government approval.

4. Exempt Transactions - Considered restricted securities and may be resold only by registration or in another transaction exempt from registration. An issuer must take reasonable care to assure against non-exempt, unregistered resales of restricted securities. These transactions include:

    a. Private Placements - Transactions by an issuer not involving any public offering. No general advertising or solicitation. Rule 506 establishes a nonexclusive safe harbor for securities without regard to the dollar amount (restricted securities). Unlimited number of "accredited investors" but no more tan 35 other purchasers. Accredited investor is any person who purchases at least $150,000 of securities but does not exceed 20% of investor's net worth, any person whose net worth exceeds $1 million, and any person with an income over $200,000.

    b. Limited Offers Not Exceeding $5 Million - Rule 505, small business like non-investment company issuer that does not exceed $5,00,000 over 12 months. Issuer is not required to believe reasonably each non-accredited investor has sufficient knowledge and experience in financial matters to be capable of evaluating the merits and risks.

    c. Limited Offers Not Exceeding $500,000 - Rule 504 provides private, non-investing company issuers exempt from registration for small issues. Securities offered and sold without general advertising. Aggregate offering price with 12 months less than $500,000. Precaution taken for non-exempt, unregistered resale. Notifies SEC of sales.

    d. Limited Offers Solely to Accredited Investors - No unaccredited investors may purchase at all.

    e. Resales of Restricted Securities - Rule 144, there must be adequate current public information about the issuer, that issuer must own the securities for at least 2 years and limited amounts sold. Notice of the sale must be provided to SEC. However, non-affiliate issuer who owned at least 3 years may sell securities in unlimited amount and is not subject to any requirements of rule 144.

5. Liability - The sanctions include administration remedies by the SEC, civil liability to injured investors and criminal penalties.

    a. Unregistered Sales - Civil liability, absolute, no defenses. Purchaser has the right to tender if back to the seller and recover the purchase price; if no longer an owner, then recover monetary damages.

   b. **False Registration Statements** - Liability is imposed on issuer, all persons who signed the statement, directors or partners, those who prepared or certified any part of the statement, and all underwriters. Defendant, other than issuer, may assert the defense of due diligence.

   c. **Antifraud Provision** - Applied to all securities. Liability extends only to the immediate purchaser, provided she did not know of the untruth or omission. Seller may avoid liability if he proved that he did not know and exercised reasonable care so could not have known of the untrue statement.

   d. **Criminal Sanctions** - On any person who willfully violates any of the provisions of the Act or the rules and regulations promulgated by SEC, fine not more than $10,000 or imprisonment of not more than 5 years.

B. **1934 Act** - Deals mainly with the secondary distribution of securities. Provides protection for holders of securities listed on national exchanges and holders of equity securities of companies traded over the counter if assets exceed $5 million, and 500 or more shareholders.

   1. **Registration and Periodic Reporting Requirements** - Requires all publicly held companies to register with the SEC. Must file specified annual and period reports to update the information contained in the original registration. Imposes penalties for filing false statements and reports, may carry a fine of less than $100,000 or imprisonment of 5 years or both.

   2. **Antifraud Provisions** - Section 10(b) of the 1934 Act and SEC Rule 10b-5 make it unlawful to: (a) employ any device, scheme, or artifice to defraud; (b) make any untrue statement of a material fact; (c) omit to State a material fact; or (d) engage in any act that operates a fraud.

      a. **Requisites of Rule 10b-5** - Requires proof of several elements: (1) a mis-statement; (2) material; (3) scienter - intentional and knowing conduct; (4) relied on; (5) connection with the purchase or sale of a security.

      b. **Insider Trading** - An insider is one who possesses material information that is not available to the public. Liable for rule 10b-5 if he fails to disclose the material nonpublic information before trading on the information unless he waits until the information becomes public. Tippee is a person who receives material, nonpublic information from insider who is also precluded from trading on that information.

   3. **Short Swing Profits** - Section 16(b) of the 1934 Act imposes liability on insiders owning 10% or more of the stock of a corporation. If the insider sells stock within 6 months from the date of its purchase, the corporation is entitled to recover all profit realized. Differences between 16(b) and 10b-5:

      a. **16b** - Applies only to transactions involving registration equity securities; definition of insiders are limited to directors, officers, owners of 10% or more of a company's stock; does not require insider possess material non-public information; applies only to transactions within 6 months; any recovery from suit is on behalf of the corporation.

      b. **10b-5** - Applies to all securities; definition of insider is much broader, may extend beyond those mentioned above; applies only to insider trading where such information is not disclosed; no such limitation; injured investors may recover damages on their own behalf.

   4. **Insider Trading Sanctions Act** - SEC is authorized by Insider Trading Sanctions Act of 1984 to bring an action in a U.S. district court to have civil penalty, which may not exceed 3 times the profit gained. The penalty is payable into the Treasury of the United States. An action must be brought within 5 years after date of purchase or sale.

   5. **Proxy Solicitations** - Proxy is a writing signed by a shareholder of a corporation authorizing a named person to vote his shares of stock at a specified meeting of the shareholders. 1934 Act makes it unlawful to solicit any proxy in contravention of such rules and regulations as the commission may prescribe.

   6. **Tender Offers** - Is a general invitation to all the shareholders of a company to purchase their shares at a specified price. The 1934 Act requires any person that makes a tender offer for more than 5% of a class of registered equity securities to file with SEC.

7. Foreign Corrupt Practices Act - As an amendment to the 1934 Act, imposes internal control requirements on companies with securities registered under 1934 Act and prohibits all domestic concerns from bribing foreign governmental or political officials.

    a. Accounting Requirement - Make and keep books in reasonable detail, accurate and fairly reflect that transactions and disposition of assets of issuer. Devise and maintain internal control to assure that transactions are executed as authorized and recorded in conformity with generally accepted accounting principles.

    b. Anti-bribery Provisions - Unlawful for any domestic concern to offer anything of value directly or indirectly to any foreign official for purpose of: (1) influencing any act of that person in his official capacity; or (2) use influence to affect a decision of a foreign government. Violation fines of up to $1 million for companies. Individuals may be fined a maximum of $10,000 and imprisoned up to 5 years or both.

C. Accountant's Liability - Legal liability is imposed by both common law at the State level and Federal securities.

    1. Common Law

        a. Contract Liability - Employment contract is subject to the general principles of contract law. Accountant is bound to perform all the duties she explicitly agrees to provide, and also implicitly agrees to complete/perform the contract in a competent and professional manner. Liable for a third party beneficiary, a non-contracting party whom the contracting parties intended to receive the primary benefit. If an accountant materially breaches his conduct, he will not be entitled to any compensation.

        b. Tort Liability - An accountant may be liable for negligence or fraud. A tort is a private or civil wrong or injury other than a breach of contract. An accountant is liable for negligence if she does not exercise the degree of care a reasonably competent accountant would. Liability extended only to the client and third party beneficiaries. An accountant who commits a fraudulent act is liable to any person who should have reasonably foreseen would be injured or misrepresented and who justifiably relied on it and is liable for both compensatory and punitive damages.

        c. Criminal Liability - Federal law of securities regulation and taxation. Penalties may be a fine not to exceed $5000 or 3 years imprisonment or both. An accountant may not disclose the contents of working papers unless: (1) client consents; (2) a court orders the disclosure; or (3) requirements of the accounting profession or GAAS.

    2. Federal Securities Law - Liability is more extensive and has fewer limitations than liability under the common law.

        a. 1933 Act - Civil liability under section 11, however, will not be liable if he can prove due diligence. Willfully violates, held criminally liable for a fine not more than $10,000 or imprisonment of not more than 5 years or both.

        b. 1934 Act - Section 18 of the 1934 Act imposes civil liability. However, an accountant will not be liable if she can prove that she acted in good faith and had no knowledge. Accountants can also held civilly liable for violations of Rule 10b-5. A willful violation is held criminally liable for fine not more than $100,000 or imprisonment for not more than 5 years or both.

DEFINITIONS

1. Blue sky laws

2. Prospectus

3. Security

4. Offering circular

5. Intrastate issue

6. Nonexclusive safe harbor

7. Restricted securities

8. Reasonable care

9. Private placement

10. Accredited purchases

11. Due diligence

12. Short swing profits

13. Insider

14. Scienter

15. Inside information

16. Tippee

17. Proxy

18. Proxy statement

19. Tender offer

20. Shelf registration

TRUE/FALSE

_____ 1. A registrant may lawfully sell its securities immediately upon filing its registration statement with the SEC.

_____ 2. Exempt securities may be resold without registration.

_____ 3. The exemption for intrastate issues is not available if one or more offerees are not a resident of the State in which the issuer is a resident.

_____ 4. Securities sold in an exempt transaction may be resold only by registration.

_____ 5. Securities sold under the private placement exemption may be purchased by an unlimited number of purchasers.

_____ 6. An issuer need not notify the SEC of sales made pursuant to an exempt transaction.

_____ 7. A person who purchases a security sold in violation of the registration requirement of the 1933 Act has the right to tender it back to the seller and recover the purchase price.

_____ 8. The Securities Exchange Act of 1934 applies only to companies whose assets exceed $3 million and who have a class of equity securities with 500 or more shareholders.

_____ 9. Under the 1934 Act, all regulated publicly held companies must make a one-time registration with the SEC.

_____ 10. Under Rule 10b-5, liability may be imposed upon buyers as well as sellers.

_____ 11. Fines imposed upon individuals for violations of the Foreign Corrupt Practices Act may not be paid by the issuing corporation.

_____ 12. The only contract duties an accountant incurs are those he explicitly agrees to render.

_____ 13. Privity of contract is a requirement to a cause of action against an accountant based upon fraud.

_____ 14. An accountant is permitted to disclose confidential communications from his client if a court orders the disclosure.

_____ 15. Scienter is required for an accountant to violate the provisions of the Foreign Corrupt Practices act.

MULTIPLE CHOICE

_____ 1. The effective date of a registration statement is:
a. the day it is filed with the SEC.
b. the tenth day after it is filed with the SEC.
c. the twentieth day after it is filed with the SEC.
d. none of the above.

_____ 2. Under Regulation A, an issuer may make a yearly offering of unregistered securities of up to:
a. $500,000.
b. $1,500,000.
c. $5,000,000.
d. none of the above.

_____ 3. The exemption for short-term commercial paper is not available if:
a. the security has a maturity at the time of issuance of less than nine months.
b. the proceeds are to be used for working capital.
c. the proceeds are to be used for the acquisition of capital equipment.
d. (a) and (c) but not (b).

_____ 4. Which of the following securities must be registered?
a. Securities of domestic governments.
b. Securities of domestic banks.
c. Securities of not-for-profit, charitable organizations.
d. None of the above.

_____ 5. Under Rule 506 of the SEC, an issuer may make a private placement of unregistered securities of up to:
   a. $500,000.
   b. $1,500,000.
   c. $5,000,000.
   d.   none of the above.

_____ 6. Violators of the 1933 Act are subject to:
   a.   administrative remedies by the SEC.
   b.   civil liability to injured investors.
   c.   criminal penalties.
   d.   all of the above.

_____ 7. There are no defenses to:
   a.   selling an unregistered security which is required to be registered.
   b.   including in a registration statement any untrue statement or omission of material fact.
   c.   selling a security by means of a prospectus which includes an untrue statement of material fact or an omission of a material fact.
   d.   (b) and (c) but not (a).

_____ 8. Corporate insiders who buy the stock of the corporation will be liable to the corporation for any profits made pursuant to a sale of that stock within:
   a.   20 days.
   b.   90 days.
   c.   6 months.
   d.   12 months.

_____ 9. Assume Y, an officer of the C corporation, buys 700 shares of C stock on January 1 for $10 per share and 800 shares of C stock on March 15 for $8 per share. If Y then sells 600 of these shares on June 30 for $12 per share and the remaining 900 shares on October 15 for $14 per share, Y will be liable to C for:
   a. $12,000.
   b. $2,000.
   c. $2,400.
   d. $4,000.

_____ 10. A person will not be liable for a violation of Rule 10b-5 if his misconduct was:
   a.   intentional.
   b.   reckless.
   c.   negligent.
   d.   none of the above.

_____ 11. Management may omit a shareholder proposal from its proxy statement if the proposal:
   a.   is a proper subject for shareholder action.
   b.   is significantly related to the business of the issuer.
   c.   relates to the conduct of the ordinary business operations of the issuer.
   d.   all of the above.

_____ 12. Which of the following is correct with respect to Section 16(b)?
   a.   It applies only to transactions involving registered securities.
   b.   It uses the same definition of "insider" as does Rule 10b-5.
   c.   It requires that an insider possess material nonpublic information.
   d.   All of the above are correct with respect to 16(b).

_____ 13. Which of the following are included within the definition of insiders for the purposes of Rule 10b-5?
   a.   Directors.
   b.   Officers.
   c.   Employees.
   d.   Directors, officers and employees are all insiders under Rule 10b-5.

_____ 14. Which rule states that solicitation of a proxy is prohibited unless each person solicited has been furnished with a written proxy statement containing specified information?
   a.   Rule 10b-5.
   b.   Rule 14a-3.
   c.   Rule 504.
   d.   Rule 505.

_____ 15. Which of the following would ordinarily not be considered a security under the Federal securities law?
   a.   A limited partnership interest.
   b.   An insurance policy.
   c.   Bonds of a corporation.
   d.   An interest in a citrus grove.

SHORT ESSAY

1. What is the primary purpose of Federal securities regulation? _____
   _____
   _____
   _____

2. What information must typically be disclosed in a registration statement? _____
   _____
   _____
   _____

3. What steps must an issuer take to assure against non-exempt, unregistered resales of restricted securities?
   _____
   _____
   _____

4. How is the profit from a short-swing sale calculated? _____
   _____
   _____
   _____

CHAPTER 41

CONSUMER PROTECTION

PURPOSE

Historically, consumers were subject to the rule of *caveat emptor* or "let the buyer beware." However, in recent years, the law has abandoned this principle in consumer transactions and today gives greater protection to consumers in statutory form. In this chapter, you study the most important Federal consumer protection statutes including the Federal Trade Commission Act, the Magnuson-Moss Warranty Act, the Equal Credit Opportunity Act, the Federal Consumer Credit Protection Act, the Truth in Lending Act and the Fair Credit Billing Act.

CHAPTER CHECKPOINTS

After reading and studying this chapter, you should be able to:

1. Discuss the Federal Trade Commission Act and list the remedies used by the FTC to enforce the act.

2. List the principle provisions of the Magnuson-Moss Act and distinguish between a full and limited warranty.

3. Summarize the major provisions of the Equal Credit Opportunity Act, the Federal Consumer Credit Protection Act, the Truth in Lending Act and the Fair Credit Billing Act.

4. Discuss the role and workings of the Consumer Product Safety Commission.

CHAPTER OUTLINE

A. Unfair and Deceptive Trade Practices - In 1914, Congress enacted Federal Trade Ccommission Act which created the FTC and charged it with the duty to prevent unfair methods of competition in commerce, and unfair or deceptive acts or practices in commerce, issue substantive rules and to conduct appropriate investigations and hearings. The FTC is the principal Federal agency concerned with the regulation of advertising -- the commission must show that the material misrepresentation of materal omission has the tendency or capacity to deceive a significant number of consumers. FTC has recently employed three other potent remedies:
   1. Affirmative Disclosure - This remedy is frequently employed by the FTC and requires the offender to provide certain information in its advertisement so that it is not deceptive.

2. Corrective Advertising - This requires disclosure in an advertisement that previous ads were deceptive.
3. Multiple Product Order - These orders require an advertiser to cease and desist from deceptive statements on all products it sells.

B. Consumer Purchases - Prohibits unconscionable contractual terms and imposes implied warranties for the protection of the purchaser.
   1. Federal Warranty Protection - To protect buyers and to prevent deception in selling, Congress in 1974 enacted the Magnuson-Moss Warranty Act. This act requires sellers of consumer products to give adequate information about warranties. This act applies to consumer products with written warranties and contains pre-sale disclosure to prevent confusion and deception and to enable purchaser to make educated product comparisons. For any product costing more than $20, must be designated on the written warranty itself to alert the consumer of legal rights. The act provides that a written warranty, full or limited, may not disclaim any warranty. The act contains remedies and the establishment, at the option of the warrantor, of an informal settlement procedure.
      a. Full Warranty - Warrantor will repair the product and if unsuccessful, will replace or refund. Warrantor cannot disclaim or limit any implied warranty.
      b. Limited Warranty - Implied warranties may be limited to a reasonable duration.
   2. Consumer Right to Rescission - Allowing a consumer a brief period of time (2-3 days) during which he may rescind a binding credit obligation. Regulation permits a consumer to rescind the door-to-door sales contract for $25 or more within 3 days. Allows a 3-day rescind; he may withdraw from credit obligation secured by mortgage on home. Interstate land Sales Full Disclosure Act applies to sales or leases of 100 or more lots of unimproved land as common promotional plan in interstate commerce. The act requires the developer to file a detailed statement. Must provide a property report. Any contract or agreement for sale or lease may be revoked within 7 days.

C. Consumer Credit Obligations - A consumer credit transaction is defined as any credit transaction involving goods, services, or land acquired for personal, household, or family purposes. 1968 FCCPA deals with effective disclosure of interest and finance charges, credit extension charges, and garnishment proceedings. UCCC integrates into one document the regulation of all consumer credit transactions and gives substantial similar regulatory to credit sales and loan transactions.
   1. Access to the Market - Equal Credit Opportunity Act prohibits all business that regularly extends credit from discriminating in extending credit on the bans of sex, marital status, race, color, religion, national origin, and age.
   2. Disclosure Requirements
      a. Truth in Lending Act - Disclosure requirements relating to credit terms for both consumer loans and credit sales. Information must be provided in a written statement presented to the consumer. Enforcement and interpretation of Truth in Lending Act was assigned to Federal Reserve Board, issued Regulation Z.
      b. Open-ended Credit - Debtor has rights to enter into a series of credit transactions.
      c. Closed-end Credit - Credit extended to debtor for a specific period of time.
      d. 1975 Fair Credit Billing Act - Procedures for the consumer to follow in making complaints about specified error in billing and requires the creditor to explain or correct such errors.
      e. Real Estate Settlement Procedures Act - to provide consumers who purchase a home with greater and more timely information on the nature and cost of the settlement process and to protect them from unnecessarily high settlement charges. This act is administered and enforced by secretary of Housing and Urban Development.
   3. Contract Terms - Impose statutory ceilings on amount that may be charged for extension of consumer credit.
      a. Balloon Payments - Loan in which the final payment is much larger than the regular payment may be prohibited. FTC adopted a rule that limits the rights of a holder in due course of an

instrument evidencing a debt that arises out of a consumer credit contract.

    b.   Fair Credit Billing Act - preserves a consumer's defense against the issuer provided the consumer has made a good faith attempt to resolve the dispute with the seller, but only if: (1) seller is controlled by the issuer; (2) card issuer included the seller's promotional literature; (3) sales involves more than $50, billing address within 100 miles of seller's place of business.

    c.   Federal Consumer Credit Protection Act - Under the FCCPA, a card holder's liability for unauthorized use of a credit card is limited to $50. Card issuer may collect up to that amount for unauthorized use only if: (1) card has been accepted; (2) issuer has provided adequate notice of potential liability to the card holder; (3) issuer provided a statement that cardholder should be notified of the loss or theft of the credit card; (4) unauthorized use occurs before the cardholder has notified of the loss; (5) provided a method by which user can be identified.

4.   Fair Reportage - The Fair Credit Reporting Act requires consumer reporting agencies to give written advance notice to consumers that an investigative report may be made.

5.   Creditors Remedies - When the consumer defaults, the creditor may declare the entire balance of debt immediately due and payable and may sue on the debt. Under the Federal Consumer Credit Protection Act, a limitation is imposed on the amount that may be deducted from an individual's wages. Garnishment is only available in a court proceeding to enforce the collection of a judgment. Fair Debt Collection Practices Act eliminates abusive, deceptive, and unfair practices in collecting consumer debts by debt collection agencies.

D.   Health and Safety - The Consumer Product Safety Act has the purposes of: (1) protecting the public against unreasonable risk of injury with consumer products; (2) assisting consumers in evaluating the comparative safety of consumer products; (3) developing uniform safety standard; (4) to promote research and investigation.

DEFINITIONS

1. Consumer transaction
2. Caveat emptor
3. Full warranty
4. Limited warranty
5. Property report
6. Open-ended credit account
7. Closed-ended credit account
8. Billing error
9. Finance charge
10. Authorized additional charge
11. Pre-payment

12. Balloon payment

13. Holder in due course

14. Delinquency charge

15. Wage assignment

16. Garnishment

17. Deficiency judgment

TRUE/FALSE

_____ 1. Orders of the Federal Trade Commission are not subject to judicial review.

_____ 2. Under the FTC Act, a person may be guilty of deceptive advertising even though no one is proved to have been actually deceived.

_____ 3. Under the Magnuson-Moss Warranty Act, a written warranty cannot disclaim or modify any implied warranty.

_____ 4. A contract subject to the Interstate Land Sales Full Disclosure Act must clearly provide that the contract may be revoked at the option of the purchaser within two years of signing the contract.

_____ 5. Violators of the Equal Credit Opportunity Act are subject to civil actions to recover actual and punitive damages.

_____ 6. Federal disclosure standards relating to credit terms for consumer loans must be complied with in every state.

_____ 7. The Fair Credit Billing Act requires creditors to explain or correct billing errors.

_____ 8. Most States impose statutory ceilings on the amount that may be charged for the extension of consumer credit.

_____ 9. Under the Fair Credit Reporting Act, a consumer is entitled to read and copy all information pertaining to him in the consumer reporting agency's files.

_____ 10. The Consumer Credit Protection Act prohibits wage assignments.

_____ 11. The Fair Debt Collection Practices Act prohibits debt collection conduct by debt collectors other than the creditor that is harrassing, oppressive, or abusive.

_____ 12. The FTC Act clearly defines the words "unfair" or "deceptive."

_____ 13. Deception may occur by a false representation, but not by a material omission.

_____ 14. The FTC ad substantiation policy requires that advertisers have a reasonable basis for their claims at the time their claims are made.

_____ 15. The remedy ordered by the FTC and sustained by the Court of Appeals in the Sears, Roebuck and Co. case was a multiple product order.

MULTIPLE CHOICE

_____ 1. Under the FTC Act, complaints are normally instituted by:
   a. the Federal Trade Commission.
   b. the injured party.
   c. the Attorney General of the State in which the injured party is resident.
   d. none of the above.

_____ 2. Under the Magnuson-Moss Warranty Act, a written warranty that limits the duration of implied warranties may be designated:
   a. "full" but not "limited."
   b. "limited" but not "full."
   c. "full" or "limited."
   d. none of the above.

_____ 3. Under the Magnuson-Moss Warranty Act, a seller may disclaim any and all implied warranties if:
   a. he gives no written warranty.
   b. the product is for personal use only.
   c. the product costs $10 or less.
   d. none of the above.

_____ 4. Under the FTC's door-to-door sales rule, a consumer may only revoke a door-to-door sales contract if:
   a. the sale is on credit.
   b. any credit obligation he incurs pursuant to the contract is secured by a mortgage on his home.
   c. the sale is for $25 or more.
   d. it is within 5 days.

_____ 5. Which of the following acts requires a creditor, within thirty days of receiving an application for credit, to notify the applicant of action taken and to provide specific reasons for a denial of credit?
   a. Consumer Credit Protection Act.
   b. Equal Credit Opportunity Act.
   c. Fair Credit Reporting Act
   d. Fair Credit Billing Act.

_____ 6. The Equal Credit Opportunity Act prohibits businesses that regularly extend credit from discriminating in extending credit on the basis of:
   a. sex.
   b. marital status.
   c. age.
   d. all of the above.

_____ 7. Under the Consumer Credit Protection Act, sales finance charges and interest rates must be quoted in terms of:
   a.   add-ons.
   b.   discounts.
   c.   annual percentage rates.
   d.   none of the above.

_____ 8. Which of the following acts prohibits kickbacks and referral fees with respect to federally related mortgage loans?
   a.   Interstate Land Sales Full Disclosure Act.
   b.   Real Estate Settlement Procedures Act.
   c.   Fair Credit Billing Act.
   d.   Consumer Credit Protection Act.

_____ 9. A creditor who fails to respond to a billing error complaint may not:
   a.   take any action to collect the disputed amount.
   b.   restrict the use of a revolving credit account because the disputed amount is unpaid.
   c.   report the disputed amount as delinquent.
   d.   all of the above.

_____ 10. The Consumer Credit Protection Act limits a credit card holder's liability for unauthorized use of a credit card to:
   a. $10.
   b. $25.
   c. $50.
   d.   none of the above.

_____ 11. Under the _____, a consumer is allowed three days during which to withdraw from any credit obligation secured by a mortgage on his home, unless the extension of credit was made to acquire the dwelling.
   a.   Interstate Land Sales Full Disclosure Act
   b.   Federal Consumer Credit Protection Act
   c.   Equal Credit Opportunity Act
   d.   Uniform Consumer Credit Code

_____ 12. Which of the following is/are included in the authority of the Consumer Product Safety Commission?
   a.   The authority to promote voluntary standards for product safety.
   b.   The authority to set and enforce mandatory standards.
   c.   The authority to ban unsafe products.
   d.   The CPSC can do all of the above.

_____ 13. Which of the following would not be prohibited by the Equal Credit Opportunity Act?
   a.   First Bank only issues its Visa cards to married women in their husband's name.
   b.   First Bank refuses to extend credit to men over the age of 70.
   c.   First Bank refuses to extend credit to people having an income of less than $12,000.
   d.   First Bank refuses to extend credit to members of the Unification Church.

_____ 14. Which of the following is/are covered by the Fair Credit Reporting Act?
   a.   Reports by credit agencies.
   b.   A creditor calling the debtor in the middle of the night.
   c.   A credit check done by a credit agency.
   d.   Two of the above, (a) and (c).

_____ 15. The FTC has issued an order of affirmative disclosure against the Warner-Lambert Company. What does the order require?
   a.   It requires a new ad that admits the prior ads were false.
   b.   It provides affirmative disclosure of the source of the information used in the original ad.
   c.   It requires that the company cease and desist from deception with regard to all products that it markets.
   d.   All of the above are required by affirmative disclosure.

SHORT ESSAY

1. What must a warrantor do to comply with the Magnuson-Moss Warranty Act? _____
   _____
   _____
   _____

2. What are the characteristics of a "full" warranty under the Magnuson-Moss Warranty Act? _____
   _____
   _____
   _____

3. What information must a creditor give to a consumer who is opening an open-ended credit account? _____
   _____
   _____
   _____

4. What information must a creditor give to a consumer who is opening a close-ended credit account? _____
   _____
   _____
   _____

5. Under what circumstances may a credit card issuer collect from a credit card holder for unauthorized use of a credit card? _____
   _____
   _____
   _____

CHAPTER 42

EMPLOYMENT LAW

PURPOSE

In this chapter, you study the State and Federal laws that direct and control employer-employee relations. Before the industrial revolution, issues relating to working conditions and employment were determined according to the law of contracts and torts. After the industrial revolution, the need for a more formal system of resolving labor-management disputes became apparent. In recent years, the need for laws governing discrimination based upon race, sex, ethnic or national origin and religion has become apparent. In this chapter, you study the common law and the statutory enactments that govern the area of employer-employee relations.

CHAPTER CHECKPOINTS

After reading and studying this chapter, you should be able to:

1. List and discuss the major Federal statutes that govern the relationship between an employer and a union representing employees.

2. List the unfair labor practices of an employer and of a union and distinguish between a closed shop and a union shop.

3. List the major Federal statutes that govern the area of employment discrimination and discuss the major provisions of each.

4. Discuss how the worker's compensation laws changed the common law with respect to injuries sustained by employes on the job.

5. List the major provisions of the OSHA and Social Security statutes and discuss the purpose and effect of OSHA on employment conditions.

CHAPTER OUTLINE

A. Labor Law - Labor law did not favor concerted activities by workers (such as strikers, picketing, and refusals to deal) to obtain higher wages and better working conditions.
   1. Norris-La Guardia Act - It was enacted in 1932 in response to the growing criticism of the use of

348

injunctions in peaceful labor disputes. Labor disputes means any controversy concerning terms or conditions of employment or union representation, regardless of whether the parties stood in an employer-employee relationship. Labor has full freedom to form unions without interference by the employer.

2. National Labor Relations Act - It is also called the Wagner Act. It marked an affirmative effort by the Federal government to support collective bargaining and unionization. It established the National Labor Relations Board (NLRB).

3. Labor-Management Relations Act - It is called LMRA or Taft-Hartley Act. It prohibits unfair union practices and separates the NLRB's prosecutorial and adjudicative functions. A closed shop contract requires the employer to hire only union members. A union shop contract permits the employer to hire nonunion members but requires that the employee must become a member of the union within a specified period of time and must remain a member in good standing as a condition of employment. A right to work law is a state statute that prohibits union shop contracts.

4. Reporting and Disclosure Act - It is also known as the Landrum-Griffin Act. It is aimed at eliminating corruption in labor unions.

B. Employment Discrimination Law
   1. Equal Pay Act - Prohibits an employer from discriminating between employees on the basis of sex by paying unequal wages for the same work. The Department of Labor is the Federal agency designated by the statute to interpret and enforce the act. In 1979, these junctions were transferred to the Equal Employment Opportunity Commission.
   2. Civil Rights Act of 1964 - It prohibits employment discrimination on the basis of race, color, sex, religion, and national origin. The Equal Employment Opportunity Commission (EEOC) is the enforcement agency. Affirmative action means the active recruitment of minority applicants.
      a. Discrimination - Disparate treatment. Present effects of past discrimination. Disparate impact.
      b. Reverse Discrimination - It refers to affirmative action that directs an employer to take the race or sex of an individual into account when hiring or promoting for the purpose of remedying under-representation of that race or sex in traditionally segregated jobs.
      c. Sexual Harassment - When the employee engaging in sexual harassment is an agent of the employer or is in a supervisory position over the victim, the employer may be liable without knowledge or reason to know.
      d. Comparable Worth - It provides that the relative values to an employer of different jobs should be measured through a rating system or job evaluation that is free of any potential sex bias.
   3. Age Discrimination in Employment Act of 1967 - It prohibits discriminating in hiring, firing, compensating or otherwise on the basis of age.
   4. Rehabilitation Act of 1973 - It attempts to provide assistance to the handicapped in obtaining rehabilitation training, access to public facilities, and employment.
   5. Executive Order - In 1965, President Johnson issued an executive order that prohibited discrimination by Federal contractors on the basis of race, color, sex, religion or national origin on any work performed by the contractors during the period of the Federal contract.

C. Employee Protection
   1. Employee Termination at Will - Under the common law, a contract of employment for other than a definite term is terminable at will by either party.
      a. Statutory Limitations - Some States have statutory limitations on termination of employment.
   2. Protection for certain employees from discriminatory discharge.
   3. Protection for certain employees in their exercise of statutory rights.
   4. Protection for certain employees from discharge without cause.
      a. Judicial Limitations - Judicial limitations on the employment-at-will doctrine have been based on contract law, tort law, or a public policy.

b.   Occupational Safety and Health Act - It assures workers of a healthy work environment. The employer is required to comply with specific safety rules.

5.   Worker's Compensation - Under the Fellow Servant Rule, an employer is not liable for injuries sustaind by an employee caused by the negligence of a fellow employee. If an employee establishes that the negligence of an injured employee caused or contributed to the injury he sustained in the course of his employment, in many jurisdictions he cannot recover damages from the employer.

D.   Voluntary Assumption of Risk - An employer is not liable to an employee for harm or injury caused by the unsafe condition of the premises if the employee, with knowledge of the facts and understanding the risks involved, voluntarily entered into or continued in the employment.

E.   Worker's compensation creates commissions or boards that determine whether an injured employee is entitled to receive compensation and if so, how much.

1.   Social Security and Unemployment Insurance - Social Security was enacted in 1935 in an attempt to provide limited retirement and death benefits to certain employees. To be fully insured, a person must be credited with forty quarters of coverage received for each $370 of earnings in a year up to a maximum of four quarters per year. An individual is currently insured if he has been credited with at least six quarters of coverage in the last three years. The purpose of the Social Security Tax is to provide unemployment compensation to workers who have lost their jobs and cannot find other employment.

2.   Fair Labor Standard Act - The Fair Labor Standards Act regulates the employment of child labor outside of agriculture. The FLSA imposes wage and hour requirements upon covered employers.

DEFINITIONS

1.   Labor dispute

2.   Unfair labor practice

3.   Affirmative action

4.   Fellow servant rule

5.   Contributory negligence

6.   Assumption of the risk

TRUE/FALSE

_____   1.   A Federal court may issue a civil injunction in a nonviolent labor dispute where there is an unfair labor practice.

_____   2.   A union may not take disciplinary action against a union member.

_____   3.   The Equal Pay Act prohibits an employer from discriminating between employees on the basis of race, color, sex, religion or national origin by paying unequal wages for equal work.

_____   4.   In a worker's compensation proceeding, the amounts recoverable for each type of injury are fixed by statute.

_____ 5. An injured employee may demand a jury trial even though he qualifies for worker's compensation.

_____ 6. Title VII does not prohibit discrimination based on age.

_____ 7. The customers at Chez Chic Restaurant prefer to be served by male waiters. The restaurant owner can refuse to hire women based upon sex being a BFOQ.

_____ 8. Sexual harassment is not covered by the Federal discrimination laws.

_____ 9. Because of the possibility of reverse discrimination, there is some conflict between the legal concepts of affirmative action and employment discrimination.

_____ 10. The National Labor Relations Act is also known as the Wagner Act.

_____ 11. To be fully insured under the Federal social security laws, a person must be credited with twenty quarters of coverage.

_____ 12. Common law employer defenses such as the fellow-servant rule, contributory negligence and voluntary assumption of the risk are eliminated by Worker's Compensation Acts.

_____ 13. Even if a person is covered by the Age Discrimination in Employment Act, the employer may refuse to hire an older worker based upon a *bona fide* occupational qualification.

_____ 14. The Equal Pay Act applies to different jobs that are comparable as well as to jobs that are equal jobs.

_____ 15. A right-to-work law prohibits union shop contracts.

MULTIPLE CHOICE

_____ 1. An employer who refuses to bargain in good faith with the duly established representatives of his employees has violated the:
   a. Norris-La Guardia Act.
   b. National Labor Relations Act.
   c. Labor Management Relations Act.
   d. Labor Management Reporting and Disclosure Act.

_____ 2. A union which goes on strike to force an employer to fire a non-union employee has violated the:
   a. Norris-La Guardia Act.
   b. National Labor Relations Act.
   c. Labor Management Relations Act.
   d. Labor Management Reporting and Disclosure Act.

_____ 3. The Federal statute that prohibits discrimination on the basis of a handicap in programs receiving Federal financial assistance is the:
a. Rehabilitation Act of 1973.
b. Civil Rights Act of 1964.
c. Age Discrimination in Employment Act of 1976.
d. Executive Order of 1965.

_____ 4. The Federal statute that prohibits the mandatory retirement of most employees under the age of 70 is the:
a. Rehabilitation Act of 1973.
b. Civil Rights Act of 1964.
c. Age Discrimination in Employment Act of 1967.
d. Executive Order of 1965.

_____ 5. An employee who sues his employer under a Worker's Compensation Act for injuries arising out of and in the course of his employment is subject to the defense of:
a. contributory negligence.
b. assumption of the risk.
c. the fellow servant rule.
d. none of the above.

_____ 6. The _____ is responsible for enforcing Federal anti-discrimination laws.
a. NLRB
b. OSHA
c. EEOC
d. Social Security Administration

_____ 7. Employees between the ages of _____ are protected under the Age Discrimination in Employment Act.
a. 18 and 45
b. 40 and no upper limit
c. 45 and 70
d. 50 and 65

_____ 8. Which of the following employees would not be protected by the Age Discrimination in Employment Act?
a. Employees between the ages of 20 and 30.
b. Employees between the ages of 40 and 50.
c. Employees between the ages of 50 and 60.
d. Employees between the ages of 70 and 80.

_____ 9. Which of the following employees would not be covered by the Rehabilitation Act of 1973?
a. An alcoholic.
b. A victim of AIDS.
c. A victim of tuberculosis.
d. A polio victim in a wheelchair.

___ 10. The National Labor Relations Act is also known as the:
    a. Norris-LaGuardia Act.
    b. Watner Act.
    c. Taft-Hartley Act.
    d. Landrum-Griffin Act.

___ 11. Which of the following may be used to pay a man more than a woman without violating the Equal Pay Act?
    a. A seniority system.
    b. A merit system.
    c. A system which measures earning by the quantity of production.
    d. All of the above may be used to allow a pay differential between a man and a woman.

___ 12. Which one of the following defenses may be used by an employer to avoid responsibility for paying an employee's claim for worker's compensation?
    a. The employee assumed the risk of the injury.
    b. The employee was contributorily negligent.
    c. A co-worker actually caused the injury.
    d. The injury did not occur on the job.

___ 13. Under the National Labor Relations Act, who supervises union elections?
    a. The Justice Department.
    b. The National Labor Relations Board.
    c. Officers of the Union.
    d. The employer.

___ 14. Which of the following is an unfair labor practice?
    a. Refusal to bargain in good faith.
    b. Discrimination against union members.
    c. Interference with the right of employees to unionize and bargain collectively.
    d. All of the above are unfair labor practices.

___ 15. In which of the following situations would the employer have liability for sexual harassment?
    a. An employee sexually harasses another employee and the employer does not take immediate action when he knows about the harassment.
    b. An employee sexually harasses another employee and the employer does not take immediate action when he should have known about the harassment regardless of whether the employer does in fact know of it.
    c. An employer would be liable in both of the above situations.
    d. An employer can never be held responsible for sexual harassment by one employee against another employee.

SHORT ESSAY

1. What are the basic defenses available to an employer who has been charged with employment discrimination? _____

_____

_____

_____

2.   What are the remedies available to an employee who brings a successful employment discrimination action?

_____

_____

_____

_____

CHAPTER 43

INTERNATIONAL BUSINESS LAW

PURPOSE

Today business requires some understanding of international business practices, because the entire global economy has become increasingly interconnected. Laws vary greatly from country to country and there is no single authority in international law. When the laws of two or more nations conflict, or when one party has violated an agreement that the other party wishes to enforce or to recover damages, it is often difficult to establish who will adjudicate the matter, which laws will be applied, what remedies will be available and where the matter should be decided. In this chapter, you study some of the basic international organizations, agreements and principles that affect international business.

CHAPTER CHECKPOINTS

After reading and studying this chapter, you should be able to:

1. List and discuss the sources and institutions of international law.

2. Discuss the purpose and major provisions of GATT.

3. Compare the doctrines of sovereign immunity and act of state, and distinguish between expropriation and confiscation.

4. Discuss the legal controls imposed on the flow of trade, labor, and capital across national borders.

5. List and briefly describe the forms that a multinational enterprise may choose when conducting its business in a foreign country.

CHAPTER OUTLINE

A. The International Environment - International law includes law that deals with the conduct and relations of nation-states and international organizations as well as some of their relations with persons. As a general rule, international law cannot be enforced, because international courts do not have compulsory jurisdiction to resolve disputes. The courts of a nation may enforce international law if the nation has adopted the international law as the law of the nation.

1. International Court of Justice - The United Nations has a judicial branch called the International Court of Justice. The ICJ consists of fifteen judges, no two of whom may be from the same sovereign state. Only nations and not private parties may be parties to an action before the court. It has jurisdiction only when nations agree to be bound by its decision, and when countries do not like its decision, they may ignore it.

2. Regional Trade Communities - International organizations, conferences, and treaties that focus on business and trade regulation are of much greater significance than the ICJ. The European Economic Community (EEC), which is better known as the Common Market, was formed in 1957 by the Treaty of Rome. It was intended to remove trade barriers between member nations and to unify their economic policies. Twelve nations are members of the EEC. They are Belgium, France, Italy, Luxemburg, the Netherlands, West Germany, Denmark, Ireland, the United Kingdom, Greece, Portugal and Spain. Other important regional trade communities are the Central American Common Market (CACM), the Carribean Community (CARICOM), the Association of South East Asian Nations (ASEAN), the Economic Community of West African States (ECOWAS), the Union Douaniere Economique de l'Afrique Centrale (UDEAC) and the Council for Mutual Economique Cooperation (COMECON).

3. International Treaties - A treaty is an agreement between or among independent nations. The United States Constitution authorizes the president to enter into treaties with the advice and consent of the Senate "providing two-thirds of the Senators present concur." The Constitution also provides that all valid treaties are the "law of the land," having the legal force of a Federal statute. Possibly the most important multilateral trade treaty is the General Agreement on Tariffs and Trade (GATT). The GATT signatories represent over four-fifths of world trade. The basic purpose of GATT is to facilitate the flow of trade by establishing agreements on potential trade barriers such as import quotas, customs, export regulations, subsidies, and import fees. GATT's most favored nation provision states that all signatories must treat each other as favorably as they treat any other country. Nevertheless, nations and may also enter into free trade areas with one or more other nations. A free trade area permits countries to discriminate in favor of their free trade partners if the agreement covers substantially all trade among the partners. Under GATT, protection given to domestic industries should be in the form of a customs tariff as opposed to other more trade-inhibiting measures.

B. Jurisdictions Over Actions of Foreign Governments - This section focuses on the power, and the limits upon the power of a sovereign nation to exercise jurisdiction over a foreign nation or to take property owned by foreign citizens.

    1. Sovereign Immunity - Every nation has absolute and total authority over what goes on within its own territory. This principle of absolute immunity of a foreign sovereign nation within a host country is known as sovereign immunity. Congress has enacted the Foreign Sovereign Immunities Act in order to establish legislatively when immunity will be extended to foreign nations.

    2. Act of State Doctrine - The act of state doctrine provides that the judicial branch of a nation should not question the validity of actions taken by a foreign government within that foreign sovereign's own borders. The U.S. Supreme Court said in 1987 that "Every sovereign State is bound to respect the independence of every other sovereign State, and the courts of one country will not sit in judgment on the acts of the government of another done within its own territory. Exceptions to the act of State doctrine include the following: (a) a sovereign may waive its right to raise the act of State defense; and (b) the doctrine may be inapplicable to commercial activities of a foreign sovereign. The doctrine will not be applied to claims to specific property located in the U.S. based on the assertion that a foreign state confiscated the property in violation of international law, unless the president determines it should apply.

    3. Taking of Foreign Investment Property - An expropriation or nationalization occurs when a government seizes foreign owned property or assets for a public purpose and pays the owner just compensation for what is taken. Confiscation is the term used when no payment (or an inadequate

payment) is given in exchange for the seized property, or when the property is seized for a nonpublic purpose. U.S. firms should obtain insurance from a private insurer or from the Overseas Private Investment Corporation (OPIC).

4. Flow of Capital - The IMF was established to facilitate the expansion and balanced growth of international trade, to assist in the elimination of foreign exchange restrictions, and to shorten the duration and disequilibrium in the international balance of payments of its members. There are also regional banks to facilitate the flow of capital and trade. A letter of credit is a promise by a buyer's bank to pay the seller provided certain conditions are met. The buyer then enters into a second contract with a local bank, called an issuer, calling for the bank to pay the agreed price upon presentation of specified documents. The commitment by the buyer's bank is the irrevocable letter of credit. Typically, a correspondent or paying bank located in the seller's country makes payment to the seller.

5. International Contracts - The legal issues inherent in domestic contracts are also inherent in international contracts. In addition, there are issues such as differences in language, legal systems and currency. The contract should specify the language and law which governs. It should also include a *force majeure* clause apportioning the liabilities and responsibilities of the parties in the event of an unforseeable occurence.

C. Transacting Business Abroad - Business abroad may involve selling goods, information or services, or investing capital or arranging for the movement of labor. This section examines the legal controls imposed on the flow of trade, labor and capital across national borders.

1. Flow of Trade - A device that is frequently applied by nations to protect domestic businesses is the tariff. A tariff is a duty or tax imposed on goods moving into or out of a country. Tariffs raise the price of imported goods, causing some consumers to purchase less expensive, domestically produced items. Nontariff barriers include unilateral or bilateral import quotas, import bans, overly restrictive safety or manufacturing standards, complicated customs procedures and subsidies to local industry. Export controls control the flow of goods out of a country. They are usually imposed for policy reasons such as national defense, foreign policy, or protection of scarce national resources.

2. Flow of Labor - Almost all countries require that foreigners obtain valid passports before entering their borders. In addition, they may issue visas to foreign citizens permitting them to enter the country for an identified purpose or specified period of time. The U.S. issues various types of visas depending on the purpose of an individual's visit.

3. Flow of Goods - The United States has ratified the U.N. Convention on Contracts for the International Sale of Goods. The CISG governs all contracts for the international sale of goods between parties located in nations that have ratified the CISG.

4. Antitrust Laws - Section 1 of the Sherman Act provides for a broad, extraterritorial reach of the U.S. antitrust laws. Recent amendments to the Sherman Act and the Federal Trade Commission Act limit their application to unfair methods of competition that have a direct substantial, and reasonably foreseeable, effect on U.S. domestic commerce, import commerce or export commerce.

D. Forms of Multinational Enterprises - Factors to be considered in determining the form of a multinational business enterprise include financing, tax consequences, legal restrictions imposed by the host country, and the degree of control over the business sought by the multinational enterprise.

1. Direct Export Sales - This is the simplest and least involved form of multinational enterprise.

2. Foreign Agents - Agency relationships are often used by companies that want limited involvement in the international market.

3. Distributorships - This is a commonly used form of multinational enterprise. Unlike an agent, a distributor takes title to merchandise it receives. This form is susceptible to antitrust violations.

4. Licensing - This involves the sale of an intellectual property right, such as patent, trademark, trade secret, or innovative production technology. The foreign firm pays royalties in exchange for the use of

the right.   Franchising is a form of licensing in which the owner grants permission to a foreign business to use the intellectual property under carefully specified conditions.

5.   Joint Ventures - In a joint venture, two or more independent businesses from different countries agree to coordinate their efforts to achieve a common result. They share profits and liabilities according to a contract. Each company can be assigned responsibility for what it does best. Regional groups and countries frequently have restrictions on foreign joint ventures to assure local control.

DEFINITIONS

1.   International law

2.   Treaty

3.   Sovereign immunity

4.   Act of State doctrine

5.   Expropriation

6.   Confiscation

7.   Tariff

8.   Letter of credit

9.   Multinational enterprise

TRUE/FALSE

_____   1.   Judgments of the International Court of Justice are enforceable in the U.S. Federal Courts.

_____   2.   Section 1 of the Sherman Act provides for a broad, extra-territorial reach of the U.S. antitrust laws.

_____   3.   Unilateral and bilateral import quotas are examples of nontarriff barriers to the flow of trade.

_____   4.   The General Agreement on Tariffs and Trade has only twelve member nations.

_____   5.   The U.S. Constitution provides that all valid treaties are "the law of the land" having the legal force of a Federal statute.

_____   6.   A simple majority of the Senators present may ratify a treaty under the United States Constitution.

_____   7.   A letter of credit transaction is an effective means of managing the risks of international trade and involves three or four different parties and three underlying contracts.

_____   8.   Under GATT's most favored nation provision, signatories are not required to treat other signatories equally with regard to privileges, immunities and favors.

_____   9.   East Germany, Hungary and Poland are all members of the European Economic Community.

____ 10. The simplest and least involved multinational enterprise is a direct export sale.

MULTIPLE CHOICE

____ 1. The EEC is better known as:
   a. the Warsaw Pact.
   b. the common market.
   c. the General Agreement on Tariffs and Trade.
   d. the International Monetary Fund.

____ 2. What is the purpose of a *force majeure* clause?
   a. It determines what law applies to a contract.
   b. It determines the method of payment for goods sold between a buyer in one country and a seller in another country.
   c. It determines the forum in which a dispute must be decided.
   d. It apportions the liabilities and responsibilities of the parties in the event of an unforeseeable occurrence.

____ 3. What international treaty governs contracts for the sale of goods between parties located in different nations that have ratified it?
   a. ICJ
   b. GATT
   c. ASEAN
   d. CISG

____ 4. One precaution that can be taken by U.S. firms to avoid the economic loss caused by the seizure of investment property by a host nation's government is to obtain insurance from either a private insurer or an agency of the U.S. government, which is known as:
   a. OPIC.
   b. ASEAN.
   c. the Commerce Department.
   d. the U.S. State Department.

____ 5. Examples of noncommercial activities to which the doctrine of _____ would extend include nationalizing a corporation, determining the limitations upon the use of natural resources, and granting licenses to export a natural resource.
   a. act of State
   b. sovereign immunity
   c.. confiscation
   d. expropriation

____ 6. Which of the following is the Soviet-Bloc counterpart to the European common market?
   a. CARICOM
   b. ANCOM
   c. COMECON
   d. ECOWAS

SHORT ESSAY

1. The Widget Corporation of America would like to begin marketing its products in the international sector. What forms of multinational business enterprise should it consider? _____

    _____

    _____

    _____

2. How do expropriation and nationalization differ? What precautions should a firm which deals in the international sector take in order to protect itself against confiscation? _____

    _____

    _____

    _____

3. Assume you are the manager of a company that has just begun the direct export of your product. What precautions can you take to assure that you will in fact be paid for your products when you have never dealt with the buyer before and you are new to the international legal environment? _____

    _____

    _____

    _____

4. What items should be specified in a contract involving the sale of goods between a seller in the United States and a buyer in a foreign country? _____

    _____

    _____

    _____

PART IX

REVIEW QUESTIONS

_____ 1. Which of the following is prohibited by the Sherman Act?
   a. A manufacturer assigns exclusive territories to each of its distributors.
   b. Two manufacturers enter into an agreement allocating exclusive territories to each manufacturer.
   c. A manufacturer suggests retail prices for its products.
   d. A manufacturer grants a franchise to a distributor and requires that the franchisee meet certain standards.

_____ 2. With regard to price fixing agreements, which of the following is generally correct?
   a. They are legal when the parties to the agreement agree to lower their prices for consumers.
   b. They are legal if they meet the rule of reason test.
   c. They are _per se_ illegal under the Sherman Act.
   d. They are legal if they benefit consumers.

_____ 3. A seller of a product conditions its sale on the buyer's purchase of a second product or service. This is an example of a:
   a. market allocation.
   b. group boycott.
   c. vertical restraint.
   d. tying arrangement.

_____ 4. Vertical price fixing is also known as:
   a. market allocation.
   b. a tying arrangement.
   c. resale price maintenance.
   d. conscious parallelism.

_____ 5. Which of the following is not exempt from the provisions of the Clayton Act?
   a. Professional organizations such as the ABA and the AMA.
   b. Labor organizations.
   c. Agricultural organizations.
   d. All of the above are exempt from the Clayton Act.

_____ 6. The FTC remedy of _____ requires that an advertiser include certain information in its advertisement so that the ad is not deceptive.
   a. corrective advertising
   b. affirmative disclosure
   c. multiple product orders
   d. injunction

_____ 7. Pursuant to Title I of the FCCPA, which is also known as the _____, the Federal Reserve Board issued Regulation Z.
   a. Equal Credit Opportunity Act
   b. Truth-in-Lending Act
   c. Magnuson-Moss Warranty Act
   d. Fair Credit Billing Act

_____ 8. Happy Homemaker requests a credit card in her own name at Marlin's Department Store. The store manager tells her the store has a policy of only issuing cards to married women in their husband's name. He says she can have a card issued in Harold's name if he completes the application. In all likelihood, Marlin's Department Store is in violation of:
    a. Title VII of the Civil Rights Act of 1964.
    b. the Fair Credit Reporting Act.
    c. the Equal Credit Opportunity Act.
    d. no laws, because this is an acceptable practice.

_____ 9. What is a "yellow dog" contract?
    a. It is a contract that allows an employer to terminate an employee at will.
    b. It is a contract that prohibits discrimination against persons of oriental heritage.
    c. It is a contract by which an employer requires his employees to promise they will not join a union.
    d. It is a contract that requires the employer to hire only union members.

_____ 10. Which of the following is prohibited by the Labor-Management Relations Act?
    a. A closed shop.
    b. Right-to-work laws.
    c. Discrimination against union members.
    d. Refusal to bargain in good faith with the duly established representatives of the employees.

_____ 11. Which law prohibits sexual harassment by a supervisor of an employee being supervised?
    a. The Equal Pay Act.
    b. Title VII of the Civil Rights Act of 1964.
    c. The Rehabilitation Act of 1973.
    d. There is no law prohibiting sexual harassment on the job.

_____ 12. Which of the following is a correct statement regarding comparable worth?
    a. It is clearly prohibited by the Equal Pay Act.
    b. Based on U.S. Supreme Court decisions, it appears to be prohibited by Title VII of the 1964 Civil Rights Act, but it has limited applicability under State discrimination statutes.
    c. It has been held by the U.S. Supreme Court to constitute reverse discrimination.
    d. It is an unfair labor practice.

_____ 13. Courts have generally interpreted the statutory definition of the term "security" found in the 1933 Securities Act to include which of the following?
    a. Limited partnership interests.
    b. Citrus groves.
    c. Real estate condominiums.
    d. All of the above have been found to be securities.

_____ 14. Which of the following transactions would not be exempt from the registration requirements found in the 1933 Securities Act?
    a. An offering to local resident investors in the city where a corporation is located and in the State in which the corporation is incorporated of $6 million in securities.
    b. An offering of stock in the Valley National Bank of Southern Minnesota.
    c. A private placement to an insurance company.
    d. An offering of limited partnerships in pecan groves to investors in two States where $6 million in the partnerships are offered.

_____ 15. Which of the following is correct with regard to Section 10(b) of the 1934 Act and SEC Rule 10b-5?
   a.   It applies to short swing profits.
   b.   It applies to proxy solicitations.
   c.   It prohibits fraud in connection with the sale of securities.
   d.   It requires the registration of certain securities.

_____ 16. Carl Contractor is a Director on the corporate board of a corporation which is covered by the Federal securities laws. He buys 2,000 shares of stock in the corporation based upon information he has received as a director.
   a.   The purchase of stock is a *per se* violation of Section 16(b).
   b.   The purchase is automatically invalid under Rule 10b-5.
   c.   The purchase is a violation of Section 4(2) of the 1934 Act and Rule 505.
   d.   The purchase is valid provided the purchase occurred after a public announcement of the information.

_____ 17. A defense which an accountant can raise under Section 11 of the 1933 Securities Act is that of:
   a.   privity.
   b.   negligence.
   c.   due diligence.
   d.   good faith.

_____ 18. Under the _____, a court in the United States should not question the validity of actions taken by a foreign government in its own country.
   a.   sovereign immunity rule
   b.   General Agreement on Tariffs and Trade
   c.   Act of State doctrine
   d.   Convention on the International Sale of Goods

_____ 19. The government of Parador seizes an American owned factory for a public purpose and pays the owner compensation for the factory based upon what it considers fair.
   a.   If the American owner is not satisfied with the compensation, it could sue in the International Court of Justice.
   b.   If the American owner is not satisfied with the compensation, it could sue in an American court under the General Agreement on Tariffs and Trade.
   c.   This is an example of a confiscation.
   d.   This is an example of an expropriation.

_____ 20. The "Good Housekeeping Seal of Approval" is an example of a:
   a.   service mark.
   b.   certification mark.
   c.   collective mark.
   d.   trademark.

INTRODUCTION TO REAL AND PERSONAL PROPERTY

PURPOSE

The concept of property is an essential concept in a democratic free enterprise society such as the one in which we live. However, in spite of its unique place in our society, "property" is not easily defined. In this chapter, you study the two forms of property -- real property and personal property. Real property, also called realty, includes land and all interests therein. Personal property includes every other thing or interest identified as property. In the case of fixtures, however, personal property may become realty.

Property can also be classified as tangible or intangible, with the later involving only a legal holding or right-of-way over the property. Transfer and taxation of property also depend on its classification.

Transfer of real property title is generally a very formal affair. This will be discussed in more detail in Chapter 47. Personal property, in contrast, may be transferred with relative ease. This transfer, however, can take many forms, which will be compared in this chapter.

CHAPTER CHECKPOINTS

After reading and studying this chapter, you should be able to:

1. Distinguish between tangible and intangible property as well as real property and personal property.

2. Explain the concept of fixture and give examples.

3. Identify and discuss the various methods of personal property transfer.

4. Define concurrent ownership and its different forms.

5. Distinguish among the rights of a finder to abandoned, mislaid, and lost property.

CHAPTER OUTLINE

I. Real Property (Realty)
    A. Forms of Real Property

      1.   Tangible - This type of property can be identified as a physical object.

      2.   Intangible - This property does not exist in physical form. The holder may have only stock certificate, promissory note, or deed granting him/her a right-of-way over the property.

      3.   Fixtures - Personal property may become realty in cases where its removal would cause damage to existing property.

  B. Ownership of Realty

      1.   Transfer - Real property can only be transferred by certain formalities which will be discussed in Chapter 47.

      2.   Taxation - Most States impose taxes on both real and personal property at varying rates, however.

II. Personal Property

  A. Transfer

      1.   Sale - A sale is a transfer of property for consideration (price).

          a.   Tangible - Goods.

          b.   Intangible - Title, rights.

      2.   Gift - A transfer without consideration is a gift. The maker of the gift, or donor, passes it to the recipient, or donee.

          a.   Delivery - A valid gift must be delivered. Its delivery is absolutely necessary to a valid gift. This includes, but is not limited to, manual transfer of the item to the donee.

          b.   Intent - The donor must clearly have intended the item to be a gift.

          c.   Acceptance - The law does not require the donee to accept an unwanted gift.

      3.   Will - Property acquired by will is property acquired by inheritance. This will be discussed in Chapter 48.

      4.   Accession - When property increases, the owner is entitled to the original property and any increase therein. Example: When a farmer's cow has a calf, the farmer owns both the cow and the calf.

      5.   Confusion - This occurs when goods belonging to two or more owners become intermixed to the point where the property of any of them can no longer be identified except as part of a mass of like goods.

      6.   Possession - In some cases, a person may acquire title by taking possession of movable personal property.

          a.   Abandond - If the property was intentionally disposed of, the finder is entitled to it.

          b.   Lost - The finder is entitled to lost property against everyone except the true owner.

          c.   Mislaid - Property that is mislaid is intentionally placed by the owner, but unintentionally left. In this case, the owner of the premises has first claim.

  B. Concurrent Ownership - Two or more owners (discussed in Chapter 46).

      1.   Joint tenancy

      2.   Tenancy in common

      3.   Tenancy in entireties

      4.   Community property

DEFINITIONS

1. Property

2. Tangible property

3.   Intangible property

4.   Real property

5.   Personal property

6.   Fixture

7.   Gift

8.   Donor

9.   Donee

10. Constructive delivery

11. Accession

12. Confusion of goods

13. Lost property

14. Concurrent ownership

TRUE/FALSE

_____ 1.   All property interests that are not classified as real property or as fixtures are classified as personal property.

_____ 2.   The intention of the parties with conflicting claims to the property, as expressed in their agreement, is controlling in determining whether personal property has become a fixture.

_____ 3.   A tenant may remove trade fixtures provided he can do so without causing material injury to the real property to which it is affixed.

_____ 4.   In general, a gratuitous promise to make a gift is binding.

_____ 5.   To be effective, a gift must be physically transferred or "delivered" to the donee.

_____ 6.   Although acceptance by the donee is a requirement of a valid gift, the law generally presumes that the donee has accepted the gift.

_____ 7.   If Fred deliberately takes Elmer's lumber and builds a boat, Fred receives title to the boat by accession.

_____ 8.   If confusion of goods results by accident and there is not enough left to distribute a full share to each owner, each party will lose his entire interest if he cannot prove his share.

_____ 9.   In general, a finder has superior title to lost property as against everyone but the true owner.

F 10. Only real property may be held concurrently by two or more persons. F

F 11. A hat left in a restaurant would be classified as abandoned property. F

F 12. The finder of lost property has a better title than the original owner. F

F 13. A copyright is an example of tangible personal property. F

F 14. When a gift is delivered by a donor, it has to be accepted by the donee. F

T 15. Hereford cattle owned by the Cartright Ranch are accidentally mixed with Hereford cattle owned by the Reagan Ranch. Neither rancher's herd can be specifically identified. If the goods can be apportioned, each ranch is entitled toits proportional share.

MULTIPLE CHOICE

C 1. An automobile is classified as:
a. tangible property.
b. personal property.
c. both (a) and (b).
d. neither (a) nor (b).

b 2. All of the following may be classified as tangible, personal property except:
a. a watch.
b. a bank check.
c. a dog.
d. a pencil.

d 3. In the absence of a binding agreement between the parties, the court, in determining whether an item is a fixture, will consider the following factors:
a. The physical relationship of the item to the land.
b. The intention of the person who attached the item to the land.
c. The interest of the person who attached the item to the land at the time of attachment.
d. All of the above.

d 4. In determining whether an item is a fixture, the testof "purpose or use" applies only if the item:
a. is affixed to the realty in some way.
b. can be removed without material injury to the realty.
c. either (a) or (b).
d. both (a) and (b).

d 5. The distinction between real and personal property is important in that legal consequences follow from it in the area(s) of:
a. transfer of property during one's life.
b. transfer of property on one's death.
c. taxation of property interests.
d. all of the above.

6. The basic distinction between a gift and a sale is that a gift:
   a. requires delivery.
   b. lacks any consideration.
   c. requires intent on the part of the donor.
   d. must be accepted by the donee.

7. Which of the requirements of an effective gift is presumed?
   a. Delivery to the donee.
   b. Intent on donor's part to make a present gift.
   c. Acceptance by the donee.
   d. None of the above.

8. Under the doctrine of title by accession, if Fred innocently took Elmer's lumber and constructed a boat, and the value of Elmer's labor is greater than the value of Fred's raw lumber:
   a. Fred is entitled to recover the boat and does not have to compensate Elmer for the reasonable value of the improvements.
   b. Fred is entitled to recover the boat but he must compensate Elmer for the reasonable value of the improvements.
   c. Fred is not entitled to recover the boat but he can seek money damages for the value of the lumber.
   d. Fred is not entitled to recover the boat and he cannot seek money damages for the value of the lumber.

9. Under the doctrine of confusion, if James, Kevin and Loren accidently commingle identical cases of beer, and there is not enough left to distribute a full share to each:
   a. the first owners proving their proportion of the whole are entitled to receive their share.
   b. the loss will be born by each in proportion to his share.
   c. no party will recover anything unless he can prove his share.
   d. none of the above.

10. Melvin promises to give a ring to Neala, but loses it before he gives it to her. Obert then finds the ring, and both Melvin and Neala claim it. Who is entitled to the ring?
    a. Melvin
    b. Neala
    c. Obert
    d. Melvin and Neala jointly.

11. Which of the following are ways by which title to personal property may be obtained?
    a. Possession.
    b. Accession.
    c. Confusion.
    d. All of the above are means by which title to personal property may be obtained.

12. Which of the following is not required for a valid gift?
    a. Intent.
    b. Deliery.
    c. An adult donor.
    d. Acceptance.

_C_ 13. Which of the following would be considered intangible personal property?
  a. A pen.
  b. A chair.
  c. A stock certificate.
  d. A lease.

_a_ 14. Which of the following would be considered intangible real property?
  a. A lease.
  b. A promissory note.
  c. A patent.
  d. A fixture.

_d_ 15. Which of the following involve(s) concurrent ownership?
  a. Tenancy in common.
  b. Joint tenancy.
  c. Tenancy by the entireties.
  d. All of the above are forms of concurrent ownership?

SHORT ESSAY

1. Distinguish between real property, personal property, and fixtures; between tangible and intangible property. What is the legal significance, if any, of these distinctions? _Real property is land building + fixtures, personal & everything else tangible is the item in fact — ____ is stock cert, patent copy right_

2. How does a court determine whether an item is personal property or a fixture? _____

3. Distinguish between a gift and a sale. _Consideration in a sale none in a gift_

CHAPTER 45

BAILMENTS AND DOCUMENTS OF TITLE

PURPOSE

In this chapter, you study the bailment relationship. A bailment is a temporary transfer of personal property without transfer of title by one person (the bailor) to another person (the bailee) after which the property is to be returned to the bailor. Bailments are a common occurrence and are of great commercial importance. Common bailments include the transportation, storage and delivery of goods; leaving an item at a shop to be repaired; and the rental of goods. Documents of title are frequently used in bailment transactions. A warehouse receipt is issued by a warehouse, which is in the business of storing goods for hire. A bill of lading is a document issued by a carrier on receipt of goods for transportation. It serves as a receipt for the goods, as evidence of the contract of carriage and as a document of title. Some bills of lading are negotiable and others are non-negotiable. To be a document of title, a document must be issued or addressed to a bailee and cover goods in the bailee's possession that are either identified or are fungible portions of an identified mass. Article 7 of the UCC deals with documents of title, warehouse receipt and bills of lading.

CHAPTER CHECKPOINTS

After reading and studying this chapter, you should be able to:

1. Discuss the essential elements of a bailment.

2. List the rights and duties on the part of the bailor and baile.

3. Discuss the duties of (a) warehouser, (b) carrier, and (c) innkeeper.

4. Define a document of title.

5. Identify and discuss the different types of documents of title and the rights acquired by due and undue negotiation of a negotiable document of title.

CHAPTER OUTLINE

I. Bailments - A bailment is the temporary transfer of personal property by one party to another.
   A. Benefit - The possession of property is delivered, without transfer of title, by one person called the

bailor to another called the bailee for the accomplishment of a certain purpose. The purpose may be to benefit either of the parties or both.

B. Essentials - The bailment must contain certain basic elements which are: (1) delivery of possession by a bailor to a bailee; (2) of personal property; (3) without ownership by the bailee; (4) for a determinable period of time; and (5) an absolute duty on the bailee to return the property or dispose of it according to the bailor's directions.

C. Rights and Duties
   1. Due Care - The bailee is under a duty to exercise due care for the safety of the property and to return it to the right person.
   2. Absolute Liability - The bailee may not limit his/her liability except in the case of prior contractual agreement with the bailor.
   3. Compensation - The bailee, who by expressed or implied agreement, undertakes to perform work or render services in connection with the bailed goods is entitled to reasonable compensation.

D. Special Types of Bailments
   1. Pledge - This is bailment for security in which the owner gives possession of his/her personal property to another (the secured party) to secure a debt or the performance of some obligation.
   2. Warehouser - This is a bailee who receives goods to be stored for compensation.
   3. Carrier - A carrier is the transporter of gods.
   4. Innkeeper - Innkeepers today are better known as hotel and motel operators.

II. Document of Title - A document of title is an instrument evidencing ownership of the document and the goods it covers.
   A. Types
      1. Warehouse Receipt - This receipt issued by a person engaged in the business of storing goods for hire.
      2. Bill of Lading - This is a document issued to the shipper by the carrier.

   B. Negotiability
      1. Due Negotiation - This is the transfer of a negotiable document in the regular course of business to a holder, who takes in good faith, without any defense of claim, and for value.
      2. Warranty - A person who negotiates or transfers a document of title for value other than a collecting bank or other intermediary incurs certain warranty obligations unless otherwise agreed.
      3. Ineffective Documents - In order for a person to obtain title to goods by negotiation of a document, the goods must have been delivered to the issuer of the document by the owner of the goods or by one to whom actual or apparent authority has been entrusted by the owner.
      4. Cost Documents - If a document has been lost, stolen, or destroyed, a claimant of the goods may apply to a court for an order directing delivery of the goods or the issuance of a substitute document.

DEFINITIONS

1. Bailment

2. Bailor

3. Bailee

4. Bailment for sole benefit of bailor

5. Bailment for sole benefit of bailee

6. Bailment for mutual benefit

7. Pledge

8. Warehouser

9. Contract carrier

10. Common carrier

11. Innkeeper

12. Document of title

13. Bill of lading

14. Warehouse receipt

15. Through bill of lading

16. Negotiability

17. Due negotiation

TRUE/FALSE

_____ 1. A bailment relationship can exist with respect to both real and personal property.

_____ 2. In order to establish a bailment relationship, the person receiving possession of the property must be under a duty to return the property.

_____ 3. The bailee has the exclusive right to possess the bailed goods for the term of the bailment.

_____ 4. Almost every State has by statute adopted the common law rule that a bailee loses his lien on the bailed goods upon their redelivery to the bailor.

_____ 5. A private carrier has no duty to accept goods for carriage except where it has agreed to do so by contract.

_____ 6. The extent of a warehouser's liability for misdelivery may be limited by a provision in the warehouse receipt fixing a specific maximum liability.

_____ 7. A warehouser has a lien on the goods to enforce the payment of his charges and any necessary expenses incurred in keeping and handling the goods.

_____ 8. The liability of the originating carrier that receives the goods from the shipper for loss or damage is limited to the period while the goods are in its possession.

_____ 9. After an indorsement in blank or to bearer, a negotiable document of title may be negotiated by delivery alone.

_____ 10. If, in the absence of a court order a carrier delivers goods to a person claiming them under a missing negotiable document, it is liable to anyone who is injured by its actions.

_____ 11. A bill of lading which specifies one or more connecting carriers is called a through bill of lading.

_____ 12. In a straight bill of lading, the carrier undertakes to deliver the goods at a destination to a named consignee at a specified destination.

_____ 13. Non-negotiable documents include a straight bill of lading and a warehouse receipt.

_____ 14. No rights are obtained to a document of title in the absence of due negotiation.

_____ 15. Fred, without compensation, loans his textbook to his friend Elmer, so that Elmer may study for a test. This is a bailment for the sole benefit of the bailee.

MULTIPLE CHOICE

_____ 1. Thomas gives his car to Colleen so that Colleen can take it to the garage to be repaired. This is an example of:
   a. a mutual benefit bailment.
   b. a bailment for the sole benefit of the bailee.
   c. a bailment for the sole benefit of the bailor.
   d. all of the above.

_____ 2. Which of the following is not an essential element of a bailment relationship?
   a. Delivery of lawful possession of specific personal property by the bailor to the bailee.
   b. Transfer of title to the property from the bailor to the bailee for a determinable period of time.
   c. An obligation of the bailee to return the property to the bailee or to one with a superior right of possession at the end of the bailment.
   d. All of the above are essential elements of a bailment relationship.

_____ 3. A mutual benefit bailment will terminate on the happening of any of the conditions listed below except:
   a. when the purpose of the bailment is fully accomplished.
   b. when the time for which the bailment was created expires.
   c. when the bailed goods are destroyed.
   d. all of the above.

_____ 4. A bailee is free from liability for casualty to the bailed goods if he exercised the requisite degree of care unless he:
   a. agrees with the bailor to insure the goods against a certain risk, then failed to do so and the casualty to the goods occurred through such a risk.
   b. used the bailed property in a manner not authorized by the bailment and damage results from that use.
   c. delivers the property to the wrong person by mistake.
   d. all of the above.

_____ 5. In order for a carrier to be subject to the rules applicable to common carriers, all of the following conditions must be present except that:
   a. the carriage must be a part of its business.
   b. the majority of the carrier's business must be as a common carrier.
   c. the carriage must be for renumeration.
   d. the carrier must represent to the general public that it is willing to serve the public in the transportation of property.

_____ 6. A bill of lading serves as:
   a. a receipt for the goods transported.
   b. evidence of the contract of carriage.
   c. a document of title.
   d. all of the above.

_____ 7. A document of title is negotiable if it is made payable to any of the following except:
   a. to a named person.
   b. to bearer.
   c. to order.
   d. a document of title is negotiable if made payable to any of the above.

_____ 8. A holder of a negotiable document of title to whom it has been duly negotiated obtains all of the following except:
   a. title to the document.
   b. proof that the document is genuine.
   c. title to the goods.
   d. the holder has all of the above rights.

_____ 9. A person who transfers a document of title for value to other than a collecting bank or other intermediary warrants to his immediate purchaser that:
   a. the document is genuine.
   b. he has no knowledge of any fact that would impair the validity of worth of the document.
   c. his transfer is rightful and fully effective with respect to the document of title and the goods it represents.
   d. all of the above.

_____ 10. A purchaser will obtain title to goods by negotiation to him of a document of title provided the goods have been delivered to the issuer of the document by:
   a. a finder of the goods.
   b. a thief of the goods.
   c. the true owner of the goods.
   d. none of the above.

_____ 11. Arthur rents a car from Ajax Rental. While the car is in his possession, it is stolen.
   a. Arthur is responsible if he did not exercise extreme care.
   b. Arthur is responsible if he did not exercise ordinary care.
   c. Arthur is responsible regardless of how much care he exercised.
   d. Arthur is responsible only if he failed to exercise slight care.

_____ 12. How does a warehouser differ from an ordinary bailee?
   a. The warehouse company is not responsible for any damage to the bailed property.
   b. The warehouse company has the power to issue a document of title.
   c. The warehouse company derives no benefit from the bailment.
   d. The warehouse company is only responsible for intentional wrongdoing that damages thewarehoused property.

_____ 13. Arthur brings his car to the garage to have some work done on it. In the trunk of the car is a set of valuable jewels. Is there a bailment relationship between Arthur and the garage?
   a. There is a bailment relationship with respect to both the car and the jewels.
   b. There is a bailment relationship for the car but not the jewels.
   c. There is a bailment relationship for the jewels but not the car.
   d. There is no bailment relationship of either the car or the jewels.

_____ 14. Which of the following is an example of an extraordinary bailee?
   a. A coat check booth at a restaurant.
   b. An appliance repair store.
   c. United Parcel Service.
   d. An automobile repair garage.

_____ 15. If the bailee misdelivers the property, the bailee is liable to the bailor for:
   a. theft.
   b. conversion.
   c. trespass to personal property.
   d. embezzlement.

SHORT ESSAY

1. Identify the four requirements for a bailment relationship to exist. _____
   _____
   _____
   _____

2. What are the three basic kinds of bailments and what standard is applied to the bailee's duty to exercise due care under each? _____
   _____
   _____
   _____

3. What does a bailor have to show to recover from the bailee for goods that are returned damaged?_____

    _____

    _____

    _____

4. Compare and contrast the duties and liabilities of a common carrier with those of a private carrier. _____

    _____

    _____

    _____

    _____

INTERESTS IN REAL PROPERTY

PURPOSE

This chapter discusses the different ways one may hold ownership or claim on real property. When the ownership is for an indefinite period of time or for the life of a person, it is known as a freehold estate. This ownership may be with or without condition, depending on the terms by which the property was acquired.

Leasehold estates, which include landlord-tenant relationships, involve obligations and rights on both ends. Concurrent ownership, which is the case with condominiums, for example, is a special type of shared ownership. Other forms will also be examined.

One may also obtain the right to use another's land for a specific purpose. This is known as a nonpossessory interest in the property. You will study the various forms of nonpossessory interests in this chapter.

CHAPTER CHECKPOINTS

After reading and studying this chapter, you should be able to:

1. Define and discuss the various freehold estates.

2. Distinguish between reversion and remainder future interests.

3. Discuss the primary rights and obligations of landlords and tenants.

4. Identify and discuss the various forms of concurrent ownership of real property.

5. Discuss the different forms of nonpossessory interests.

CHAPTER OUTLINE

I. Freehold Estates - Ownership of real property for an indefinite time or for the life of a person.
    A. Fee Estates - Includes absolute ownership and qualified fee ownership which is subject to being taken away upon the happening of an event.

    B.   Life Estates - Ownership for the life of a designated person. They may be created by voluntary act or by law, as in the case of a wife's dower rights to her husband's property.

    C.   Future Interests - Not all interests in property are subject to immediate use and possession, even though the right and title to the interest are absolute. For example, property may be willed "to A for his life and then to B for her heirs." B has future interest while A is still alive.
        1.   Reversion - Grantor's right to property upon termination of another estate.
        2.   Remainder - Held by a person other than the grantor or his/her successors.

II. Leasehold Estates - Right to possess real property.
    A.   Creation and Duration - The landlord, or owner of land grants a leasehold interest to the tenant for a definite or ascertainable period of time.

    B.   Transfer - Both the tenant's interest in the leasehold and the landlord's reversionary interest in the property may be freely transferred in the absence of contractual or statutory prohibition. The tenant may transfer all of his/her leasehold interest by assignment, or sublease and retain some interest.

    C.   Tenant's Obligations - The tenant has an obligation to pay specified rent at specified times, as well as any other provisions covered in the lease agreement.

    D.   Landlord's Obligations - The landlord's obligations are few. He/she must give the tenant a right to possession, but often not actual possession. The landlord is bound to provide the tenant with quiet and peaceful enjoyment.

III. Concurrent Ownership
    A.   Joint Tenancy - The most significant feature of joint tenancy is survivorship. On death of one tenant, ownership passes to survivor(s).

    B.   Tenancy in Common - Each tenant holds an interest with no right of survivorship.

    C.   Tenancy by the Entireties - Co-ownership by spouses.

    D.   Community Property - Rights by spouses in property is acquired by the other in marriage.

    E.   Condominiums - The purchaser acquires separate ownership to the unit and becomes a tenant in common with respect to the common facilities.

    F.   Cooperatives - An indirect form of common ownership. A cooperative, usually a corporation, purchases or constructs the dwelling units and leases to its shareholders as tenants, who acquire the right to use and occupy their units.

IV. Nonpossessor Interests
    A.   Easements - A limited right to use the land of another in a specific manner.

    B.   Profits a Prendre - The right to remove the produce from the land of another.

    C.   Licenses - Permission to use one's land which is subject to revocation by the owner at any time.

DEFINITIONS

1. Freehold estate

2. Leasehold estate

3. Fee simple estate

4. Qualified fee estate

5. Conventional life estate

6. Future interest

7. Reversion

8. Remainder

9. Estate for years

10. Periodic tenancy

11. Tenancy at will

12. Tenancy at sufferance

13. Assignment of a lease

14. Sublease

15. Constructive eviction

16. Tenancy in common

17. Joint tenancy

18. Tenancy by the entireties

19. Community property

20. Condominiums

21. Cooperatives

22. Easements

23. Profit a prendre

24. License

TRUE/FALSE

_____ 1. Both freehold estates and leasehold estates are regarded as possessory interests in property.

_____ 2. A fee simple estate is created by any words which indicate an intent to convey absolute ownership.

_____ 3. A widow's common law dower is subordinate to claims that were not reduced to a judgment before marriage.

_____ 4. A reversion, a life estate, and a remainder are all considered future interests.

_____ 5. A lease is both a contract and a grant of an estate in land.

_____ 6. A lease that does not specify any duration is treated as a tenancy at sufferance.

_____ 7. Unless specifically permitted in the lease, leases are not freely assignable without the landlord's consent.

_____ 8. A tenant is under no duty to make any repairs to the leased premises unless the lease expressly so provides.

_____ 9. Like joint tenants, tenants in common are persons who hold undivided interests in the property, each having the right to possession, but neither claiming any specific portion of the property.

_____ 10. A tenancy by the entireties can only be created in a conveyance to a husband and wife.

_____ 11. The purchaser of a cooperative acquires separate ownership to the unit and becomes a tenant in common in the common facilities.

_____ 12. It is generally the responsibility of the owner of the servient parcel to maintain the easement and keep it in repair.

_____ 13. The rental of a hotel room is a typical example of a license.

_____ 14. Appurtenant easements are the most common type.

_____ 15. The land which is subject to an easement is the dominant parcel.

MULTIPLE CHOICE

_____ 1. All of the following conveyances will create an unqualified fee simple estate in the transferee except:
   a. "To B."
   b. "To B forever."
   c. "To B so long as she does not remarry."
   d. "To B in fee simple."

_____ 2. If B is given a life estate in Blackacre by A, and B then sells his entire interest in Blackacre to C, C's interest in Blackacre is:
a. a fee simple estate.
b. a qualified fee simple estate.
c. a life estate for B's life.
d. a life estate for C's life.

_____ 3. O conveys Greenacre "to A for life, then to B." What interest, if any, does B have in Greenacre?
a. A reversion.
b. A vested remainder.
c. A contingent remainder
d. No interest.

_____ 4. A leases a factory to B for 3 years. The written lease provides that rent is to be paid on the first day of each month, and that either party may terminate the lease at any time. The lease can best be described as:
a. an estate for years.
b. a periodic tenancy "from year to year."
c. a periodic tenancy "from month to month."
d. a tenancy at will.

_____ 5. After he conveys the leasehold interest, the landlord may transfer to a third party his:
a. reversionary interest in the leasehold.
b. right to rent to be paid by the tenant.
c. neither (a) nor (b).
d. both (a) and (b).

_____ 6. If a tenant assigns his leasehold interest without the written consent of the landlord as required by the lease, the assignment is:
a. valid and enforceable.
b. void and unenforceable by either party.
c. voidable at the landlord's election.
d. treated as a sublease.

_____ 7. A tenancy in common requires which of the following "unities?"
a. Time.
b. Title.
c. Interest.
d. Possession.

_____ 8. A conveys "the back forty" to B. The parcel is bordered on three sides by the remainder of A's farm and on the fourth by a river. At present, B has no access to the highway and the deed from A grants none. Which of the following is correct?
a. B has an express easement across A's land to the highway.
b. B has an implied easement across A's land to the highway.
c. B has an easement by necessity across A's land to the highway.
d. B has no right to cross A's land to the highway.

9. If A gives B permission to extract oil from his land, he has given B:
    a. an easement in gross.
    b. a license.
    c. a profit a prendre.
    d. none of the above.

10. A theatre ticket is an example of:
    a. an easement in gross.
    b. a license.
    c. a profit a prendre.
    d. none of the above.

11. How may an easement be created?
    a. By express grant or reservation.
    b. By implied grant or reservation.
    c. By prescription.
    d. An easement may be created by any of the above methods.

12. Which of the following is correct with regard to a *profit a prendre*?
    a. Unless it is clearly designated as exclusive, it is subject to similar use by the owner.
    b. It is sometimes difficult to distinguish from a license.
    c. It is the right to remove the produce from another's land.
    d. All of the above are correct.

13. Catherine tells David that he may cross her land to pick hickory nuts.
    a. This is an easement by prescription.
    b. This is a license.
    c. This is an easement by dedication.
    d. This is an easement by express grant or reservation.

14. How does a joint tenancy differ from a tenancy in common?
    a. A joint tenancy has the right of survivorship.
    b. Unlike a joint tenancy, the only prerequisite for a tenancy in common is the unity of possession.
    c. Joint tenants hold an undivided interest in the same property.
    d. Two of the above, (a) and (b).

15. Sam Student and two of his friends rent an apartment near the campus of Ivory Towers University. When winter comes and the outside temperature is below zero, they discover that the furnace does not work. They notify the landlord, but he says that is not his problem. Does the landlord have any responsibility to maintain the furnace?
    a. Yes, because of his obligation of quiet enjoyment.
    b. Yes, because of the implied warranty of habitability.
    c. Yes, because of his obligation of repair.
    d. Two of the above, (b) and (c).

SHORT ESSAY

1. What are the basic characteristics of a fee simple estate? How do these estates differ from a qualified fee

simple estate? _____
_____
_____
_____

2. Distinguish among a reversion, a possibility of reverter, and a remainder. _____
_____
_____
_____

3. How do the rights and duties of the parties to an assignment of a lease differ from those of the parties to a sublease? _____
_____
_____
_____

4. What are the rights and duties of the landlord and tenant at common law? How have most jurisdictions changed these rules? _____
_____
_____
_____

5. What are the two types of easements? How do they differ from each other? From a profit prendre? From a license? _____
_____
_____
_____

TRANSFER AND CONTROL OF REAL PROPERTY

PURPOSE

The transfer of title of real property can be a difficult and time-consuming process. In this chapter, we examine the various ways to transfer possession of realty along with the public and private controls which affect its acquisition.

The first requirement of property sale is the formation of a contract. The contract should include the names of both or all parties involved as well as a description of the property involved. The contract should also specify the time of conveyance, or closing of the sale, and the type of deed to be given.

The deed itself can take different forms, each with its own conditions. The deed must meet statutory requirements which may vary from State to State. Delivery and recordation of the deed transfer should follow due process. Transactions of realty may be secured, in the case of a mortgage, for example. In these cases, the real estate itself is used to secure the buyer's obligation. Foreclosures, such as those of many farms, have resulted from such an agreement.

Another factor which tends to slow down the process of acquiring or developing real estate is the presence of public and private controls such as zoning restrictions. These controls, their different forms, and implications will be discussed in this chapter.

CHAPTER CHECKPOINTS

After reading and studying this chapter, you should be able to:

1. List the essential elements in the formation of a contract of sale.

2. Distinguish among the following types of deeds: (a) warranty; (b) special warranty; (c) quitclaim.

3. Describe the fundamental requirements of a valid deed.

4. Explain what is meant by a secured transaction.

5. Discuss public zoning restrictions along with some of their exceptions.

6.   Define and give an example of eminent domain.

7.   Describe the nature and types of restrictive covenants.

CHAPTER OUTLINE

I.   Transfer
     A.   Contract of Sale
          1.   Formation - The contract should be written and signed by both parties in order to be enforceable. The simplest agreement should include: (a) the names and addresses of the parties; (2) a description of the property; (c) the time for the conveyance (closing); and (d) type of deed to be given.
          2.   Marketable Title - Should be free from any defects or encumbrances such as mortgages, easements, liens, leases, and restrictive covenants.
          3.   Implied Warranty of Habitability - The builder-seller of a dwelling implied warrants that a newly constructed house is free from latent defects -- those that are not visible upon a reasonable inspection of the house.

     B.   Deeds - A formal document transferring any type of interest in land.
          1.   Types
               a.   Warranty Deed - The grantor (seller) promises the grantee (buyer) that he/she has a valid title to the property, without defect.
               b.   Special Warranty Deed - The seller promises only that he/she has not impaired the title.
               c.   Quitclaim Deed - The seller transfers whatever claim (interest) he/she has in the property.
          2.   Requirements - The transfer must be in writing to be within the Statute of Frauds. The transfer document should contain all information pertinent to the property, as stated above under formation of contracts.
          3.   Delivery - An intent that the deed take effect as evidenced by acts or statements of the grantor.
          4.   Recordation - Consists of delivery of a duly executed and acknowledged deed to the recorder's office in the county where the property is located.

     C.   Secured Transactions - Many people must borrow money or defer payment of real estate over a period of time. In these cases, the real estate itself is used to secure the obligation, which is evidenced by either a mortgage or a deed of trust.
          1.   Form of Mortgages - The written document is in the form of a conveyance from the mortgagor to the mortgagee. It provides security for the payment of a debt.
          2.   Rights and Duties - May depend on whether the mortgage is viewed as creating a lieu or as transferring legal title to the mortgagee.
          3.   Transfer of Interests - If the purchaser assumes the mortgage, he/she becomes personally liable to pay the debt. A transfer subject to the mortgage does not obligate the mortgagee to payment, but the property remains subject to the mortgage.
          4.   Foreclosure - Sale of the mortgaged property arising from default to satisfy the debt.

     D.   Adverse Possession - Involves acquisition of title to land by open, continuous, and often hostile occupancy for a statutorily prescribed period.

II. Public and Private Controls
     A.   Zoning - The principal method of public control over private land use, concerned with regulation rather than acquisition.

1. Legislation - Power to zone is generally delegated to local authorities by statutes known as enabling acts. Under these powers the local authorities may enact zoning ordinances.
2. Variance - In cases of particular hardship caused by legislation, land use may differ from ordinance provisions.
3. Nonconforming Uses - Uses existing prior to an ordinance must be permitted to continue for at least a reasonable time.
4. Judicial Review - Zoning ordinances may be reviewed in the event that they are invalid, unreasonable, or too restrictive.
5. Master Plans - Municipalities are granted the authority to subdivide land into plats.

B. Eminant Domain - The power to buy private land for public use. Such is the case with housing projects being constructed in place of condemned or vacant areas. However, the owners of the property taken must receive just compensation.

C. Private Restrictions
1. Nature - Private restrictions, known as restrictive covenants are, in a sense, easements to the extent that they impose a limitation on the use of the land.
2. Type - There are many types of restrictive covenants, the most common ones either limit the use of property to residential purposes, restrict the lot on which a structure can be built, or provide for a special type of architecture.
3. Termination - A restrictive covenant may end by the terms of the original agreement.
4. Validity - Although not always popular, restrictions are usually enforced when they are to the general benefit of the owners affected.

DEFINITIONS

1. Marketable title

2. Warranty deed

3. Special warranty deed

4. Quitclaim deed

5. Mortgagor

6. Mortgagee

7. Deed of trust

8. Right of redemption

9. Adverse possession

10. Variance

11. Non-conforming use

12. Eminent domain

13. Restrictive covenant

TRUE/FALSE

_____   1.   Title to land may only be transferred by deed.

_____   2.   To be enforceable, a contract for the sale of an interest in land must be in writing and signed by the party against whom enforcement is sought.

_____   3.   At common law, when the contract of sale is entered into, the risk of loss or destruction of the property passes to the purchaser.

_____   4.   In most jurisdictions, consideration must pass between the parties for a deed to be valid.

_____   5.   A deed is not effective to pass title unless and until it is both delivered and recorded.

_____   6.   The provisions of Article 9 of the U.C.C. govern real estate mortgages and trust deeds.

_____   7.   A mortgagee has the right to assign the mortgage to a third person without the consent of the mortgagor.

_____   8.   When the power of eminent domain is exercised, the award of compensation is given to the holders of all vested and contingent interests in the condemned property.

_____   9.   In a notice-race State, an unrecorded deed is invalid against any subsequent purchaser without notice who records first.

_____   10.   Under a special warranty deed, the grantor obligates himself to make the grantee whole if the latter suffers any damage because the grantor's title was defective.

_____   11.   A mortgagor's right of redemption cannot be extinguished except by operation of law.

_____   12.   Transfer of title by adverse possession requires no contract, deed, or other formality.

_____   13.   A court will enforce a restrictive covenant regardless of whether circumstances have changed to make the covenant inequitable and oppressive.

_____   14.   A restrictive covenant prohibiting the owner of property from selling to someone of a particular race or ethnic background will be upheld by the courts.

_____   15.   A builder-seller of residential dwellings impliedly warrants that a newly constructed house is free of latent defects.

MULTIPLE CHOICE

_____ 1. After a contract of sale is entered into but before the deed has been delivered, the risk of loss or destruction of the property is:
   a. entirely upon the seller.
   b. entirely upon the purchaser.
   c. shared equally by the seller and the purchaser.
   d. none of the above.

_____ 2. A marketable title is one that is free from all of the following except:
   a. encumberances, such as mortgages and leases.
   b. defects in the chain of title appearing in the land records.
   c. any defects that would subject the purchaser to the inconvenience of having to defend his title in court.
   d. existing zoning restrictions that are not noted on the deed.

_____ 3. Which of the following deeds conveys an after-acquired title to the grantee?
   a. A warranty deed.
   b. A special warranty deed.
   c. A quitclaim deed.
   d. None of the above.

_____ 4. In order for a deed to be effective, it must be:
   a. exchanged for consideration.
   b. delivered.
   c. recorded.
   d. all of the above.

_____ 5. A State in which an unrecorded deed is invalid against any deed recorded before it is:
   a. a notice State.
   b. a notice-race State.
   c. a race State.
   d. all of the above.

_____ 6. Which of the following are elements of a secured transaction?
   a. A debt or obligation to pay money.
   b. An interest of the creditor in specific property which secures performance of the obligation.
   c. neither (a) nor (b).
   d. both (a) and (b).

_____ 7. The mortgagor retains title to the property in:
   a. a "lien" theory State.
   b. a "title" theory State.
   c. neither (a) nor (b).
   d. both (a) and (b).

_____ 8. The mortgagor's right to relieve his mortgaged property from the lien of a mortgage by payment of the indebtedness that it secures is called the right of:
   a.   rescission.
   b.   redemption.
   c.   renegotiation.
   d.   renovation.

_____ 9. In many States, if a person openly and continuously occupies the land of another for a statutorily prescribed period, that person will gain title to the land by:
   a.   foreclosure.
   b.   redemption.
   c.   eminent domain.
   d.   adverse possession.

_____ 10. Most zoning ordinances provide for the elimination of non-conforming uses:
   a.   when the use is discontinued.
   b.   when a non-conforming structure is destroyed or is substantially damaged.
   c.   when a non-conforming structure has been permitted to exist for the period of its useful life.
   d.   all of the above.

_____ 11. A restrictive covenant is enforceable only if:
   a.   the restriction was intended to benefit the seller of any lot in the tract.
   b.   the restriction appears somewhere in the chain of title to which the land of the person seeking to enforce the covenant is subject.
   c.   neither (a) nor (b).
   d.   both (a) and (b).

_____ 12. Which of the following is/are typically found in the enabling statutes which delegate zoning power to local authorities?
   a.   The power to regulate and limit the height and bulk of buildings.
   b.   The power to set standards to which buildings must conform.
   c.   The power to restrict the location of trades and industries.
   d.   All of the above are typically found in enabling statutes.

_____ 13. Andrew Attorney does a title search on property that Ron Realtor wishes to purchase. The search indicates a title defect, because the abstract shows that Carl Contractor could possibly have an interest in the land even though he is not the seller. What type of deed should Ron ask Carl to give him in order to clear up the title defect?
   a.   A warranty deed.
   b.   A special warranty deed.
   c.   A quit-claim deed.
   d.   A contract for deed.

_____ 14. Which of the following is generally not required in order to get title to property by adverse possession?
   a.   Actual possession of the property in question.
   b.   Continuous possession of the property in question for a prescribed period of years.
   c.   Hostile or adverse possession of the property in question.
   d.   A written deed.

_____ 15. Alicia purchases Brad's house and in so doing assumes the mortgage. Which of the following is correct regarding the assumption of the mortgage?
   a.   Alicia is personally liable to pay the mortgage.
   b.   Brad is personally liable to pay the mortgage.
   c.   Brad is relieved of his obligation to pay the mortgage.
   d.   Both Alicia and Brad are personally liable to pay the mortgage.

SHORT ESSAY

1.   What are the two essential documents involved in the transfer of real estate? What must or should each document contain? _____

_____

_____

_____

2.   What are the three types of deeds? How do they differ in effect? _____

_____

_____

_____

3.   Discuss briefly what is necessary to deliver effectively a deed? _____

_____

_____

_____

4.   Discuss what is meant by a restrictive covenant. How is one terminated? _____

_____

_____

_____

CHAPTER 48

TRUSTS AND WILLS

PURPOSE

The transfer of real property may take the form of a will or trust, in which the property is given to a party for their benefit. This transfer is usually created by the settler, or original owner of the property. In the absence of an expressed intent, the courts will sometimes impose a trust on property if the situation warrants.

Descendent's estates, or wills, are written instruments conveying the disposition of one's property to take effect after his/her death. Wills are executed with the formalities required by statutes, therefore certain conditions and requirements must be met. We will discuss these in this chapter. In addition, we will examine the general course of descent and administration of wills, all of which are subject to State limitations.

CHAPTER CHECKPOINTS

After reading and studying this chapter, you should be able to:

1. Describe the differences between an expressed and implied trust.

2. List the essential elements of a trust.

3. Discuss the formal requirements of making a valid will and how a will may be revoked.

4. Define and describe a codicil.

5. Discuss the general rules of intestate succession.

CHAPTER OUTLINE

I. Trusts - Transfer of property to one party for the benefit of another.
    A. Types
        1. Express - Established by voluntary action by the settler (creator) of the trust.
        2. Implied - In the absence of any expressed intent, the courts will sometimes impose a trust on property if the situation warrants.

B.   Creation - Each trust has: (1) a settler; (2) a "corpus" or trust property; (3) a trustee or holder of legal title; and (4) a beneficiary.

C.   Termination - Normally, the instrument creating a trust establishes a termination date, and the trust terminates at the stated time without complication. Any other action would be up to the courts.

II. Decedent's Estates
A.   Wills - A written instrument executed with the formalities required by statutes, whereby a person makes a disposition of his/her property to take effect after his death.
1.   Mental Capacity - The power to make a will is granted by the State to persons believed generally able to handle their affairs.
2.   Formal Requirements of a Will - First of all, the will must be in writing and must include the signature of the testator (creator). Also, the will must be attested, or certified, by witnesses.
3.   Revocation - A will is revocable only by the testator and, under certain circumstances, by operation of law.
4.   Special Types - Special types of wills are binding only in specific and isolated situations, and they may have limitations.
5.   Codicils - An addition to or revision of a will, generally by a separate instrument, in which the will is expressly referred to and incorporated.

B.   Intestate Succession - Generally, the property of the deceased will pass as he/she directs, subject only to limitations by the State.
1.   Course of Descent - The rules of descent vary widely from State to State, but generally the intestate property passes in equal shares to each child of the descendent, that is, after the widow's dower rights have been settled.
2.   Administration - The rules controlling management of an estate are also statutory and therefore varied. In all cases, the court supervises the procedure. Often the executor is named in the will.

DEFINITIONS

1.   Trust

2.   Trustee

3.   Beneficiary

4.   Settlor

5.   Express trust

6.   Implied trust

7.   Constructive trust

8.   Resulting trust

9.   Charitable trust

10. Spendthrift trust

11. Totten trust

12. Trust corpus

13. Testamentary trust

14. *Inter vivos* trust

15. Ademption

16. Abatement

17. Nuncupative will

18. Holographic will

19. Codicil

20. Intestate succession

21. *Per stirpes*

22. *Per capita*

23. Probate

24. Executor

25. Administrator

TRUE/FALSE

_____ 1. Legal title to property may be held by one or more persons while at the same time its use, enjoyment and benefit belong to one or more others.

_____ 2. An express trust must be in writing in order to be valid.

_____ 3. A constructive trust is created by express language of the settlor, written or oral, by which specific property is transferred to a trustee for the use and benefit of one or more beneficiaries.

_____ 4. A resulting trust is founded on a presumed intent out of the acts of the parties.

_____ 5. Consideration is an essential element of an enforceable trust.

_____ 6. Anyone legally capable of holding title to and dealing with property may be a trustee.

_____ 7. The death of a trustee destroys the trust.

_____ 8. In general, unless the settlor reserves a power of revocation, a trust once validly created is irrevocable.

_____ 9. A will is generally revocable by the testator at any time during his lifetime.

_____ 10. A will must always be in writing to be effective.

_____ 11. A holographic will does not need to be witnessed to be valid.

_____ 12. A codicil must be executed with all of the formal requirements of a will.

_____ 13. Legally adopted children are generally recognized as lawful heirs of their adopting parents.

_____ 14. The rules of descent are uniform throughout the United States.

_____ 15. A marriage generally revokes a will executed before the marriage.

MULTIPLE CHOICE

_____ 1. The party holding legal title to the property in trust is known as:
   a. the beneficiary.
   b. the trustee.
   c. the settlor.
   d. the creator.

_____ 2. If a director of a corporation is found to have taken advantage of a "corporate opportunity," the court will impose:
   a. an express trust.
   b. a constructive trust.
   c. a resulting trust.
   d. a charitable trust.

_____ 3. All of the following are correct statements concerning a resulting trust except:
   a. it serves to carry out the true intent of the parties in those cases where the intent was inadequately expressed.
   b. it is created by implication and operation of law.
   c. it is designed to rectify fraud, duress, or a breach of confidence.
   d. none of the above.

_____ 4. A spendthrift clause in a trust instrument will insulate income already received from the trust by the beneficiary from:
   a. the claims of the beneficiary's creditors.
   b. the beneficiary's control.
   c. neither (a) nor (b).
   d. both (a) and (b).

_____ 5. A trust created by a settlor's will is:
  a. a resulting trust.
  b. a charitable trust.
  c. a testamentary trust.
  d. an *inter vivos* trust.

_____ 6. Which of the following is not a duty of a trustee?
  a. To carry out the purposes of the trust.
  b. To act with prudence and care in the administration of the trust.
  c. To exercise a high degree of loyalty toward the beneficiary.
  d. To act as a guarantor for the liabilities of the trust.

_____ 7. In order to make a valid will, the testator must have:
  a. the "power" to make a valid will, as defined by State law.
  b. the "capacity" to make a valid will.
  c. either (a) or (b).
  d. both (a) and (b).

_____ 8. To incorporate by reference a memorandum into a will, all of the following conditions must exist except:
  a. it must be in writing.
  b. it must be in existence when the will is executed.
  c. it must be physically attached to the will.
  d. it must be adequately described in the will.

_____ 9. Which of the following will result in the revocation of a will?
  a. The testator is divorced after having executed the will.
  b. The testator executes a codicil.
  c. The testator marries after having executed the will.
  d. The testator tears the will in half thinking that it is a void "I.O.U."

_____ 10. If A executes a will leaving "Blackacre" to B, but then sells the land for $20,000 before he dies, on A's death, B will receive:
  a. Blackacre.
  b. $20,000.
  c. Green Acre.
  d. nothing.

_____ 11. In which of the following situations will a will be declared invalid?
  a. The testator was incompetent most of the time, but executed the will during one of his periods of lucidity.
  b. The will was executed under fraudulent circumstances.
  c. A will is invalid in both of the above circumstances.
  d. A will is not invalid under either of the above circumstances.

_____ 12. A _____ is a separate written instrument that amends or revokes provisions in a will.
  a. devise
  b. hologram
  c. codicil
  d. settlor

_____ 13. Which of the following is generally correct regarding the course of descent?
    a.   At common law, property could not lineally ascend to one's parents.
    b.   At common law, a stepchild was considered an heir.
    c.   All States distribute property on a per capita basis.
    d.   None of the above is correct.

_____ 14. What is another name for the personal representative of an estate?
    a.   The testator.
    b.   The settlor.
    c.   The executor.
    d.   The decedent.

_____ 15. Which of the following will not automatically revoke a will?
    a.   The execution of a second will.
    b.   The tearing, burning or otherwise destroying of a will.
    c.   The divorce of a spouse.
    d.   In each of the above situations, evidence of intent to revoke would need to be shown before the act would revoke the will.

SHORT ESSAY

1. What are the four essential elements of a trust? _____
_____
_____
_____

2. Distinguish between a constructive trust and a resulting trust. _____
_____
_____
_____

3. How is a trust created? How is one terminated? _____
_____
_____
_____

4. What are the requirements of a valid will? When does it become effective? _____
_____
_____
_____

5. Outline briefly the steps involved in the administration of an estate. _____
_____
_____
_____

INSURANCE

PURPOSE

Insurance covers a vast range of contracts, each of which distributes risk among a large number of members through an insurance company. The members are the insured, and the company is the insurer. An insurance policy is a contractual undertaking by the insurer to pay a sum of money or give something of value to the insured or a beneficiary upon the happening of a contingency or fortuitous event which is beyond the control of the parties. Because the insurance relationship arises from a contract of insurance between the insurer and the insured, the law of insurance is a branch of contract law. The rules applicable to contracts in general are equally applicable to insurance contracts. In this chapter, you study the various kinds of insurance and the nature of insurance contracts.

CHAPTER CHECKPOINTS

After reading and studying this chapter, you should be able to:

1. Identify the McCarren Ferguson Act and explain what the act did with respect to regulation of the insurance industry.

2. List and define the 13 types of insurance contracts discussed in this chapter.

3. Distinguish between an endowment contract and an annuity contract.

4. Explain what an insurable interest is and why it is required by the law.

5. Distinguish between waiver, estoppel, representations and warranties as they affect forfeiture and avoidance of an insurance policy.

CHAPTER OUTLINE

A. Kinds of Insurance
   1. Life Insurance – Called death insurance because it is a contract by the terms of which insurers will pay a specified sum of money on the death of the insured to a named beneficiary who is a privilege of the owner of the policy.

    a.   Ordinary Life - A form of saving or investment, because insured has a right to borrow from the insurer an amount not to exceed the cash surrender value of the policy. Low interest is charged. It is designed to run for the entire life of the insured and payment of premium until his death. Limited payment life policies require payment of premiums only for a fixed number of years. For single premium life insurance, the entire premium is prepaid in one lump sum.

    b.   Term Life - Issued for a limited number of years. Proceeds are paid only if the insured dies within the specified time period. The insurer may not be obligated to pay out anything on the policy, carry a provision to review the policy.

2.   Endowment and Annuity Contracts - Endowment contract is an agreement by the insurer to pay a lump sum of money to the insured when she reaches a certain age or to a beneficiary in the event of premature death. Annuity contract is an agreement by the insurer to pay fixed sums to the insured at periodic intervals after a designated age.

3.   Accident and Health Insurance - Really insurance against losses due to accidents and sickness and provides for reimbursement of specific expenses in the event of illness or accidental injury.

4.   Fire and Property Insurance - Fire insurance protects the real or personal property against loss resulting from damage to or destruction of the property by fire and certain related perils. Fire insurance policies are standardized but coverage is enlarged by an endorsement or rider. Policies are written for periods of 1 or 3 years.

5.   Co-insurance - Sharing the risk between insurer and insured, in which a person insures property for less than its full or stated value and agrees to share the risk of loss.

Recovery = Face value of policy/(Fair market value of property x co-insurance) x loss

Recovery under non-life insurance policies is limited by other insurance clauses which require liability be distributed pro rata among various insurers.

6.   Casualty Insurance - Covers loss due to the damage or destruction of personal property by various causes other than fire or the elements.

7.   Automobile

    a.   Collision Insurance - Protects the owner of an automobile against the risk of loss or damage due to contact with other vehicles or objects.

    b.   Liability Insurance - Provides indemnification against loss by reason of liability of the insured for damages resulting from injuries to another person or property. It is carried by owners and lessees of property.

    c.   No-fault Insurance - Compensating victims of automobile accidents regardless of liability. Coverage is provided to the named insured.

8.   Title Insurance - Provides indemnity against loss arising from defects in the title to real estate or due to liens or encumbrances on the property.

9.   Group Insurance - Covers a number of individuals, all with some common interest, under a blanket or single policy.

B.   Nature of Insurance Contracts - Basic principles of contract law apply to insurance policies but insurance policies are standardized.

1.   Offer and Acceptance - The applicant who makes the offer, and contract is created when that offer is accepted by the company.

    a.   Binding Receipt - Acknowledging payment of the premium and providing for the issuance of a standard policy effective from the date of the medical examination.

    b.   Binder - Making an agreement legally binding until the completion of the formal contract.

2.   Insurable Interest - A financial interest or close personal relationship in someone's life or property that justified insuring the life or property. To eliminate gambling and to lessen the moral hazard.

    a.   Property Insurance - A right deriving from a contract concerning the property also gives rise to an insurable interest. Its policies are not assignable before loss ocucrs but are freely assignable after the loss.

      b.   Life Insurance - Only close relatives, creditors, and business associates or employees may take out insurance on another's life. An insured may assign the life policy proceeds to a third person who has no insurable interest.

3.   Premiums - Amount to be paid, often in installments, for an insurance policy, which is calculated on the basis of: (a) mortality rates; (b) interests; (c) expense. The regulatory authorities are under a duty to require that companies' rates be reasonable, not unfairly discriminatory.

      a.   Double Indemnity - Twice the face amount of the policy, in the event of accidental death or death that results directly and independently of all other causes from bodily injuries.

4.   Defenses for the Insurer

      a.   Misrepresentations - For a representation to have legal consequences, it must have been relied on by the insurer as an inducement to enter into the contract and it must have been substantially false when made, to the insured's knowledge. The principal remedy of the insurer on this is rescission of the contracts and must return all the premiums that have been paid.

           1)   Incontestability Clause - The prohibition of an insurer to avoid an insurance policy after a specified period of time.

           2)   Innocent Misrepresentation - An innocent misrepresentation of a material fact is a sufficient ground for avoidance of a policy by the insurer.

           3)   Immaterial Misrepresentation - An immaterial misrepresentation is not a ground for avoidance of the policy.

      b.   Breach of Warranty - Warranty are conditions that must exist before the contract is effective or before insurer's promise to pay is enforceable. Failure of the condition to exist relieves the insurer from any obligation to perform its promise. Insured is not liable unless the suit is brought within 12 months from the date of the occurence of the loss.

      c.   Concealment - Failure of an applicant for insurance to disclose materal facts that insurer does not know.

      d.   Waiver and Estoppel - Waiver is the intentional relinquishment of a known right. Estoppel means that a person is prevented by his own conduct from asserting a position that is inconsistent with acts of his that another person justifiably relied on. Insureds have the right to rely on representations made by the insurer's employees if acting within the scope of his authority binds the principal.

5.   Termination and Performance - Due performance terminates the insurer's obligation.

      a.   Cancellation - By mutual consent, the insurer must return the unearned portion of the premium. To rescind a policy, insurer must return all premiums.

      b.   Notice - After the occurence of the insured event, required to give notice, proof of loss within a specific time. In liability policies, notice within a reasonable time. Automobile liability policies require immediate notification.

DEFINITIONS

1.   Insurance

2.   Insured

3.   Beneficiary

4.   Life insurance

5.   Whole life insurance

6. Cash surrender value

7. Term life insurance

8. Endowment contract

9. Annuity contract

10. Co-insurance

11. Casualty insurance

12. Collision insurance

13. No-fault insurance

14. Title insurance

15. Insurable insurance

16. Double indemnity

17. Incontestability clause

TRUE/FALSE

_____   1. Insurance is a contractual undertaking.

_____   2. Insurance is regulated primarily by federal law.

_____   3. With whole-life insurance, the insured has a right to borrow from the insurer an amount not to exceed the cash surrender value of the policy.

_____   4. Proceeds from a term life insurance policy will be paid only if the insured dies within the period specified by the policy.

_____   5. Credit insurance protects debtors against loss due to the insolvency of their creditors.

_____   6. Title insurance protects property owners against loss arising from defects in the title to real estate, but not against defects due to liens or encumbrances on the property.

_____   7. An insurance agent's solicitation of a person to purchase an insurance policy usually constitutes an offer by the company to the person that can be accepted by completing the application form.

_____   8. Property insurance policies are not assignable before loss occurs, but they are freely assignable after the loss.

_____   9. An insured may not assign the proceeds of his life insurance to a third person who has no insurable interest.

_____ 10. The principal remedy of the insurer upon discovery of a misrepresentation by the insured is rescission of the contract.

_____ 11. An "incontestability clause" makes a life insurance policy unassailable by the insurer, even if the insured misrepresents his age.

_____ 12. In order to invalidate an insurance policy, a non-disclosure must generally be both material and fraudulent.

_____ 13. Ordinary life, or whole-life, is often considered a form of savings or investment, because the insured has a right to borrow money from the insurer.

_____ 14. Under no-fault insurance, a victim of an automobile accident is compensated regardless of liability.

_____ 15. Credit life insurance protects the creditor and the debtor by providing for the payment of an indebtedness of the insured in the event of his death before the debt has been paid.

MULTIPLE CHOICE

_____ 1. The type of life insurance that has a cash surrender value is known as:
   a.   term life insurance.
   b.   ordinary life insurance.
   c.   casualty insurance.
   d.   all of the above.

_____ 2. An agreement by an insurer to pay a lump sum of money to the insured when he reaches a certain age or to a beneficiary in the event of premature death is called:
   a.   an annuity contract.
   b.   an endowment contract.
   c.   a life insurance contract.
   d.   none of the above.

_____ 3. If a building valued at $20,000 is covered by a $12,000 fire insurance policy with an 80 percent co-insurance clause and the building suffers $10,000 damage by fire, the insurer would pay:
   a. $3,750.
   b. $7,500.
   c. $8,000.
   d. $10,000.

_____ 4. Under a "no-fault" insurance policy, coverage is provided for personal injury to:
   a.   the named insured and passengers in the motor vehicle.
   b.   pedestrians injured by the motor vehicle.
   c.   authorized operators of the motor vehicle.
   d.   all of the above.

_____ 5. An insurance contract generally becomes binding upon the insurer when:
   a. the insurance agent solicits the contract.
   b. the insured completes the application form and submits it to the insurer.
   c. when the insurer accepts the application of the insured.
   d. none of the above.

_____ 6. A person does not have an insurable interest in the life of:
   a. his debtor.
   b. himself.
   c. his business partner.
   d. his neighbor.

_____ 7. An insurable interest in property must exist at:
   a. the time that the insurance contract is entered into.
   b. the time that the property loss occurs.
   c. either (a) or (b).
   d. both (a) and (b).

_____ 8. An insured may assign the proceeds of a life insurance policy:
   a. to himself.
   b. to anyone with an insurable interest in the insured.
   c. to anyone, including persons with an insurable interest in the insured.
   d. it may not be assigned prior to loss.

_____ 9. A representation by or on behalf of an applicant will have legal consequences if:
   a. it was relied upon by the insurer as an inducement to enter into a contract.
   b. it must have been substantially false when made or it must have become so with the insured's knowledge before the conract was created.
   c. either (a) or (b).
   d. both (a) and (b).

_____ 10. An contestability clause does not prevent the insurer from contesting the policy on which of the following grounds?
   a. Failure to pay the premiums.
   b. Misrepresentation of age.
   c. Lack of insurable interest by the policy owner.
   d. all of the above.

_____ 11. To what does co-insurance refer?
   a. It refers to a policy in which the insured agrees to bear a portion of the loss.
   b. It refers to the requirement that the insured must maintain more than one policy on the same property in order to ensure complete coverage.
   c. It refers to the fact that a person with property insurance will not be able to recover more than the value of his actual loss.
   d. It refers to the requirement that an insured must show proof of coverage to a mortgage holder.

_____ 12. Bradley buys an insurance policy which at its maturity in twenty-five years will pay him $10,000 each year after that.
   a.   Bradley has purchased an annuity.
   b.   Bradley has purchased a whole life policy.
   c.   Bradley has purchased a term life policy.
   d.   Bradley has purchased a co-insurance policy.

_____ 13. Arthur owns a piece of property on which he has a co-insurance policy for fire and property damage. The property is valued at $100,000 and the policy is in the amount of $60,000. If the property is 50% destroyed by fire, how much can Arthur recover from the insurance company?
   a. $30,000
   b. $37,500
   c. $40,000
   d. $48,000

_____ 14. Christopher has a life insurance policy that has two components -- life insurance protection and savings. The life insurance component is provided by renewable term insurance; the savings component is an extra portion of the premium beyond what is necessary to buy the term life. What kind of insurance does Christopher have?
   a.   An endowment policy.
   b.   A limited-payment life policy.
   c.   A straight-life policy.
   d.   A universal life policy.

_____ 15. How are life insurance premiums calculated?
   a.   They are calculated based on mortality rates.
   b.   They are calculated based on interest.
   c.   They are calculated based on expenses.
   d.   All of the above are considered by an insurance company in settling its rates.

SHORT ESSAY

1. Distinguish between ordinary life insurance and term life insurance. _____
_____
_____
_____

2. How do endowment contracts and annuity contracts differ from life insurance contracts? _____
_____
_____
_____

3. Describe briefly the concept of insurable interest. What purpose does it serve? _____
_____
_____
_____

4.   Of what significance are warranties in insurance contracts?   How do they operate? _____
_____
_____
_____
_____

5.   Distinguish between waiver and estoppel. _____
_____
_____
_____

PART X

SAMPLE EXAMINATION

_____ 1. Which of the following would be considered intangible personal property?
   a. A book.
   b. A lease.
   c. A copyright.
   d. A pet dog.

_____ 2. Which of the following would be considered tangible personal property?
   a. A Siamese cat.
   b. A lease.
   c. A promissory note.
   d. All of the above.

_____ 3. A _____ is a transfer of property from one person to another without consideration.
   a. sale
   b. gift
   c. bailment
   d. trust

_____ 4. The creator of a trust is known as the:
   a. trustee.
   b. beneficiary.
   c. settlor.
   d. executor.

_____ 5. When Arthur dies and his will is probated, Brad receives a life estate in Arthur's house. What happens to the house when Brad dies, if no one else is mentioned in the will as receiving an interest in the house?
   a. It goes to Brad's heirs.
   b. It reverts to Arthur's heirs.
   c. It goes to the State.
   d. It is shared by Brad's heirs and Arthur's heirs.

_____ 6. When Arthur dies and his will is probated, Brad receives a life estate in Arthur's house. The will also states that on Brad's death, the house will go to Clark. Clark's interest in the house is known as a:
   a. possibility of reverter.
   b. vested remainder.
   c. contingent remainder.
   d. periodic tenancy.

_____ 7. Albert conveys part of his land to Barbara. The part conveyed to Barbara is so situated that Barbara would have no access to it except across Albert's remaining land. Under these facts, Barbara has an easement by:
   a. express grant or reservation.
   b. implied grant or reservation.
   c. necessity.
   d. prescription.

_____ 8. Albert grants to Brian, an adjoining landowner, the right to cross his land and to gather black walnuts from the trees located there. Brian has a/an:
   a. easement by prescription.
   b. *profit a prendre.*
   c. license.
   d. either a *profit a prendre* or a license.

_____ 9. Bill Businessman rents a car from Ajax Car Rental while on a business trip to Los Angeles. This is an example of a/an:
   a. extraordinary bailment.
   b. constructive bailment.
   c. gratuitous bailment.
   d. bailment for mutual benefit.

_____ 10. Sarah Salesclerk's Siamese cat gives birth to a litter of five kittens. Sarah owns the kittens by reason of:
   a. confusion.
   b. accession.
   c. possession.
   d. gift.

_____ 11. Neil Neighbor borrows Harold Homemaker's snowblower to clear his own driveway of snow. This is an example of a:
   a. bailment for mutual benefit.
   b. bailment for the benefit of the bailor.
   c. bailment for the benefit of teh bailee.
   d. gift.

_____ 12. Which of the following is correct regarding a trade fixture?
   a. It is considered to be personal property belonging to the tenant.
   b. It belongs to the landlord upon termination of the lease agreement.
   c. It becomes so attached as to be considered part of the real property.
   d. Two of the above, (b) and (c) are both correct.

_____ 13. Hal Hoodlum steals a car from Harold Homemaker, then brings it to his chop shop where he takes it apart and sells the parts to Al's Auto Repair. Bill Businessman brings his car to Al's shop to have a new transmission installed, and Al installs the transmission from the stolen car into Bill's car. Bill pays for the work and takes the car home. Who owns the transmission?
   a. Harold Homemaker, because he is the true owner of the stolen car.
   b. Bill, because he paid Al for it and Al bought it from Hal.
   c. Bill, because he has become the owner by accession.
   d. Bill, because he has become the owner by confusion.

_____ 14. Sam Student rents an apartment from Ron Realtor. The lease is for a six month period with rent due on the first of each month. The rental agreement is for a:
   a. periodic tenancy.
   b. tenancy from month to month.
   c. tenancy at will.
   d. tenancy at sufferance.

_____ 15. Sam Student rents an apartment from Ron Realtor. The lease is for a six month period with rent due on the first of each month. At the end of six months, Sam continues in possession of the

apartment with the permission of Ron and the rent is paid on a monthly basis, but no new lease is drafted and signed by either party. The rental agreement is for a:
a.   periodic tenancy.
b.   tenancy from month to month.
c.   tenancy at will.
d.   tenancy at sufferance.

_____ 16. Lyle Landowner has a building valued at $100,000. He has an 80% co-insurance policy on the property in the face amount of $80,000. If the building is totally destroyed by an earthquake, Lyle will be able to recover what amount of money?
a. $64,000
b. $72,000
c. $80,000
d. $100,000

_____ 17. Lyle Landowner has a building valued at $100,000. He has an 80% co-insurance policy on the property in the face amount of $65,000. If the building is totally destroyed in an earthquake, Lyle will be able to recover what amount of money?
a. $64,000
b. $65,000
c. $81,250
d. $100,000

_____ 18. An ordinary life insurance policy divided into two components, which consist of term insurance and an investment portfolio, is known as:
a.   universal life.
b.   an annuity policy.
c.   an endowment contract.
d.   co-insurance.

_____ 19. The Individual Indemnity Insurance Company wishes to deny a claim and pay nothing at all. In which of the following situations would it be likely to successfully avoid all liability on a claim involving life insurance?
a.   The applicant lied about her age in order to obtain the policy.
b.   The applicant knew he had AIDS at the time he applied for the policy, but lied about it to the agent.
c.   The policy has an incontestability clause.
d.   The applicant had another policy with a different insurance company.

_____ 20. Sarah Salesclerk and her boyfriend go to a restaurant for dinner. While washing her hands in the restroom, Sarah removes her watch and accidentally leaves it there. Later in the evening, a waitress finds it and turns it over to the restaurant owner. The owner puts it in the restaurant safe and then forgets about it until six months later when the cleaning lady finds it there and shows it to the restaurant manager. Assuming that Sarah never returned to the restaurant to look for the watch, who has first claim to it?
a.   The waitress.
b.   The restaurant owner.
c.   The cleaning lady.
d.   None of the above, because Sarah is the true owner and has only mislaid the property.

ANSWERS TO CHAPTER TESTS

CHAPTER 1

True/False:

1.	T	6.	T	11.	T
2.	F	7.	F	12.	F
3.	F	8.	F	13.	F
4.	T	9.	T	14.	F
5.	T	10.	T	15.	F

Multiple Choice:

1.	b	6.	a	11.	c
2.	d	7.	b	12.	a
3.	d	8.	a	13.	c
4.	d	9.	d	14.	d
5.	c	10.	b	15.	c

Short Essay:

1. In civil law systems, the legislatures create the laws and the judges initiate and conduct the litigation through the inquisitional method of adjudication. In common law systems, the legislatures, administrative agencies and the judges create the laws, the parties initiate and conduct the litigation through the adversary system, and the judges act as referees to insure that the parties follow the procedural rules.

2. When a court decides a case, not only does it resolve the immediate conflict, but it also indicates to the public how the court is likely to decide similar cases in the future. Thus, people gain a better understanding of their rights and responsibilities and are better able to conform their conduct to the requirements of the law. To the extent that courts do not adhere to their precedents and decide similar cases with different results, people cannot be sure whether they were conforming to the law. This would undermine people's confidence in the law.

3. By administering statutes which apply to specific areas of government control, these expert bodies regulate and supervise complicated areas of the economy that are beyond the effectiveness of the traditional branches of government. Thus, they are intended to insure the orderly flow of commerce, the safety of consumers and workers, and the efficient use of resources.

4. They define the structure of a government, the nature and extent of a government's power, and the rights and liberties of the people. In short, they limit the power of a government to enact laws which restrict the rights and liberties of the people.

5. They are similar in that they were both drafted by legal scholars who were concerned that legal rules be good rules that have wide applicability nationwide. They are different in that the Restatements of Law are not law in and of themselves, but are statements of what legal scholars believe the common law to be and where there is more than one rule in existence in the common law what they believe the law should be. In contrast, the UCC is State statute in every State except Louisiana, because the UCC has been adopted by the various State legislatures.

CHAPTER 2

True/False:

1.	T	6.	T	11.	T
2.	F	7.	T	12.	T
3.	T	8.	F	13.	F
4.	F	9.	F	14.	F
5.	T	10.	F	15.	F

Multiple Choice:

1.	c	6.	b	11.	a
2.	b	7.	a	12.	c
3.	c	8.	d	13.	c
4.	d	9.	b	14.	b
5.	c	10.	c	15.	b

Short Essay:

1. An appeal by right is an appeal which the U.S. Supreme Court must hear. Such appeals usually concern the constitutionality of Federal or State statutes. An appeal by writ of certiorari is a discretionary appeal. Such appeals are more likely to be heard if they concern a Federal question of substantial importance or a conflict in the decisions of th U.S. Circuit Courts of Appeal.

2. The judge assumes that all the evidence introduced by the non-moving party is true. He then asks himself whether this evidence, if true, would be sufficient for the jury to find in favor of the non-moving party. If the evidence of the non-moving party, assumed to be true, is not sufficient for the jury to find in favor of the non-moving party, then there is no point in requiring the moving party to try to disprove that evidence. Thus, the moving party will be entitled to a directed verdict.

3. The essential elements are: (1) the relevant facts; (2) a duty owed by the defendant to the plaintiff; (3) the defendant's breach of that duty; (4) injury to the plaintiff proximately caused by the breach; and (5) prayer for relief.

4. The Federal court system includes: (a) District Courts, which are trial courts; (b) Appeals Courts for each circuit in the U.S.; (c) the U.S. Supreme Court, which for the most part hears cases by writ of certiorari on appeal from the various Courts of Appeal. It can also hear some cases on appeal from a State Supreme Court. A typical State court system includes: (a) Municipal Courts or some other type of special local court; (b) District Courts, which are trial courts of general jurisdiction (this court is usually the equity court; in California, it is called the Superior Court and in New York, it is called the Supreme

Court); (c) an intermediate appellate court exists in most States (in some States, the court listed in (b) has some appellate jurisdiction); and (d) a State Supreme Court (in New York, this court is known as the Court of Appeals).

5. (a) Pleadings - service of a Summons and Complaint and of an Answer, Reply and/or Counter-claim; (b) Possible Dumurrer or Motion to dismiss for failure to state a claim; (c) Discovery in the form of depositions, interrogations, requests for admission, and examinations of various sorts; (d) Pre-trial conference to clarify issues and set a date for a trial; (e) Trial - consists of jury selection or voir dire, opening statements, examination and cross-examination of witnesses, closing statements, jury instructions and verdict; (f) Motion for a new trial or executing of judgment if no appeal; (g) Appeal.

CHAPTER 3

True/False:

1.	F	6.	T	11.	F
2.	T	7.	T	12.	F
3.	F	8.	T	13.	F
4.	F	9.	F	14.	T
5.	F	10.	T	15.	F

Multiple Choice:

1.	d	6.	c	11.	a
2.	d	7.	a	12.	c
3.	b	8.	b	13.	d
4.	c	9.	d	14.	b
5.	d	10.	c	15.	d

Short Essay:

1. The United States Supreme Court held in the <u>Sullivan</u> case that for a "public official" to be defamed, the statement must have been made with actual malice. Essentially, this requires the plaintiff to prove that the defendant had knowledge that the statement was false or that she acted in reckless disregard of the truth. The court has extended the actual malice rule to cover candidates for public office and public figures.

2. Substantive due process involves the requirement that a law or governmental action be compatible with fundamental constitutional rights. Procedural due process refers to the governmental process by which substantive legal rights are enforced and the means by which a person is deprived of life, liberty, or property.

3. The rational relationship test is applied to economic legislation. It must be conceivable that the legislation bears a rational relationship to a bona fide governmental interest. The strict scrutiny test is more stringent and is applied to legislation affecting fundamental rights, e.g., right to vote, right to privacy, and free speech.

4. By exercising its constitutional power granted to enact legislation, Congress may create law that is in conflict with State statutes. In such cses, the State law must give way to the Federal law due to the importance of recognizing the Constitution as the supreme law of the land.

5. A State may not regulate activities if it would produce an undue burden on interstate commerce. The

Supreme Court considers whether the regulation is necessary as well as the burden it would impose on interstate commerce. Note that States may not tax goods that continue to remain in the stream of commerce. Taxes may only be imposed after the movement of the goods has ceased.

CHAPTER 4

True/False:

1.	F	6.	F	11.	F
2.	F	7.	F	12.	F
3.	T	8.	T	13.	T
4.	T	9.	T	14.	F
5.	F	10.	F	15.	T

Multiple Choice:

1.	c	6.	c	11.	d
2.	c	7.	d	12.	b
3.	a	8.	a	13.	d
4.	d	9.	d	14.	d
5.	b	10.	b	15.	c

Short Essay:

1. (a) Arrest and booking of suspect; (b) initial appearance at which notice of charges is given and bail is set; (c) preliminary hearing to determine whether probable cause exists to continue the prosecution; (d) arraignment and entry of plea; (e) hearings on evidentiary and other matters; (f) pre-trial conference; (g) trial; (h) possible appeal, if none and there is a finding of guilt, sentencing.

2. Deadly force may be used to protect oneself against an attack that threatens bodily harm or death.

3. If a person voluntarily becomes intoxicated, this test does not allow intoxication to stand as a valid defense. However, if a person is forced against his will to drink alcohol, he can raise involuntary intoxication as a defense.

4. A search warrant is not required in the following situations: (a) hot pursuit of a fugitive; (b) voluntary consent is given; (c) an emergency; (d) search incident to a lawful arrest; (e) criminal evidence in plain view of a law enforcement officer; (f) a delay which would hinder an investigation.

5. A tort is a civil wrong whereas a crime is a wrong against all of society. A tort case can result in a civil judgment awarding money damages. A criminal case can result in a fine and/or imprisonment of the defendant.

CHAPTER 5

True/False:

1.	F	6.	T	11.	F
2.	F	7.	T	12.	T
3.	T	8.	T	13.	T
4.	F	9.	F	14.	F
5.	F	10.	F	15.	T

Multiple Choice:

1.	c	6.	d	11.	c
2.	a	7.	a	12.	b
3.	c	8.	c	13.	b
4.	b	9.	b	14.	d
5.	d	10.	d	15.	b

Short Essay:

1. Trespass is an interference with a person's right to the exclusive possession of his property, while nuisance is an interference with a person's right to use and enjoy his property. Trespass usually occurs when the wrongdoer attempts to exercise possession of the land by actally coming onto the land. Nuisance, on the other hand, usually occurs when the wrongdoer makes it difficult or impossible for the property owner to use or enjoy his land by subjecting it to such irritants as dirt, smoke, noise, or unpleasant odors.

2. For purposes of tort law, a wrongdoer intends to commit a particular tort if he acts with the purpose or motive of achieving the tortious result or with the knowledge that such tortious result is substantially certain to occur as a natural consequence of his actions. For example, if A throws a rock at B, hoping to hit her, he has acted with the purpose of battering her and so he has the requisite intent. If, however, A throws a rock into a large crowd at a rock concert, not hoping to hit anyone at all, he can hardly be surprised when someone is in fact hit. Thus, he will have acted with the knowledge that a battery was substantially certain to occur as a natural consequence of his action and so he would have the requisite intent.

3. In general, one's conduct is privileged if it furthers an interest of such social importance that the harm to an individual is outweighed by the benefit to society. For example, a person may enjoy absolute immunity from liability for defamation even though the defamed individual is harmed because of the overriding public policy which favors complete freedom of speech.

4. (a) Arnold has probably committed assault, battery and conversion, because he put Arnold in fear for his life or safety, inflicted offensive bodily harm and permanently deprived him of his property in the form of the wallet. (b) Arnold has committed the crimes of assault, theft, and robbery. (c) Benjamin can use reasonable force not intended or likely to cause death or serious bodily harm to defend himself. (d) Carl can use the same amount of force to defend Benjamin that Benjamin could use to defend himself.

CHAPTER 6

True/False:

1.	T	6.	F	11.	T
2.	F	7.	T	12.	T
3.	F	8.	T	13.	T
4.	T	9.	F	14.	F
5.	T	10.	T	15.	T

Multiple Choice:

1.	d	6.	c	11.	c
2.	c	7.	d	12.	c
3.	b	8.	c	13.	b

4.	b	9.	c	14.	c
5.	a	10.	a	15.	b

Short Essay:

1. The reasonable man standard is ordinarily used to determine a defendant's negligence by comparing what the defendant did to what a reasonable man acting prudently and with due care under the circumstances would have done. Some statutes impose a specific standard of care upon certain classes of defendants for the protection of certain classes of plaintiffs. Thus, the courts may take the requirements of a statute as the applicable standard of care in determining the negligence of a particular defendant if the defendant violated a statute which is intended to protect a particular class of persons of which the plaintiff is a member against the particular hazard and kind of harm which resulted.

2. The elements are: (1) defendant's legal duty; (2) breach of that duty; (3) the breach proximately caused plaintiff's injuries; (4) which are protected against negligent interference.

3. A person's actions are a cause in fact of an event whenever the event would not have occurred but for those actions or if those actions were a substantial factor in bringing about the event. A person's actions are the proximate cause of an event whenever the consequences of the event are sufficiently closely related to the actions to hold that person legally responsible for those consequences. Thus, proximate cause tends to limit the liability of a person for the consequences of those events which his actions have in fact caused.

4. (a) Engaging in abnormally dangerous activities; (b) keeping of wild animals or of domesticated animals with violent tendencies; (c) manufacturing or selling a defective product that is unreasonably dangerous to the user or consumer.

5. When the standard is applied to children, the individual child's age, experiences and background are considered. When the standard is applied to persons of mental deficiency, they are held to the same standard as a person of normal intelligence.

PART I - SAMPLE EXAM

1.	c	8.	a	15.	b
2.	a	9.	d	16.	d
3.	a	10.	b	17.	a
4.	b	11.	d	18.	c
5.	c	12.	c	19.	b
6.	d	13.	d	20.	b
7.	b	14.	c		

CHAPTER 7

True/False:

1.	F	6.	F	11.	T
2.	T	7.	T	12.	F
3.	F	8.	F	13.	F
4.	F	9.	F	14.	T
5.	T	10.	T	15.	T

Multiple Choice:

1.	a	6.	d	11.	d
2.	b	7.	c	12.	a
3.	d	8.	c	13.	c
4.	b	9.	c	14.	d
5.	a	10.	d	15.	a

Short Essay:

1. The law of contraIts is governed primarily by State common law. An often-cited source of this law is found in the Restatements of the Law of Contracts promulgated by the American Law Institute. The Restatement, Second, of Contracts was adopted by the Institute on May 17, 1979. In all States except Louisiana, however, Article 2 of the Uniform Commercial Code governs sales. A sale is a conract involving the transfer of title to movable, tangible personal property from seller to buyer for a price. In all transactions to which Article 2 does not apply, and in all those governed by Article 2 but where general contract law has not been specifically modified by the Code, contract common law continues to apply.

2. The contract to provide accounting services to Clem for $15,000 does not depend upon mere formality for its legal validity, and therefore is classified as an informal contract. Moreover, the contract involves an oral manifestation of willingness by both parties to enter into a contract, and therefore it is express, even though not in writing. The contract also involves an exchange of promises -- Arthur's accountant's promise to provide accounting services for 1 year in exchange for Clem's promise to pay $15,000 to Arthur -- and therefore is bilateral. There is no evidence that the contract is void, voidable, or otherwise unenforceable. Finally, since, at its inception, neither party has performed any of its duties, the contract is executory.

3. In the nineteenth century, almost total freedom in forming contracts was the rule. The rule of caveat emptor prevailed. The twentieth century has seen a rise in consumer protection and the demise of the total freedom of contract that formerly prevailed. Many of the formalities of contract formation have been relaxed. The narrow view of contract damages of the nineteenth century has been expanded. The doctrine of privity of contract which formerly restricted which parties could enforce contract rights has given way to the current view that permits intended third-party beneficiaries to sue in their own right. Earlier contract theory did not require good faith and fair dealing among contracting parties who dealt at arm's length. Today, the duty of good faith is imposed on parties to a contract and the doctrine of unconscionability protects against grossly unfair dealings.

4. A contract is a binding agreement that the courts will enforce. The Restatement more precisely defines a contract as "a promise or a set of promises for the breach of which the law gives a remedy, or the performance of which the law in some way recognizes as a duty." The four essential ingredients of a binding contract are: (1) manifestation of mutual assent; (2) consideration; (3) legality of object; and (4) capacity of the parties. A quasi contract is an implied in law contract. It is not a contract, because it is not based on an express or implied promise, but it is enforced by the law as if it were a contract in order to avoid injustice.

5. (a) The common law of contracts; (b) the UCC; (c) the common law; (d) the common law.

CHAPTER 8

True/False:

1.	F	6.	T	11.	T
2.	T	7.	T	12.	T
3.	F	8.	F	13.	F
4.	F	9.	F	14.	T
5.	T	10.	T	15.	F

Multiple Choice:

1.	d	6.	c	11.	c
2.	d	7.	d	12.	c
3.	a	8.	d	13.	c
4.	c	9.	c	14.	c
5.	c	10.	b	15.	b

Short Essay:

1. In order for an offer to have legal effect and thereby confer upon the offeree a power of acceptance: (1) it must be communicated to the offeree; (2) it must manifest an intent to enter into a contract; and (3) it must be sufficiently definite and certain in its terms. In order to have the mutual assent requisite to the formation of a contract, the offer must be communicated to the offeree by the offeror or by one authorized to do so on the offeror's behalf. Moreover, the offeree must have knowledge of the offer because he cannot agree to something about which he does not know. The offer must also manifest an intent to enter into a contract. Whether a proposal contains such an intent is judged according to an objective, reasonable person standard, rather than according to the subjective intentions of either party. Finally, the offer must be reasonably certain in its terms so as to provide a court with a basis for determining whether a contract actually exists and for giving an appropriate remedy. If the parties intended to form a contract, it will be supplied by course of dealing, usage of trade, or by inference.

2. An offer may lapse either upon the running of the period of time specified in the offer itself, or if no such time is stated, upon the expiration of a reasonable period of time. The offeror may also revoke his offer at any time prior to acceptance unless the offer is held open by an option contract, is a merchant's firm offer under the Code, is statutorily irrevocable, or is for a unilateral contract and the offeree has begun the requested performance. An offeree's power of acceptance may also be terminated by the offeree's communicated rejection. The rejection is effective from the moment that it is received by the offeror. A counter-offer or a conditional acceptance both indicate an unwillingness to agree to the terms of the offer and, therefore, operate as a rejection. They are to be distinguished, however, from mere inquiries about the possibility of obtaining new or different terms for the contract, as these do not terminate the offer. Finally, an offer will be terminated by the death or insanity of the offeror or of the offeree, or by the destruction of the specific subject matter of the contract, or if performance of the previously valid offer is subsequently made illegal.

3. Under the common law "mirror image" rule, an acceptance must be positive and unequivocal. It may not change any of the terms of the offer, nor add to, subtract from, or otherwise qualify the terms of the offer in any way. Any communication that attempts to do so is not acceptance but rather is a mere counter-offer. In contrast, the Code modifies this rule to account for the realities of modern business practices, the most notable being the extensive use of the standardized business form. The Code focuses on the intent of the parties; if the offeree definitely and reasonably expresses his acceptance of the offer and does not expressly make his acceptance conditional on the buyer's assent to the additional or different terms, then a contract is formed. Here the issue becomes whether the seller's different or additional terms become part of the contract. The Code provides rules to resolve these disputes depending on whether the parties are merchants and on whether the terms are additional or different terms.

4. A revocation is the cancellation of an offer by an offeror. A rejection is the refusal of an offeree to accept an offer. In both cases, the power of acceptance is terminated. A counter-offer by the offeree operates as a rejection.

5. (a) The common law follows the mirror image rule which states that offers and acceptances must be mirror images of each other. In 2-207 (the battle of the forms section), the Code allows for the acceptance of an offer where the terms of the acceptance vary from those of the offer. (b) The common law required definiteness and certainty in the terms of an offer. The UCC has "gap filler" provisions in 2-305, 2-308 and 2-309 that allow a contract to exist when certain terms are left open. (c) At common law, an offer which says it will be kept open for a specified period of time can be terminated at any time in the absence of consideration. Under UCC 2-205, a firm offer in wrting by a merchant is binding even without consideration. (d) At common law, an offer must be accepted in the manner specified. Under the UCC, an offer may be accepted in any manner and by any medium reasonable under the circumstances. In general, the Code looks at whether the parties intended to form a contract rather than at technical rules regarding the exact moment of acceptance of an offer.

CHAPTER 9

True/False:

1. T	6. F	11. T
2. F	7. T	12. T
3. F	8. F	13. T
4. T	9. T	14. F
5. F	10. F	15. F

Multiple Choice:

1. a	6. d	11. c
2. c	7. d	12. c
3. c	8. b	13. c
4. d	9. a	14. d
5. c	10. b	15. b

Short Essay:

1. There are two basic types of duress: The first occurs when a party is compelled to assent to a contract through physical force. This form of duress renders the purported agreement void. The second type of duress involves the use of improper threats to compel a person to enter into a contract. The threat may be explicit or inferred from words or conduct. A subjective test is used to determine whether the threat actually induced assent on the part of the person claiming to be the victim of duress. Duress of this kind renders the resulting contract voidable at the option of the coerced.

2. (a) A false representation; of fact; that is material; and made with knowledge of its falsity and the intention to deceive; that is justifiably relied on. (b) In general, a statement of opinion cannot constitute fraud in the inducement. However, a statement of opinion by an expert is treated as being a statement of fact. (c) Puffing is rather general and is considered to be "sales talk." A statement such as "This is the best car in town" is puffing. A statement such as "Consumer Reports rates this the best car of the year" is a statement of the fact that it has in fact been so rated by Consumer Reports.

3. The contract is voidable due to mutual mistake of fact. The contract here entered into was based upon a mutual mistake of material fact.

4. A person under duress does not voluntarily enter into an agreement and thus needs to be protected by the use of the subjective standard. In the case of fraud in the inducement, the justifiable reliance standard is necessary to protect a buyer from inadvertently making a fraudulent statement to a buyer with more knowledge.

5. A person who enters into a contract under duress by threats of physical force has no free will in making the agreement. What seems like consent is merely an attempt to avoid bodily harm. A person who enters into a contract by improper threats can refuse without incurring harm to his person.

CHAPTER 10

True/False:

1.	F	6.	T	11.	T
2.	F	7.	F	12.	F
3.	F	8.	T	13.	T
4.	F	9.	T	14.	T
5.	T	10.	F	15.	F

Multiple Choice:

1.	d	6.	b	11.	b
2.	c	7.	d	12.	c
3.	a	8.	b	13.	d
4.	b	9.	b	14.	c
5.	d	10.	a	15.	b

Short Essay:

1. Mutuality of consideration means that the promises or performance of both parties to a contract must be legally sufficient for the contract to be enforceable by either. To be legally sufficient, a promise or performance must be either a legal benefit to the promisor or a legal detriment to the promisee. In this regard, legal benefit means the obtaining by the promisor of that which he had no legal right to obtain. A legal detriment means the doing of that which the promisor was under no prior legal obligation to do, or the refraining from doing that which he was previously under no legal obligation to refrain from doing.

2. The two essential elements of consideration are (1) legal sufficiency (value) and (2) bargained-for exchange. In short, consideration is a bargained-for exchange of value. The adequacy of consideration, however, is irrelevant and the subject matter that the parties respectively have exchanged need not have approximate value. Rather, the law will treat the parties as having considered the subject of the exchange adequate by reason of their having freely agreed to the exchange.

3. Illusory promises are not enforceable because their performance is entirely optional in the discretion of the promisor. As such, the promisor suffers no legal detriment by his promise nor does he confer legal benefit. In short, an illusory promise is not legally sufficient. Output and requirements contracts differ from illusory promises in that the promisor agrees to sell all of his output or to purchase all of his supplies of a particular kind rather than to sell or to buy as much as he desires. Moreover, the Code imposes an obligation of good faith on requirements and output contracts to insure against an unfair result.

4. Sam has detrimentally relied upon Big Bucks' promise of a job. He can sue to enforce the contract

based upon his detrimental reliance.

5. (a) No consideration necessary to enforce a firm offer (2-205). (b) No consideration necessary to enforce a modification of a pre-existing contract (2-209). (c) A written waiver or renunciation to settle a dispute is binding without consideration (1-107). (d) Outputs and requirements contracts (2-306(1)). (e) Exclusive dealing contracts (2-306(2)).

CHAPTER 11

True/False:

1.	T	6.	F	11.	F
2.	F	7.	F	12.	T
3.	T	8.	T	13.	F
4.	F	9.	T	14.	T
5.	F	10.	F	15.	T

Multiple Choice:

1.	d	6.	b	11.	b
2.	b	7.	d	12.	a
3.	a	8.	c	13.	d
4.	c	9.	d	14.	c
5.	b	10.	a	15.	b

Short Essay:

1. An essential requirement of a binding promise or agreement is legality of objective. Thus, a contract, by definition, is a legal and enforceable agreement. Illegal agreements are not enforceable in order (1) to discourage such undesirable conduct in the future, and (2) to avoid the inappropriate use of the judicial process in carrying out the socially undesirable bargain.

2. The two types of licensing statutes are those which are regulatory in nature and those enacted in order to raise revenue. A regulatory licensing statute is one designed to protect the public against services provided by unqualified individuals. If violated, there can be no recovery for professional services rendered by a person not having the required license. A revenue-raising licensing statute is one designed solely to raise revenue, and does not seek to protect the public from services provided by incompetents. Accordingly, agreements by persons not having the license required by such a statute are enforceable.

3. It is an agreement often in connection with the sale of a business that the seller will not compete against the buyer for a specific period of time and within a specific geographical area. They are enforceable if they are reasonable. An agreement to refrain from a particular trade, profession or business is effective if (a) the purpose of the restraint is to protect a property interest of the promisee; and (b) the restraint is no more extensive than is reasonably necessary to protect that interest.

4. Section 2-302 of the UCC states that a court may refuse to enforce an unconscionable contract or any part of the contract found to be unconscionable. Section 208 of the Restatement, Second of Contracts has a similar provision. Neither the Code nor the Restatement defines the word "unconscionable."

CHAPTER 12

True/False:

1.	F	6.	T	11.	T
2.	T	7.	T	12.	T
3.	T	8.	F	13.	F
4.	T	9.	F	14.	F
5.	F	10.	F		

Multiple Choice:

1.	d	6.	d	11.	b
2.	b	7.	d	12.	c
3.	a	8.	b	13.	d
4.	c	9.	d	14.	c
5.	b	10.	d	15.	a

Short Essay:

1. Necessaries are generally regarded as those things needed by a person to maintain his particular station in life. Obviously included, therefore, are those items necessary for subsistence and health, such as food, lodging, clothing, and medical services. Other items essential to a person's ability to earn a livelihood may also be included.

2. If a minor disaffirms a contract, most States require only that the minor return any property that he has received from the other party provided it is in the minor's possession at the time of disaffirmance. If an incompetent disaffirms a contract, however, the duty is somewhat different. If the contract is fair and if the competent party had no reason to suspect the other's incompetency, the incompetent must restore the competent party to its status quo by a return of the consideration received or its equivalent in money. Finally, with regard to intoxicated persons, the courts enforce the requirement of restitution even more strictly than with regard to incompetents.

3. Although minors are generally liable for their torts, there is a doctrine in law that if a tort and a contract are so connected or "interwoven" that to enforce the tort action the court must enforce the contract, the minor is not liable in tort.

4. States do not agree whether a minor who misrepresents his age has the power to disaffirm a contract. Under the prevailing view, Tim may disaffirm the contract. However, some States would not allow Tim to disaffirm if the bank officer in good faith relied upon the misrepresentation.

CHAPTER 13

True/False:

1.	F	6.	F	11.	F
2.	T	7.	T	12.	F
3.	T	8.	T	13.	F
4.	F	9.	F	14.	F
5.	F	10.	F	15.	F

Multiple Choice:

1.	c	6.	d	11.	c
2.	b	7.	c	12.	c
3.	d	8.	d	13.	b

4.	b	9.	b	14.	d
5.	b	10.	c	15.	c

Short Essay:

1. An original promise, which is within the Statute of Frauds, is one in which the promisor himself is primarily liable. A collateral promise, by contract, is one in which the promisor is secondarily liable.

2. As a general rule, a promise to transfer an interest in land is within the Statute of Frauds and therefore must comply with its requirements. There are two exceptions to that rule, however. The first involves a promise to make a short term lease. In most States, this is defined by statute to include leases that are for one year or less in duration. The second involves an oral contract that may be enforced if the party seeking enforcement has so changed his position in reasonable reliance upon the contract that injustice can only be prevented by enforcing the contract.

3. The general contract Statute of Frauds requires that an agreement be in writing to be enforceable. The writing has to be signed by the party to be charger or his agent; specify the parties to the contract; and specify with reasonable certainty the subject matter and the essential terms of the unperformed promises. The Statute of Frauds provision under the U.C.C. is more liberal. The Code requires only a writing that is sufficient to indicate that a contract has been made between the parties; signed by the party against whom enforcement is sought or by his authorized agent; and specify the quantity of goods to be sold. An oral contract for the sale of goods may comply with the requirements of the Code in the following four instances: (1) where written confirmation of a contract between merchants is sent and no objection is made within 10 days; (2) where the party defending against the contract admits it by pleading, testimony, or otherwise in court; (3) under certain circumstances, where the goods are to be specially manufactured; and (4) where there has been payment or delivery and acceptance.

4. The parol evidence rule does not apply in the following six situations: (1) where the contract is partly written and partly oral; (2) where there is a clerical or typographical error which obviously does not represent the agreement of the parties; (3) where there is a lack of contractual capacity on the part of one of the parties; (4) where there is a defense asserted of fraud, duress, undue influence, mistake or illegality; (5) a condition precedent agreed upon and to which the entire agreement was made subject; (6) a subsequent mutual rescission or modification of the written contract.

CHAPTER 14

True/False:

1.	T	6.	T	11.	T
2.	F	7.	T	12.	F
3.	T	8.	T	13.	F
4.	F	9.	T	14.	T
5.	F	10.	F	15.	F

Multiple Choice:

1.	a	6.	b	11.	c
2.	c	7.	d	12.	c
3.	d	8.	c	13.	a
4.	a	9.	a	14.	b
5.	d	10.	c	15.	d

Short Essay:

1. An assignment of rights is the voluntary transfer to a third party (the assignee) of the rights arising from a contract. A delegation of duties, on the other hand, is a transfer to a third party (the delegatee) of the contractual duty to perform. An effective assignment extinguishes the assignor's right of performance by the obligor. Therefore, only the assignee has a right to the obligor's performance. A delegation of duty, however, does not extinguish the delegator's duty to perform, but only results in an additional party, the delegatee, also being obligated.

2. Notice to the obligor is not a precondition to a valid assignment. Nevertheless, notice of the assignment should be given because in its absence, an assignee will lose his rights against the obligor if the latter pays the assignor without notice of the assignment. Moreover, the obligor's set-offs and counterclaims against the assignor that arise out of separate transactions and after notice has been given cannot be used against the assignee.

3. The majority American rule regarding the successive assignment of the same contractual rights provides that a prior assignee is entitled to the assigned right and its proceeds to the exclusion of a subsequent assignee. The rule, however, does not apply where the prior assignment is revocable or voidable by the assignor. It also does not apply where the subsequent assignee in good faith and without knowledge of the prior assignment gives value and obtains payment or satisfaction of the obligor's duty; obtains a judgment against the obligor; obtains a novation with the obligor; or obtains possession of a writing of a type customarily accepted as a symbol or as evidence of the right assigned.

4. An intended creditor beneficiary is a third person to whom the promisee owes a legal duty that the performance of the promise is intended to satisfy. An intended gratuitous (or donee) beneficiary, on the other hand, is a third party to whom the promisee intends to make a gift by way of the performance of a bargained-for promise by the promisor. While an intended gartuitous beneficiary only has rights against the promisor, an intended creditor beneficiary has rights against the promisee based upon the original obligation and against the promisor based on the third party beneficiary contract.

CHAPTER 15

True/False:

1.	T	6.	F	11.	T
2.	F	7.	T	12.	T
3.	T	8.	F	13.	T
4.	F	9.	T	14.	F
5.	T	10.	F	15.	T

Multiple Choice:

1.	b	6.	b	11.	b
2.	c	7.	d	12.	c
3.	d	8.	b	13.	d
4.	c	9.	c	14.	c
5.	a	10.	c	15.	b

Short Essay:

1. There is an important difference between the effect of the breach or non-performance of a contract and the effect of the failure or non-occurrence of a condition. A breach of contract, on the one hand,

subjects the promisor to liability. Moreover, depending upon its materiality, the breach may excuse the promisee for non-performance of his duty under the contract. The occurrence or non-occurrence of a condition, on the other hand, either prevents the promisee from acquiring a right or deprives him of a right. It does not, however, subject either party to liability.

2.   At common law, a party was discharged from his duty to perform under the contract on grounds of impossibility only if it was objectively impossible for anyone to perform. The courts also generally regarded frustration of purpose as a discharge where the purpose of the contract was frustrated by fortuitous circumstances that deprived the performance of the value attached to it by the parties. The Restatement and the Code positions, however, are that literal impossibility is not required, and that commercial impracticability resulting from a supervening event will excuse non-performance. The supervening event, however, must have been a "basic assumption" that both parties made when they entered into the contract.

3.   The Code requires that a seller tender goods that conform exactly to the contract. Common law requires a material breach before a party could sue.

4.   Subjective impossibility means that performance can be done, but not by the party to the contract. Objective impossibility means that no one (or virtually no one) can perform as agreed. It does discharge contractual obligations.

CHAPTER 16

True/False:

1. T	6. F	11. T
2. F	7. T	12. F
3. F	8. F	13. T
4. F	9. T	14. F
5. T	10. F	15. T

Multiple Choice:

1. a	6. a	11. c
2. d	7. d	12. b
3. b	8. d	13. c
4. c	9. a	14. d
5. c	10. a	15. d

Short Essay:

1.   Damages are only recoverable for a loss resulting from a breach of contract to the extent that the party in breach had reason to foresee that such loss would be a probable result of such a breach when the parties entered into the contract. The test of foreseeability is an objective one based upon what the breaching party had reason to foresee. A foreseeable loss is one which follows a breach in the ordinary course of events, or from special circumstances of which the party in breach either knew or had reason to know.

2.   Under the doctrine of mitigation of damages, the party injured by a breach of contract must take such steps as may be reasonably calculated to lessen the damages that he may sustain. Damages are not recoverable for losses that the injured party could have avoided without undue risk, burden or

humiliation.

3. The two major equitable remedies applicable to a breach of contract are the decree of specific performance and the injunction. A decree of specific performance orders a breaching party to render the performance promised under the contract. In contrast, an injunction is an order issued by a court of equity commanding a person to refrain from doing a specific act or engaging in specified conduct. Generally, both are available only where damages for a breach would be inadequate. However, a court will not decree specific performance of a contract for personal services. Nor will it issue an injunction to enforce an exclusive personal service contract if the probable result would be to leave the employee without other reasonable means of making a living.

4. Restitution is a return to the aggrieved party of the consideration, or its value, that he gave to the other party. It is available as a remedy in several contractual situations: (1) as an alternative remedy for a breach of contract; (2) for a party in default; (3) for a party who may not enforce a contract because of the Statute of Frauds; and (4) upon the avoidance of a voidable contract.

PART II - SAMPLE EXAM

1. c	8. d	15. b
2. b	9. a	16. b
3. c	10. d	17. b
4. a	11. d	18. d
5. b	12. c	19. d
6. c	13. b	20. b
7. c	14. a	

CHAPTER 17

True/False:

1. T	6. T	11. T
2. T	7. F	12. F
3. F	8. F	13. T
4. F	9. T	14. T
5. T	10. T	15. F

Multiple Choice:

1. b	6. b	11. b
2. a	7. b	12. c
3. d	8. b	13. c
4. d	9. d	14. d
5. c	10. a	15. b

Short Essay:

1. Article 2 of the Uniform Commercial Code is expressly applicable to contracts for the sale of goods, as it defines those terms. General contract law, however, continues to govern apsects of the sale of goods not specifically modified by the Code as well as contracts outside the scope of the Code. These include transactions other than sales, such as bailments, leases and gifts, as well as sales of things other than goods, such as services, real property, and intangibles. Nevertheless, the Code is often applied by analogy to non-sales transactions, thereby expanding the scope of its principles and policies.

2. At common law, the "mirror image" rule required that an acceptance not vary from the terms of the offer. The Code, in contrast, has taken a more liberal approach necessitated by the realities of modern business practices, most notably the standardized business form utilized in most commercial transactions. Accordingly, the Code provides that unless the language in the offer or the surrounding circumstances clearly indicate otherwise, an offer to make a contract invites acceptance in any manner and by any medium reasonable in the circumstances.

3. All transactions within the scope of the Code are subject to a requirement of "good faith" which is defined as "honesty in fact in the conduct or transaction concerned." In addition, in the case of a merchant, the "good faith" standard requires that the merchant observe "reasonable commercial standards of fair dealing in the trade." The first standard is a subjective one, focusing as it does on the motives of the parties involved. The second, however, is an objective standard by which the merchant is held to a standard considered fair in the trade.

4. A firm offer is a written offer by a merchant to buy or to sell goods that states it will be kept open for a period of time of up to three months. Under 2-205 of the Code, such offers are binding on the merchant and cannot be revoked for the time stated or if no time is stated, for a reasonable period of time.

CHAPTER 18

True/False:

1.	T	6.	F	11.	F
2.	F	7.	F	12.	T
3.	F	8.	T	13.	T
4.	T	9.	F	14.	F
5.	T	10.	F	15.	F
				16.	T

Multiple Choice:

1.	b	6.	b	11.	c
2.	d	7.	d	12.	d
3.	a	8.	c	13.	b
4.	b	9.	d	14.	b
5.	b	10.	c	15.	d

Short Essay:

1. At common law, risk of loss was placed upon the party that had title to the goods at the time in question. The Code, however, employs a transactional approach that diminishes the importance of the concept of title. Accordingly, the Code sets forth a detailed set of rules for allocating risk of loss depending on whether there has been a breach of the sales contract. In the absence of a breach, the Code attempts to place the risk of loss upon the party who is more likely to have greater control over the goods or is better able to prevent the loss.

2. A shipment contract is one that authorizes the seller to send the goods to the buyer but does not require the seller to deliver the goods to a particular destination. A destination contract, by contrast, requires the seller to deliver the goods to a particular destination. Under the former, title and risk of loss pass to the buyer at the time and place that the seller delivers the goods to the carrier; under the latter, title and risk of loss pass to the buyer upon tender of the goods to him at that destination.

3. A void title to goods is not title and therefore the holder of void title cannot transfer any interest in the goods. A voidable title is one acquired under circumstances that permit the former owner to transfer and revest himself with title. A holder of voidable title has the power to resell the goods to a bona fide purchaser for value and without notice of any infirmity in the title. If such a subsequent sale takes place, the original seller's right of rescission is cut off and the subsequent bona fide purchaser acquires good title.

4. If goods are held by a bailee and are to be delivered without being moved, risk of loss passes to the buyer on his receipt of a negotiable document of title if one is involved in the transaction. If, however, a non-negotiable document of title is utilized by the bailee as a receipt for the seller's goods being stored, risk of loss passes to the buyer upon tender to him of the document, unless he reasonably objects. If no documents of title are involved, risk of loss passes upon either (a) the delivery by the seller to the bailee of a writing that directs the bailee to transfer the goods to the buyer, or (b) an acknowledgement by the bailee of the buyer's right to possession of the goods.

CHAPTER 19

True/False:

1. T	6. F	11. T
2. F	7. T	12. F
3. F is correct but the question should be qualified		
	8. F	13. F
4. T	9. F	14. T
5. F	10. T	15. F

Multiple Choice:

1. b	6. d	11. b
2. c	7. a	12. c
3. d	8. c	13. a
4. b	9. c	14. d
5. d	10. a	15. d

Short Essay:

1. As a general rule under the Code, a seller's opinion of the goods he sells does not create a warranty. Two exceptions to this rule, however, are: (a) if the seller is an expert and gives his opinion as such, he may be liable; and (b) if an ordinary seller misrepresents his opinion.

2. Under the implied warranty of merchantability, a merchant seller impliedly warrants that the goods that are of the kind in which he deals are merchantable -- i.e., that they are reasonably fit for the general purpose for which they are manufactured and sold, and also that they are of fair, average, and merchantable quality. The warranty may apply to second hand goods, and it can be disclaimed, unless barred by the Magnuson-Moss Act, by a conspicuous writing containing language that specially includes merchantability or a similar oral disclaimer. Under the implied warranty of fitness for a particular purpose, any seller, whether a merchant or a non-merchant, impliedly warrants that the goods are reasonably fit for the particular purpose of the buyer for which the goods are required provided at the time of contracting the seller has reason to know such particular purpose and that the buyer is relying upon the seller's skill and judgment to furnish suitable goods. The disclaimer of an implied warranty to fitness for the particular purpose must be in writing and conspicuous.

3. In order to recover under a theory of strict liability in tort, a seller must show that: (1) the defendant

sold the product in a defective condition; (2) the defendant was engaged in the business of selling such a product; (3) the defective condition was one that made the product unreasonably dangerous to the user or consumer or to his property; (4) that the defect in the product existed at the time it left the hands of the defendant; (5) the plaintiff sustained physical harm or property damage by use or consumption of the product; and (6) the defective condition was the proximate cause of such injury or damage. Many of the traditional obstacles to recovery are not applicable to a claim of strict liability in tort. Liability cannot generally be modified or disclaimed, and there is no requirement of horizontal or vertical privity. Moreover, contributory negligence is, for the most part, not recognized as a valid defense; comparative negligence, however, has on occasion been applied to limit a plaintiff's recovery to account for his degree of fault. Finally, voluntary assumption of the risk is a valid defense to an action based on strict liability in tort.

4.   (a) Manufacturing defects occur when the product is not properly made and fails to meet its own manufacturing specifications. (b) Design defects occur when a product is produced as specified but is dangerous or hazardous because its design is inadequate. (c) Inadequate warnings or instructions are considered a defect when as a result of a failure to warn or to provide adequate directions for safe use, the product becomes dangerous.

CHAPTER 20

True/False:

1. T	6. F	11. T
2. F	7. T	12. T
3. T	8. T	13. T
4. F	9. T	14. F
5. F	10. F	15. F

Multiple Choice:

1. c	6. c	11. a
2. c	7. a	12. d
3. c	8. b	13. b
4. b	9. d	14. c
5. d	10. d	15. d

Short Essay:

1.   The seller's basic performance obligation is to tender delivery of conforming goods to the buyer. He is required to put and to hold goods that conform to the contract at the buyer's disposition and to give the buyer notification reasonably necessary to enable her to take delivery. The buyer has two basic performance obligations: to accept conforming goods tendered by the seller, and to pay for them according to the terms of the contract. Unless the parties otherwise agree, tender of payment or payment by the buyer is a condition to the seller's duty to tender and to complete any delivery.

2.   Unless the parties otherwise agree, the place for delivery of goods is the seller's place of business. Under a shipment contract, however, the seller is obligated to send the goods to the buyer (although he is not required to deliver them to a particular place as in a destination contract). Discharge of his duty of performance under a shipment contract requires the seller to: (1) deliver the goods to a carrier; (2) make a reasonable contract for their shipment; (3) obtain and promptly deliver or tender to the buyer any documents necessary to alow the buyer to obtain possession of the goods from the carrier; and (4) promptly notify the buyer of the shipment.

3. The doctrine of "cure" is a modification of the buyer's right to reject goods upon the seller's failure to comply with the perfect tender rule. When the buyer refuses to accept a nonconforming tender of goods, the seller may, by acting promptly and within the time allowed for performance, make a proper tender or delivery of conforming goods and thereby cure his defective tender or performance. Secondly, the Code allows the seller to cure a non-conforming tender that he had reasonable grounds to believe would be acceptable with or without disclosing the existence of a curable defect to the seller, or if he refuses to accept the seller's attempted cure, the buyer may not assert the defect as an excuse for not accepting the goods or as a breach of contract by the seller if the defect is one that is curable.

4. A rejection is a manifestation by the buyer of his unwillingness to become owner of the goods. To be effective, it must be made within a reasonable time after the goods have been tendered or delivered and the seller must be reasonably notified. A buyer may rightfully reject goods that do not conform to the contract, but any exercise of ownership of the goods by the buyer after rejection is wrongful as against the seller. Finally, a buyer's duty after rejection varies depending on whether or not he is a merchant. A revocation of acceptance is a manifestation of unwillingness to remain the owner of the goods after the buyer has already accepted them. A buyer may revoke his acceptance of nonconforming goods only if the nonconformity substantially impairs the value of the goods and the acceptance was (a) based on the reasonable assumption that the seller would cure the nonconformity and did not, or (b) without discovery of the nonconformity and such acceptance was reasonably induced by the difficulty of discovery before acceptance or by assurances of the seller. Upon revocation of acceptance, the buyer is in the same position with respect to the goods and has the same rights and duties with regard to them as if he had rejected them.

5. The parties to a contract can be relieved of their obligations of full performance in three instances. The first is if there has been a loss of goods that were identified when the contract was made, and the loss occurred without the fault of either party and before risk of loss passed to the buyer. If the loss was total, the contract is avoided; if partial, it is voidable at the election of the buyer. The second instance is upon the non-happening of a presupposed condition that was a basic assumption of the contract. The parties are relieved from their obligation of performance, however, only to the extent of the non-happening of the condition. Finally, where neither party is at fault and the agreed manner of delivery of the goods becomes commercially reasonable, can be tendered by the seller and accepted by the buyer.

CHAPTER 21

True/False:

1.	T	6.	F	11.	F
2.	F	7.	T	12.	T
3.	F	8.	T	13.	F
4.	T	9.	F	14.	T
5.	T	10.	T	15.	T

Multiple Choice:

1.	c	6.	b	11.	c
2.	b	7.	d	12.	c
3.	d	8.	a	13.	a
4.	c	9.	a	14.	d
5.	a	10.	d	15.	c

Short Essay:

1. If a buyer has rightfully rejected the seller's non-conforming tender of goods, the buyer has several non-exclusive remedies for the seller's contract breach. First, the buyer may cancel the contract. He may also recover any payments already made, and establish a security interest in any of the seller's goods that are already in his possession to the extent of any payment of the price already made. Finally, he may also cover and recover damages or simply seek market price damages for the seller's breach.

2. All of the remedies outlined in question 1 are available to a buyer if the seller repudiates a contract, and several more are also available. First, the buyer may mainain an action for replevin of goods that have been identified to the contract if th buyer after a reasonable effort is unable to effect cover for such goods, or if the goods have been shipped under reservation of a security interest in the seller and satisfaction of this security interest has been made or tendered. In addition, if the goods are unique or if money damages would not be an adequate remedy, the buyer may seek specific performance.

3. Several remedies are available to the seller after buyer has wrongfully rejected a conforming tender of goods. First, the seller may cancel the contract. He may also withhold delivery of additional goods and identify goods to the contract. He may resell and recover damages or just recover market price damages. Finally, if appropriate, a seller may bring an action for price -- this is most likely to occur if conforming goods have been lost or damaged after the risk of loss has passed to the buyer, or where goods have been identified to the contract and there is no ready market available for their resale at a reasonable price.

4. A person may sue for specific performance when the goods are unique or in "othe proper circumstances" according to 2-716. The decree may include terms and conditions as to payment of the price, damages, or other relief.

5. The parties may expressly limit or exclude consequential damages unless such limitation or exclusion would be unconscionable. The limitation of consequential damages for personal injury from breach of warranty in the sale of consumer goods is always unconscionable. Limitations of such damages in a commercial contract is not.

PART III - SAMPLE EXAM

1. c	8. d	15. a
2. a is correct but d is better.	9. c	16. c
3. b	10. b	17. d
4. d	11. d	18. c
5. c	12. d	19. b
6. b	13. c	20. a
7. b	14. c	

CHAPTER 22

True/False:

1. T	6. T	11. T
2. F	7. T	12. T
3. T	8. T	13. F
4. F	9. T	14. T
5. F	10. F	15. T

Multiple Choice:

1.	b	6.	c	11.	c
2.	a	7.	a	12.	d
3.	d	8.	c	13.	b
4.	d	9.	d	14.	d
5.	b	10.	b	15.	a

Short Essay:

1. By postdating it.

2. It is non-negotiable because it is not payable to order or to bearer.

3. The requirements of negotiability are: (a) the instrument must be in writing; (b) the insrument must be signed; (c) the instrument must contain a promise or order to pay; (d) the instrument must be unconditional; (e) the instrument must be for a sum certain in money; (e) the instrument must contain no other promise to order; (f) the instrument must be payable on demand or at a definite time; (g) the instrument must be payable to order or to bearer.

4. The notation does not violate the particular fund doctrine and does not destroy the negotiability of the draft. It is a mere bookkeeping notation.

CHAPTER 23

True/False:

1.	F	6.	F	11.	F
2.	T	7.	T	12.	T
3.	T	8.	F	13.	F
4.	F	9.	T	14.	T
5.	T	10.	F	15.	T

Multiple Choice:

1.	c	6.	b	11.	d
2.	b	7.	d	12.	d
3.	a	8.	c	13.	c
4.	d	9.	b	14.	b
5.	c	10.	a	15.	c

Short Essay:

1. Not if you are worried about its being lost or stolen. Remember that bearer paper runs to whoever is in possession of it, so that a finder or thief is entitled payment. On the other hand, if an order instrument such as a check is lost or stolen, the finder or thief is not a holder and is thus not entitled to payment.

2. (1) Blank - merely the indorser's signature makes the instrument bearer paper. (2) Special - designates the person to whose order the instrument is payable. (3) Restrictive - attempts to restrict the rights of the indorsee in some fashion (four different types).

3. A transferee becomes an assignee in two situations: (1) when an instrument that is not negotiable is transferred; and (2) when a negotiable instrument is improperly negotiated such that the transferee is not a holder as where an order instrument is either not indorsed or where it is improperly indorsed.

4. No, negotiation of a negotiable instrument is separate from the underlying contractual transaction. This rule is followed in order to allow negotiable instruments to move freely in the marketplace. It is this feature of negotiability that gives the holder of an instrument the right to payment and that allows a holder in due course a unique legal position in that the holder in due course has greater rights in the instrument than the transferee from whom he received it.

CHAPTER 24

True/False:

1.	T	6.	F
2.	T	7.	T
3.	F	8.	F
4.	T	9.	T
5.	T	10.	F

11.	F
12.	F
13.	T
14.	F
15.	T

Multiple Choice:

1.	a	6.	c
2.	d	7.	d
3.	c	8.	a
4.	a	9.	b
5.	b	10.	c

11.	d
12.	c
13.	b
14.	c
15.	b

Short Essay:

1. Anyone who meets the following requirements may be a holder in due course: (a) a holder who takes the instrument, (b) for value, (c) in good faith and, (d) without notice that there is anything "wrong" with it.

2. A mere holder is nothing more than an assignee. Thus, he takes the rights his transferor had and is subject to the claims and defenses that could be asserted against his transferor. A holder in due course, on the other hand, takes the instrument free from any claims and free from most defenses. Thus, a holder in due course will be entitled to payment in many cases where a mere holder would not be.

3. A holder in due course takes an instrument free from defenses only with respect to parties with whom he has not dealt.

4. In general, when an instrument is incomplete, it may be completed in accordance with the authority given and is then valid and effective as completed. Even the signature may be made by an authorized agent, but you may have a hard time proving to your local merchant that you have authority to sign someone else's checks. The signature notwithstanding, you could legally spend the check by filling in the date, the payee, and the amount of the purchase when your roommate's items have been totalled at the cash register.

CHAPTER 25

True/False:

1.	F	6.	F
2.	T	7.	T
3.	F	8.	T

11.	T
12.	F
13.	F

4.	F	9.	T	14.	T
5.	F	10.	T	15.	F

Multiple Choice:

1.	d	6.	d	11.	a
2.	d	7.	b	12.	a
3.	c	8.	b	13.	c
4.	d	9.	c	14.	d
5.	d	10.	a	15.	b

Short Essay:

1. Yes, when the forgery is that of an indorser's signature (under the presenter's warranty as well as possibly under the imposter of fictitious payee rule), or the drawer's signature if the forgery was due to the drawer's negligence. The drawee can also recover under the presenter's warranty for material alteration of the instrument and against the drawer if the material alteration was due to the drawer's negligence.

2. A drawer is only relieved of liability to the extent of any loss suffered by reason of the delay.

3. Under primary liability, one is absolutely and unconditionally liable, while under secondary liability, one is only liable upon the happening of certain specified events.

4. A drawee is not liable on an instrument until it has accepted it. Under the Code, certification is acceptance. Once a bank or other drawee has certified or accepted an instrument, it is primarily liable on it and the holder must seek payment from the bank rather than the drawer or indorsers.

CHAPTER 26

True/False:

1.	T	6.	T	11.	T
2.	F	7.	F	12.	T
3.	F	8.	T	13.	T
4.	F	9.	F	14.	T
5.	T	10.	T	15.	T

Multiple Choice:

1.	c	6.	a	11.	d
2.	d	7.	d	12.	b
3.	b	8.	c	13.	d
4.	a	9.	c	14.	b
5.	c	10.	a	15.	a

Short Essay:

1. In general, if you do not indorse your check by the time you deposit it, your bank may indorse it for you.

2. The drawer of a check is secondarily liable on the check, so that a holder may sue the drawer for the

amount of the check if the drawee refuses to pay it. Normally, the drawer stops payment in the first place because of a claim or defense against the payee. Such a defense would be valid against the payee or a mere holder, but would not prevent a subsequent holder in due course from obtaining payment.

3. Arthur must examine his bank statement and report the payment of the forged check to the bank. The bank will in all likelihood bear the loss, unless it can find Carl, who will have liability for the forgery both criminally and based upon several of the civil provisions in the Code. The forged signature is that of Carl even though he signed Brad's name. Carl has also breached both the indorser's warranties and the presenter's warranties and thus has liability based on both the contract of indorsement and the warranty provisions of the Code. The bank has liability to Brad for conversion.

4. David is liable for only $50, because he immediately notified the bank within two days of learning of the loss or theft. If he had not immediately notified the bank, his liability would have been for $500. If he had failed to notify the bank within sixty days, he would bear the entire loss.

PART IV - SAMPLE EXAM

1. a	8. a	15. c
2. b	9. b	16. a
3. c	10. b	17. c
4. c	11. c	18. b
5. b	12. d	19. d
6. b	13. b	20. a
7. d	14. b	

CHAPTER 27

True/False:

1. F	6. F	11. T
2. F	7. F	12. T
3. T	8. T	13. T
4. T	9. F	14. F
5. T	10. F	15. F

Multiple Choice:

1. c	5. d	8. b
2. b	6. b is correct; d is possible	9. d
3. d	7. a is correct; d is better	10. c
4. d		

Short Essay:

1. A fiduciary duty arises when one person is entitled to place his trust and confidence in another. Because of this relationship, the agent does not deal with his principal at arm's length. Thus, the agent owes his principal at all times the duties of loyalty, good faith, and full disclosure.

2. An agent may not (a) represent his principal in any transaction in which he has a personal interest; (b) take a position in conflict with the interests of his principal; (c) compete with his principal; (d) act on behalf of a competitor or for persons whose interests conflict with those of the principal; (e) use for his own benefit, and contrary to the interests of his principal, information obtained in the course of the

agency; or (f) make a secret profit out of the subject matter of the agency.

3. In an employer-employee relationship, which is also referred to as the master-servant relationship, the employer has the right to control the physical conduct of the employee. In an employer-independent contractor relationship, the person who engages the independent contractor does not have the right to control the conduct and activities of the independent contractor in the performance of his contract.

4. The principal is under a duty to reimburse his agent for authorized payments made by the agent on behalf of the principal and for authorized expenses incurred by the agent.

CHAPTER 28

True/False:

1.	T	5.	F	8.	F
2.	T	6.	F	9.	T
3.	T	7.	T	10.	F
4.	T				

Multiple Choice:

1.	d	5.	c	8.	a
2.	c	6.	b	9.	a
3.	c	7.	c	10.	c
4.	d				

Short Essay:

1. Actual authority is based upon words or conduct of the principal manifested to the agent. Apparent authority is based upon words or conduct of the principal which manifests to a third person that the agent has actual authority. Actual authority gives an agent both the power and the right to bind his principal in legal relations with third persons, while apparent authority gives the agent the power but not necessarily the right to bind his principal.

2. An agent has the power to bind her principal when the principal is legally bound by the act of the agent. An agent has the right to bind her principal whenever she may do so without violating her duty of obedience by exceeding her actual authority. For example, when an agent has apparent authority but not actual authority, she has the power but not the right to bind her principal. Thus, the principal is legally bound by the act of the agent, but by exceeding her actual authority, the agent has violated her duty of obedience and is liable to the principal for any resulting loss.

3. The obvious answer is that the employer is liable for the torts of his employee, provided, of course, that at the time of the wrongful act the employee was acting within the scope of his employment. The rationale of respondeat superior, however, is to make the employer's vicarious liability the price which the employer must pay for the privilege of enlarging the scope of his business activities through the use of employees. In short, the employer is supposed to treat his vicarious liability as just another business expense which is added to the cost of his products. Thus, the people who end up buying his products, through the higher prices they must pay, are the ones who ultimately bear the loss of the employee's negligence.

4. An agent is personally liable for his tortious acts that injure third persons, whether or not such acts are authorized by the principal and whether or not the principal may also be liable. A principal may be

held liable in damages for his own negligence or recklessness in carrying on an activity through employees or agents. A principal who authorizes his agent to commit a tortious act concerning the property of another is liable for the injury or loss sustained by that person. An independent contractor is generally not the agent or employee of the person for whom he is performing work. Hence, the doctrine of respondeat superior does not apply to torts committed by an independent contractor.

PART V - SAMPLE EXAM

1. T	8. F	15. c
2. F	9. F	16. a
3. T	10. F	17. c
4. T	11. d	18. b
5. T	12. d	19. d
6. F	13. b	20. c
7. T	14. b	

CHAPTER 29

True/False:

1. T	6. T	11. T
2. T	7. F	12. T
3. F	8. T	13. F
4. F	9. F	14. F
5. F	10. T	15. F

Multiple Choice:

1. d	6. c	11. a
2. b	7. b	12. d
3. d	8. d	13. b
4. a	9. d	14. b
5. d	10. d	15. c

Short Essay:

1. The court will look for a community of interest for business purposes. Specifically, the court will determine whether there exists: (a) A business -- an intention to acquire profits; a continuous series of commercial activities. (b) Co-ownership -- a community interest in the capital employed in the business; a sharing of profits and losses; a community of authority to conduct the business activities.

2. When times are good and the business is making money, an employee may want to prove that he is a partner so that he may share in the profits. On the other hand, when times are bad and the business is losing money, creditors may want to prove that an employee or an investor is a partner and thus liable for the debts of the partnership.

3. A partnership is recognized as a legal entity in certain respects, but as an aggregation of individuals in others. For example, a partnership is considered an entity in that: (a) every partner is considered its agent; (b) its assets, liabilities, and business transactions are considered separate from those of its partners; (c) it may hold title to real estate, sue, and be sued in its own name. On the other hand, a partnership is considered an aggregation in that: (a) its existence is tied to the continued participation of its partners; (b) its debts are ultimately the debts of its partners; (c) its income is taxed to the individual

partners.

4. It's a close question. Although co-ownership alone is not sufficient to establish the existence of a partnership, the sisters here have co-ownership and the sharing of profits. The carrying on of a rental business that is jointly owned where there is a sharing of the profits would seem to establish the existence of a partnership. The sharing of profits and/or losses is considered to be strong evidence of the existence of a partnership where there is co-ownership of property.

CHAPTER 30

True/False:

1. T	6. T	11. F
2. F	7. F	12. T
3. T	8. F	13. T
4. T	9. T	14. F
5. F	10. T	15. F

Multiple Choice:

1. d	6. c	11. c
2. c	7. b	12. b
3. d	8. b	13. d
4. d	9. a	14. c
5. b	10. b	15. c

Short Essay:

1. Partners may by agreement vary their legal rights and obligations so long as the rights of third parties are not affected and standards of fairness among the partners are maintained.

2. Partners may agree to: (a) share profits and losses unequally; (b) pay interest on capital contributions; (c) pay salaries to one or more of the partners; (d) share management responsibilities unequally; (e) keep the books of the partnership somewhere other than the principal place of business and to limit partners' access to them.

3. A partner has actual implied authority to: (a) hire and fire employees whose services are necessary to carry on the business of the partnership; (b) purchase property necessary for the business; (c) make repairs reasonably necessary for the proper conduct of the business; (d) make contracts which are incidental to the business; (e) sell goods in accordance with the purposes for which the business is operated; (f) receive payment of sums due the partnership; (g) pay debts due from the partnership arising out of the business enterprise; (h) direct the ordinary operations of the business.

4. In the absence of an agreement on the sharing of profits, the UPA provides that profits must be shared equally, regardless of the capital contribution of each of the partners. Each partner would receive $12,000.

CHAPTER 31

True/False:

1. T	6. F	11. T

2.	T	7.	F	12.	F
3.	F	8.	F	13.	T
4.	F	9.	T	14.	F
5.	F	10.	T	15.	T

Multiple Choice:

1.	b	6.	d	11.	a
2.	c	7.	a	12.	d
3.	a	8.	c	13.	d
4.	c	9.	d	14.	c
5.	c	10.	b	15.	b

Short Essay:

1. Winding up a partnership involves: (a) completing unfinished business; (b) collecting receivables; (c) reducing assets to cash; (d) taking inventory; (e) auditing the partnership books; (f) paying creditors; (g) distributing the remaining assets to the partners.

2. Dissolution may be brought about by: (a) an act of the parties; (b) operation of law; (c) court order.

3. The order of distribution of an insolvent partner's assets is: (a) debts and liabilities owing to non-partnership creditors; (b) debts and liabilities owing to partnership creditors; (c) contributions owing to other partners by reason of payments by them to partnership creditors in excess of their respective share of the liabilities of the firm.

4. The order of distribution of a general partnership's assets is: (a) to creditors other than partners; (b) to partners other than for capital and profits; (c) to partners in respect of capital; (d) to partners in respect of profits. The $123,000 would be distributed as follows:

    ```
    123,000
    -40,000    to outside creditors
     83,000
     -2,000    expenses of winding up
     81,000
    -15,000    loan by Elvis and Fred
     66,000
    -45,000    return of partners' capital
     21,000    divided by 3 = $7,000 profit to each of the three partners
    ```

CHAPTER 32

True/False:

1.	T	6.	F	11.	F
2.	F	7.	T	12.	F
3.	T	8.	F	13.	F
4.	F	9.	T	14.	T
5.	T	10.	F	15.	T

Multiple Choice:

1.	d	6.	b	11.	d
2.	a	7.	c	12.	b
3.	b	8.	b	13.	a
4.	c	9.	d	14.	c
5.	d	10.	d	15.	d

Short Essay:

1. A limited partner may rightfully demand the return of his contribution upon: (a) dissolution of the partnership; (b) the date specified in the certificate for its return; (c) six months' written demand if no time is specified in the certificate for the return of the contribution or for dissolution.

2. A limited partner is protected against unlimited personal liability only if the following conditions are met: (a) there is substantial compliance in good faith with the requirement that a certificate of limited partnership be filed; (b) the surname of the limited partner does not appear in the partnership name; (c) the limited partner does not take part in control of the business.

3. A limited partnership is dissolved: (a) at the time, or upon the happening of the events, specified in the certificate; (b) upon the unanimous written consent of all the parties; (c) upon the withdrawal of a general partner; (d) by a decree of judicial dissolution.

4. (a) fiduciary duty; (b) duty of obedience; (c) duty of care.

PART VI - SAMPLE EXAM

1.	b	8.	c	15.	c
2.	d	9.	b	16.	d
3.	b	10.	d	17.	d
4.	c	11.	d	18.	b
5.	a	12.	a	19.	b
6.	c	13.	c	20.	c
7.	c	14.	d		

CHAPTER 33

True/False:

1.	T	6.	F	11.	T
2.	F	7.	F	12.	T
3.	T	8.	F	13.	T
4.	T	9.	F	14.	F
5.	T	10.	T	15.	T

Multiple Choice:

1.	a	6.	d	11.	b
2.	d	7.	a	12.	a
3.	c	8.	b	13.	a
4.	c	9.	d	14.	d
5.	c	10.	a	15.	d

Short Essay:

1. A corporation is created by statutory authorization; it is a legal entity; it may be perpetual; its shareholders are not generally liable for its debts; its stock is freely transferable; its business is managed by a board of directors; its shareholders are not its agents; it may sue and be used in its own name. A partnership, on the other hand, is created by agreement of the partners; it is a legal entity for some, but not all purposes; it is dissolved by the withdrawal of a partner; its partners are subject to unlimited liability for its debts; the interest of a partner is transferable subject to certain conditions; each partner is entitled to participate in the management of the business; each partner is an agent of the partnership; all partners are parties in actions brought by or against the partnership.

2. A de facto corporation may be formed if: (a) there exists a general corporation statute; (b) there is a bona fide attempt to comply with that law in organizing a corporation under that statute; (c) there is actual exercise of corporate power by conducting a business in the belief that a corporation has been formed.

3. A court will pierce the corporate veil where the shareholders have not: (a) provided an adequate financial basis for the business; (b) conducted the business on a corporate basis.

CHAPTER 34

True/False:

1.	F	6.	T	11.	F
2.	F	7.	F	12.	T
3.	T	8.	T	13.	F
4.	T	9.	F	14.	T
5.	T	10.	T	15.	F

Multiple Choice:

1.	c	6.	b	11.	c
2.	d	7.	d	12.	b
3.	a	8.	c	13.	c
4.	c	9.	a	14.	c
5.	b	10.	b	15.	c

Short Essay:

1. A shareholder has the right to: (a) participate in control of the corporation; (b) participate in the earnings of the corporation; (c) particpate in the residual assets of the corporation upon dissolution.

2. Preferred stock is usually issued with a par value because such stock usually has a liquidation preference which, for all practical purposes, acts as a par value. For example, when stock has a par value, only the consideration received for the stock in excess of par value may be allocated to capital surplus. Likewise, when stock has a liquidation preference, only the consideration received for the stock in excess of the amount of liquidation preference may be allocated to capital surplus, and, when a liquidation preference is provided, preferred stock usually has priority over common to the extent of the par value of the stock.

3. A court will grant an injunction where: (a) demand has been made upon the directors before commencement of the suit; (b) earnings or surplus are available out of wich a dividend may be declared;

(c) the earnings or surplus is in the form of available cash; (d) the directors have abused their discretion in withholding dividend.

4. The transferor warrants that: (a) the transfer is effective and rightful; (b) the security is genuine and has not been materially altered; (c) he knows of no fact that might impair the validity of the security.

CHAPTER 35

True/False:

1. F	6. T	11. T
2. T	7. F	12. T
3. F	8. F	13. F
4. F	9. T	14. F
5. T	10. T	15. F

Multiple Choice:

1. c	6. a	11. b
2. a	7. b	12. b
3. b	8. d	13. c
4. a	9. b	14. b
5. c	10. c	15. d

Short Essay:

1. A shareholder may only inspect the books and records of the corporation for a proper purpose. Thus, a shareholder may be denied his right if he attempts to obtain the information for such improper purposes as use by a competitor or sale to a third party.

2. Shareholder approval is required to make certain fundamental changes in the corporation. These changes include: (a) amending the articles of incorporation; (b) reducing the stated capital; (c) effecting a merger; (d) effecting a consolidation; (e) selling or leasing all or substantially all of the assets of the corporation other than in the usual and regular course of business; (f) effecting a compulsory share exchange.

3. The board of directors has general authority to manage the business and affairs of the corporation. This authority invests the board with the power to: (a) select and remove officers; (b) set management compensation; (c) determine the capital structure; (d) declare dividends; (e) amend the bylaws.

4. Directors and officers are required to be: (a) obedient; (b) reasonably diligent; (c) completely loyal.

5. Directors and officers are required to perform their duties with such care as an ordinarily prudent person in a like position would use under similar circumstances.

CHAPTER 36

True/False:

1. T	6. T	11. T
2. F	7. F	12. F
3. T	8. T	13. T

4. T	9. T	14. F
5. T	10. T	15. F

Multiple Choice:

1. d	6. c	11. d
2. d	7. b	12. c
3. c	8. a	13. d
4. a	9. b	14. c
5. d	10. c	15. d

Short Essay:

1. Fundamental changes include: (a) charter amendments; (b) mergers; (c) consolidations; (d) dissolution; (e) sale or lease of all or substantially all of the corporation's assets not in the usual and regular course of business; (f) compulsory share exchange.

2. Under modern statutes, the typical procedure involves: (a) adoption of a resolution by the board setting forth the proposed amendment; (b) approval by a majority vote of the shareholders; (c) execution and filing of articles of amendment with the secretary of state; (d) issuance of the certificate of amendment by the secretary of state.

3. This may be accomplished by: (a) purchase or lease of the assets; (b) purchase of a controlling stock interest in the other corporation; (c) merger with the other corporation; (d) consolidation with the other corporation.

4. A dissenting shareholder must: (a) file with the corporation a written objection to the proposed corporate action prior to the vote of the shareholders; (b) refrain from voting in favor of the proposed corporate action either in person or by proxy; (c) make a written demand upon the corporation on a form provided by that corporation within the time period set by the corporation, which may not be less than thirty days after the corporation mails the form.

PART VII – SAMPLE EXAM

1. b	8. c	15. a
2. a	9. d	16. c
3. d	10. a	17. d
4. c	11. d	18. b
5. c	12. c	19. b
6. b	13. a	20. a
7. c	14. d	

CHAPTER 37

True/False:

1. T	6. F	11. F
2. F	7. F	12. T
3. F	8. F	13. F
4. F	9. T	14. F
5. T	10. T	15. T

Multiple Choice:

1.	c	6.	d	11.	c
2.	d	7.	c	12.	c
3.	a	8.	c	13.	b
4.	a	9.	d	14.	c
5.	b	10.	b	15.	a

Short Essay:

1. There are two steps that a lender must execute in order to obtain a perfected security interest in the boat as collateral for a loan. The first is to create a security interest and have it "atach" to the collateral the boat. Attachment occurs upon: (1) the giving of value by the secured party (the lender); (2) the debtor acquiring rights in the boat; and (3) the secured party takes possession of the boat or a security agreement is entered into which is in writing and which contains a description of the collateral and is signed by the debtor. The second step is for the secured party to perfect the security interest. In this case, where the collateral is a boat, perfection is most likely to be effected by filing a financing statement, signed by the debtor, in the appropriate offices. However, perfection can also be obtained by possession or by automatic perfection if the lender satisfies the requirements of a PMSI in consumer goods.

2. (a) Transactions involving real estate are not within the scope of Article 9 of the Code, but instead are subject to State law governing security interests in real property. (b) A sewing machine would be treated the same as the boat. (c) In most States, security interest in motor vehicles must be perfected by a notation on the certificate of title rather than by filing a financing statement. (d) Shares of stock are classified as "instruments," and with two exceptions, the only way to perfect a security interest in them is to take possession of them.

3. A purchase money interest in consumer goods is one in which a seller of consumer goods retains an interest in them by way of a security agreement or by which a lender loans funds for the debtor to purchase the goods. A purchase money security interest in consumer goods is perfected automatically and immediately upon attachment without the necessity of filing a financing statement.

CHAPTER 38

True/False:

1.	F	6.	F	11.	T
2.	T	7.	T	12.	F
3.	T	8.	F	13.	F
4.	F	9.	F	14.	T
5.	T	10.	F	15.	F

Multiple Choice:

1.	b	6.	b	11.	d
2.	a	7.	b	12.	a
3.	d	8.	c	13.	d
4.	c	9.	d	14.	c
5.	d	10.	d	15.	a

Short Essay:

1. The bankruptcy process commences with the filing of either a voluntary or an involuntary petition. This filing operates as a stay against attempts by both secured and unsecured creditors to begin or continue to recover claims against the debtor, to enforce judgments against the debtor, or to create or enforce liens against property of the debtor. A trustee is then appointed by the court (he is selected by a vote of the creditors in proceedings under Chapter 7) to collect, liquidate and distribute the debtor's estate.

2. Discharge is the termination of all debts of the debtor for allowed claims. A discharge of a debt voids any judgment obtained at any time with respect to that debt and operates as an injunction against the commencement or continuation of any action to recover that debt. An agreement between a debtor and a creditor permitting the creditor to enforce a discharged debt is enforceable to the extent permitted by State law, but only if: (a) the agreement was made before the discharge has been granted; (b) the debtor has not rescinded the agreement within 30 days after it becomes enforceable; (c) the court has informed a debtor who is an individual that he is not required to enter into such an agreement and explains the legal effect of the agreement; and (d) if the debt is a consumer debt, the court approves the agreement as not imposing an undue hardship upon the debtor and in the debtor's best interest.

3. The trustee in bankruptcy is made an ideal lien creditor. He possesses every right and power conferred by the law of the State upon its most favored creditor who has acquired a lien by legal or equitable proceedings. He need not locate an actual existing lien creditor, for he assumes the rights and powers of a purely hypothetical lien creditor.

4. A trustee in bankruptcy can recover a preferential transfer from the debtor to a creditor if the transfer was made to or for the benefit of a creditor; for or on account of an antecedent debt owed by the debtor before such transfer was made; made while the debtor was insolvent; made on or within 90 days before the date of the filing of the petition; and that enables such creditor to receive more than he would have received under Chapter 7.

5. At least three non-bankruptcy forms of compromise have been developed to provide relief to debtors. The first is a composition which is a contract or agreement between the debtor and his creditors by which the latter receive a pro rata portion of their claims and the debtor in turn is discharged from the balance of the claims. A second is an assignment for the benefit of creditors, which is a voluntary transfer by the debtor of some or all of his property to a trustee who applies the property to pay all of the debtor's debts. Finally, a court of equity can appoint a disinterested person called a receiver to collect and preserve the debtor's assets and income, and then to dispose of them at the direction of the court that appointed him.

PART VIII - SAMPLE EXAM

1.	c	8.	b	15.	d
2.	b	9.	d	16.	b
3.	a	10.	d	17.	c
4.	a	11.	d	18.	d
5.	c	12.	d	19.	b
6.	a	13.	a	20.	c
7.	d	14.	d		

CHAPTER 39

True/False:

1.	F	6.	F	11.	T
2.	T	7.	T	12.	T

3.	T	8.	T	13.	F
4.	F	9.	f	14.	T
5.	F	10.	F	15.	T

Multiple Choice:

1.	d	6.	c	11.	a
2.	b	7.	b	12.	c
3.	d	8.	d	13.	c
4.	b	9.	c	14.	c
5.	d	10.	a	15.	c

Short Essay:

1. Federal and State antitrust statutes are designed to prevent unreasonable concentration of economic power which would weaken or destroy free and open competition in the marketplace.

2. Economic theory predicts that the goal of every monopolist is to utilize its power to limit production and increase prices. Thus, a monopolistic market will produce fewer goods at a higher price than a competitive market.

3. Monopolization requires: (a) sufficient monopoly power; (b) unfair conduct in attaining or using that power.

4. An attempt to monopolize requires: (a) proof of a specific intent to monopolize; (b) a dangerous probability of achieving monopoly power.

CHAPTER 40

True/False:

1.	F	6.	F	11.	T
2.	T	7.	T	12.	F
3.	T	8.	F	13.	F
4.	F	9.	T	14.	T
5.	F	10.	T	15.	F

Multiple Choice:

1.	c	6.	d	11.	c
2.	b	7.	a	12.	a
3.	c	8.	c	13.	d
4.	d	9.	c	14.	b
5.	d	10.	c	15.	b

Short Essay:

1. The primary purpose of Federal securities regulation is to prevent fraudulent practices in the sale of securities and thereby maintain public confidence in the securities markets.

2. A registration statement usually includes: (a) a description of the registrant's properties and business; (b) a description of the significant provisions of the security to be offered for sale, and its relationship to

the registrant's other capital securities; (c) place a legend on the securities certificate stating that the securities have not been registered and that they are restricted securities.

3. An issuer must take reasonable care to assure against such sales. Reasonable care includes, but is not limited to, the following: (a) making reasonable inquiry to determine if the purchaser is acquiring the securities for herself or for other persons; (b) providing written disclosure prior to the sale to each purchaser that the securities have not been registered and therefore cannot be resold unless they are registered or an exemption from resale is available; and (c) placing a legend on the securities certificate stating that the securities have not been registered and that they are restricted securities.

4. The profit is calculated by subtracting the lowest purchase price from the highest sale price that occur within six months of each other. No offset is permitted for losses.

CHAPTER 41

True/False:

1.	F	6.	F	11.	T
2.	T	7.	T	12.	F
3.	T	8.	T	13.	F
4.	F	9.	F	14.	T
5.	T	10.	F	15.	T

Multiple Choice:

1.	a	6.	d	11.	b
2.	b	7.	c	12.	d
3.	a	8.	b	13.	c
4.	c	9.	d	14.	d
5.	b	10.	c	15.	a

Short Essay:

1. A warrantor must: (a) disclose in clear and understandable language the warranty that is to be offered; (b) describe the warranty as either "full" or "limited"; (c) not disclaim implied warranties if a written warranty is given.

2. Under a "full" warranty, the warrantor must: (a) agree to repair without charge the product to conform with the warranty; (b) not limit the duration of any implied warranty; (c) give the consumer the option of a refund or replacement if repair is unsuccessful; (d) not exclude consequential damages unless conspicuously noted.

3. The creditor must disclose: (a) the cost of the credit; (b) when the finance charge is imposed and how it is computed; (c) what other charges may be imposed; (d) whether a security interest is retained or acquired by the creditor.

4. The creditor must disclose: (a) the total amount financed; (b) the cash price; (c) the number, amount, and due dates of installments; (d) delinquency charges; (e) a description of the security, if any.

5. The card issuer may collect up to $50 if: (a) the card has been accepted; (b) the issuer has furnished adequate notice of potential liability to the cardholder; (c) the issuer has provided the cardholder with a statement of the means by which the issuer may be notified of the loss or theft of the card; (d) the

unauthorized use occurs before the card holder has notified the issuer of the loss or theft; (e) the issuer has provided a method by which the user can be identified as the person authorized to use the card.

CHAPTER 42

True/False:

1.	T	6.	T	11.	F
2.	F	7.	F	12.	T
3.	F	8.	F	13.	T
4.	T	9.	T	14.	F
5.	F	10.	T	15.	T

Multiple Choice:

1.	b	6.	c	11.	d
2.	c	7.	b	12.	d
3.	a	8.	a	13.	b
4.	c	9.	a	14.	d
5.	d	10.	b	15.	c

Short Essay:

1. The basic defenses are: (a) a bona fide seniority system; (b) a bona fide merit system; (c) a bona fide occupational qualification; (d) a professionally developed ability test; (e) a system based on quantity or quality of production; (f) any reasonable system which does not discriminate on a prohibited basis.

2. The remedies are: (a) recovery of back pay; (b) injunctive relief; (c) affirmative action; (d) reinstatement.

CHAPTER 43

True/False:

1.	F	5.	T	8.	F
2.	T	6.	F	9.	F
3.	T	7.	T	10.	T
4.	F				

Multiple Choice:

1.	b	3.	d	5.	b
2.	d	4.	a	6.	c

Short Essay:

1. There are many forms of multinational enterprises. They include: (a) direct export sales; (b) the use of foreign agents; (c) the use of foreign distributors; (d) licensing to a foreign firm; (e) joint ventures; and (f) the use of a wholly owned subsidiary. As a company just entering the foreign market, WCA should first look at direct export, the use of a foreign agent or the use of a foreign distributor. If it considers the use of a foreign agent or the use of a foreign distributor, it should carefully study the agent or the distributor before entering into agreements and should consult legal counsel regarding the laws of the

particular country in which it wishes to do business with particular reference to any special provisions regarding the termination of an agent or distributor.

2. Expropriation is a governmental taking of foreign-owned property for a public purpose. When property is expropriated by a foreign government, the government must pay for it. Confiscation is a governmental taking of foreign-owned property without payment or with inadequate payment. To protect itself, a company should take out insurance with the Overseas Private Investment Company.

3. The company should have a good working relationship with a bank that deals in the international sector and that has correspondent banks around the world. The company should consider requiring the buyer to furnish a letter of credit, which is a promise by a buyer's bank to pay the seller provided that certain conditions are met. A letter of credit transaction affords the seller protection against the possibility of nonpayment when dealing in the international sector.

4. A contract involving the sale of goods between a seller in the United States and a buyer in a foreign country should consider such items as: (a) the official language of the contract; (b) the law that governs any breach and if the other country is a party to th CISG whether that will govern the transaction; (c) how any disputes will be settled; (d) acceptable currencies and methods of payment; and (e) a force majeure clause apportioning liabilities and responsibilities in the event of any unforeseen occurrences.

PART IX - SAMPLE EXAM

1. b	8. a	15. c
2. c	9. c	16. d
3. d	10. c	17. c
4. c	11. b	18. c
5. a	12. b	19. d
6. b	13. d	20. b
7. b	14. d	

CHAPTER 44

True/False:

1. T	6. T	11. F
2. T	7. T	12. F
3. T	8. F	13. F
4. F	9. T	14. F
5. F	10. F	15. T

Multiple Choice:

1. c	6. b	11. d
2. b	7. c	12. c
3. d	8. c	13. c
4. d	9. b	14. a
5. d	10. a	15. d

Short Essay:

1. Real property consists of all interests in land. Personal property, in contrast, is every other thing or interest identified as property. A fixture is an item of personal property that has been attached to realty

so that an interest in it arises under real property law. These classifications are significant in that real and personal property rights are governed by different principles of law. Tangible property is property that exists in a physical form; all other property is classified as intangible property. Once again, the determination of various property rights can depend on whether property is classified as tangible or intangible.

2. A fixture is an article or piece of personal property that has been attached in some manner to land or a building so that an interest in it arises under real property law. The intent of the parties as expressed in their agreement will control that determination, but in the absence of an agreement, the courts will look to: (1) the physical relationship of the item to the land; (2) the intention of the person who attaches the item to the land; (3) the purpose served by the item in relation to the person who brought it there; and (4) the interest of that person in the land at the time of the attachment of the item.

3. A gift is a transfer of property from one person to another without consideration. A sale, on the other hand, is a transfer of title to specified existing goods for a consideration. The basic difference then, is the lack of consideration needed for an effective gift; in its place, however, is substituted a requirement of completed delivery of the gift.

CHAPTER 45

True/False:

1.	F	6.	T	11.	T
2.	T	7.	T	12.	T
3.	T	8.	F	13.	T
4.	F	9.	T	14.	F
5.	T	10.	F	15.	T

Multiple Choice:

1.	c	6.	d	11.	b
2.	b	7.	a	12.	b
3.	d	8.	b	13.	b
4.	d	9.	d	14.	c
5.	b	10.	c	15.	b

Short Essay:

1. The four essential elements of a bailment are: (1) the delivery of lawful possession of (2) specific personal property by the bailor to the bailee (3) without transfer of title for a determinable time (4) at the end of which the bailee is obligated to return the property either to the bailor or to a person having a superior right of possession.

2. The three kinds of bailments are those for the benefit of the bailee, those for the benefit of the bailor, and mutual benefit bailments. In a mutual benefit bailment, the bailee must exercise the degree of care that a reasonably prudent person would exercise under the same circumstances. If the bailment is one for the benefit of the bailee only, a higher degree of care is expected, and if for the bailor's benefit only, a lower degree of care.

3. Since it is often difficult to show that a bailee's lack of care was the cause of the injury to the bailed goods, the bailor is afforded a presumption that the bailee was at fault. The bailor only needs to show that the goods were delivered by way of bailment and that the bailee failed to return them or that they

were returned in a damaged condition. The burden then rests upon the bailee to prove that he exercised the degree of care required him.

4.   Common carriers and private carriers are both bailees, but the common law imposes an extraordinary liability upon the common carrier because of the public nature of its services. For example, a common carrier has a duty to serve the public to the limits of its capacity and, within those limits, to accept for carriage goods of the kind that it normally transports. A private carrier, however, has no duty to accept goods for carriage except where it agrees to do so by contract. A private carrier generally is held liable as an ordinary bailee with respect to the goods that it undertakes to carry. The common carrier, on the other hand, is held to a stricter duty that approaches that of an insurer of the safety of the goods. Finally, both common and private carriers are under an absolute duty to deliver the goods to the person to whom they are consigned by the shipper.

CHAPTER 46

True/False:

1.	T	6.	F	11.	F
2.	T	7.	F	12.	F
3.	F	8.	T	13.	T
4.	F	9.	T	14.	T
5.	T	10.	T	15.	F

Multiple Choice:

1.	c	6.	c	11.	d
2.	c	7.	d	12.	d
3.	b	8.	c	13.	b
4.	d	9.	c	14.	d
5.	d	10.	b	15.	b

Short Essay:

1.   The two basic characteristics of the fee simple estate are the holder's absolute rights of transferability and of transmitting by inheritance. In contrast, a qualified fee is one that it is possible to convey or will to another to enjoy absolutely, subject, however, to the possibility that it will be taken away at a later date if a certain event takes place.

2.   A reversion is the general interest that the grantor retains if he conveys away less than his entire estate. It is a present estate to be enjoyed in the future. A possibility of reverter exists when the property conveyed may return to the grantor or his successor in interest because of the happening of an event upon which a fee simple estate was to terminate. A possibility of reverter is just an expectancy and is not a present estate. Finally, a remainder is an estate in property that, like a reversion, will take effect in possession if at all upon the termination of a prior estate created by the same instrument. Unlike a reversion, however, a remainder is held by a person other than the grantor or his successors. There are two kinds of remainders -- vested and contingent.

3.   Under an assignment, both the assignee and the assignor are bound to the obligation to the landlord, as well as with respect to any violations of other covenants that run with the land. A sublease, however differs from an assignment in that it involves the transfer of less than all of the original tenant's rights in the lease. Moreover, a sublessee's obligations run solely to the original tenant who in turn remains liable to the lessor, and the lessor has no right or action against the sublessee under any of the covenant

contained in the original lease.   The original tenant, however, remains liable to the landlord in all respects.

4.   At common law, a tenant has an implied obligation to pay a reasonable rent at the end of the term. Moreover, a landlord could not remove a tenant for non-payment of rent, but most jurisdictions today have changed that rule by statute.   The tenant at common law is not relieved of his liability for rent nor is he allowed to terminate the lease if the premises are destroyed.   Similarly, the landlord had few implied duties or rights under the common law of leaseholds.   He must give the tenant a right to possession at the beginning of the lease, but in most States he is not required to give the tenant actual possession.   Moreover, he has an implied duty to provide for the tenant's right to "quiet enjoyment" of the premises.   He is, however, under no obligation to maintain the premises in a tenantable condition or to make them fit for any purpose, although some courts have abandoned this rule as it applies to residential leases.   Finally, except for the common areas remaining under his control, the landlord has no duty to repair the premises.

5.   The two types of easements are the easement appurtenant and the easement in gross.   The former is more common and the rights created by it pertain to the land itself and not to the particular individuals that create them.   Moreover, both the burden and the benefit of an appurtenant easement pass with the land.   An easement in gross, however, is personal to the particular individual that received the right.   It does not depend upon the ownership of the land, and therefore amounts to little more than an irrevocable personal right to use the land.   A profit aprendre is a right to remove the produce of another's land.   Like an easement, a profit may arise by prescription, but if the act of the parties, it must be created with all of the formalities of a grant of an estate in real property.   Finally, unless clearly designated as exclusive, a profit is always subject to a similar use by the owner of the land.   A license is merely permission to make use of one's land.   It creates no interest in the property and is terminable at the will of the grantor.   Finally, no formality is necessary to create or to destroy one.

CHAPTER 47

True/False:

1. F	6. F	11. T
2. T	7. T	12. T
3. T	8. F	13. F
4. F	9. T	14. F
5. F	10. F	15. T

Multiple Choice:

1. b	6. d	11. d
2. d	7. a	12. d
3. a	8. b	13. c
4. b	9. d	14. d
5. c	10. d	15. d

Short Essay:

1.   The two essential documents involved in the transfer of real estate are the contract of sale and the deed. The conduct of sale must be in writing to satisfy the Statute of Frauds.   Moreover, it should contain the names and addresses of the parties, a description of the property to be conveyed, the time for the conveyance, the type of deed to be given, and the price and manner of payment.   A deed must contain a description of the property that is sufficiently clear and certain to permit identification of the property

conveyed. It will also usually describe the quantity of the estate conveyed. It will also contain the appropriate covenants of title, if any. Finally, it must be signed by the grantor, and for purposes of recordation, it must be acknowledged before a notary public.

2. The three types of deeds are the warranty deed, the special warranty deed, and the quitclaim deed. By the warranty deed, the seller promises that he has title to the property and that he will do what is necessary to make the grantee whole if the latter suffers any damage because the grantor's title was defective. A warranty deed also conveys after-acquired title. In contrast, a special warranty deed is one that warrants only that the title has not been impaired, encumbered or rendered defective by any act or omission of the grantor. The grantor does not warrant that the title may not be defective by reason of the acts or omissions of others. Finally, a quitclaim deed is used to convey all of one's interest in certain property, whatever it might be. No warranties of title are made.

3. A deed is not effective until it is delivered. "Delivery" means an intent that the deed will take effect and is evidenced by the acts or statements of the grantor. Manual or physical transfer of the deed is usually the best evidence of this intent, but it is not necessary to effect delivery. The deed may be given to a third party escrow agent or even retained in the possession of the grantor. It is treated as delivered when the grantor intends it to be delivered, provided he acts accordingly.

4. A restrictive covenant is a limitation upon the use of one's land -- in essence, a negative easement. The restriction is enforceable against all landowners by all landowners in a subdivided common plat to which the restriction applies provided it appears that the restriction was intended to benefit the purchaser of any lot in the tract, and that the restriction appears somewhere in the chain of title to which the lot is subject. There are basically two ways that a restrictive covenant can be terminated. First, if it can be shown that there has been a long acquiescence by neighbors in numerous violations of the covenant in the past. Second, the covenant can be terminated if it can be shown that the circumstances that gave rise to the covenant no longer exists.

CHAPTER 48

True/False:

1.	T	6.	T	11.	T
2.	F	7.	F	12.	T
3.	F	8.	T	13.	T
4.	T	9.	T	14.	F
5.	F	10.	F	15.	T

Multiple Choice:

1.	b	6.	d	11.	b
2.	b	7.	d	12.	c
3.	c	8.	c	13.	d
4.	c	9.	c	14.	c
5.	c	10.	d	15.	d

Short Essay:

1. The four essential elements of a trust are as follows. First, the trust must have a creator, known as the settlor. Second, there must be a subject matter of the trust, or the trust "corpus" or "res," that is definite and certain. Third, there must be a trustee, but the trust will not fail for want of a trustee because the court will appoint one. Finally, there must be a beneficiary of the trust.

2. A constructive trust is one imposed upon a party to remedy the abuse of a confidential relationship. The property is held in trust by the abusing party for the benefit of the aggrieved party. A resulting trust, however, serves to carry out the true intent of the parties in those cases where the intent was inadequately expressed. Both constructive and resulting trusts are created by implication and operation of law and, therefore, neither has to be in writing.

3. A trust need not be created by particular words provided that the intent of the settlor to establish a trust is unmistakable. Moreover, consideration is not required. A trust may be terminated in one of several ways. First, a designated time period may expire or the designated purpose of the trust may end. A trust is irrevocable by the settlor, however, unless he specifically reserves the right, and the trust will not terminate on the death of the trustee or the beneficiary unless their lives are used to measure the duration of the trust.

4. In order to have a valid will, the testator must have both the power and the mental capacity to do so. Moreover, the will must be in writing, signed by the testator, and attested by the State required number (generally two or three) disinterested witnesses. But even if all these requirements are satisfied, a will is revocable by the testator and does not become effective until his death.

5. The first step involved in administering an estate is to see if the deceased left a will. If so, the named executor will handle the administration. If there is no will, the court will appoint an administrator. If there is a will, it is submitted to probate by the personal representative, who then must file an inventory of the estate. Assets are then collected, debts paid, and the remainder disbursed according to either the terms of the will, or if there is no will, the laws of intestate succession.

CHAPTER 49

True/False:

1.	T	6.	F	11.	F
2.	F	7.	F	12.	T
3.	T	8.	T	13.	T
4.	T	9.	F	14.	T
5.	F	10.	T	15.	T

Multiple Choice:

1.	b	6.	d	11.	a
2.	b	7.	b	12.	a
3.	b	8.	c	13.	b
4.	d	9.	d	14.	d
5.	c	10.	d	15.	d

Short Essay:

1. Ordinary life insurance is insurance that accumulates a cash surrender value over time as premiums are paid, but then pays the face value of the policy to the designated beneficiary upon the death of the insured. Term life insurance, however, is issued for a limited number of years. It too will pay proceeds to the designated beneficiary if the insured dies within the specified time period, but it does not accumulate a cash surrender value.

2. Life insurance contracts pay out the face value of the policy to the designated beneficiary upon the death of the insured. An endowment contract contains many similar provisions, but agrees to pay a

lump sum of money to the insured when he reaches a certain age or to a beneficiary in the event of the insured's premature death. Finally, an annuity contract is an agreement by the insurer to pay fixed sums at periodic intervals to the insured after he reaches a certain age.

3. An insurable interest is a relationship that a person has to another person, or to certain property such that the happening of a possible specific damage causing contingency would result in direct loss or injury to him. The purpose of the concept is to ensure that insurance is used as protection against the risk of loss resulting from the happening of an event, not the realization of profit from idle wagering.

4. Warranties operate as conditions that must exist before the contract of insurance is effective or before the insured's obligation to pay is enforceable. Failure of a certain condition to exist or to occur relieves the insurer from any obligation to perform its promise.

5. Waiver is the intentional relinquishment of a known right; estoppel, on the other hand, means that a person is precluded by his own conduct from asserting a position that is inconsistent with his acts and which have been justifiably relied upon by another.

PART X – SAMPLE EXAM

1. c	8. b	15. b
2. a	9. d	16. c
3. b	10. b	17. b
4. c	11. c	18. a
5. b	12. a	19. b
6. b	13. c	20. b
7. b	14. a